THE *HISTORY* OF ZONARAS

While an exile from Constantinople, the twelfth-century Byzantine functionary and canonist John Zonaras culled earlier chronicles and histories to compose an account of events from creation to the reign of Alexius Comnenus. For topics where his sources are lost or appear elsewhere in more truncated form, his testimony and the identification of the texts on which he depends are of critical importance.

For his account of the first two centuries of the Principate, Zonaras employed now-lost portions of Cassius Dio. From the point where Dio's *History* ended, to the reign of Theodosius the Great (d. 395), he turned to other sources to produce a uniquely full historical narrative of the critical years 235–395, making Books XII.15–XIII.19 of the *Epitome* central to the study of both late Roman history and late Roman and Byzantine historiography.

This key section of the *Epitome*, together with Zonaras' *Prologue*, here appears in English for the first time, both complemented by a historical and historiographical commentary. A special feature of the latter is a first-ever English translation of a broad range of sources that illuminate Zonaras' account and the historiographical traditions it reflects. Among the authors whose newly translated works occupy a prominent place in the commentary are George Cedrenus, George the Monk, John of Antioch, Peter the Patrician, Symeon Magister, and Theodore Scutariotes. Specialized indices facilitate the use of the translations and commentary alike.

The result is an invaluable guide and stimulus to further research for scholars and students of the history and historiography of Rome and Byzantium.

Thomas M. Banchich is Professor of Classics and History at Canisius College, Buffalo, New York. His research interests include ancient philosophy, history, and historiography.

The late **Eugene N. Lane** was Professor of Classics at the University of Missouri, Columbia.

Routledge Classical Translations

THE *HISTORY* OF ZONARAS

From Alexander Severus to the death
of Theodosius the Great

Translation by
Thomas M. Banchich and
Eugene N. Lane

Introduction and commentary by
Thomas M. Banchich

Routledge
Taylor & Francis Group

LONDON AND NEW YORK

First published 2009
by Routledge
2 Park Square, Milton Park, Abingdon, Oxon OX14 4RN

Simultaneously published in the USA and Canada
by Routledge
270 Madison Ave, New York, NY 10016

Routledge is an imprint of the Taylor & Francis Group, an informa business

© 2009 Thomas M. Banchich and Eugene N. Lane

Typeset in Garamond 3 by
Florence Production Ltd, Stoodleigh, Devon

British Library Cataloguing in Publication Data
A catalogue record for this book is available from the British Library

Library of Congress Cataloging in Publication Data
Zonaras, Joannes, 12th cent.
[Epitome historion. English]
The history of Zonaras: from Alexander Severus to the death of Theodosius
the Great/translation by Thomas M. Banchich and Eugene N. Lane;
introduction and commentary by Thomas M. Banchich.
p. cm.
Includes bibliographical references.
1. Emperors—Rome. 2. Rome—History—Severans, 193–235.
3. Rome—History—Period of military anarchy, 235–284.
4. Rome—History—Empire, 284–476. I. Banchich, Thomas, 1949–.
II. Lane, Eugene, 1936–. III. Title.
DG298.Z613 2009
937'.08—dc22 2008036721

ISBN10: 0–415–29909–8 (hbk)
ISBN10: 0–203–88204–0 (ebk)

ISBN13: 978–0–415–29909–1 (hbk)
ISBN13: 978–0–203–88204–7 (ebk)

CONTENTS

ACKNOWLEDGMENTS

Dean Paula McNutt and Canisius College deserve thanks for several grants and two sabbatical leaves, which greatly facilitated the research for and writing of this book. I am deeply appreciative, too, of the support afforded me daily by my colleagues in the Departments of History and Classics. Barbara Boehnke, Sally DiCarlo, Ruth McGuire, and many other members of the staff of the Andrew L. Bouwhuis Library at Canisius, along with their counterparts at the Lockwood Library of the State University of New York at Buffalo, satisfied an incessant series of requests for books, articles, and microfilms. On the lone occasion when their combined efforts failed, Philip Rousseau and Lenore Rouse took their time to track down a passage from an obscure text in the Department of Rare Books and Special Collections at the Mullen Library of Catholic University. Scott Clark negotiated every technological obstacle. The far longer labors of David Bard, then my student assistant, have not been forgotten. Richard Stoneman, who was my first editor at Routledge, exhibited a level of patience surpassed only by that of my family. Ultimately, Routledge's Lalle Pursglove tightened the reins just enough to bring me to my destination and Fiona Isaac supervised the final phases of production.

Dr Ernesto Milano of the Bibliotheca Estense Universitaria kindly arranged for the Studio Fotografico Roncaglia to supply me with photographs of several pages of that library's beautifully illustrated manuscript of Zonaras, one of which graces the cover of this volume. Katrina Hofmann of Walter de Gruyter saw to permission for the publication of my translations of a broad range of Greek and Latin texts to which that esteemed publisher holds copyright. In the few cases of translations of texts not under the purview of de Gruyter, every effort has been made to secure like authorization. Any oversights brought to our attention will be remedied in future editions.

Along the way, I have benefited from more than my share of extraordinary teachers. Fred D. Miller, Jr, has been unstintingly supportive. Robert K. Sherk, who will not remember doing so, first steered me toward historical epitomes; George L. Kustas led me through Ammianus Marcellinus and Eunapius. I wish that Leendert G. Westerink were here to accept my gratitude for his guidance and his example of great learning combined with kindness and good humor. Finally, Lawrence J. Daly, who introduced me to the study of the ancient world and pointed me toward Julian the Apostate and the theme of *paideia*, deserves my special thanks.

ABBREVIATIONS

For the few abbreviations not listed below, see the *OCD*[3], pp. xxix–liv.
See the corresponding bibliographic entries, pp. 277–287, for details.

Agath.	Agathias
Alex. Mon.	Alexander the Monk
AM	*Anno Mundi*
Amm. Marc.	Ammianus Marcellinus
Anon. Cont.	Anonymous Continuator of Cassius Dio
Art. Pass.	John of Rhodes *S. Artemii Passio*
Aur. Vict.	Aurelius Victor
Basil. Libri	*Basilicorum Libri LX*
BHG	*Bibliotheca hagiographica Graeca*
BJ	Josephus *De Bello Iudaico Libri VII*
BMCR	*Bryn Mawr Classical Review*
BNJ	*Brill's New Jacoby*
BNP	*Brill's New Pauly*
CAH	*Cambridge Ancient History*
Ced.	Cedrenus
CFHB	*Corpus Fontium Historiae Byzantinae*
Chron. 354	*Chronographus Anni CCCLIIII*
CMH	*Cambridge Medieval History*
Cod. Theod.	*Theodosian Code*
CP	*Chronicon Paschale*
Cramer	*Anecdota Graeca*
CSHB	*Corpus Scriptorum Historiae Byzantinae*
De Matr. Sobr.	John Zonaras, *De Matrimonio Sobrinorum*
D-L	Michael H. Dodgeon and Samuel Lieu, *The Roman Eastern Frontier and the Persian Wars*
EEC	*Encyclopedia of the Early Church*

EH	*Excerpta historica iussu Imperatoris Constantini Porphyrogeniti confecta*
EI	*Excerpta de Insidiis*
ELGR	*Excerpta de legationibus gentium ad Romanos*
ELRG	*Excerpta de legationibus Romanorum ad gentes*
Epit. de Caes.	*Epitome de Caesaribus*
ES	*Excerpta de Sententiis*
Eun. *Hist.*	Eunapius *History*
Eun. *VS*	Eunapius *Vitae sophistarum*
Eus.	Eusebius
Eutr.	Eutropius *Eutropi Breviarium ab Urbe Condita*
EV	*Excerpta de Virtutibus et Vitiis*
Exc. Hist. Eccl.	*Excerpts from an Ecclesiastical History*
FCH	Roger C. Blockley, *The Fragmentary Classicising Historians of the Later Roman Empire*
FgrH	*Die Fragmente der griechischen Historiker*
FHG	*Fragmenta Historicorum Graecorum*
GCS	*Die Griechischen Christlichen Schriftsteller*
Gel. Caes.	Gelasius of Caesarea
Gel. Cyz. *Comm.*	*Gelasii Cyziceni Actorum Concilii Nicaeni Commentarius*
Gel. Cyz. *HE*	Gelasius Cyzicenus, *Anonyme Kirchengeschichte*
Get.	Jordanes *Getica*
Greg. Naz.	Gregory of Nazianzus
GVC	*Guida Life of Constantine*
HE	*Historia ecclesiastica*
JA	Josephus *Antiquitatum Iudicarum Libri XX*
Jer. *Chron.*	Jerome *Chronica*
Jord.	Jordanes
Lactant. *De Mort. Pers.*	Lactantius *De Mortibus Persecutorum*
LCL	*Loeb Classical Library*
LIM	*Laterculus Imperatorum Malalianus*
L-M	Samuel Lieu and Dominic Montserrat, *From Constantine to Julian*
Malal.	John Malalas
MGH	*Monumenta Germaniae Historica*
Naz.	Nazarius
Nov. *Theod.*	*Leges Novellae*
NPNF	*Nicene and Post-Nicene Fathers*

*OCD*³	*Oxford Classical Dictionary*, 3rd edition
ODB	*Oxford Dictionary of Byzantium*
Orig. Const.	*Excerpta Valesiana*
Paean.	Paeanius
Pap. Ox.	*Oxyyrhynchus Papyri*
Pass. Art.	*Passion of St Artemius*
PBW	*Prosopography of the Byzantine World*
Pet. Patr.	Peter the Patrician
PG	*Patrologia Cursus Completus*
Philost.	Philostorgius
Photius *Bibl.*	Photius *Bibliotheca*
PIR	*Prosopographia Imperii Romani*
PLRE	*Prosopography of the Later Roman Empire*
Plut.	Plutarch
Pol. Sil.	Polemius Silvius
Porphyry *Vit. Plot.*	Porphyry *Life of Plotinus*
RE	*Paulys Realencyclopädie der classischen Altertumswissenschaft*
Rom.	Jordanes *Romana*
R-P	*ΣΥΝΤΑΓΑΜΑΤΑ ΤΩΝ ΘΕΙΩΝ ΚΑΙ ΙΕΡΩΝ ΚΑΝΩΝ* eds G. A. Rhalles and M. Potles
Salmasian John	John of Antioch
Scut.	Theodore Scutariotes
SHA	*Scriptores Historiae Augustae*
Soc.	Socrates Scholasticus
Soz.	Sozomenus
Sym.	Symeon Magister
Theod. Lect.	Theodore Anagnostes
Theod.	Theodoret of Cyrrhus
Theoph.	Theophanes
TTH	*Translated Texts for Historians*
Xiphil.	John Xiphilinus
Zon.	Zonaras *Epitome of Histories*
Zos.	Zosimus *Historia Nova*

INTRODUCTION

The *Epitome of Histories*

John Zonaras' *Epitome of Histories* recounts events from creation through the death of the emperor Alexius Comnenus in 1118—about 6,619 years by Byzantine reckoning. Composed in the first half of the twelfth century and the most substantial extant historical work written in Greek between Cassius Dio's *Roman History* of the early third century AD and the fall of Constantinople, it comprises three substantial volumes and slightly more than 1,700 pages of text in its best modern edition.[1] The production of the original copy would have required much time, labor, and expense: the large number of manuscripts of the *Epitome* and its early translation into a number of languages are measures of the esteem it long commanded.[2] Yet since the advent of modern scholarship in the nineteenth century, few have thought there was any good reason to read the whole *Epitome*, fewer have attempted to do so, and fewer still have finished the job.

This was not so much because the *Epitome* was dull or inaccurate as because it was largely derivative. Indeed, Zonaras explains in his *Prologue* that he aimed at originality only in his wish to make earlier histories more accessible by presenting them in a new fashion. For him this entailed staking out a middle ground between barebones abbreviation and overly detailed recapitulation. He would eschew speeches and learned excurses, but, at the same time, maintain a style, tone, and level of engagement with his material worthy of an intelligent readership. In the event, the outcome was neither proper history in a classicizing mode nor chronicle, but a unique epitome of histories, and it is precisely this that effected the neglect into which the *Epitome* eventually fell, for why read the *Epitome* when other, better guides—sometimes Zonaras' actual sources—were available?[3]

But before this could happen, those sources had to be identified and weighed against the content of the *Epitome*. Much scholarly

1

energy was and, as evidenced by this book, continues to be expended in this exercise of *Quellenforschung*. On three points consensus has emerged: Zonaras' treatment of the Roman republic, dependent on lost books of Cassius Dio, is fundamental to our knowledge of that period; Zonaras' account of Roman history from Alexander Severus through Theodosius the Great—our most detailed continuous Byzantine narrative of that span and one that depends on sources no longer extant—is equally important for a historical understanding of that period and for a critical assessment of the historiographical traditions upon which our literary sources for the era depend; and Zonaras' account of Alexius Comnenus is highly distinctive and, perhaps, uniquely informative.[4]

For Byzantinists, this last consideration has resulted in an increased interest in other sections of the *Epitome* as a way to gauge whether some of Zonaras' negative comments about Alexius are part of a broader historically and constitutionally based critique of the position of emperor and of individual emperors, prompted, perhaps, by the impact of Alexius on Zonaras' own life.[5]

John Zonaras

Zonaras' reputation as a writer rested among his contemporaries, as it rests today, on his exegesis of sacred canons and on his *Epitome of Histories*. We know little about his life. The offices of Grand Commander of the Palace Watch (*Megas Drouggarios tês Biglas*) and First Secretary of the Chancery (*Prôtoasêkritês*), both duly noted in headings of several manuscripts of his works, mark the apex of his public career.[6] They betray his elite origins and, by their wholly legalistic functions, offer our only clue to his formal education, though they by no means imply that Zonaras had a narrow legal training.[7] After all, the same system had produced the historians John Scylitzes and Michael Attaliates, the former a Grand Commander of the Palace Watch, the latter a distinguished judge.[8] Within this curriculum, history functioned as a repository of *exempla*, a guide to precedent and tradition, and a means of judging the original contexts of specific laws and the powers and prerogatives behind them. Concord between canon and secular law, when both were properly understood, would have been an unstated assumption: in his capacity as a high-ranking civil servant, Zonaras' duty would have been to Church and State, a unity subsumed under the umbrella of Orthodoxy. At some point—perhaps only then taking the name John—he retreated to the monastery of St Glyceria on present-day Ineir Adasi in the Bay of Tuzla, where he completed his *Epitome of Histories* in time for the mid-twelfth-century historian Michael Glycas to quote him by name.[9] The date, place, and circumstances of his death are unknown.[10]

Scholars most often set Zonaras' service in the imperial court during the reign of Alexius Comnenus (1081–1118). His withdrawal from public life they regularly link to intrigue contingent on the accession of John II Comnenus in the face of opposition from Nicephorus Bryennius, Alexius' caesar and the husband of Anna Comnena, daughter of Alexius and sister of John. Zonaras, they hold, had backed the wrong horse, and, in a fate parallel to that of Anna, was sentenced by her brother to trade court for cloister.[11]

The principal reasons for the association of Zonaras' career with Alexius' reign are the terminus of the *Epitome of Histories*, which abruptly ends with Alexius' death, and its sometimes-harsh portrait of that emperor and his policies. However, Zonaras is explicit that his departure from Constantinople was his own decision, made in light of personal losses. If we take him at his word, this voluntary retirement might just as easily have occurred before or shortly after Alexius won the throne from Nicephorus III Botaniates (r. 1078–1081).[12] After all, Botaniates' views on the proper constitutional relationship between emperor, senate, and church correspond closely to Zonaras' own but clash with those of Alexius.[13] By the same token, Zonaras' public career and withdrawal could fall in the reign of Alexius' successors John (1118–1143) or, less likely, Manuel Comnenus (1143–1180).

Prosopographic data afford only minimal help. Sources often fail to differentiate between several types of *drungarii*. To complicate matters, because *drungarii* had no set tenure, one cannot simply weigh the relative merits of those years in which no *drungarius* is named to choose a niche for Zonaras. Only two Grand Commanders of the Palace Watch—John (perhaps Scylitzes), from the theme Thrakesion, who, in March 1092, had bumped heads with Alexius Comnenus over the issue of the dissolution of betrothals, and Nicholas Mermentolus, who attended the Synod of the Blachernae in 1094–1095—can be securely dated to Alexius' reign.[14] Among the prominent members of the Zonaras family active between *ca.* 1075 and the reign of Manuel Comnenus, Naucratius Zonaras, a highly esteemed monk of St Glyceria and former *drungarius* who helped finance the reconstruction of a church in the monastery around the late 1120s, is particularly noteworthy. This Naucratius may be Nicholas Zonaras (Nikolaus 20158, *PBW*), though that would put two Zonarases—John and Naucratius/Nicholas—who had been *drungarius* in St Glyceria at or about the same time. On the other hand, Naucratius may, in fact, be John, author of the *Epitome*.[15] Even so, this would still not tell us when he arrived, though it would rule out the reign of Manuel Comnenus.

Additional clues from the *Epitome* may permit greater precision. Zonaras states that a long interval separated his retreat from public life and the beginning of his work on the *Epitome*, the result of the incessant promptings of friends. Furthermore, his description of himself as at that time "intellectually lax . . . and passing life in lethargy" implies that significant time had elapsed since he had engaged in any writing (*Prologue* 1 [I, p. 3.2] and 2 [I, p. 7.10–12]). This is a far cry from the situation he says prevailed when he turned to interpretation of the canons:

> Let no one accuse me of rashness. For I did not undertake the work on my own initiative, but, when I had been summoned, I shouldered the burden and devoted myself to the job, in order that I not be condemned because of inattentiveness.
>
> (R-P II, pp. 1–2)

In this case, it was probably an emperor who "summoned" Zonaras to canonical exegesis and whose potential condemnation "because of inattentiveness" worried him, while a real or feigned concern with being judged rash by his colleagues, in turn, fits a man just entering his prime as *drungarius* rather than a seasoned retiree in a monastery.

On the basis of this reconstruction, Manuel Comnenus appears impossibly late to deserve consideration as the ruler who pointed Zonaras to the canons. His reign commenced in 1143 and the *Epitome* was available to Glycas by the middle of the twelfth century. Botaniates' reign (1078–1081), on the other hand, seems too early to have Zonaras win that emperor's confidence and then, after retirement, produce a substantial number of compositions over what obviously was a significant duration of time. Alexius Aristenus, who joins Zonaras and Theodore Balsamon to form the trio of great Byzantine canonists, probably took his mandate from John II Comnenus, and it is difficult to imagine that John would have set both Zonaras and Aristenus to the same task.[16] Conversely, Alexius Comnenus' reign is the most suitable, not only on chronological grounds, but in light of Zonaras' comments about the patriarchs Cosmas I (1075–1081), Eustratius (1081–1084), Nicholas III (1084–111), and John IX Agapetus (1111–1134).

4

In a passage that reflects the standard literary assessment of Cosmas, Zonaras describes him as a monk unversed in intellectual matters but of exemplary virtue.[17] By comparison, his judgments of Eustratius as a eunuch monk both unversed in intellectual matters and incompetent when it came to practical affairs, "a dunce and more suited for solitude or some corner," and of Nicholas as "a monk, nicknamed 'the Grammarian,' . . . not unfamiliar with intellectual culture, though he did not partake of this to a high degree" are pointed and personal.[18] Zonaras never names John Agapetus, but contrasts him with his predecessors:

> [John] was, on the one hand, one of the clergy of the church and, indeed, of the degree of the deacons and ranked among the patriarchal officials, one the other, he was a nephew of the one then in charge of the church in Chalcedon [*Anonymus* 6073, *PBW*], reared in secular and sacred matters of the intellect, the sovereign himself having attended the church and selected him therein.
>
> (XVIII.25.8 [III, p. 2–8])

The tenures of Nicholas and John, a period of negotiation between the church and Alexius, saw a growing concern with interpretation of the sacred canons on the part of both interested parties, and Zonaras' comments likely reflect his recollections of his perceptions as a *drungarius*, confident of his own cultural refinement and dismissive of what he perceived as monkish ignorance: they afford a convincing context for Zonaras' summons to the study of the canons.[19] Attempts between 1089 and 1112 to define more clearly the relationship between the bishops of Rome and Constantinople also mesh with Zonaras' carefully considered comments on this issue.[20] This does not require Zonaras' completion of his canonical commentaries before his retirement, only that the work was well under way and finished in time to allow for the interval of inactivity—a time when Zonaras confesses that his mind was not employed in any worthy task— which preceded the composition of the *Epitome*. Before that break must also have been the occasion for his other treatises, some tending toward the historical, but all closely concerned with matters more appropriate to a monk than a *drungarius*.[21]

By the time Zonaras turned to the reign of Alexius Comnenus, about a quarter of a century would have passed since his departure from Constantinople. One might expect to detect some differences in his exposition of matters at court after this withdrawal, as a consequence of his reliance on informants or written sources as opposed to autopsy, and such appears to be the case from Zonaras' account of the defeat of the Frank Bohemund in 1107 (XVIII.25.7 [III, p. 750.15–17]) to the end of Book XVIII. Chronological vagueness, confusion about incidents and personalities, and the omission of significant events are commonplace.[22] Of course, some of this would have been the result of Zonaras' own hazy recollections of the distant past and of old axes to grind. At the same time, one must not forget that Zonaras was an epitomizer: he brought special qualities to that role, but he was not a historian. Whatever the precise explanation behind specific passages that exhibit these qualities, their ubiquity, particularly when opposed to the vivid precision of the initial portion of Book XVIII, points again to the final years of the patriarchate of Nicholas or the very beginning of that of John as the time when Zonaras took his leave of the Queen of Cities. His criticisms of Alexius and some of what transpired during his reign are not due to harsh feelings that resulted from some hypothetical exile at the emperor's command nor, since the finished *Epitome* would antedate Anna Comnena's *Alexiad*, do they represent a rejoinder to Anna's laudatory portrait of her father; they reflect the considered judgment of Zonaras the *drungarius* as remembered by Zonaras the monk.

The sole obstacle to this reconstruction occurs at the end of Zonaras' interpretation of Canon 6 of the Council of Caesarea:

"A presbyter is not to celebrate weddings of those marrying twice. Since, when the twice-married is petitioning repentance, who will be the presbyter, he, through the celebration, sanctioning the weddings?"

Zonaras: "The second marriage is subject to penalty, for it is barred from Holy Communion for a year. That being the case, 'What sort of priest will he be, seeming to condone the second marriage through his presence?' says the canon. That is to say, how will one, approving the second marriage through his presence, not be ashamed penalizing one who is twice-married? But these are in writing [*i.e.* they are dead-letter]. By us a patriarch was seen, and various metropolitans, engaging in [wedding] festivities with a sovereign who had been married twice?" (R-P II, p. 80])

Some have identified Manuel Comnenus as the "sovereign who had been married twice." If this is correct, Manuel's marriage in

1161 would furnish a *terminus ante quem* for this interpretation and perhaps, by extension, for Zonaras' activity as a canonist. However, "But these things are in writing. By us a patriarch was seen, and various metropolitans, engaging in [wedding] festivities with a sovereign who had been married twice" may well be an interpolation rather than Zonaras' sentiment. Its opening is unparalleled in Zonaras' exegesis, and the sentiment is as much a reaction to the body of the gloss as it is to the actual canon. Moreover, if Zonaras is the author, the emperor in question may be Nicephorus Botaniates.

Botaniates, in fact, married three times. His second wife, Vevdene, became empress when Botaniates was crowned, and she died shortly thereafter. He then married Maria Alania, former wife of the vanquished Michael VII Ducas, Botaniates' exiled adversary. Though Zonaras does not mention the second marriage, his censure of the third as "boldfaced adultery" reveals he knew of it. In light of the other evidence for the chronology of Zonaras' life, then, the case for the wedding of Botaniates to Vevdene as the inspiration for the closing comments of the interpretation of Canon 7 is far stronger than is that for the second marriage of Manuel Comneus.[23] Thus, if it tells us anything about Zonaras' life, it would be that Zonaras himself saw the patriarch Cosmas and various metropolitans at the marriage of Botaniates and Vevdene in 1078.

On this reckoning, Zonaras was probably in his twenties around 1079. The prime of his public life would have been during the patriarchate of Nicholas and, perhaps, early in that of John Agapetus, at which time, probably on Alexius' orders, he began his work on the sacred canons. When, late in Nicholas' tenure, or early in John's, *ca.* 1112, some personal loss precipitated his retirement, he would have been in his fifties. He initially produced several modest works and, if he had not already completed his canonical commentaries, finished this project. Subsequent to a period of inactivity, he was convinced to begin the *Epitome*. Sometime before 1134, when, after a lengthy period of composition, Zonaras brought this work to its abrupt conclusion, he would have been in his seventies. He allows that there was more ground to cover, but it was not "profitable or opportune" to do so. This has generally been understood as a reference to the uncertainty of current events—some military campaign, for example. However, Zonaras could just as easily be referring to himself: the labor he had expended had served its purpose and, either because of his age or health, he decided to put down his pen.

Zonaras and *Quellenforschung*

Quellenforschung is the investigation of interrelationships between extant sources, the delineation of traditions evidenced by those sources, and the identification and reconstruction of missing links in those traditions. A series of articles by Edwin Patzig set the course of modern investigations of Zonaras' sources, the sources drawn upon by other Byzantine historians and chroniclers, and their connections. One of Patzig's most important conclusions with regard to Zonaras' account of AD 222–395 was that comparison between the *Chronicle* of Leo Grammaticus (read in Bekker's deeply flawed Bonn edition and now properly edited as the work of Simeon Magister [mid-tenth c., *ODB* III, pp. 1982–1983, *s.v.* Symeon Logothete]), George Cedrenus (twelfth c., *ODB* II, p. 1118), the *Synopis Chronikê* first published by Constantine Sathas (now identified as the work of Theodore Scutariotes [thirteenth c., *ODB* III, pp. 1912–1913]), and, as they appeared in Müller's *FHG*, the fragments of John of Antioch (seventh c., *ODB* II, p. 1062) and the so-called *Anonymus post Dionem* or Anonymous Continuator of Cassius Dio (the latter now regularly identified with Peter the Patrician [sixth c., *ODB* III, p. 1641]) revealed three lost sources, dubbed by Patzig the *Synopsisquelle*, the *Leoquelle*, and the *Zwillingsquelle*. Patzig further maintained that when Zonaras reached the point in his narrative where he could no longer rely on Dio and Herodian he took the *Synopsisquelle* as one of his principal guides. From Diocletian's through Theodosius' reigns and beyond, however, Patzig held that the influence of the *Synopsisquelle* was relatively minor compared to that of the *Leoquelle* and *Zwillingsquelle*. Finally, he argued for the identification of the *Leoquelle* with John of Antioch, who, Patzig thought, had used the Anonymous Continuator (= Peter the Patrician) as one of his guides.[24]

Almost a century after Patzig, Michael DiMaio revisited the source problem and, once again, argued for Zonaras' indebtedness to John of Antioch, who, DiMaio thought, had transmitted to Zonaras material from Greek translations of Eutropius' *Breviarium* and Ammianus Marcellinus' *Res Gestae*. Furthermore, DiMaio sought to demonstrate that Zonaras had directly consulted a number of sources —for example, Julian the Apostate and Philostorgius—considered by Patzig to have been known to Zonaras only indirectly through the hypothesized *Synopisquelle*, *Leoquelle*, and *Zwillingsquelle*.[25]

The connection between John of Antioch and Zonaras, so central to the views of Patzig and DiMaio, was broken, so it seemed, by Panagiotis Sotiroudis.[26] Both Patzig and DiMaio had known full well that a large number of the fragments of John as printed by Müller were preserved in the *EH* of Constantine Porphyrogenitus but that another substantial group survived separately in what had come to be referred to as the *Excerpta Salmasiana*, named for Claude de Saumaise (1588–1653), who had copied them from the sole manuscript in which they survived.[27] Patzig himself had noted that correspondences between John and the *Leoquelle* almost always involved these Salmasian fragments. Thus, when Sotiroudis made a strong case against assigning the Salmasian excerpts to John of Antioch, it necessarily followed that the *Leoquelle*, too, had to assume a new identity.

Bruno Bleckmann proposed Virius Nicomachus Flavianus (15, *PLRE* I, pp. 347–349), an identification that attracted as much support from continental scholars as it did opposition from their Anglophone counterparts.[28] Bleckmann's argument accepted Patzig's *Leoquelle* but, in place of the apparently discredited connection with John of Antioch, substituted Nicomachus as filtered partly through Peter the Patrician and the Salmasian excerpts. The opposition generally directed its attacks against the identification of Nicomachus but accepted that Sotiroudis had effectively eliminated John of Antioch from consideration.

Umberto Roberto's first critical edition of the fragments of John has now demonstrated that Sotiroudis was mistaken and returned the debate to the state it was in prior to the now unnecessary distinction between John of Antioch and the author of the Salmasian excerpts.[29]

But how did Byzantine authors know John's work? The compilers of the *EH* had it before them, but, as is evident from a comparison of excerpts in the *EH* from authors who survive independently, *e.g.* Thucydides, they routinely adapted passages for incorporation into the various volumes of the *EH*. Likewise, the lexicographers of the *Suda*, who drew the bulk of their historical entries, including portions of John of Antioch, from the *EH* rather than directly from the texts of the historians in question, regularly further altered their material. The paradoxical result is that texts of authors thought to have drawn directly upon works otherwise preserved in the *EH* and *Suda* may more accurately reflect their sources than do the actual "fragments" of those sources.[30] This alone makes it dangerous to evaluate the relationship between the *Epitome* of Zonaras and the lost *Chronicle* of John of Antioch simply on the basis of a comparison of sections of the *Epitome* with the fragments of John. Assembling parallels between Zonaras and such authors as Symeon Magister and

Theodore Scutariotes (Patzig's Leo and *Synopsis Chronikē*) may provide a control, though strictures identical to those that apply to Zonaras would hold equally true for them, and, of course, the greater the remove either forward or backward in time from John's text, various permutations of intermediate adaptations become ever more probable.

Additional and too-often-forgotten complicating factors are mistakes of the eye or ear or intentional adaptations in the process of manuscript transmission. Numbers and names are notoriously susceptible to scribal error or alteration. Interpolation poses another, particularly serious, obstacle to the deduction of sources through the standard method of a comparison of texts. Because parallels may result from the insertion of material from a manuscript of a later author into a manuscript of an earlier author, equal attention must be paid to the relative chronologies of manuscripts and of authors. Distinctive accounts of identical subjects in manuscripts of the same author, too, may arise from interpolation. Thus, those manuscripts that provide the fullest detail are not necessarily the safest guide to what their author wrote. Staffan Wahlgren's excellent critical edition of Symeon Magister, for instance, has revealed that Bekker's text, the basis for the so-called *Leoquelle*, was replete with interpolations and, consequently, grossly unsuited to serve the role it has played since Patzig's day. Indeed, this great advance warns that, even with the publication of Wahlgren's Symeon, Roberto's John of Antioch, and Raimondo Tocci's Scutariotes, the conclusions of any investigation of Zonaras' sources for his account of AD 222–395 will be severely compromised so long as there is no scholarly edition of the *Chronicle* of George Cedrenus. Even then, the elucidation of broad strands of tradition and the identification of some of the authors who comprise them may well be the greatest degree of precision the evidence allows.[31]

One further, and potentially important, observation remains. David Pingree has convincingly argued that the horoscope attributed to Valens and noted both by Zonaras and Cedrenus was cast around 990.[32] Since the *EH* of Constantine Porphyrogenitus (r. 908–959, sole emperor 945–959) predates the horoscope, it is possible that the common source of Zonaras and Cedrenus had access to the *EH*. Within each thematic volume of the *EH*, excerpts are organized by author and, so far as we can tell, reflect the order in which they appeared in each author's work. This arrangement would lend itself to the discovery of variant versions of the same topic or of unique information within a particular category, both distinguishing features of the *Epitome*. Likewise, use of the *EH* or of a source that has used the *EH* would result in a pastiche of material from those authors included in the *EH*, another characteristic of the *Epitome*. Of course, Zonaras' or his sources' direct consultation of a range of works in the course of researching specific individuals and events would yield identical results. Nonetheless, use of the *EH*, especially by a source shared by Zonaras and Cedrenus, must be reckoned a very real possibility and dictates an adjustment to the application of the techniques of *Quellenforschung* to Zonaras.

Principles of translation

Despite its significance for late antique history and historiography, since the sixteenth century there has been no translation of or commentary on Books XII.15–XIII.19 of the *Epitome* in any modern language other than Iordanes Gregoriades' modern Greek version.[33]

The immediate impetus to remedy this situation came in the form of a suggestion from Michael DiMaio to Banchich that they revise and perhaps expand DiMaio's earlier translation of and commentary on Zonaras' account of the Neo-Flavians.[34] Banchich proposed the chronological termini of Alexander Severus and Theodosius largely due to his interest in source problems associated with that section of the *Epitome*. At that point, DiMaio invited Eugene Lane, Jacqueline Long, and William Leadbetter aboard. Ultimately, this translation-by-committee approach fell by the wayside and Banchich returned to the Greek to produce a wholly new translation of Zonaras' *Prologue*, Books XII.15–XIII.19, and *Postscript*, all of which Lane alone critiqued. The resultant translation, then, is Banchich's, often adjusted and improved in response to suggestions by Lane. When ill health eventually forced Lane (d. January 1, 2007) to become a silent partner in work on the translation, Banchich saw this facet of the project through to its end. Complaints about the result should be set at his door.

The basis of the translation of Zonaras is the edition of Pinder and Büttner-Wobst. This applies, too, to chapter divisions and pagination, the latter given within brackets throughout the translation, to proper names—for example, "Gallerius" rather than "Galerius" and "Constas" rather than "Constantius Chlorus"—and to the distinction between numerical notation as opposed to names of numbers. Most proper names appear in their Latinate forms—for example, "Aurelianus" rather than "Aurelian"—the principal exceptions being Diocletian, Constantine, and Julian the Apostate. References in the commentary or index of proper names to *PIR*, *PLRE*, or *EEC* entries should eliminate confusion. "Sovereign" renders the Greek *basileus*, Zonaras' term for a broad range of rulers, and "usurper" *tyrannos*.[35]

The translation preserves the syntax of the original, not because of stylistic virtuosity on Zonaras' part but rather because shifts in diction and vocabulary may suggest shifts in sources, changes in Zonaras' estimation of how to present a particular topic, or some other variable. Moreover, this approach maximizes the potential to appreciate, even in translation, the relationship between the *Epitome of Histories* and the broad range of parallel texts translated in the accompanying commentary. Of course, this would be true only if translations of those texts adhered to the same principles as those employed in the translation of Zonaras himself. Such, indeed, has been the case with regard to all texts translated in the commentary, many of which appear there for the first time in any modern language. Even where excellent translations existed—for example, Roberto's Italian John of Antioch, Paschoud's French or Ridley's English Zosimus, or Amidon's English Philostorgius[36]—the purpose of their comparison with Zonaras and one another necessitated re-renderings into English governed by common principles. In the few instances where Greek words have been retained, they are transliterated.

Scope and purpose of the commentary

The commentary's foremost aim is to elucidate Zonaras' testimony in so far as it pertains to historical and historiographic issues. It provides only enough information about the historical context of the content of particular passages—who was doing what to whom at what time and where—to achieve that end. Issues of why things happened or why people behaved as they did take a back seat throughout to the issue of why Zonaras says what he says. For the history of the period, as opposed to Zonaras' take on that history, scholarship abounds.[37]

This focus explains why the commentary only incidentally mentions epigraphic, papyrological, and archaeological evidence and takes no notice of numismatic evidence, for, though central to modern historical research and reconstruction, these are almost absent from the pages of the *Epitome*. Though the commentary rarely refers to literary evidence that does not contribute to understanding Zonaras, it does direct readers toward appropriate entries in the standard prosopographies, repositories of such information.

The period from Alexander Severus through Theodosius is a subject of immense international interest, which manifests itself in erudite articles and monographs, in the publication in various forms of new evidence or collections of evidence, and in broad, sometimes highly interpretive, narrative accounts. The fires of international scholarship have been fueled by learned commentaries on key texts (François Paschoud's on Zosimus, for example), more-accurate or first-ever translations (pride of place in the English-speaking category occupied by the volumes of the *TTH* series), and the replacement of antiquated and often substandard editions by their first modern counterparts. The scholarly literature on AD 222–395 is, then, immense. That said, this commentary offers only slim guidance to modern scholarship. The justification is threefold: only rarely do judgments in the commentary about what Zonaras says and why derive from modern scholarship as opposed to autopsy of primary texts; the inclusion of mainly illustrative bibliographic entries, no matter how useful, would have necessitated a much, much bigger book; and, finally, several repositories of such references already exist.[38]

As the commentary took shape, each chapter of Zonaras and a broad range of ancient texts that dealt with the same content were studied in the original and points of contact, agreement, divergence, and outright contradiction duly noted. Historical glosses—dates, comments on and identification of people and places, and the like— were added. When this lengthy process was complete, the results for each chapter were compared and broader patterns of relevance or irrelevance for the business of understanding Zonaras' *Epitome* began to emerge. There followed a pruning of much of the material collected earlier but subsequently revealed as irrelevant or tangential to the commentary's concerns. Of course, what has been jettisoned must not be automatically equated with what Zonaras himself or his sources knew but chose to ignore or omit.

The commentary consequently changed from a kind of variorum collection of literary sources for the period in question to an exposition and analysis of material important for understanding the *Epitome*. In the process, it became clear that Zonaras, Symeon Magister (earlier scholarship's Leo Grammaticus), George Cedrenus, and Theodore Scutariotes (the author of an anonymous chronicle previously referred to by the name of Constantine Sathas, its initial editor), though independent of one another, reflect a common tradition. It also became obvious that Theodore Lector's *Historia Tripartita* (sixth c., *ODB* III, p. 2042) was an important element in the tradition upon which the *Epitome* depends. To a degree, this was nothing new. However, scholars generally had been more concerned with working backward for the sake of getting closer to earlier strata of sources than in appreciating the nexus of sources closest in time to Zonaras, whether before or after he wrote, and Zonaras' place in it. Yet the commentary regularly demonstrates that it is the light shed on Zonaras by those chronologically closest to him that illuminates most clearly certain of their shadowy predecessors. This would seem to offer an opportunity for those involved in study of such matters to reassess and, perhaps, refine their reconstructions of the historiographical traditions upon which Zonaras depended.

To this end, a prominent feature of the commentary is the presentation of translations in parallel columns. When so arranged, texts appear in ascending chronological order from left to right. Because so many of the authors referred to are unfamiliar except to specialists, most of the commentary's citations of primary sources are more precise than is normally necessary. This applies especially to fragmentary authors, whose remains often appear in multiple collections of such material, each with its own special merits. In contrast, in the case of mainstream classical authors such as Homer and Plutarch or a few late antique texts available in multiple critical editions *and* in translations that include detailed textual divisions—for example, Ammianus Marcellinus—citations generally provide only standard textual divisions without the volume numbers and pagination of specific editions or translations.

In matters of absolute chronology, the commentary generally follows Dietmar Kienast's *Römische Kaisertabelle*, the *PIR* or *PIR*[2], and, for dates later than 260, *PLRE*, all sometimes supplemented by D-L for military campaigns and for ecclesiastical chronology by the *EEC*. For the chronology of the tetrarchic period, the reigns of Constantine and his sons, and ecclesiastical matters during the reign of Constantius II, Timothy Barnes' *New Empire of Diocletian and Constantine* and *Athanasius and Constantius* were sure guides.[39]

While the commentary's repeated references to the *PIR*, *PIR*[2], and *PLRE* both secure the identity of specific individuals and lead those interested to citations of primary evidence critical for the careers of those same individuals but outside the purview of the commentary itself, the primary rationale for references to the *EEC* is its sound treatments of individuals and events and its up-to-date bibliographies in a number of languages. The few instances where the commentary cites modern studies indicate particular indebtedness, originality, or thoroughness. That such references are almost always to scholarship in English, should not obscure the international character of the best research on Roman, Late Antique, and Byzantine history. The decision not to include maps was made easier by the fact that most locations mentioned by Zonaras seem to have been little more than names to him: for such matters readers should consult the authoritative *Barrington Atlas* and the series of maps in the relevant volumes of Paschoud's Zosimus.[40] They would be well advised, too, to read the *Epitome* with a list of emperors and usurpers between 222 and 395 at hand in order to gauge who is missing from Zonaras' emperor-centered history.[41] The "Index of passages cited" (pp. 290–301) contains some basic information about the authors listed therein.

Notes

1 *Ioannis Zonarae Epitomae Historiarum*, ed. M. Pinder and T. Büttner-Wobst. 3 vols *CSHB* (Bonn: Weber, 1841–1897).

2 For cost, see "Book Trade" and "Parchment," *ODB* I, pp. 308–309 and III, p. 1587, respectively. For manuscripts, over seventy, and early translations, see H. Hunger, *Die Hochsprachliche Profane Literatur der Byzantiner*, 2 vols (Munich: C. H. Beck, 1978), I, p. 418, and P. M. L. Leone, "La tradizione manoscritta dell' *Epitome historiarum* di Giovanni Zonaras," *Syndesmos. Studi in onore di Rosario Anastasi*, 2 vols (Catane: Facoltà di lettere e filosofia, Istituto di studi bizantini e neoellenici, 1991), pp. 221–262. For the last reference, I thank Bénédicte Berbessou Broustet, whose research promises to shed new light on the manuscript tradition of Books X–XI of the *Epitome*.

3 See especially *Prologue* 1–2 (I, pp. 4.7–9.7). Zonaras nowhere gives his work a formal title, though he says at *Prologue* 1 (I, p. 7.5–6) that he eventually took the advice of friends "to publish a concise history" (*syntomos historia*). Two of the key manuscripts—*Parisiensis Regius* 1715 and *Vindobonesis* 16—use the title *Epitome of Histories*. Cf. the *apparatus criticus* of Pinder and Büttner-Wobst at Vols I, p. 2, and II, p. 298. On the genre "Chronicle" and Zonaras, see E. M. Jeffreys, "The Attitudes of Byzantine Chroniclers towards Ancient History," *Byzantion* 49 (1979), pp. 199–238, and R. Macrides and P. Magdalino, "The Fourth Kingdom and the Rhetoric of Hellenism," *The Perception of the Past in Twelfth-Century Europe*, ed. P. Magdalino. (London and Rio Grande: Hambledon Press, 1992), pp. 117–156. For Zonaras' qualities as a writer, see I. Grigoriadis, *Linguistic and Literary Studies in the* Epitomê Historiôn *of John Zonaras* (Thessalonica: Byzantine Research Centre, 1998).

4 Vols I–II of the Loeb edition of Cassius Dio's *Roman History*, ed. and trans. E. Cary, 9 vols (Cambridge MA: Harvard University Press, 1914–1927), give the text with translation of the pertinent sections of the *Epitome*. On the account of Alexius in Zon. XVIII.20–29 (III, pp. 726–768), see R. Tada, *John Zonaras' Account of the Reign of Alexius I Comnenus (1081–1118): Translation and Commentary* (University of Washington MA thesis, 1999).

5 On this issue, see P. Magdalino, "Aspects of Twelfth-Century Byzantine *Kaiserkritik*," *Speculum* 58 (1983), pp. 326–346.

6 For Zonaras' comments on the sacred canons, see R-P; for Zonaras' titles, *cf.* Pinder's *apparatus criticus* to the prologue of the *Epitome* (Vol. I, p. 3) and R-P II, p. 1.

7 R. Macrides, "Perceptions of the Past in the Twelfth-Century Canonists," *Byzantium in the Twelfth Century: Canon Law, State and Society*, ed. N. Oikonomides, Society of Byzantine and Post-Byzantine Studies 3 (Athens, 1991), pp. 589–599. P. Magdalino, *The Empire of Manuel Komnenos, 1143–1180* (Cambridge: Cambridge University Press, 1993), pp. 356–360, provides an insightful sketch of special relevance to Zonaras.

8 For Attaliates and Scylitzes, see *ODB* I, p. 229, and III, p. 1914.

9 For the location, see R. Janin, *Les Églises et les Monastères des Grands Centres Byzantins, La Géographie Ecclésiastique de l'Empire Byzantin* (Paris: Institut Français d'Études Byzantines, 1975), pp. 54, 56–57. K. Ziegler's reservations, "Zonaras," *RE* X A.1 (1972), col. 722, are unwarranted. Glycas names Zonaras at pp. 266.7–8, 350.16–17, 546.8–9, and 551.22, ed. I. Bekker, *CSHB* (Bonn: Weber, 1836).

10 The claim of the sixteenth-century Franciscan traveler A. Thevet (*Les Vrais Pourtraits et Vies des Hommes Illustres*, 2 vols, reprint of 1584 edn (Delmar, NY: Scholars' Facsimiles & Reprints, 1973), I, p. 27) that Zonaras died at Mt Athos, where his epitaph could be seen, is suspect, given Thevet's demonstrable inclination to embellishment.

11 So, to mention one particularly influential example, Ziegler, "Zonaras," cols 720–721.

12 Zon. *Prologue* 1, I, pp. 3.1–4.4.

13 M. Angold, *Church and Society in Byzantium Under the Comneni, 1081–1261* (Cambridge: Cambridge University Press, 1995), pp. 38–39.

14 See *Jus Graecoromanum*, ed. J. Zepos and P. Zepos (Athens: George Fexis Cie, 1931), Vol. I, p. 319, with discussion by Angold, *Church and Society in Byzantium under the Comneni*, pp. 409–410, for John. See P. Gautier, "Le synod des Blachernes (fin 1094). Étude prosopographique," *Revue des Études Byzantines* 29 (1971), pp. 213–284, for Nicholaus 104, *PBW*.

15 Nicolaus Zonaras (Nikolaus 20158, *PBW*) was a *drungarius ca.* 1075 and early in the twelfth century was styled *nobelissimos*. Nicolaus Zonaras (Nikolaus 198) was *prôtoasêcrités* in the mid to late twelfth century. For other Zonarases, see Basileios 20107, *ca.* 1090; Christopher 20135, *ca.* 1150; Nikolaus 205, late eleventh century; and Nikolaus 20159, *ca.* 1100. For Naucratius, see C. Mango, "Twelfth-Century Notices from Cod. Christ Church Gr. 53," *Jahrbuch der Österreichischen Byzantinistik* 42 (1992), pp. 221–228, especially 221–222 and 226–227.

16 On Aristenus and Balsamon, see *ODB* I, pp. 169 and 249, respectively, For Balsamon's description of the commission in his case, see R-P I, pp. 31–33.

17 With Zon. XVIII.18.3 [III, p. 717.17–18], and Anna Comnena *Alexiad* II.12.5, p. 86, *cf.* Scylitzes Continuatus p. 176.6–13:

> the sovereign [Michael VII Ducas] selected another, not one of the senate, not of those of the church, not another of the Byzantines notable and far-famed from work and deed, but Cosmas, a monk who had come from the Holy City and was held in the greatest esteem by the sovereign through the virtue manifest in him. For if he was without a taste of secular wisdom and uninitiated, yet he preened himself in diverse virtues.

18 Zon. XVIII.21.22 (III, p. 734.9–11) and XVIII.21.24 (III, p. 734.14–16).
19 On matters of church, state, and canon law under Alexius, see Magdalino, *The Empire of Manuel I Komnenos*, pp. 267–275.
20 For Zonaras' position, see R-P II, p. 173, translated below in n. 28 of the commentary on Zon. XIII.3, p. 19. For the context, see J. M. Hussey, *The Orthodox Church in the Byzantine Empire* (Oxford: Oxford University Press, 1990), pp. 168–171.
21 Works that probably fall in this period are: treatises on nocturnal emissions, *Oratio ad Eos Qui Naturalem Seminis Fluxum Immunditiem Existimant*, *PG* 119, cols 1011–1031, and on hymns and on the marriage of cousins, *De Canone, Hirmo, Tropario et Oda* and *De Matrimonio Sobrinorum*, *PG* 135, cols. 422–428 and 429–438, respectively; a memoir on Sophronius, bishop of Jerusalem, *HYΠOMNHMA EIΣ TON OΣION ΠATEPA HMΩN ΣΩΦPONION*, ed. A. Papadopoulos-Kerameus, Vol. V of *ANAΛEKTA IEPOΣOΛYMITIKHΣ ΣTAXYOΛOΓIAΣ* (Reprint of 1888 edn; Brussels: Culture et Civilisation, 1963), pp. 137–150; and, if by Zonaras, a biography of Silvester, bishop of Rome, *BIOΣ KAI ΠOΛITEIA TOY EN AΓIOIΣ ΠATPOΣ HMΩN ΣIΛBEΣTPOY ΠAΠA PΩMHΣ*, *Roma e l'Oriente* 6 (1913), pp. 340–376. See further K. Krumbacher, *Geschichte der byzantinischen Litteratur*, 2 vols (reprint of 1897 edn; New York: Burt Franklin, 1970), I, pp. 135, n. 6, 139, n. 4, 374–375, and II, pp. 679–682. On the *Lexicon* sometimes attributed to John, see K. Ziegler, "Zonarae Lexicon," *RE* XA.1 (1972), cols 732–763.
22 *E.g.* the conflation of Bohemund's failure in 1107 with end of Nicholas' patriarchate in 1111 at XVIII.25.7 (III, p. 750.15–1); vague temporal expressions at XVIII.25.9 (III, p. 751.9), 26.1 (p. 752.10), 26.9 (p. 753.11), 26.21 and 23 (p. 755.7 and 14), and 27.8 (p. 757.3); the failure to note the death of Alexius' son Andronicus in 1116; and the conflicting accounts of Alexius' death at XVIII.28.19–21 (pp. 761.17–762.16).
23 Zon. XVIII.19.13–14 (III, p. 722.15–15): "The undertaking was boldfaced adultery. And hence, he who had finalized the sacred vow for them was banished from the priesthood." With this *cf.* Scylitzes Continuatus, pp. 181.22–182.6–7, which names Vevdene and concludes: "and the priest immediately was suspended, since an adultery had been profanely finalized" (p. 182.6–7); Nicephorus Bryennius, *Hylê Historias* III.25, pp. 126.8–127.8; and A. E. Laiou, "Imperial Marriages and Their Critics in the Eleventh Century: The Case of Skylitzes," *Dumbarton Oaks Papers* 46 (Dumbarton Oaks, Washington DC: Trustees for Harvard University, 1992), pp. 165–176, especially pp. 173–174.
24 E. Patzig, "Über einige Quellen des Zonaras," *Byzantinische Zeitschrift* 5 (1896), pp. 24–53, and 6 (1897), pp. 322–356. W. A. Schmidt, "Ueber die Quellen des Zonaras," *Zeitschrift für die Altertumswissenschaft* 30–36 (1839), pp. 238–285, reprinted in *Ioannis Zonarae Epitome Historiarum*, ed. L. Dindorf (Leipzig: B. G. Teubner, 1874), Vol. VI, pp. iii–lx, remains valuable.
25 M. DiMaio, "The Antiochene Connection: Zonaras, Ammianus Marcellinus, and John of Antioch on the Reigns of the Emperors Constantius II and Julian," *Byzantion* 50 (1980), pp. 158–185; "Infaustis Ductoribus Praeviis: The Antiochene Connection, Part II," *Byzantion* 51 (1981), pp. 502–510; and "Smoke in the Wind: Zonaras' Use of Philostorgius, Zosimus, John of Antioch, and John of Rhodes in his Narrative on the Neo-Flavian Emperors," *Byzantion* 58 (1988), pp. 230–255.

26 *Untersuchungen zum Geschichtswerk des Johannes von Antiocheia*, *ΕΠΙΣΤΗ-ΜΟΝΙΚΗ ΕΠΕΤΗΡΙΔΑ ΤΗΣ ΦΙΛΟΣΟΦΙΚΗΣ ΣΧΟΛΗΣ* 67 (Thessalonica: ΑΡΙΣΤΟΤΕΛΕΙΟ ΠΑΝΕΠΙΣΤΗΜΙΟ ΘΕΣΣΑΛΟΝΙΚΗΣ, 1989).

27 On the *Excerpta Salmasiana*, see *Ioannis Antiocheni Fragmenta ex Historia Chronica. Texte und Untersuchungen zur Geschichte der altchristichen Literatur 154* , ed U. Roberto, (Berlin and New York: Walter de Gruyter, 2005), pp. liii–lxxvii.

28 *Die Reichskrise des III. Jahrhunders in der spätantiken und byzantinischen Geschichtsschreibung. Untersuchungen zu den nachdionischen Quellen der Chronik des Johannes Zonaras* (Munich: tuduv, 1992).

29 *Ioannis Antiocheni Fragmenta ex Historia* (Berlin and New York: Walter de Gruyter, 2005). For a summary of Roberto's conclusions, see Alan Cameron's review, *BMCR* 2006.07.37, available at http://ccat.sas.upenn.edu/bmcr/2006/2006-07-37.html.

30 See further T. M. Banchich, *The Historical Fragments of Eunapius of Sardis*, 1985 State University of New York at Buffalo PhD dissertation (Ann Arbor MI: University Microfilms International, 1986), pp. 39–66. For possible evidence of the excerptors' methods, see P. Schreiner, "Die Historiker-handschrift Vaticanus Graecus 977: ein Handexemplar zur Vorbereitung des Konstantinischen Exzerptenwerkes?," *Jahrbuch der Österreichischen Byzantinistik* 37 (Wein: Österreichischen Akademie der Wissenschaften, 1987), pp. 1–29.

31 *Symeonis Magistri et Logothetae Chronicon*, ed. S. Wahlgren, *CFHB*, *Series Berolinensis* 44.1 (Berlin: Walter de Gruyter, 2006), reviewed by T. M. Banchich, *BMCR* 2007.09.34, available at http://ccat.sas.upenn.edu/bmcr/2007/2007-09-34.html; Tocci, "Zu Genese und Compositionsvorgang der ΣΥΝΟΨΙΣ ΧΡΟΝΙΚΗ des Theodoros Skutariotes," *Byzantinische Zeitschrift* 98 (2005), pp. 551–568, and *Theodori Scutariotae Chronica*. ed. R. Tocci, *CFHB*, *Series Berolinensis* 46 (Berlin: Walter de Gruyter, forthcoming, 2008). The list of pertinent authors in need of new editions could be extended. See, for example, D. Afinogenov, "Le manuscrit grec Coislin. 305: la version primitive de la *Chronique* de Georges le Moine," *Revue des Études Byzantines* 62 (2004), pp. 239–246.

32 "The Horoscope of Constantinople," *ΠΡΙΣΜΑΤΑ: Naturwissenschafts-geschichtliche Studien*, eds Y. Maeyama and W. G. Saltzer (Wiesbaden: Franz Steiner, 1977), pp, 305–315. See further n. 24 on Zon. XIII.3, p. 15.

33 John Zonaras, Ἐπιτομὴ Ἱστοριῶν, ed. trans. I. Gregoriades, 3 vols, *Keimena vyzantines logotechnias* 5 (Athens: Kanake, 1995–2001). Krumbacher, *Geschichte der byzantinischen Litteratur*, I, p. 374, lists early Italian and French translations. Agnes Wenman (d. 1617) produced an English translation of the French version of Jan de Maumont:

> The translation is preserved in manuscript in the Cambridge University Library, in two large folio volumes, and is entitled "The Historyes and Chronicles of the World. By John Zonaras . . . Digested into three Books. Done out of Greek into French. . . . And done into English by the noble and learned lady Agnes Wenman . . ." The volumes appear to have been transcribed from Lady Wenman's autograph, of which a portion . . . is in another manuscript in the library."
>
> (E. Carlyle, "Agnes Wenman," *The Dictionary of National Biography*, eds L. Stephen and S. Lee, 22 vols [Oxford: Oxford University Press, 1921–1922], XX, p. 1166)

18

An electronic search of various catalogues of the Cambridge libraries yielded no results for Wenman's translation.

34 *Zonaras' Account of the Neo-Flavian Emperors: A Commentary*, 1977 University of Missouri PhD dissertation (Ann Arbor MI: University Microfilms International, 1992).

35 For these and other terms, see "Zonaras' military and administrative terminology," pp. 288–289.

36 Roberto, *Ioannis Antiocheni Fragmenta; Zosime Histoire Nouvelle*, ed. and trans. F. Paschoud, 3 vols, Collection Budé (Paris: "Les Belles Lettres," 1971–2003); Zosimus, *New History*, trans. R. T. Ridley (Canberra: Australian Association for Byzantine Studies, 1982); and Philostorgius, *Church History*, trans. P. R. Amidon (Atlanta GA: Society of Biblical Literature, 2007).

37 *E.g.* A. Demandt, *Die Spätantike: Römische Geschichte von Diocletian bis Justinian, 284–565 n. Chr.* (Munich: C. H. Beck, 1978); *The Late Empire, A.D. 337–425*, Vol. XIII of *CAH*, 2nd edn, eds A. Cameron and P. Garnsey (Cambridge: Cambridge University Press, 1998); P. Southern, *The Roman Empire from Severus to Constantine* (London and New York: Routledge, 2001); N. Lenski, *Failure of Empire* (Berkeley CA: University of California Press, 2002); D. Potter, *The Roman Empire at Bay* (London and New York: Routledge, 2004); *The Crisis of Empire*, Vol. XII of *CAH*, 2nd edn, eds A. K. Bowman, P. Garnsey, and A. Cameron (Cambridge: Cambridge University Press, 2005); and S. Mitchell, *A History of the Later Roman Empire* (Oxford: Blackwell Publishing, 2007).

38 Along with the notes and bibliographies in Paschoud's Zosimus and in the works listed above in n. 37, see S. Brecht, *Die römische Reichskrise von ihrem Ausbruch bis zu ihrem Höhepunkt in der Darstellung byzantinischer Autoren. Althistorische Studien der Universität Würzburg*, Vol. I (Rahden, Westf.: Verlag Marie Leidorf GmbH, 1999).

39 D. Kienast, *Römische Kaisertabelle*, 3rd edn (Darmstadt: Wissenschaftliche Buchgesellschaft, 2004), T. D. Barnes, *The New Empire of Diocletian and Constantine* (Cambridge MA and London: Harvard University Press, 1982) and *Athanasius and Constantius* (Cambridge MA: Harvard University Press, 1993).

40 *The Barrington Atlas of the Greek and Roman World*, ed. R. J. A. Talbert (Princeton NJ: Princeton University Press, 2000).

41 See, for example, *Chronologies of the Ancient World, BNP, Supplement I*, eds W. Eder and J. Renger, trans. and ed. W. Henkelman (Leiden and Boston MA: Brill, 2007), pp. 272–280, or Kienast, *Römische Kaisertabelle*.

EPITOME OF HISTORIES

Collected and composed
by the monk John Zonaras
formerly Grand Commander of the
Palace Watch and First Secretary
of the Chancery

PROLOGUE

1

[3] On target one might, in mockery, say, "Diversion is of greater importance to you than work. For, since I had, in truth, long since forsworn matters of business, forborne to be disturbed, absented myself from public life, chosen to live alone, and sentenced myself to perpetual exile—for thus had the One above us arranged our affairs, since He broke my bonds, when, for reasons which He alone understood, He (painfully for me, but nevertheless beneficially) deprived me of those most dear—, it became necessary that I pursue naught but those things which restore a soul and cleanse [4] it of deeds which have, by virtue of their pettiness, defiled it, and those things which appease the Divine concerning the things which, because I had transgressed Its injunctions and ordinances, I did to anger It, and thus to seek forgiveness for my missteps. And I, apathetically disposed toward my work as a result of my indifference to fine things, expended my energy on diversion.

But in order to defend myself even a bit further, I did not rush of my own volition to this undertaking, but men who were my friends urged me to it, observing me at leisure and saying, "Use your leisure for work of general benefit and recompense will be laid up for you before God from this, too."[1] For they added how those who have labored on histories and have written what happened long ago, have, some of them, written in great detail both the various deeds of the men of old and their stratagems, detailing dispositions and clashes of armies, encampments, fortifications, entrenchments, and if there was anything connected with these, and, in addition to them, descriptions of locales, difficulties of routes, fortifications of cities, steep and trackless mountains, narrowness of passes, heights of towers lofty and, as some say, ethereal; while by others, displaying their level of power with regard to writing, compositions also have

23

been composed for show, [5] and, as a result, they place public speeches center stage and have employed language very discursively or even very rhetorically; for some their love of distinction actually culminated in dialogues, with the result that, wherever they are writing of those who hold heterodox views and who are in error about correct doctrines, they compose lectures for them as for people present, refute their base opinion, and adduce proofs from the Holy Scripture, or even speak against Jews, showing them to be willing evildoers unless they accept our mystery, and they have employed prophetic oracular responses, and have, moreover, set themselves in opposition to Hellenes, brought their nonsense into public, ridiculed those things related by them as myths, and adduced their writings as evidence of their base opinion, and in places they even speak in maxims and write with a moral purpose.[2] By the majority, not to say perhaps by all of those who have read the compositions of those histories, these things are regarded as tiresome and off-putting because they both require a surfeit of leisure and because, even if some who apply themselves to the histories manage to be so fortunate, the effort expended on them turns out vain, since the lengthy expositions about alignments and wars and the soldiers' orders-of-battle and of the rest of such things elude their memory, and, in truth, the public speeches and the lectures verge on the useless for those who apply themselves to what is [6] being recounted. "For," they say, "for whom will there be any advantage as a result of knowing what this demagogue said to the people, what the general said to the soldiers, or what that emperor said to the ambassadors from the Persians, or another to those from the Celts or Scythians or perhaps to those from Egypt or those from the Dacians and Triballians, and how another, delivering a speech, conversed with the senatorial council or the plebeian throng?"[3] Some, they said, had published compositions of histories of this sort, quite obviously embellished and tending toward the ornate, while others, antithetically opposed to these with regard to the compilation of their histories, having employed succinctness of speech, and thence, as concerns matters of import, penalizing those who have paid serious attention to their compositions, seeing that they omitted, too, very important actions of the men who were being written about—some, moreover, very praiseworthy—having stated things as briefly as possible about them, and these neither clarifying their character, nature, or purpose nor how each of those who have reigned gained sovereignty, nor who he was before this, nor from whom he was descended. They regularly added that some of these compositions have been published in an excessively simple style, and that these have been very clumsily produced and constructed in phrases crude or sometimes even barbarous, with the result, therefore, that men familiar with literature are repelled by them.[4] [7] Saying things of this sort and assailing historical compositions as has been described, they constantly prodded me to take books in hand and, having omitted much indeed, some of which, through its quantity, did not naturally cling to the memory, and other things which end in nothing beneficial, and having abridged their obviously embellished narrative, to publish a concise history, the composition succinctly instructing its users about the accomplishments of—or, on the other hand, what has befallen—those about whom the compilation speaks.

So then, they kept inciting me to strip down for such a work and to set upon such a composition.

2

But, for one thing, being intellectually lax (for the truth will be told) and passing life in lethargy, and, for another, seeing that the matter required work and many books, I kept hesitating and shrinking from the attack. But those who were goading me did not let up, and eventually, by the incessancy of their prodding, they roused me to the task. For if a raindrop's persistence is able to hollow the rigidity and hardness of the rock, incessant speech, tapping at the ears, is able to arouse a mind's lethargy and lazy inclination. Then, too, it came to mind that the labor and busywork connected with the compilation would not be unprofitable with regard to spiritual benefit. For the spirits of evil are more accustomed to blow on the mind at rest and rouse waves of base concerns and, from time to time, worries, and [8] to immerse it by the incessancy of their assaults, and either to make it glide off toward sins—even if not in deeds but, in fact, in assents to deeds—or, at times, to wash over it a great gale and tumult. If the mind is engrossed with something, it is prone, on the whole, to escape the inundation of many worries and base concerns. So then, through the stimulus from my friends and through the frightening away of my sordid or, indeed, vain concerns, I committed myself to this study.

Now thus did it happen that I undertook the present composition. If I shall not relate in great detail the history of each of the particulars narrated therein, I beg those who will read it to grant me pardon. For perhaps it will not befall me, spending my time at the very present in this out-of-the-way place, to have possession of all the books which are useful to me for the purpose of my composition, nor did all the writers of the histories write the same things about the same matters, but, in instances, if not most often, they disagree. And even if I should actually wish to do a thorough treatment of each of the things recounted, and to clarify what a particular writer says about this and what another writer says about the same thing, I would myself also make the treatment of each many lines long. On this account, it has seemed best to me to omit things about which those who have written about the same matters were in opposition, unless it is something very worthy of attention, which, being omitted, will ruin the compilation with regard to matters of import. If the impression of my language is variegated and not throughout [9] internally consistent, let no one fault my language or its father, me. For, having collected the histories from many books, in many instances, indeed, I might use the formulations and phrases of those writers, and also, too, in what I myself might parody or paraphrase, I shall adapt the form of the language I use to their character, lest my writing itself seem internally discordant.[5]

3

But, before the history, let me state in a very summary fashion what will be recounted, in order that those who are going to read the composition know that they will become knowledgeable of many and, among them, most indispensable histories. Indeed, then, encompassed in the *Epitome* is the *Octateuch* and as much as is recounted in it. The books of *Kings* are likewise embraced, and, in addition to these, *Chronicles* and as much as the Hebrew Josephus, discussing antiquities, otherwise stated beyond the more ancient ones, whether he recounted something more discursively or differently compared with these.[6] The matters of Esdras are recounted, and the matters of the captivities of the Hebrews—of the earlier, the one of the ten tribes, which was brought about by the Assyrian Salmanasar, after he had taken Samaria by siege and had captured the people and had led it away and settled it beyond the Euphrates, and had resettled in Samaria some peoples named Chuthaei,[7] then, [10] too, the one brought by Nebuchadnesar upon Jerusalem, and how the city became deserted, the temple was burned, and the entire people enslaved,[8] how, after seventy years, according to the predictions of the prophets, it was granted to the people by Cyrus, after he had destroyed the sovereignty of the Assyrians, to return to Jerusalem, to rebuild the city, and to renovate the temple—; who Cyrus was, how he dissolved the Assyrians' sovereignty, and who gained the sovereignty after him;[9] how and by whom the building of the city was hindered, and by whom, in turn, its construction was granted;[10] about Daniel the prophet, how he interpreted the dreams of Nebuchadnesar and the vision of Balthasar, when that barbarian saw the "wrist of the hand" writing on the wall, about certain visions of the prophet, which are all recounted with an abbreviated exegesis;[11] about the three boys and the extraordinary things that, by God, came to pass for them or through them;[12] about Esther and how she rescued the race of the Hebrews from total annihilation;[13] about Judith, who, having outwitted Holophernes, killed him and delivered his army to perdition;[14] about Tobith and how, having been struck by blindness and carried off from wealth to abject poverty, through good work he again, by God's providence, gained vision and received an abundance of wealth.[15] But Alexander of Macedon's affairs, too, [11] have here been abbreviated, the history having necessarily taken note of him both for other reasons and because he sojourned in Jerusalem after his initial defeat of Darius at Issus and especially honored the high priest; and how he ended the Persians' sovereignty and made it subject to himself, how long he reigned, and how, when he died, his sovereignty was divided into four realms;[16] and what came to pass for the Jews from Antiochus Epiphanes, who happened to be a descendent of one of Alexander's successors;[17] how the Hasmonaeans rose against him and redeemed those of their race from the tyranny that had resulted from him, who they were, how they led their tribesmen and for how long; how, after its return to Jerusalem from its captivity under the Assyrians, the people of the Jews was not governed by a sovereign, but ruled by its high priests; that the descendants of the aforementioned Hasmonaeans, being invested with the highpriestly honor and guiding the affairs of the people, even bestowed a diadem on themselves;[18] and how, after the brothers Hyrcanus and Aristobulus had quarreled about the Judaean sovereignty, Pompey the Great, being then in command of Romans, after he had been summoned by the siblings to arbitrate, seized the city of Jerusalem and subjected the people to the Romans;[19] how Herod, the son of Antipater, came subsequently into control of the sovereignty of the Jews, who this man was, [12] whence he came, his domestic affairs, and how long his descendants were in control of the sovereignty;[20] for what cause and from which time governors were dispatched from Rome to Judaea;[21] what Josephus wrote about our Savior Jesus Christ, but moreover, about John the Baptist, too;[22] and through what reasons the Judaeans refused to submit to the

Romans; and how their people was warred upon by the Romans, and by whom and how Jerusalem suffered its final, irrevocable sack.[23]

4

Because the history had taken note of Romans and of Rome, I thought it necessary for me to write about these, too, and to hand down whence and from what the people of the Romans had its beginning; by whom the region of Italy was previously inhabited; whence Romulus, the man who became the founder of Rome, was brought forth to the light of day; how Remus, his brother, was killed and then, too, how the former disappeared; how the city itself was first ruled; what manners and customs it employed;[24] how Tarquinius Superbus, after he had changed the sovereignty to a tyranny, was deposed; how many and what sort of wars Rome waged as a result of his deposition; how conditions for Romans were changed to aristocracy and then democracy, with consuls and *dictatores*, then tribunes, too, [13] performing the administration of public affairs;[25] what the consulship was in olden days, what the dictatorship was, and what the work of the censors was; what term was assigned to each of these offices; what a triumph was like among them and whence this name was introduced;[26] what sorts of things, even if not everything—through lack of books detailing these things— happened in the times of the consuls;[27] how, from these, rule for the Romans later changed to monarchy; how, even if not clearly, Gaius Julius Caesar first pretended to this, then, after he had been killed upon the speaker's platform by those who clung to liberty, Augustus Octavius Caesar, who was a nephew of the slain Caesar and who had been given to him in adoption, pursued the killers of his adoptive father, having Antony, too, participating with him in the work, and how, when he had afterwards quarreled also with him, he had been victorious in a naval battle off Actium, and then, when he had overtaken him after he had fled to Alexandria with Cleopatra, he brought the man to such a degree of necessity that he even killed himself; the extent of Roman losses in these civil wars, first when Octavius and Antony took the field against Brutus, Cassius, and Caesar's other killers, and then when these men battled against one another; how Cleopatra, Egypt's queen, a descendant of the Ptolemies, was taken alive [14] how she, too, killed herself, so it was concluded, by the bite of an asp; and that thus, after he had returned to Rome with brilliant victory celebrations, Octavius pursued absolute rule and transformed the leadership of the Romans into a genuine monarchy;[28] who were monarchs after him, how each reached the position, how and for how long he ruled, and what sort of end of life he met; who, during their reigns, after the revered apostles, adorned the thrones of the four great churches (I am speaking of Rome, Alexandria, Antioch, and Jerusalem) and which of them was deemed worthy of a martyr's end;[29] how, more than the others, Diocletian and Maximianus Herculius raged against Christians; how, having laid aside their office, they picked others in their own stead as Caesars, one of whom was Constantius Chlorus, the father of Constantine the Great, the rule of Gaul and Britain having been assigned to him; how he, dying, made successor of his own office his firstborn son—this none other than Constantine, the Equal of the Apostles; how, after he had defeated the rest, when the cruciform star had appeared to him through the stars in the heaven, he established himself monarch; how he came to Christ and spread the faith, having given license for the preaching of the Gospel; how he constructed a city named after himself in Byzantium, having dubbed it New Rome, [15] and transferred the sovereignty from the senior Rome to it; and who reigned therein after him, of what sort each was with respect to their characters—in addition, with respect to their piety, too—, how long each was in control of the realm, and how each departed life; and who were in charge of the church in Constantinople, how long each was, who of them adhered to right doctrine, who had become heterodox, and how each of these departed from here; and under what emperors and patriarchs and against whom the synods were summoned.[30] And thus, the account, descending as far as those who have become emperors in our own time, concludes the compilation, having been mindful of many well-known histories and others obscure.[31] For me, making a beginning of this compilation, it is necessary to begin with the ineffable first beginning, the cause of all things, the beginning both without beginning and without duration, and the production and genesis of what has been produced by it from the state of not-being toward subsistence and essentiality.

[Now the Divine eternally was, beyond every cause and power, shining timelessly, perpetually moved by the beauty of its own glory and brilliance, without beginning and without duration, neither having previously subsisted earlier from some other essence nor having come to be spontaneously later from things not being and advancing toward a consummation of Its own glory [16] gradually, but eternally being and abiding, because the All Holy Spirit alone, examining all things, supernaturally knew the depths of the Deity, co-eternally rejoicing and reveling in these. And when, through utmost goodness, immense mercy, and ineffable compassion, It chose to model this visible cosmos and to bring the Second thence to the forefront by Its creation, and also a cosmos first and extraordinary by Its Grace, inasmuch as It, too, has been fashioned according to God's image—I say, in fact, man—, just as having employed the very best course toward Its construction, It earlier subordinated the immaterial powers and the celestial unit commanders, simply thinking, having advanced, swifter than a word, from Its contemplation to work.][32]

POSTSCRIPT
Book XVIII.29

[768] Let this be the limit of the writing for me and let the course of the history here conclude—a course which has been prolonged at length. For I have not judged it profitable or opportune to commit what remains to writing. Now if the result of my labor appears helpful to any, thanks be to God, through whom all good is accomplished. But if it makes no contribution, let the fault be ours and the offspring return to me, its father, to be fuel for my memory.[33]

COMMENTARY ON
PROLOGUE AND
POSTSCRIPT

1 Similar sentiments appear in Zonaras' *Proem* to his *Commentary on the Canons of the Apostles* (R-P II, pp. 1–2): "Let no one accuse me of indiscretion. For I did not on my own assume the task, but, when I had been summoned, I submitted and devoted myself to the toil, lest, through inattentiveness, I be condemned." *Cf.* Scut. pp. 3.1–4.18:

> [3] With regard to the present work, someone might perhaps accuse us of making our own narrative things which have been described often by many and which are, therefore, known nearly to all. And someone else, too, might say we are ostentatious and showy, reveling in the words of others as of our own, and, like the jackdaw of the tale, winning our own reputation by others' wings. But I both steadfastly deny that I have made this narrative in ostentation and that I have any deep knowledge whatsoever with reference to its contents, and I grant to him who wishes to name whom he wishes the book's father. For I am very far removed from disputing these things and, as one might say, from imparting luster to them. Thus has all covetousness of things terrestrial been shunned by me. Confessing at the outset, that do I submit. Now these things have been related, my good fellow, by a number significant not only numerically but also with respect to power of speech and elegance of exposition, and composing in many works strategic and soldierly [4] forays and studies, and further, too, expostulating a mass of speeches and breadth of dialogues, like the one who chooses to wish to unroll entire books and to traverse in detail the action and administration of some single reign. But this is burdensome to the masses and also impossible, perhaps, for those for whom culture is not an acquaintance, as is the

case for worshippers who, transgressing the contents of the scriptures, inasmuch as they have fallen short of the Word, to be sure, have fallen short of their own rational disposition. But we, having synopsized the many and gathered the contents of many books into one, and having served-up this same, single work, how each administered the realm and tended his subjects, whether manifestly in piety and justness, or turned aside from the right and neglected the just. But, in truth, having avoided the entanglement of speeches and the sublimity of ideas, in common and familiar diction, to those who wish we have served seasoning and sauce sufficient for the meal, beginning whence we men, too, have had our beginning—Adam, of course—and concluding in the pious sovereigns who bear the scepters in our day.

On the *Prologue* in general, see I. Grigoriadis, "A Study of the *Prooimion* of Zonaras' *Chronicle*," *Byzantinische Zeitschrift* 91 (1999), pp. 327–344.

2   Zonaras describes the content of his work by saying what it will not contain and, in the process, reveals something of what he thought his readers might expect from a work of history. He does indeed avoid detailed descriptions of the first sort he mentions, typical of the genres of *Strategica* and *Tactica*. Likewise, with respect to the second type of historiographical excess, Zonaras includes few speeches. As for his comments about dialogues in historical works, it is difficult to tell precisely what he or his friends had in mind—perhaps passages such as Plutarch's dialogue between Alexander the Great and the gymnosophists (*Alex.* 64), reduced by Zon. IV.14 to a single sentence. On the other hand, he may be thinking of works such as Theodoret of Cyrrhus' *Eranistes* (*EEC* II, pp. 828–828; *PG* 83, cols 27–336), Macarius of Magnesias' *Apocriticus* (*EEC* I, p. 514; eds C. Blondel and P. Foucart, *Macarii Magnetis quae supersunt ex inedito codica* [Paris: Typographia Publica, 1876]), or even the so-called *Adamantius Dialogue* sometimes attributed to Origen (*PG* 11, cols 1713–1884) and portions of Origen's own *Against Celsus* (ed. P. Koetschau, *Contra Celsum*, 2 vols, *Origenes Werke*, *GCS* 2–3 [Berlin: Akademie Verlag, 1899]). The sorts of "dialogues" to which he refers certainly seem of a different kind than the brief, unique discussion between Philosophy and History with which Theophylact Simocatta prefaced his *History* (ed. C. de Boor, pp. 20–22; trans. Michael Whitby and Mary Whitby, *The* History *of Theophylact Simocatta* [Oxford: Oxford University Press, 1986], pp. 3–5).

3   Separate volumes of the *EH* produced in the reign of Constantine VII Porphyrogenitus (945–959)—the *ELGR* and *ELRG*—contain speeches of Roman legations to foreigners and foreign legations to Romans and reflect the ubiquity of and interest among Byzantines in these rhetorical displays.

4   Comparison between Zonaras, Symeon Magister, Cedrenus, and Theodore Scutariotes is instructive. Where dependent on a common source or tradition, Zonaras regularly offers more detail more fully integrated into a historical narrative. His dissatisfaction with the sparseness of accounts such as those of George the Monk and Syncellus, in fact, rather than any critical appraisal of their historical accuracy, doubtless contributed to Zonaras' rejection of the historiographical tradition preserved in such authors and his attraction to that reflected in Symeon, Cedrenus, and Scutariotes.

5   Note that Zonaras' point is not that his style will be uniform throughout the *Epitome* but rather that as he shifts sources he will adapt his style to theirs. This has obvious and important implications for any analysis of his sources. That Zonaras' metaphorical reference to himself as the "father" of his work also appears at the very end of his final book (XVI.19, translated above) suggests that he composed his *Preface* and closing comments at the same or about the same time.

6   Zonaras drew liberally from both the *JA* and the *BJ* of Flavius Josephus (b. AD 37/38). The "more ancient ones" are the biblical writers themselves. *2 Chronicles* ends with the destruction of the temple and the beginning of the Babylonian Captivity in 587 or 586 BC under Nebuchadnezzar, on whom see below, n. 8.

7   Josephus *JA* IX.14.1 (II, pp. 324–325) = Zon. II.22–23. Salmanasar V (r. 726–722 BC) probably captured Samaria, capital of the Kingdom of Israel, in 722. The Cuthaei are the Samaritans. Josephus *JA* XI.5.1–5 (III, pp. 27–35) = Zon. IV.5 derives from the apochryphal *1 Esdras*.

8   Josephus *JA* X.8.1–6 (II, pp. 358–363) = Zon. II.25. Nebushadnesar is Nebuchadnezzar, King of Babylon (r. 605/604–562 BC). The destruction of the temple occurred in 587 or 586 BC. The deportation of the Jews began the so-called Babylonian Captivity.

9   Zon IV.1 = Josephus *JA* XI.1.1–3 (III, pp. 4–7). Cyrus the Great, founder of the Achaemenid Dynasty of Persia (r. 559–530 BC), captured Babylon in 539/8.

10   Zon. IV.1. The Cuthaei opposed the rebuilding of Jerusalem (*JA* XI.2–3 [III, pp. 7–18]), approved by the Persian King Darius (r. 522–486 BC).

11   Zon. III.2–10 = Josephus *JA* X.10–11 (II, pp. 370–392). The exegesis consists of Zonaras' comments mixed with an abbreviation of portions of the *Interpretatio in Danielem* of Theodoret (*PG* 81, cols 1255–1546).

12   Shadrach, Meshach, and Abnednego. Zon. III.2 = Josephus *JA* X.10.1 (II, pp. 370–371).

13   Zon. IV.6–7 = *JA* XI.6.2–13 (III, pp. 41–60).

14   Zon. III.12. The apochryphal *Judith* 8–16 recounts the Jewish heroine's murder of Holophernes, Nebuchadnezzer's general, of which Josephus is silent.

15   Zon. III.13–14 abbreviates the apochryphal *Tobit*. Josephus does not mention Tobit.

16   Zon. IV.8 and IV.15, following Josephus *JA* XI.8.2–5 (III, pp. 62–68), deals with Alexander's probably apocryphal visit to Jerusalem, which he places after the defeat of Darius at Issus in 333 BC but before the end of the siege of Tyre (333–332). In Zonaras' view, it is Alexander's sojourn in Jerusalem that makes the Macedonian conqueror historically relevant. Zon. III.6 describes the four realms— Ptolemy's Egypt, Seleucus' Syria, Antigonus' Asia, and Antipator's Macedon—in the context of his account of Daniel's vision (*Daniel* 7.2–27/Josephus *JA* X.11.7 [II, pp. 387–392]). Zonaras found the identification of the four beasts of the dream with the four kingdoms of the Diadochs in Theodoret's *Interpretatio* (*PG* 81, cols 1417B–C and 1444A–B).

17   Antiochus IV Epiphanes, of the Seleucid dynasty, ruled from 176 to 164 BC. Reaction among some Jews against Seleucid rule and Greek cultural inroads among fellow Jews led to open violence under the leadership of Matthias of the Hamonaean priestly family. After the

death of Mattathias, his son Judah Maccabee won a series of victories against Antiochus' commanders that contributed by 142 BC to some sort of *modus vivendi* between a Hasmonaean-directed Judaea and the current Seleucid ruler, Demetrius II (r. *ca.* 161–125 BC). Zonaras' account (IV.18–V.2) depends on Josephus *JA* XII.4.11–13.2 (III, pp. 111–162), and on *BJ* I.

18   In 140 BC the Hasmonaean Simon became both high priest and King of Judaea.

19   In 67 BC John Hyrcanus II and Aristobulus II, sons of the Hasmonaean ruler Alexander Janneus (r. 104/103–76 BC) and Queen Salome Alexandra vied for the throne. Pompey the Great, whose campaigns against Mithridates of Pontus had brought him to the Near East, was asked to intervene and threw his support to John, whom he perhaps viewed as more easily manipulated than Aristobulus.

20   Zon. V.5–VI.3/Josephus *JA* XIV.1.3–17.13 (III, p. 240–IV, p. 137). When the Parthians installed a certain Antigonus, a Hasmonaean, as King of Judaea in 40 BC, Rome countered with her own appointee, Herod the Great (r. 37–4 BC), son of the Idumenaean Antipater and a proven supporter of Roman interests. Herod, who took a Hasmonaean wife, ruled until his death. Augustus then divided the kingdom among Herod's sons Philip, Herod Antipas, and Archelaus. Archelaus, who had been granted the southern portion of Herod's realm—Judaea proper, Samaria, and Idumaea— eventually fell into disfavor and was banished by Augustus in AD 6, at which time Judaea became a Roman province.

21   Zon. VI.3 = Josephus *JA* XVIII.1 (IV, pp. 140–141). Zonaras takes care to mention every Roman administrator whose name he found in Josephus *JA* and *BJ*.

22   Zon. VI.4 = *JA* XVIII.3.3 (IV, pp. 151–152), the latter often suspected to be a Christian addition to Josephus' text, and Zon. VI.6 = *JA* XVIII.5.2 (IV, pp. 161–162).

23   Titus' capture and sack of Jerusalem in AD 70 is the subject of Josephus' *BJ* V = Zon. VI.18–29.

24   Zonaras ends Book VI with a transition from the Roman campaign in Judaea to an account of the history of Rome herself, which

Book VII.1–10 brings up to the reign of Tarquinius Superbus, traditionally dated 534–510 BC.

25   These changes had special significance for Zonaras, who found in Theodoret's *Interpretatio* (*PG* 81, col. 1420A) connections between alterations in the government of Rome and the imagery of the dream of Daniel. Zonaras says at III.3, "And someone who consults the pertinent ancient composition will discover that these things have occurred very often in the Roman constitution."

26   Zonaras treats consuls at VII.19, dictators at VII.13, and censors at VII.19. His digressions on the triumph appear at VII.21 and XII.32, for which see n. 139 on the latter passage.

27   Zonaras records nothing of Roman history between the sacks of Corinth and Carthage in 146 and the rise of Pompey the Great—the latter drawn from Plut. *Pomp.*—with which he begins Book X. This gap corresponds exactly to a portion of Dio's *History* no longer extant and clearly also missing from the text consulted by Zonaras. However, at the conclusion of his treatment of Republican Rome (IX.31), Zonaras gives other reasons for these omissions:

> Now what had been accomplished up to this point by the Romans, I, having chanced upon books of the men of old who had investigated these ancient things, have appropriated from them in abbreviated form and have placed in this composition, and in addition to these in sequence the things which were accomplished by the consuls and dictators as long as affairs were being administered by those in these offices in Rome, lest anyone fault me as having passed over these matters either in disdain or laxness or lethargy and having permitted the composition to be incomplete. For not in carelessness have the omissions gone unnoticed by me nor have I willingly bequeathed the work half finished, but by a shortage of books which, indeed, recount these things for me, having often sought, but nevertheless not having discovered, these books—I know not whether because these do not survive, the extent of time having destroyed them, or because those to whom I had entrusted it had perhaps not very carefully done a search of these, myself being an exile and passing time far from the city on a little island. Indeed now, because it was not granted to me to

chance upon these books, the history has, as a result, become incomplete with respect to the deeds of the consuls, but moreover also those of the dictators. Therefore, having passed over these, even reluctantly, I shall write up those of the emperors, having related beforehand certain details, in order that the course by which the Romans were brought to autarchy from aristocracy or from democracy, too, be clear to those who are going to read the composition and at the same time, besides, that the writing also possess continuity.

Among the works that Zonaras may have employed in place of Dio are Appian's *Civil Wars* and a series of Plutarch's biographies. This said, it is evident that in Zonaras' view this period of Roman history was unimportant within the framework of the workings in history of the Christian god and could, therefore, be passed over. The same applies to other notable minimizations: mention of the Trojan War only in connection with the story of Aeneas taken from a lost book of Dio (VII.1/*cf*. Boissevain, Vol. I, p. 1); of Sparta only in connection with an alleged mid-second-century BC alliance with the Jews also recounted by Josephus (*JA* XIII.5.8 [III, pp. 180–182] = IV.24); of Athens only in connection with a very brief mention in the context of a list of Achaemenid kings and of Xerxes' invasion of Europe and defeat at Salamis (III.6), her reconciliation in 335 BC with Alexander after his destruction of Thebes (IV.9, from Plut. *Alex*.13.1, her friendship with Rome in 228 BC (VIII.19) from a lost book of Dio (*cf*. Boissevain, Vol. I, p. 182), her reception of Pompey in 67 BC (X.3, from Plut. *Pomp*. 27.3), the honors she granted to Cassius and Brutus (X.18, from Dio XLVII.4), Valerianus' repair of her walls (XII.23), and the character of the Empress Eudocia (XIII.22); and of Philip II of Macedon (IV.8) only in connection with Alexander's life as recounted by Plutarch.

28   Book X ends with the death of Augustus and the birth of Jesus. Here again, Zonaras' concept of a Christian history is evident.

29   Zonaras once more exhibits his Christian historiographical concerns. Through the reign of Alexander Severus he largely combines material from the *Ecclesiastical History* of Eusebius of Caesarea, from Herodian, and from John Xiphilinus the Younger's eleventh-century epitome of Books XXXVI–LXXX of the *Roman History* of Dio.

30   For Zonaras, post-Constantinian history is almost exclusively an account of the empire of Constantinople, her rulers and patriarchs, and of the triumphs of Orthodoxy over a series of heresies. He usually notes other matters only in so far as they impinge on these interrelated themes. All else is historically irrelevant.

31   Zonaras ends with the death of Alexius Comnenus and the accession of John Comnenus in AD 1118.

32   These theological observations appear only in some manuscripts and, as a result, Pinder and earlier editors have bracketed them as an addition by a later hand. "Celestial unit commanders" probably refers to the archangels Michael, Gabriel, and, perhaps, Raphael.

33   For Zonaras' closing metaphor of "fuel" for memory, *cf.* Gregory of Nazianzus *Or.* 8.22, *PG* 35, col. 813C, and *Or.* 24.2, *PG* 35, col. 1172B.

BOOK XII.15–35

15

[571] After Pseudo-Antoninus[1] had been eliminated, Alexander, the son of Mamaea, his *anepsios*—for this word, which now means "nephew," was used by the ancients to mean "cousins"—was allotted the rule.[2] He immediately proclaimed Augusta his own mother, Mamaea, who had handled affairs of state, and she gathered wise men around her son in order that his mores be modulated by them, and from the senate she selected the best counselors, with whom she shared all that had to be done. When the command of the guardsmen and the administration of the treasury had been entrusted to Domitius Ulpianus, he corrected many of Sardanapalus' deeds. He killed Flavianus and Chrestus in order to succeed them, and not much later was attacked by the guardsmen by night and slaughtered. While Ulpianus still lived, there was, as the result of some trivial confrontation, violence between the people and the guardsmen, and for three days they battled one another. When the soldiers were getting the worst of things and set fire to some houses, the people, in fear for the city, reluctantly retired. Although other uprisings occurred, they were supressed.[3]

[572] Alexander's mother, addicted to riches, amassed wealth from all quarters. She presented to her son a bride, whom she did not assent to be called Augusta, but whom, after a brief interval, she detached from her son and relegated to Libya, though she was the object of his affection. He was unable to oppose his mother, who controlled him.[4]

Now then, Artaxerxes the Persian, who was from an obscure and inglorious family, gained possession of the Parthian realm for the Persians and ruled them. From him Chosroes' family, too, is said to be descended. After the death of Alexander of Macedon, his Macedonian successors long ruled both the Persians and the Parthians and the other tribes, but, of course, they marched against one another and destroyed each other. When they had been weakened thus, first Arsacides the Parthian attempted rebellion from them, won control of the Parthians, and left his realm to his descendants, the last of whom was Artabanus. After he had defeated him in three battles, the aforementioned Artaxerxes captured and killed him. Then he marched against Armenia, too, and was beaten when the Armenians and the Medes, with the sons of Artabanus, attacked him. After he had recovered, he, in turn, watched for an opportunity to set upon Mesopotamia and Syria with a larger force and threatened that he would recover everything bequeathed to the Persians from their ancestors.[5]

[573] Then Artaxerxes, with the Persians, overran Cappadocia and besieged Nisibis.[6] Now Alexander, seeking peace, sent ambassadors to him. The barbarian did not receive the delegation, but dressed four hundred of his grandees in costly robes, put them on horses from the choice mounts, adorned them with glittering arms, and dispatched them to Alexander, thinking that he would thus frighten him and the Romans. When they had arrived and come into Alexander's presence, they said, "The Great King Artaxerxes orders the Romans to abandon Syria and all Asia opposite Europe and to concede to the Persians to rule as far as the sea." Alexander arrested them, stripped them of their arms and robes, deprived them of their horses, dispersed them into many villages, and compelled them to till the soil. For he did not consider it pious to kill them.[7] He divided his own forces into three groups and launched a triple attack against the Persians. And while much destruction of Persians resulted, very many Romans also perished, not so much at the hands of their enemies as in the return through the mountains of Armenia. For, since the mountains were very frigid, the feet of the marchers and even the hands of some, blackened and morbid, were amputated as a result of the cold. And, on account of this, Alexander became a ground for complaint to the Romans. Hence, out of despondency, or even from the change of climate, he became very ill.[8]

When he had recovered, he attacked the Germans and harassed them with his javeliniers and archers. He also sent a delegation to them about sureties [574] in exchange for subsidies. As a result, the soldiers became enraged and contemplated rebellion.[9] And, ostensibly against his will, they grabbed a certain Maximinus, a Thracian by extraction, who as a child had been assigned to herd sheep and subsequently had become a soldier, and named him emperor. He took those who had proclaimed him and headed off immediately to where Alexander was staying. When Alexander learned of this, he exhorted the soldiers with him to his aid, and they promised to help. When Maximinus approached, Alexander assembled his army and ordered it to attack Maximinus' men. But they both reproached and disparaged his mother for her greed, and insolently turning on him they abandoned him as a coward and began to depart. When he saw himself bereft of aid, he withdrew to his tent, embraced his mother, and began weeping. Maximinus sent a centurion and killed Mamaea, Alexander, and those with him, and he came into control of the realm.[10]

Mamaea, Alexander's mother, had pursued virtue and a reverent life. While accompanying her son in Antioch, she learned about Origen and summoned him from Alexandria. By him she was taught the word of the faith and became very devout, as Eusebius recounts and certain other writers say. On this account, not only did the contemporary persecution of the Christians subside but also those revering Christ were deemed most worthy of honor.[11]

[575] At that time, while Urbanus was the bishop in charge of the city of Rome, Hippolytus flourished, a man most holy and wise, who became bishop of the port of Rome, composed many writings, and explicated various points of the divine. Asclepiades was in charge of Antioch and was directing the church of the faithful there. And Sardianus of Jerusalem.[12]

16

After he had led the Romans for ten years, Alexander was disposed of in the manner described, and Maximinus received the empire.[13] Immediately he both aroused a persecution against the Christians and commanded that those in charge of the churches be killed on the grounds that they were teachers and preachers of the mystery according to Christ. It is said that he initiated the persecution because of his hatred toward Alexander, since the latter honored those who revered Christ. For he was angry with that ruler because, when he had been selected general by him and campaigned against the Persians and had been disgracefully defeated, he endured imperial ire. There was also a second cause of the persecution: many throughout Alexander's household had recognized Christ as God.[14] At that time Ambrose, a learned man, who inspired Origen to exegesis of the divine scripture and provided lavish outlays for him and supplied to him seven tachygraphers [576] who were engaged in the writing by turns according to appointed times, and no fewer scribes and maidens trained as calligraphers, is said to have been adorned with the crown of martyrdom, together with Protoctetus, a presbyter.[15]

When he had become ruler, Maximinus at once wrote to the senate, disclosing to it his acclamation by the soldiers. He was oppressive and cruel not to Christians alone, but also to all his subjects, for he was both violent and greedy, and consequently very unjust, a perpetrator of murders, and an outright tyrant, who at any reasonable opportunity resorted to rapes and men's murders. To such a degree did he career toward bloodguilt that he did not even spare his own wife, for he murdered her. Concealing his ignoble pedigree as much as possible, he dishonored the elite and socialized with men of obscure station. For this, therefore, he was despised.[16]

He campaigned against the Germans and plundered their territory, while not one of the barbarians showed himself. Then they appeared around the swamps and the dense forests, and, when the Romans advanced there, a great number were killed. Thus did Maximinus, when he had conquered, return, bringing a throng of prisoners.[17] Appropriating all the possessions of his subjects and enriching himself from all quarters, he did not even refrain from the temples. Then, while everyone was blaming the soldiers who had acclaimed him, those who were stationed in Libya [577] contemplated rebellion when they learned of this and because they had been aroused for another additional reason. For at any reasonable opportunity the guardians of the affairs of Libya were confiscating the wealth of her elite and killing those who possessed it. Consequently, having been compelled, those there rebelled, seized from the senate a certain aged and unwilling man called Gordianus, put a diadem on him, dressed him in purple, and proclaimed him emperor and Augustus. He came to Carthage. And all willingly accepted him because of their hatred for Maximinus. He then wrote to the senate and dispatched men to announce his acclamation to those in Rome.[18] When the envoys were a long time in their voyage, those in Rome, unable to endure Maximinus' tyranny, were moved to rebellion, toppled his statues, and reviled the tyrant. Then, when they had come to the realization that, if Maximinus should survive, there would be no hope of salvation for them, they put forward Maximus and Albinus, two generals, and both enrolled in the senate. Some recorded that they were proclaimed Caesars by the senate since it had not yet learned of the acclamation of Gordianus.[19]

At any rate, Maximinus learned of this and rushed toward Italy, having made many threats against the senate. Knowing that Maximus was advancing against him—for Albinus, for defense of Rome, had remained [578] there—he veered toward Aquileia, having Moors with him, hastening to get possession of the town. Aquileia is said to be the present Venice. But he was repulsed, since those within bravely resisted him. After he had been repulsed from Aquileia and had attacked Maximus' adherents, he was beaten. He then withdrew to his own tent. When his soldiers and his guardsmen had revolted against him, he came before the tent with his son for the purpose of a parley with them. But they immediately attacked both of them and killed them. Maximinus was five-and-sixty years old, of which he ruled six. The heads of those who had been killed were cut off, exhibited to those in Aquileia, and sent on to Rome. Those in Rome stuck the head of Maximinus on a pole in the Forum in order that it be conspicuous to everyone.[20]

17[21]

Subsequently, Maximus returned to Rome, and Albinus met him, and the people and the senate received him with hymns and applause. Both ruled together and ruled nobly. But the soldiers, at any rate, were vexed that not they but the senate and people had proposed these emperors. Then even the sovereigns themselves had disagreements with one another, and this became the cause of their ruin. For when the soldiers realized that they were at odds they attacked them and, after they had bound both, they led them through [579] the entire city, abused and mocked and, in truth, tortured. Then, when they learned that the Germans planned to rescue them and save them from death, in order that this not happen, they executed them. Of these, Maximus was seventy-four years old, Albinus sixty. According to some they reigned about twenty-two days, but according to others not quite three months.[22]

After them, some have written that a certain Pompeianus grasped the empire of the Romans, but that he lost control of it quickly, as if he had gained his power in a dream, for two months had not yet passed when he was deprived, in addition to the monarchy, of his life, too, and killed—by whom and through what reason, I myself, having been unable to discover, have omitted mention—, but others have written that another took control. After him, they write that Publius Balbinus was installed, and that he too tasted a tiny bit of the rule, for they delimit for him a reign of about three months, and that he also was killed as soon as Gordianus from Libya, who, as I have already said, was proclaimed there, gained control.

They write that Gordianus, after he had arrived at Rome, became ill, in part because he was elderly—for he had lived seventy-nine years—and in part because he was exhausted, having been a long time at sea en route, and that he died from this disease, having passed only twenty-two days in it. And they write that he designated his own son successor to the realm, and that he too was called Gordianus and was named for his own father.[23]

[580] Now some have recorded that these things happened thus, while others say that some rebelled against the elder Gordianus when he had been proclaimed in Libya, and that, when battle was joined, Gordianus' men were beaten and many of them, and, in truth, his own son, were killed. And they record that, being sorely pained, he hanged himself and thus betook himself from life.[24]

Those who assign to his son, young Gordianus, the leadership of the Romans after the death from disease of the elder Gordianus have written that the former campaigned against the Persians, engaged them, and, riding his horse in the battle and encouraging his own men and stirring them toward courage, that his thigh broke when the horse slipped and fell upon him, that he was thus conveyed toward Rome, and that he died from the break, having ruled about six years.[25]

Urbanus, the archpriest of Rome, who had served as archpriest for eight years, died during Maximinus' reign. Pontianus succeeded him. After Philetus, Zebinus was in charge of the church of the Antiochenes.[26] Precisely under Gordianus the youth, Pontianus, who had been in charge of the faithful in Rome, quit life and, having occupied his office six years, had as successor Anteros. In fact, Anteros, after he had directed the church for the very briefest moment, departed for another life. After him, Flavianus chanced by divine lot on the archpriesthood, as Eusebius recorded. For it is said that when the [581] faithful had been gathered in order to select from those beside them who was going to direct the episcopacy, that Flavianus too was present, coming just then from the field. Now then, it is said that there had not been a word from anyone about his being put in charge of the church, but that there were others about whose candidacy the assembly was concerned. In such a circumstance, a dove flew down and perched upon Flavianus' head. Subsequently, all those gathered there employed one voice exactly as if from a signal and shouted to him, "You are worthy!" and they bore him to the throne of the archpriest, with no hesitation at all.[27] At that time Zebinus, the man in charge of the church of the faithful in Antioch, departed life and was succeeded by Babylas. Origen, staying at that time around Caesarea in Palestine, acquired many pupils from all over, and he even had the great Gregory the Wonderworker and his brother, Athenodorus, as auditors of his words. At that time Africanus the historian also was noteworthy.[28]

18

After the youth Gordianus, another Gordianus, in turn, obtained the empire, in lineage, as word has it, related to the departed Gordians. He campaigned against the Persians, did battle with them—Sapor, the son of Artaxerxes being in command of the nation—, defeated his opponents, and, in turn, recovered for the Romans Nisibis and Carrhae, which had been snatched by the Persians under Maximinus.[29] [582] Then, when he had reached Ctesiphon, as a result of a conspiracy of Philippus, prefect of the guard, he was killed.[30] For this Gordianus, when he had become ruler, chose as prefect his own father-in-law, called Timesocles. Now, as long as he was around, matters having to do with resources were fine for the emperor and affairs of state flowed smoothly for him, but when Timesocles died, Philippus was chosen prefect. Since he wished the soldiers to rebel, he reduced their rations, so implying that the emperor had ordered this. But others say that he withheld the supplies being brought to the camp, with the result that the soldiers were oppressed and, in consequence, were stirred to rebellion. Having rebelled against the emperor, they attacked him as the cause of the famine which had befallen them, and having attacked him, they killed him, after he had been in charge about six years.[31] Philippus immediately made a dash for the empire. When the murder of Gordianus was announced to the senate, it aroused it to select another emperor. It immediately acclaimed Caesar a certain philosopher, Marcus. He died suddenly, staying in the palace, before getting a firm foot in his rule.[32] With him dead, Severus Hostilianus controlled the leadership of the Romans. But he too, almost before he had obtained it, paid his debt. For he became ill, was bled, and died.[33] [583]

19

Then, after he had returned, Philippus came into control of the empire of the Romans. During his return, he appointed his son Philippus colleague in his sovereignty. After he had established a truce with Sapor, the ruler of the Persians, he concluded the war against the Persians, having ceded to them Mesopotamia and Armenia. When he recognized that the Romans were upset because of the transfer of the territories, after a bit he set the treaties aside and seized the territories. Sapor, as has been recorded, was of enormous bodily size, and such a man had never before been seen.[34]

Having embarked for the return, Philippus was well disposed to the Christians and even, according to some, also assented to the faith of Christ, with the result that he joined Christians in prayers in a church and there gladly admitted all his sins. For not otherwise would he have been received into communion by the leader of the church, unless he had confessed and enrolled himself among those seeking forgiveness. And it is said that he obeyed him who was in authority.[35] Now then, some say that he was the father of the martyr Eugenia. But concerning this opinion, they have been misled. For it has been recorded that that man too had been a commander, but of Egypt, and not of the guard. And after his declaration of faith in Christ, he, after he had renounced his office because of his pledge to Christ, played the man and was adorned with martyrdom.[36]

[584] After he had undertaken a war against the Scythians, the emperor Philippus returned to Rome.[37] In Moesia, Marinus, a unit commander, was chosen by the soldiers to reign. On account of this, Philippus was troubled and conversed with the senate about the revolt. While the others were silent, Decius told him that he did not need to be concerned about Marinus, as he would be killed by the soldiers themselves, since he was unworthy of the realm— which is what happened a little later according to his prediction.[38] Then, on account of this, Philippus admired Decius and urged him to depart to Moesia and to punish the instigators of the revolt. But he asked to be excused from the mission, saying that to go there benefited neither himself nor him who sent him. But even yet, Philippus kept urging him. Though unwilling, he departed. After he had departed, the soldiers immediately hailed him sovereign. When he declined, they drew their swords and forced him to accept the empire. Then from there he wrote to Philippus not to be troubled, for if he advanced on Rome, he would set aside the trappings of sovereignty. But distrusting this, Philippus took the field against him. When he had attacked Decius' men, he fell fighting in the front ranks. With him too was killed his son, Philippus. With them dead, all went over to Decius.[39] According to some, he reigned for five years, but according to others six months in addition to these. He was a native of Bostra, where, after he had become sovereign, he constructed a city named for himself, having named it Philippoupolis.[40] [585]

20[41]

At any rate, Decius, as has been said, after all the soldiers had gone over to him, returned to Rome and came into control of the leadership. After he had contemplated the weight of his office and the management of affairs of state, as some say, he appointed Valerianus over the administration of affairs of state.[42] After they had mutually encouraged one another toward fighting God, they immediately aroused a very violent persecution against those bearing the name Christian. There are some who say that Decius set upon the Christians as a result of his hatred for Philippus, since he had revered them. At any rate, he raged against all the faithful. At that time Flavianus, who had been put in charge of the church in Rome, met with a martyr's death, and Babylas, who directed the church of the faithful in Antioch, and Alexander, the bishop of Jerusalem—who then not for the first time strove on behalf of his faith in the Lord Savior, but earlier, too, as has already been said—, was imprisoned in a dungeon and then died.[43] But the great Cyprianus, too, who was bishop of Carthage, then strove on behalf of his faith in Christ. When the aforementioned archpriests had quit life, in Rome, in place of Flavianus, Cornelius became bishop, and in Antioch, in place of Babylas, Flavianus, and in Alexandria, Dionysius, and in Jerusalem, in place of Alexander, Mazabanes. Very many others were then deemed worthy of martyrdom.[44]

[586] At that time Origen was brought before the tyrannical tribunal on the grounds that he was revering Christ, but he did not attain a martyr's death, I think because God did not judge him worthy of this because of the wretched fellow's perversity with regard to orthodox doctrines. For he broke ranks, and this after an ordeal of tortures.[45] As has been said before, after he had become great in words and thence mighty and pretentious, he did not follow the doctrine of the holy fathers prior to him, but, relying on himself, he reckoned himself an innovator of novel doctrines, and vomited forth from the evil treasure of his heart blasphemies both toward the holy trinity and toward the divine incarnation, and he became the founder of virtually every heresy. For he both taught that the only begotten Son of God was created and estranged him of his glory and his paternal essence, and he debased the Holy Spirit from the rank of the Father and of the Son, saying that neither is the Son able to behold his Father nor, indeed, the Spirit the Son, exactly as the angels are not able to behold the Spirit nor humans the angels. While these were the blasphemies of Origen about the holy and

consubstantial trinity, he did indeed blaspheme about the incarnation of the Son of God, impiously teaching that Christ did not receive flesh animated from the Holy Virgin. For he fabricated a tale that before the foundation of the universe the only-begotten Son of God was united with Intellect, which, as chosen and not submitting to disturbance, he reshaped, and with it to the utmost degree he was made man and [587] took on flesh distinct from intellectual and rational soul. And he taught that the Lord would again set aside the flesh and that his reign would have an end. For he instructed that there was going to be a restoration of the demons, and a temporal, but not everlasting, retribution, and that it would exist for the sake of a purification of sins, and that, after they had been purified, all, both humans and demons, would be restored to the "Unity." The particulars about this "Unity," which require a surfeit of words to clarify its nonsense, were omitted, just as were others of his blasphemies, too.

Now this was the situation with regard to Origen, whom they also called "Adamantine." [46] And then too did Navatus, a presbyter of the church at Rome, become the originator of a heresy and founder of those who call themselves "Pure Ones," and denied repentance to those who, after they had done obeisance before and offered sacrifice to the idols, were then returning and confessing, and did not admit those who prostrated themselves before him and who, in repentance and contrition, were seeking a remedy for their error. Against him there convened in Rome a synod, in charge of which was Cornelius. It was decreed therein that it was necessary that those who had fallen by the wayside in the time of the persecution, when they had returned, be re-admitted, and that it was necessary to relieve them with the remedies of repentance. But since he did not obey the decrees, those divine fathers expelled Navatus from the church and banished him as a "brother hater." [47]

[588] Eusebius mentions an account of the following sort from a letter of Dionysius, who served as bishop of the church of the Alexandrians. For he says that Dionysius wrote these things verbatim:

There was a certain Serapion among us, a faithful old man, who had lived blamelessly, but had fallen into temptation. He was often in need, and no one attended to him because he had sacrificed. Having become ill, he endured three successive days speechless and senseless. On the fourth day, having briefly recovered, he summoned his daughter's son and said, "Make haste! Call one of the elders for me!" And again he was voiceless. The boy ran to the elder. And, though he was unable to come (for he was infirm), having previously received an injunction from me that those departing life, if ever they were in need, and most of all if they had happened previously to have been suppliants, be absolved, in order that they depart in good hope, he gave a bit of the Eucharist to the child, having ordered him to soak it and to let it drip into the old man's mouth. The boy returned bearing it. And when he was near, before he entered, Serapion, having again come to, said, "Are you come, child? Since the elder is not able to enter, you do with haste what he ordered and let me depart." The boy soaked it and at once poured it into the mouth of the old man, and when he had swallowed a morsel, straightway he gave up the ghost. Was he not obviously preserved and did he not remain alive until he was absolved and, with his sin absolved, until he could be acknowledged for the many fine things he had done?

These things did the letter of Dionysius relate.[48]

[589] Decius, being so disposed toward those revering Christ, before he had completed two whole years in his rule of the Romans, died most shamefully. For when barbarians were plundering the Bosporus, Decius engaged them and killed many. When they were hard pressed and offered to surrender all their loot if they were allowed to withdraw, Decius did not give in, but posted Gallus, one of the men of the senate, on the route of the barbarians, ordering him not to let them pass. But Gallus, betraying Decius, proposed to the barbarians that, since a deep swamp was nearby, they deploy there. When the barbarians had so deployed and turned their backs, Decius pursued them. And both he, with his son, and a multitude of Romans fell into the swamp and all perished there, with the result that their bodies, interred in the slime of the swamp, were not found.[49]

21

Then Gallus, whom some writers say was also called Volusianus as a second name, came to power. But others have written that his son was Volusianus and that he ruled with him.[50] Further, when he had gained control of the empire of the Romans, Gallus made a treaty with the barbarians on condition that they receive from the Romans an annual tribute and not plunder the possessions of Romans, and, having so arranged, he returned to Rome and proclaimed his son, Volusianus, Caesar.[51] He too became a burden to the Christians, no less than Decius, arousing a persecution against them and killing many. And during his reign there began anew the [590] Persians' unrest, and Armenia was subdued by them, its king, Teridates, having fled, and his children going over to the Persians. Also Scythians, a multitude almost overwhelming in number, made inroads into Italy and overran Macedonia, Thessaly, and Greece. It is said that one group of them, having traversed the Bosporus and crossed over Lake Maeotis, arrived at the Euxine Sea and plundered many lands. At that time, too, many other peoples attacked the Roman dominion. Plague also then befell the lands, starting from Ethiopia and spreading over almost every land, both East and West, and, lasting for fifteen years, denuded many of the cities of their inhabitants.[52]

So then, the Scythians, taking annually what had been arranged by the Romans according to treaty, came to receive these things, and, saying that what was given to them was less than what had been promised, departed under threats. A certain Aemilianus, a Libyan man, commander of the army of Moesia, promised that he would give the soldiers all that had been given the Scythians, if they would engage in war with the barbarians. Catching the Scythians by suprise, they killed all but a few and collected much booty from them, overrunning their territory.

Subsequently, when he became haughty in his success, Aemilianus canvassed the soldiers under him. They proclaimed him emperor of the Romans.[53] He [591] immediately roused his forces and hastened to occupy Italy. Then indeed, when these matters came to Gallus' attention, he too, having prepared himself on the opposite side, arrayed himself against Aemilianus. When the armies had engaged in combat, Gallus' men were beaten, and being beaten, they attacked their own emperor. When they had killed him and his son, whose reigns had been two years and eight months, they attached themselves to Aemilianus and they too voted him the realm.[54]

22

After he had thus been proclaimed emperor, Aemilianus wrote to the senate, promising that he would rid Thrace of barbarians, that he would campaign against Persia, and that, having turned the realm over to the senate, he would do everything and fight as their general.[55] But he did not get around to doing any of the things he said, since there rose up against him Valerianus, who, commander of the forces beyond the Alps, when he had learned about Aemilianus, himself also became a usurper. After he had concentrated the forces under him, he hastened toward Rome. Then, in fact, those who served with Aemilianus, when they had recognized that they were no match in battle for the army of Valerianus, judging that it was not pious that Romans destroy and be destroyed by one another, that wars be joined between men of the same race, and otherwise reckoning, too, that Aemilianus was unworthy of the realm both as ignoble and groveling, and, to be sure, considering that [592] Valerianus was better suited for the rule because he would, for certain, assume affairs in a more authoritative fashion, killed Aemilianus, who had not yet reigned four months and was forty years of age. They submitted themselves to Valerianus and entrusted the empire of the Romans to him without a fight.[56]

When, as has been said, Flavianus had been martyred under Decius, Cornelius received the pastoral office of Rome and, having been distinguished in this for three years, he measured out his lifespan. Lucius was elevated to the throne of the archpriesthood, and, before he had fulfilled his eighth year in the episcopacy of Rome, died. Stephanus succeeded to the office of the pastoral post, from whom there happens to be a directive not to baptize Christians who had converted from heresies, but to purify them by prayer through a laying on of hands. A letter of his about this to the holy martyr Cyprianus is recorded.[57] When Stephanus had gone to his rest after two years, Xystus occupied the archpriestly throne of Rome. Then, too, the heresy according to Sabellius was stirred up in Ptolemais of the Pentapolis.[58]

Thus did matters stand with regard to the archpriests of Rome.

23

Valerianus, when he had assumed the leadership of the Romans with Galienus, his son, also set in motion a most violent [593] persecution against Christians. Many became martyrs in various locations, performing feats of various types in behalf of their faith in Christ.[59] Then, too, when under him there was an uprising of the peoples, affairs were dire for the Romans. For the Scythians, crossing the Ister, once more enslaved the Thracian territory and besieged the illustrious city of Thessalonica, but nevertheless did not take it. They threw everyone into such great panic that the Athenians rebuilt their city's wall, which had been dismantled from the times of Sulla, and the Peloponnesians built a wall across the Isthmus from sea to sea.[60]

In addition, the Persians, too, with Sapor their king, overran Syria, ravaged Cappadocia, and were besieging Edessa. Valerianus was hesitating to meet the enemy. When he learned that the soldiers in Edessa had made a sally from the city, engaged the barbarians, and were killing many and taking much booty, he took heart and, having departed with the army that was with him, engaged the Persians. They, being more numerous, encircled the Romans, and many died and some also fled, and Valerianus, with those about him, was captured by the enemy and led off to Sapor. Since he had gained control of the sovereign, he thought that he was in control of everything. And being savage already, hereafter he became worse by far.[61]

That Valerianus was taken thus as a prisoner of war [594] by the Persians some record, while others say that Valerianus voluntarily went over to the Persians because, while he was living in Edessa, famine befell the soldiers, and from this they were roused to rebellion and sought to kill the emperor. But, because he feared the uprising of his soldiers, he fled to Sapor, lest he be destroyed by his own men, having betrayed to the enemy not only himself but, so far as it lay in his power, the Roman forces, as well. To be sure, the soldiers were not destroyed, but, when they learned of his treachery, they fled after a few of them had been killed.[62] But whether the sovereign was taken by the Persians as a prisoner of war or whether he voluntarily put himself in their hands, he was treated ignominiously by Sapor.[63]

The Persians, attacking the cities with complete impunity, took both Antioch on the Orontes and, of the cities of Cilicia, the very renowned Tarsus, and Caesarea in Cappadocia.[64] When they had collected a multitude of captives, they did not provide them rations, except the tiniest amount in order for them to stay alive, neither did they allow them to partake of enough water to quench their thirst, but once a day their guards drove them to water just like cattle. Caesarea, being very populous—for it is said that about 400,000 men dwell in it—they did not take—those in it having nobly resisted their enemies and being commanded by a certain Demosthenes, a man brave and intelligent—before a man who had been taken prisoner, [595] a physician, unable to endure the insults leveled at him, suggested a certain spot by which the Persians entered in the night and killed everyone. In fact, their general, Demosthenes, after he had been encircled by many Persians who had been ordered to take him alive, mounted his horse, grasped his naked sword, and flung himself into the midst of the enemy. After he lay many low, he escaped from the city and managed to get away. [65] With matters having befallen the Persians thus, they dispersed through the entire eastern territory subject to the Romans and plundered it with impunity.

Now then, the Romans who had fled, so it is said, appointed a certain Callistus as their general. When he had observed the Persians dispersing and recklessly attacking the territories because they did not think that anyone would oppose them, he quickly attacked them, wrought a massive slaughter of the barbarians, and captured the concubines of Sapor, together with much wealth. So he, greatly pained by these things, turned hastily homeward, bringing along Valerianus, who ended his life in Persia, reviled and mocked as a captive. [66]

Not only did Callistus then excel against the Persians, but so did a certain Palmyrene man called Odenathus, who, allying himself with the Romans, destroyed many of the Persians, attacking them as they were returning via the Euphrates territory. Galienus, rewarding him for his generalship, appointed him General of the East. [67]

[596] Moreover, among the dead of the Persian army who were being stripped, women, too, are said to have been found who had been dispatched and equipped in the fashion of men. Some women of this sort were also taken alive by the Romans. [68] Sapor, on his return, when he happened upon a deep ravine which his baggage train was unable to cross, commanded that captives be slain and tossed into the ravine in order that, once its depth had been filled with the dead bodies, their baggage train thus cross. And it is so recorded that he crossed the ravine. [69]

Thus were the affairs of Valerianus. Xystus was the leader of the church of the Romans, and of the church of the Antiochenes, Demetrianus, having succeeded Flavianus, and of the church of Jerusalem, Hymenaeus, Mazabanes having died, and Dionysius was in charge of the church in Alexandria. [70]

24

After Valerianus, Galienus, his son, assumed the leadership of the Romans. [71] His father, campaigning against the Persians, left him in the West to resist those lying in wait in Italy and those plundering Thrace. Attacking the Alamanni, who were about 300,000 strong, around Mediolanum, he was victorious with 10,000. Then, too, he proceeded against the Aerouli, a Scytho-Gothic race, and prevailed. He also warred against the Franks. [72]

[597] Auriolus, being from a Getic territory later named Dacia and of undistinguished lineage—for he previously was a mere shepherd—, but with fortune resolved to lift him to greatness, became a soldier and, when he had become very adept, was chosen as attendant of the imperial horses. Doing an excellent job with them, he seemed pleasing to the ruler. When the soldiers in Moesia had rebelled and had proclaimed Ingenuus emperor, and when Galienus had taken the field against him near Sirmium with the other soldiers and was leading the Moors, who are said to be descended from Medes, Auriolus, commanding the cavalry, after he had battled nobly with his horsemen, annihilated many of Ingenuus' adherents and turned the remainder to flight, with the result that Ingenuus himself fled in desperation and, as he fled, was killed by his own guardsmen.[73]

Then Postumus next revolted against Galienus. For the emperor, having a son by the same name, both clever and handsome, whom he held as successor of the realm, left him behind in the city of Agrippina to aid the Gauls, who were being raided by Scythians. On account of his son's youth, he also set over him a certain person called Albanus. Postumus, who had been left to guard the Rhine River so as to impede the crossing into Roman territory for the barbarians dwelling beyond, attacked some, who, after they had crossed unnoticed, were taking much plunder as they were returning, and he killed many [598], recovered all the plunder, and immediately apportioned it to his soldiers.

Albanus, when he had learned this, sent messengers and demanded that the plunder be brought to him and to the young Galienus. Postumus called his soldiers together and exacted from them their shares of the plunder, scheming to incite them to rebellion. And that is exactly what happened. With them he attacked the city of Agrippina, and the inhabitants of the city surrendered to him both the son of the sovereign and Albanus, and he executed them both.[74]

Galienus, when he had learned of these things, proceeded against Postumus, and, when he had engaged him, was initially beaten and then prevailed, with the result that Postumus fled. Then Auriolus was sent to chase him down. Though able to capture him, he was unwilling to pursue him for long, but, coming back, he said that he was unable to capture him. Thus Postumus, having escaped, next organized an army. Galienus again marched upon him and, after he had penned him in a certain city of Gaul, besieged the usurper. In the siege, the sovereign was struck in the back by an arrow and, having become ill as a result, broke off the siege.[75]

Another war against Galienus was incited by Macrinus, who, having two sons, Macrianus and Quintus, attempted a usurpation. Because he was lame in one leg, he did not don the imperial mantle, but clad his sons in it. [599] The people of Asia joyfully received him. After he had lingered a little on the Persian front, he began to make preparations about Galienus and appointed Ballista, whom he selected cavalry commander, to face the Persians, and left behind his son, Quintus, with him.[76.] Then the sovereign sent Auriolus, with other generals, too, against Macrinus and his son Macrianus. They engaged them, surrounded them, and killed some. For they spared them since they were members of the same race, and they hoped that they would desert to the sovereign. They would not surrender. But in consequence of a certain fortuitous circumstance they all went over to the sovereign. For while on the march, those near the usurpers were holding their standards erect, and one of the standard-bearers, stumbling over his own feet as he marched, fell, and when he fell his standard dropped. Then the rest of the standard-bearers, seeing the fallen standard and not knowing how it had fallen, assumed that the man holding it had purposely lowered it, switching over to the sovereign. And immediately they too lowered and flung down all of theirs and hailed Galienus, the Pannonians alone having remained on Macrinus' side. Then, when even they were considering changing sides, Macrinus, with his son, entreated them not to surrender them, but to kill them first and thus to join the sovereign. When they had done this, the Pannonians surrendered themselves.[77]

To be sure, Quintus, the younger son of Macrinus, was in the East [600] with Ballista, and had made almost all of it subject to himself. Against them Galienus sent Odenathus, who was in command of the Palmyrenes. When the defeat of the Macrini which had occurred in Pannonia was announced to Quintus and Ballista, many of the cities under them rebelled. They were quartered in Emesa. When he arrived there, Odenathus attacked them, was victorious, and himself executed Ballista. But the people of the city executed Quintus. The sovereign, repaying Odenathus for his courage, appointed him general of the entire East.[78]

This Odenathus, after he had become great, faithful to Romans, and had distinguished himself in many wars of sundry peoples and against the Persians themselves, ultimately was murdered by his own brother's son. For the latter, in the company of his uncle on a wild animal hunt, when a beast leaped out, was the first to attack and, having made his cast, killed the beast. Odenathus became annoyed and threatened his nephew. But he did not stop, but did this a second and third time. Odenathus, enraged, took away his horse. This is reckoned a great insult for the barbarians. Accordingly, the youth, being vexed, threatened his uncle. On this account, he imprisoned him. Then the elder of Odenathus' sons petitioned his father that the prisoner be released. When he had been released, at a dinner party he attacked Odenathus with a sword and killed both him and his son, with whose help he had been released. He too was killed, when some men attacked him.[79]

25

[601] Moreover, there occurred another uprising against Galienus, arranged by Auriolus, commander of all of the cavalry and a very powerful man. He seized the city of Mediolanum and prepared to engage the sovereign. The latter, too, when he had arrived with a force and taken the field against the usurper, destroyed many of the opposition. Then Auriolus was wounded and penned in Mediolanum, besieged there by the sovereign. While Galienus was making sorties against some of the enemy, the empress was on one occasion exposed to danger. For she was present with him. For as the sovereign had sallied forth with the majority of his troops, very few were stationed about his camp. The enemy, when they noticed this, attacked the sovereign's tent, intending to snatch the empress. One of the soldiers who had been left behind had seated himself in front of the tent, removed one of his shoes from his foot, and was mending it. Then, as he saw the enemy attacking, he grabbed a shield and dagger and bravely rushed against them. He struck one and a second and blocked the remainder, who had shied away before his charge. And so, when more soldiers had raced to the spot, the sovereign's wife was saved.[80]

While the sovereign was still besieging Mediolanum, there came to him with horsemen Aurelianus, with whose aid the grandees planned to kill him.[81] But they were putting off the scheme until he took Mediolanum. When they learned that their treason had been discovered, [602] they accelerated the conspiracy. They dispatched some men who announced to Galienus that enemies were attacking. He rushed out against them immediately—the hour already being about mealtime—and with a few men accompanying him. Horsemen met him as he was departing. When they were not far distant and had neither dismounted from their horses nor done anything else which was customarily done in the sovereign's presence, he asked those at hand, "What do they wish?" They replied, "To remove you from office." He immediately gave his horse the rein and turned to flight. He would have even escaped the conspirators by the speed of his horse had he not chanced upon a channel of water. For the horse shied away from crossing it and balked, and thus did his pursuers capture him. One of them hurled his spear at him. The wounded man fell from his horse, and, after he had lingered for a little while, died as a result of loss of blood, having reigned fifteen years, including those of his father. He was magnanimous in outlook and wished to please all, and no one who petitioned him was unsuccessful, even to the extent that he did not punish either those who had opposed him or those who had associated with the would-be usurpers.

Now some record that Galienus died thus, but others say he was slaughtered by Heraclianus, the prefect. For when Auriolus, serving as general in Gaul, had rebelled against him and arrived in Italy with his forces, Galienus, too, [603] rushed out against him. By night Heraclianus approached him as he slept in his tent, having shared the conspiracy also with Claudius, a man most suited for command, and reported that Auriolus was attacking with a heavy force. Confused by the suddenness of the report, he leaped from his bed and, half-naked, began demanding his weapons. Heraclianus struck him a mortal blow and slew him. [82]

In his times, Xystus, when he had led the church of the Romans for eleven years, died, and Dionysius succeeded him. But when the shepherd of Christ's flock in Antioch, Demetrianus, also had measured out his life, Paul of Samasota received the church, he who taught lowly things about Christ: that he had become a common man by nature, and not a god. The pastors of the rest of the churches convened a synod against him in which were present both Gregory the Wonderworker and his brother Athenodorus, censured him for thinking evilly about Christ, and publicly renounced him. Since he was not persuaded to leave his church, Aurelianus, then in control and having received from the orthodox a petition about this matter, issued a directive that the church be allotted to those whom the bishops in Rome and Italy appointed. Thereupon, Paul was ignominiously driven from his church, and Domnus took over.[83]

26

Now then, when Galienus had been killed, Claudius was acclaimed [604] Caesar. Auriolus laid down his arms and was obedient to him. It was he who, again attempting a usurpation, was killed by his soldiers.[84] Claudius, who was a good man and in step with justice, forbade anyone to petition from the sovereign another's possessions. For it had been customary that sovereigns were empowered to bestow as gifts even the property of others, whence the laws still in place in the state had their origin. Thereupon, a woman came forward whose estate he had received through royal dispensation prior to his reign and said, "Claudius the cavalry commander did me an injustice." He replied, "Precisely what Claudius, while a private citizen, took away when the laws were of no concern to him, this, having become sovereign, does he restore."[85]

In Rome, in fact, the senate, when it had learned of Galienus' death, executed his brother and son.[86] Now then, while Postumus was still exercising illegitimate power, and when barbarians had crossed Lake Maeotis to both Europe and Asia and were plundering these areas, and when a council convened to decide what type of war had to be undertaken first, Claudius said, "The war against the usurper is my concern, the one against the barbarians, the state's, and it is proper that that of the state take precedent."

The barbarians overran many areas, and, in fact, besieged Thessalonica, which in the old days is said to have been called Emathia but had its name changed to Thessalonica, from Thessalonica, the daughter of Philip and wife of Cassander.[87] But they were repulsed from that [605] city and, having attacked Athens, captured her. When they had collected all the books in the city, they were planning to burn them. But one of those who among them seem to be wise dissuaded his tribesmen from their undertaking, saying, "Since they devote their leisure to these, the Greeks are unconcerned with military matters and, thus, become very easily controllable."[88] Cleodemus, an Athenian man who had managed to get away, attacked them with boats from the sea and killed many, with the result that even the survivors fled from there.[89]

When he had hastened against them after they had been dispersed into many areas, Claudius at one time was victorious in naval battles and at another time in battles joined on land. Storms afflicted them and famine befell them and destroyed them.[90] While staying in Sirmium, Claudius took sick, and, after he had summoned those of the army who were most renowned, had a discussion with them about a sovereign, and he said that Aurelianus happened to be worthy of the realm. There are those who say that, forthwith, he also proclaimed him sovereign.[91] And some say that the senate in Rome, when it had learned of Claudius' death, because of its longing for Claudius deemed Quintilianus, his brother, worthy of the realm, and that the military acclaimed Aurelianus.[92] When Quintilianus, naive and by nature unsuited for the management of affairs, had learned of the acclamation of Aurelianus, he killed himself, severing the vein of his own wrist and, as a result of the hemorrhage there, [606] expired, after he had for but seventeen days, as it were, dreamt his rule.[93] But the sources are not in accord with one another about the duration of Claudius' reign, for some record that he ruled about one year, others, among whom is Eusebius, two.[94]

Constas Chlorus, the father of Constantine the Great, was the son of the daughter of the sovereign Claudius' daughter.[95]

27

Aurelianus, after he had assumed the leadership of the Romans, asked those in office how he ought to rule. One of them said to him, "If you want to rule nobly, you must ring yourself with gold and iron, employing the iron against those who cause you discomfort, repaying with gold the very men who do you service." He first, so it is said, had the benefit of his own advice, since he felt the iron not soon thereafter.[96]

Initially this emperor dealt mildly with those revering Christ, but, as the duration of his reign progressed, he changed, and he even resolved to rouse a persecution against the faithful, and forthwith began drawing up edicts, too. But divine justice checked the fury of his evil against those who revered Jesus Christ, cutting short his life.[97]

[607] But not yet about his end, it being necessary to discuss what he did in his reign. For, being a commander most able, he won many wars. For he both subdued the Palmyrenes and defeated and subdued their queen, Zenobia, who had gained control of Egypt and had captured Probus, who was then commander there, himself taking the field against her.[98] Some say that she was led off to Rome and she was wed to a man, one of the nobles; others say that she died en route, wracked by the change of her fortune, that Aurelianus took one of her daughters for a wife, and that the rest he paired with distinguished Romans.[99]

He also again returned to the Romans' control Gaul, which had for many years been controlled by various men exercising illegitimate power, and, after he had appointed commanders for it, he returned to Rome and entered in triumphal procession upon a chariot drawn by four elephants.[100] He also prevailed over the Gauls, who had then become restless. But when he set his army against the Scythians, he was killed while he was at Thracian Heracleia. For there was a certain man called Eros, who was a reporter of public gossip and, as some record, an eavesdropper, who reported to the sovereign whatever anyone said about him. When Aurelianus had become angered at him, he plotted against him. He forged his handwriting and composed a certain document that contained the names of some powerful individuals, commanding that they be put to death. By showing this to them, he provoked them [608] to the murder of the emperor. For these men, in fear of their lives, set upon Aurelianus and killed him, six years minus a few months after he had assumed sovereignty.[101]

28

Tacitus, an elderly man, succeeded him. For it is written that he was seventy-five years old when he was chosen for monarchy. The army recognized him, though he was absent, for he was then residing in Campania. When he received the decision there, he entered Rome in private dress and, with the consent of the Senate and the People, donned the imperial garb.[102]

The Scythians, having crossed Lake Maeotis and the Phasis River, attacked Pontus, Cappadocia, Galatia, and Cilicia. Tacitus, who had joined battle with them, and Florianus, who was prefect, slew many, and the remainder sought safety in flight.[103] Tacitus appointed Maximinus, one of his kinsmen, as governor of Syria. But, when he behaved badly in his office, he was killed by his soldiers. Those who had killed him, frightened that the emperor would not leave them unpunished, set out after him too and killed him, not yet seven months after he had assumed sovereignty, but according to some not quite two years.[104]

29

When he had been slaughtered, two sovereigns were chosen at the same time: Probus by the soldiers in the East, and, by the senate in Rome, Florianus. Both continued to rule: Probus [609] in Egypt, Phoenicia, Syria, and Palestine, and Florianus, in fact, from Cilicia as far as Italy and the Hesperiae. But the latter, not quite three months after he had assumed his reign, departed from life and power at the same time, killed by soldiers reportedly sent by Probus.[105]

When he had died as described, Probus invested himself with full power. It is recorded that he was of the highest repute and that he erected trophies of victory against many peoples and that he rounded up the soldiers who had murdered Aurelianus and Tacitus, severely rebuked them, and had them executed.[106]

When Saturninus the Moor, who was his very close friend, attempted to usurp power, he did not believe the news and punished the man who reported it. But Saturninus was killed by the soldiers.[107] Some other fellow in Britain, whom the sovereign had put in charge of this province because Victorinus the Moor, who was close to him, had so requested, studied the possibility of rebellion. Probus, upon learning of this, blamed Victorinus. But he requested that he be sent to the man, departed—ostensibly fleeing the emperor—, and was gladly received by the usurper. After he had murdered him in the night, he returned to Probus. Probus was regarded fondly by all as gentle, kind, and beneficent.[108]

Facing the people of the Germans who were attacking cities under the Romans, because the war had lasted a long time, he came to be in a predicament, since famine had befallen [610] his army. Then it is said that a violent rainstorm fell on his camp, and that much grain fell with the shower, if anyone could believe this. The army, when it had collected it, was fed, escaped its peril, and routed its opponents.[109]

There was another rebellion against him. For Carus, who was in command of portions of Europe, recognized that the soldiers under him wished to proclaim him emperor and revealed this to Probus, begging that he be recalled from there. But Probus was not willing to remove him from office. Then the soldiers surrounded Carus, compelled him reluctantly to receive the empire of the Romans, and immediately hastened with him against Italy. Probus, when he had learned of this, sent an army with a commander to oppose him. As soon as those dispatched had drawn near Carus, they arrested their commander and surrendered him and themselves to Carus. Probus was killed by his own guardsmen, who had learned of the desertion of the soldiers to Carus. The duration of Probus' sole rule had been not quite six years.[110]

30

When he had come into control of the realm, Carus crowned his own two sons, Carinus and Numerianus, with an imperial diadem. Together with one of the boys, Numerianus, he immediately marched against the Persians, and captured Ctesiphon and [611] Seleucia.[111] But the army of the Romans had a close brush with danger. For they were encamped in a gully, and the Persians, when they observed this, by means of a trench diverted toward the gully the river flowing nearby. But Carus charged the Persians, met with success, and routed them. He returned toward Rome leading a multitude of captives and much booty.[112] Then, when the people of the Sarmatians rebelled, he engaged them too, was victorious, and brought the people into line.[113] He was a Gaul by ancestry, but brave and accomplished in matters of warfare. The account of his death has been variously composed by those who have done historical research. Some say that, having campaigned against the Huns, he was killed there. Others say that he was encamped by the River Tigris and that there, in the place where his army had thrown up a palisade, his tent was struck by lightning, and they record that, along with it, he too was destroyed.[114]

When his lifetime had expired, whether in this or another way, Numerianus, his son, survived in the camp as sole sovereign. He immediately campaigned against the Persians. When war had erupted and the Persians had gotten the upper hand and the Romans had turned tail, some record that he was captured in flight, that the hide was stripped from his body in the fashion of a wineskin, and that he perished thus. But others have written that, while returning from Persia, he developed ophthalmia and was murdered by his own father-in-law, Prefect of the Camp, who, having coveted his sovereignty, nevertheless he did not gain it. For the army [612] chose Diocletian sovereign, since he was there at the time and had exhibited many acts of courage against the Persians.[115]

Carinus, of course, the other of Carus' sons, living in Rome, presented a menace to the Romans, since he had become brutal, cruel, and vindictive. He was killed by Diocletian, who had come to Rome. The duration of their reign did not, all told, come to three years.[116]

In these times, Manes, the thrice-accursed, slunk from the Persians into the habitable world about us and spewed forth in this his own venom, from which, up to the present, the Manichaeans name did not vanish. It was he who at one time used to dub himself Paraclete and Holy Spirit—He in whom the spirit of evil manifestly dwelt!—and at another was calling himself Christ—He! The one appointed by the demons to their service!—and brought with him twelve disciples—communicants and preachers of his nonsense, which he used to concoct from many godless dogmas of now extinguished heresies![117]

Now then, when Dionysius, the one tending the faithful in Rome, had completed nine years in this office and had given way, Felix received the holy throne of Rome. When he died after a five-year period, Eutychianus was deemed worthy of the episcopacy of Rome. But this man, too, after he had been bishop not yet ten months, quit his life, and Gaius was introduced into the office of pastor. After he had been in charge of the church about fifteen years [613], Marcellinus became successor. These men lived in the times of the persecutions.[118]

Now then, in the church of Antioch Timaeus was bishop after Domnus, and Cyrillus succeeded Timaeus, and after Cyrillus the throne received Tyrannus, under whom the assault of the churches had its acme and the tyranny became insufferable. And after Hymenaeus, Zabdas was in charge of the church of Jerusalem, after whom, when he had gone to his rest not much later, Hermon adorned this throne. In Alexandria, when Maximus, the one who had obtained the priesthood eighteen years after Dionysius, had served off his debt, Theonas was bishop. He was followed by Peter, who, having been beheaded, took the crown of martyrdom.[119]

Thus, then, were the successions of these archpriests.

31[120]

Diocletian, who obtained the leadership—a Dalmatian by race and of obscure lineage (some say that he was a freedman of Anulinus, a member of the senatorial order)—, had become *dux* of Moesia from the ranks of the enlisted men.[121] Others say that he became *comes* of the *domestici*. Some believe that *domestici* were the cavalry.[122] He addressed the soldiers and assured them that he had had no part in the murder of Numerianus. As he was saying this, he turned to Aper, who was commander of the army, said, "This is his murderer," [614] and, with the sword in his hand, immediately killed him. When he had arrived in Rome, he took upon himself the affairs of the empire and put his hand to their management.[123] Considering the excessive size of the realm, in the fourth year of his leadership, or, according to others, in the second, he chose as his colleague Maximianus Herculius, reasoning that he himself was not adequate for the management of so large an empire.[124]

So then the pair conspired and roused against Christians a persecution more violent and fierce than all those which had gone before, for eagerly—more accurately, maniacally—they rushed to obliterate from all the earth the salvific name of our God, Jesus Christ. Whereupon in every city and countryside so many people stood up manfully in behalf of their pledge to Christ that it was close to impossible to count them, for they considered this activity more important than all their other business.[125]

When Busiris and Coptos, Egyptian cities in the vicinity of Thebes, had inclined toward rebellion, Diocletian campaigned against them, took them, and razed them.[126] Then, in turn, Alexandria and Egypt lifted their hand against the Romans, a certain Achilles having incited the Egyptians to this. But when the Romans came against them under Diocletian, they did not resist for very long, and many of those responsible for the revolt were killed, including Achilles.[127]

Diocletian and Maximianus appointed [615] their sons-in-law Caesars: Diocletian appointed Maximinus Gallerius, joining to him in marriage his own daughter, Valeria, and Herculius Maximianus appointed Constans, who was called Chlorus because of his paleness, grandson on his mother's side of the Claudius who, as I have already said, had reigned a bit earlier, likewise promising him his daughter Theodora. Both of these Caesars had wives, but rejected them in order to be in-laws of the sovereigns and married the sovereigns' daughters.[128]

When a certain Amandus rebelled in Gaul, Maximianus went there and suppressed the rebellion. The prefect Asclepiodotus executed Crassus, who had held Britain for three years. When some of the Quinquegentiani occupied Africa, Herculius defeated them.[129]

Now the Caesar Constans, while fighting in Gaul with the Alemanni, was vanquished and victorious on the same day. For first, when the Alemanni fell upon his army with violent force, they all turned to flight. Constans himself, fleeing with them, was almost captured. For, coming back, he found the gates of the city closed. His pursuers, drawing near, were ready to apprehend him, and he would have been led off as a prisoner, except that ropes were lowered from the wall above and used to pull him up. After he had been rescued and entered the city thus, having immediately assembled the army, [616] roused it to action with encouraging words, and, so to speak, breathed courage into it, he straightway went forth, joined with the enemy, and won a famous victory, with the result that about 60,000 of his opponents fell.[130]

When Narses was sovereign of Persia, he who is listed as the seventh to reign in Persia after Artaxerxes, whom the writer of this history previously mentioned as having again renewed the realm for the Persians (for after this Artaxerxes or Artaxares—he had two names— Sapor ruled Persia, and after him Hormisdas, then Vararanes, and after him Vararakes, and then another Vararanes, and finally, Narses), moreover, with Narses then plundering Syria, Diocletian, as he was traversing Egypt against the Ethiopians, dispatched with an adequate force his own son-in-law Gallerius Maximinus to engage him. He joined battle with the Persians, was defeated, and fled. Diocletian dispatched him again with a larger army. Then, when he attacked them again, he won such an outstanding victory that the earlier defeat was canceled out. He killed the greater part of the Persians and, having pursued Narses, who was wounded, into the interior of Persia, led off his wives and children and sisters as captives, and captured all the riches that Narses had brought with him for his campaign, as well as many people of distinction in Persia.[131] After he had recovered from his wound, Narses sent delegations to [617] Diocletian and Gallerius, asking that his children and wives be returned to him and that a peace treaty be made. He gained his request, ceding to the Romans whatever they wanted.[132]

Diocletian and Maximianus successfully prosecuted many other wars, some by themselves or their Caesars, some by means of generals, and they expanded the boundaries of the realm.[133] Diocletian, when he had become elated and arrogant as a result, no longer tolerated being addressed by the senate as before, but made it a custom to receive obeisance, adorned his clothing and shoes with gold and precious stones and pearls, and introduced greater extravagance into the imperial insignia. For the previous sovereigns had been honored in the fashion of consuls and had as a sign of their sovereignty only a purple robe.[134]

32[135]

When the persecution had become more severe and countless men and women were dying for the sake of their pledge to Christ, and when the faithful still increased in number, these tyrants, going mad, in about the nineteenth year of the reign of Diocletian published proclamations everywhere commanding that the churches of the Christians be pulled down and razed, that their books be burned, their priests, too, as teachers and preachers of the faith, be ruthlessly wiped out, and, of the remainder, [618] that those who had been enrolled in governmental or military positions be dishonorably discharged from the civil service and military, and that those of private station be enslaved.[136]

When Diocletian had already completed his twentieth year in office, both rulers laid aside their sovereignty by agreement, stating publicly that they were jettisoning the burden of affairs, but to those to whom they disclosed the secrets of their hearts they admitted that they put aside their office out of distress since they were unable to gain the upper hand over Christians or extinguish the Christian gospel, and chose not to enjoy their sovereignty. By agreement they laid aside their office on the same day, the one in Nicomedia, the other, Maximianus, in Mediolanum, and, becoming private persons, Diocletian resided in Salona, a city of Dalmatia, which was also his hometown, and Herculius in Lucania.[137] Before they abdicated their office, they returned to Rome and celebrated a triumph for the victory over the Persians, in which they led in triumph Narses' wives and children and relatives, as well as leaders of other peoples, and the wealth which they had plundered from the Persians.[138]

But here it would be a good idea to clarify whence the name of the "triumph" is derived. Now they say it took this name from the *thria*, which are the leaves of the fig tree. For before masks were devised for actors, they covered their faces [619] with fig leaves and jested in iambs. The soldiers in victory processions, too, put fig leaves on their faces and made jests about those who held the parades. Thence it is thought that victory parades were named *thriamboi*.[139] But others say that the triumph was so named because those who made up the procession were composed of a "trio"—the senate, the people, and the soldiers—and, as a result of the three orders banding together, it was called a sort of *triambos*, but that theta replaced the tau for greater euphony.[140]

After this victory parade, they resigned their authority and appointed the Caesars rulers, dividing the empire among them, allotting the eastern portion, together with Illyricum, to Gallerius Maximinus, and to Chlorus Constans assigning the West, together with Africa. When these things had happened thus, in Rome the soldiers who used to be called *praetoriani* proclaimed sovereign Maxentius, the son of Herculius Maximianus.[141]

Now of these three Constans, who was in control in Britain and the Cottian Alps and Gaul, behaved very leniently toward those revering Christ, as, indeed, to all those under his sway, and was disdainful of riches. Maximinus, Commander of the East, both roused a very burdensome persecution against Christians and behaved very harshly toward his other subjects.[142] [620] Being extremely woman-crazy and promiscuous, not only did he seize common women against their will and have sex with them, but also forcefully dragged the wives of prominent men away from their husbands, and, after assaulting them, returned them to their own spouses.[143] He was so addicted to divinations that he did not do the slightest thing without divinations, and those who carried out the secret rites were held in honor by him. He decreed the total destruction of the pious and decided to confiscate their properties, imputing no blame against the blameless except their knowledge of God and their faith in Christ.[144]

33

In Rome, Maxentius, for his part, turned out to be no more moderate a tyrant to his subjects, but he managed affairs of the empire in the same way as Maximinus, raging likewise against the Christians under his control, subjecting them to all kinds of injuries, and being of a most bitter disposition toward everyone under his sway. He arranged the slaughter of very many prominent men with no proper trial, dared on a daily basis to have sex with noble women and to ruin maidens, outraging them most shamelessly, seized unjustly the fortunes of the well-to-do, and oppressed his subjects with new and heavy imposts.[145]

In Rome, having fallen desperately in love with a woman very noble but, moreover, modest, too, who was married to one of the prominent men of Rome, [621] he sent those who tended to such things for him to bring him the woman. But when she discovered that the procurers were standing at her house door, had learned the reason for their visit, and realized that her departure for the tyrant was unavoidable (for her husband, cowering in fear of death, was permitting them to take his wife and lead her away), and that she had no assistance from elsewhere, she requested that a moment be granted her that she might adorn herself and then depart with them. The woman both revered Christ and had been initiated into the divine mystery. She then entered her bedroom and, being left alone, did away with herself in order that she remain undefiled and not forfeit her modesty, having chosen voluntary death, and having left behind her dead body for the procurers and her vile lover.[146]

Thus, then, did they rule, but both Diocletian and Maximianus died as private citizens. Authors disagree about their end. For Eusebius says in the eighth book of his *Ecclesiastical History* that Diocletian took leave of his wits and that, with his body wasted by a chronic disease, he violently vomited up his wretched soul, and that Maximianus Herculius actually departed this life by hanging himself.[147] But others do not relate that they died in this way, but that, after they had reconsidered, resolving to possess the empire again, they were apprehended and executed by a decree of the senate.[148]

There are also those who say that Herculius, seeking the imperial power again [622], shared with Diocletian the renewed attempt to recover the realm, and that he refused.[149] They say that he went before the council of the Romans and said that his son was not adequate for the management of public affairs; and that, when the soldiers had been moved to anger at his speech on grounds that he was usurping the office, Herculius feared the danger and said that he was not really of that opinion, but that he had said these things making trial of the troops, to see how they were disposed toward his son. And they say that thus he suppressed the tumult among the soldiers; then that he went to Gaul, to Constantine the Great, who was also an in-law of his through his daughter Fausta, plotting against him too and trying to seize his realm, and also that he was discovered, repulsed from his undertaking, and so hanged himself.[150]

But while these men measured out their life spans in just one of the ways described, Constans, in the eleventh year of his reign since he had been proclaimed Caesar, having ruled gently and mildly, came to the end of his life while residing in Britain, having, because of his goodness, bequeathed grief for himself among those he ruled, first having appointed successor the elder of his own sons, namely Constantine the Great, whom he begat by his first wife.[151] He also had by his second wife, Herculius' daughter Theodora, other sons, Constantinus, Hannibalianus, and [623] Constantius. Constantine the Great was preferred over them, since they were judged by their father to be unsuited for sovereignty.[152] The entire business was arranged by God on behalf of the Divine Gospel, or rather on behalf of all those subject to the empire of the Romans, so that through him the tyrannies might be destroyed. For it is said that when Constans was ill and disheartened over his misfortune in the case of his other children, an angel stood by him, bidding him to bequeath his authority to Constantine.[153]

Constantine, when he was still a lad, was actually given by his father as a hostage to Gallerius, in order that, serving as a hostage, at the same time he be trained in the exercise of the soldierly art. But he, seeing him to be highly skilled, and being envious, plotted against him. First, while fighting the Sarmatians, he ordered him to attack their leader, who stood out because of his armor. Constantine attacked him, took him alive, and brought him to Gallerius. Then he ordered him to take on a lion, a dreadful and violent beast. He accomplished this labor, too, which was admittedly dangerous, but with divine grace preserving him. Knowing from these things that he was envied and plotted against by Gallerius, he escaped by night with some men in whom he had confidence and returned to his father.[154]

Thus did he escape danger [624] and was judged worthy of his father's realm.

34

Maximinus took as colleague in his rule Licinius, who derived his lineage from the Dacians and was the brother-in-law of Constantine the Great.[155] After he had made him colleague in his sovereignty and left him in Illyricum to defend the Thracians, who were being plundered by barbarians, he himself proceeded to Rome, to battle against Maxentius. Then, being suspicious of his own soldiers and fearing lest they desert to the enemy, he desisted from battle and departed.[156] He regretted his appointment of Licinius, first plotted secretly against him, and then openly joined battle with him. He attacked him, was repulsed, defeated, and fled, and in his flight did away with himself.[157]

Now some historians stated that Maximinus brought his life to an end in a conclusion of this sort, but others have related that, because he was raving against Christians, divine justice overtook him. For they relate that a severe ulcer beset him in the groin and genitals and devoured the organs of his licentiousness. And that from the putrefaction of these parts worms emerged, and that his suffering was incurable. As to his doctors, they relate that those who immediately gave up the idea of operating were savagely slain, but those who attempted, yet were unable to affect a cure, were killed most pitilessly, because they did not accomplish the impossible. They relate, then, that the tyrant suspected [625] that he was paying the penalty for the unjust murders of those who revered Christ, that he published decrees everywhere commanding that the persecution of the Christians cease, that they live and worship however they wished, and that they pray on his behalf.[158] Here, too, two stories are told. One says that, contrary to all expectations, he was freed of the suffering, then roused the persecution once more and remained incorrigible until he drank the dregs of the cup in the Lord's hand; the other denies the impious fellow any recovery, maintaining that he died of the aforesaid illness, after he had vomited worms from his mouth.[159]

He, then, violently terminated his life in one or the other of the ways recounted. [In Rome, Eusebius took charge of the church of the faithful after Marcellinus, who had performed the service for two years, and, when he died a year later, Miltiades succeeded him.

After Miltiades had been in charge of the faithful in Rome for four years, Silvester became his successor. In Antioch, after Tyrannus, who had been bishop for thirteen years, Vitalius was chosen and, after he had completed six years, Philogenes succeeded him, and, after the passage of five more years, Paulinus became his successor. Hermon was allotted the archpriestly throne of Jerusalem after Zabdas, who served for ten years. Of Alexandria, after the holy martyr Peter had adorned its throne for eleven [626] years, Alexander held the archpriesthood. In Rome, after Silvester, who had served twenty-eight years, Julius took charge of the church for fifteen years. After him, Liberius completed his sixth year, and Damasus, who was pastor for twenty-eight years, succeeded him, and Siricius, who served for sixteen years, succeeded him. Then Innocentius was chosen, who taught the Lord's people for fifteen years. Zosimus was set on the throne of the church of the Romans at the death of Innocentius. When he had completed his twelfth year, Celestinus, who was conspicuous in the archpriesthood for ten years, succeeded him. Xystus became his successor, lasting eight years. Then Leon replaced him, defending correct doctrines for twenty-four years. At the decease of Leon, Hilarion, who finished his sixth year, was set on the throne in his place. In his stead, Simplicius was appointed, who himself, after he had performed the pastoral function for nineteen years, passed on, and Felix replaced him. And this man, when he died in his ninth year, left the honor to Gelasius, who enjoyed it for five years. After him, Anastasius was chosen. After four years, he was succeeded by Symmachus. When he had spent twelve years in the archpriesthood, Hormisdas' name was drawn. After he had performed the service for ten years, he departed [627] life, and the throne of the Roman church received John for three years. After him, Felix was in charge of the faithful in Rome, enjoying the honor for four years. Then Boniface was deemed worthy of the leadership for two years, and, after him, Agapetus was chosen. And after he had shepherded the flock of Christ, the chief pastor, for two years in Rome, he paid his dues, and Silverius was appointed archpriest of Rome. When he had served one year as archpriest, he measured out his life span. Vigilius became his successor. When he had completed eighteen years in the office, Pelagius was chosen. After he had devoted himself to this service for five years, he departed, and the archpriestly seat of Rome received John for eight years, and, after him, Gregory for fifteen years. After him, those in charge of the church of Romans can no longer be found in a continuous series. In Antioch in Coele Syria, Eustathius succeeded Paulinus, who had devoted himself to the service for five years, and, after Eustathius had shepherded the faithful for eighteen years, Euphronius served eight years. After him Flacitus completed a twelfth year. Then Stephanus, an Arian heretic, introduced corruption to the church for three years, and after him Leontius was brought in. After he had been bishop for eight years, he departed this life, and, after him, Eudoxius led the church of Antioch for two years, and, after Eudoxius, Arrianus was bishop for four years, and after him Meletius for twenty-five years. [628] After him, Flavianus was in charge of those of Christ's name for twenty-six years. Then Theodotus undertook the service and completed four years in it. John was brought in to replace him and lasted eighteen years. In John's place Domnus was appointed, and he survived his appointment by eight years. In his place Maximus was seated on the throne of the church of the Antiochenes and remained in charge for four years. He was succeeded by Martyrius, who completed nine years in office. Then Julian sat upon this archpriestly seat for six years and had Peter for successor. After a duration of three years, Stephanus succeeded him and was archpriest for the same number of years. Calandion became Stephanus' heir. After four years, another Peter became heir and tended the church for a duration of three years. Palladius became his successor and completed ten years in office. Then Flavianus was chosen and served as archpriest for thirteen years. After him, Severus, having served seven years, left the sacred seat to Euphrasius. After five years, Ephraimius succeeded him. He lasted ten years in service.][160]

COMMENTARY ON
BOOK XII.15–35

1   Parallels between George the Monk (ninth c., *ODB* II, pp. 836–837, *s.v.* George Hamartolos), Symeon, Cedrenus, and Theodore Scutariotes are one of several factors that strongly suggest that the close correspondences between Zonaras, Herodian, and Eusebius result from Zonaras' use of an intermediate chronological source that integrated secular and ecclesiastical events and that itself depended for secular events from *ca.* 222 up to *ca.* 238 on a tradition that derived, in part, from Herodian.

George the Monk, p. 460.14–19: And after Antoninus, Alexander the son of Mamaea reigned 13 years and was slaughtered with his mother Mamaea as a result of a plot of Maximinus, a general. Under him, Narcissus [*EEC* II, p. 528, *s.v.* Narcisus], bishop of Jerusalem, when the oil of unction had run out during baptism, ordered water to be thrown into the font and, having prayed, turned this to oil.	Sym. 73, p. 98: Alexander, son of Mamaea, reigned 13 years, 8 months. Under him there was a famine in Rome with the result that people even consumed human flesh. When he [Alexander] had campaigned against Persians, the soldiers put forward Maximinus. Mamaea, Alexander's mother, happened to be god-fearing, and while in Antioch she summoned Origen to her to be taught the mystery according to Christ.	Ced. p. 450.3–12: Alexander, the son of Mamaea, *exadelphos* of Avitus [*i.e.* Elagabalus], reigned 13 years, 8 months. Under him there was a famine in Rome with the result that people even consumed human flesh. When he had campaigned against Persians, he was beaten in battle and, having been despised, was slaughtered with his mother. She happened to be a Christian and while in Antioch she summoned Origen to herself, wishing to be taught the mystery according to Christ. Under him, Narcissus,

bishop of Jerusalem, when the oil of unction had run out during baptism, ordered water to be thrown into the font, and thus, having prayed, turned it into oil.

Scut. p. 35.1–18:

Alexander, the *exadelphos* of Heliogabalus, son of Mamaea, twelve years. He did all things wisely, adorned with words most excellent and with wisdom, revering his mother, excelling in virtue and solemnity of life. She opened the affairs of state to the wise, and she herself was a co-auditor of legal cases and surreptitiously observed everyone, with the result that nothing unjust was able to escape her notice. Laws and decrees were explicated through her, she appointed the legislators to teach laws. When he had campaigned against the Persians with his mother, in Antioch he selected as general Maximinus, who, having attacked Persians, was beaten, as a result of which the sovereign was vexed. When he had learned from Rome that war was underway with the German race, after he had made peace with Persians, he went off against the Germans. And Maximinus immediately thereafter usurped power and was proclaimed sovereign by the army and marched upon Italy. And Alexander, having learned of this and attacked him, was beated and slaughtered with his mother, being in his 39th year. She happened to be a Christian, so Eusebius says. For, in Antioch, having summoned Origen, she was instructed in the mystery according to Christ.

Varius Avitus, perhaps a native of Emesa in Syria, was linked to the Severan family through his mother, Julia Soaemias (*PIR*[2] I 704). Before his elevation to Augustus (May 16, 218), he had served in that city as a priest of the sun god Helagabal, whence his sobriquet Heliogabalus or Elagabalus. As emperor he took the name M. Aurelius Antoninus and, in order to maintain a semblance of dynastic continuity, stories were circulated that he was an illegitimate son of his predecessor M. Aurelius Antoninus Caracalla. In the course of the subsequent struggle for the throne between Elagabalus and his Severan rival and adopted son Alexander, attempts were made to discredit the former's connection to the imperial family and he became styled Pseudo-Antoninus. His perverse behavior won him another nickname, Sardanapalus, the semi-legendary figure, perhaps inspired by the ninth-century Assyrian king Ashurbanipal, who had become synonymous with luxury and excess. Zonaras would have found the name in his source. See, *e.g.*, Xiphil. 355.25, p. 729. Elagabalus died in Rome on March 11 or 12, 222, murdered with his mother by the Praetorian Guard.

2 Before his adoption by Elagabalus and elevation to Caesar (June 221), M. Aurelius Severus Alexander (*PIR* A 1610) had been called Bassianus Alexianus. His father was Gessius Marcianus (*PIR*² G 171). His mother Julia Avita Mamaea (*PIR*² I 649) was a niece of Elagabalus' mother. He was hailed *Imperator* by the Praetorians (March 13, 222) and the following day recognized by the senate as Augustus.

Salmasian John *fr.* 134 Müller *FHG* IV, p. 590—"After him, Alexander, Mamaea's son, his *exadelphos*, 14 years."—is actually a gloss between excerpts of John in the Paris manuscript *Cod. Reg.* 1763. *Cf.* the *apparatus* to John *fr.* 218.35 Roberto, p. 386. Sym. 72.2, p. 92, calls Alexander Elagabalus' *exadelphos*; Herodian V.7.1 and Xiphil. 352.19, p. 728, his *anepsios*; George Syncellus (d. *ca.* 810, *ODB* II, p. 839) p. 437.16, his *adelphidous*. If *SHA Alex. Sev.* 49.5 (= Dexippus *FgrH* 100 F 14) can be trusted, the question of Elagabalus' precise relationship to Alexander had prompted Dexippus to assert: "Antoninus Heliogabalus was Alexander's uncle (*patruum*), and not the son of his mother's sister."

At IX.25 (II, p. 280.2–3), from a lost section of Dio on the young Antiochus IV, Zonaras glosses *anepsios* "for thus the ancients used to call *exadelphoi*." At V.22 (I, p. 453.7), where he has taken from Josephus *JA* XVII.19.4 the application of *anepsia* to one of Herod's wives, Zonaras adds "clearly *exadelphê*" and continues: "For the ancients used to call *exadelphai anepsiai*, as it is possible to find often both in Plutarch and the law books [*e.g. Basil. Libri LX* 28.5.1 (IV, p. 1342.11)]." Zonaras again refers to "law books" at VII.3 (II, p. 10.15–17), where, in connection with Plut. *Rom.* 13.2, he writes: "And he [Romulus] named the *dêmos* [Plutarch has *plêthos*] 'populace,' whence also in the law books the demotic action has been called 'popular' [*popoularia*]." *Cf. Digest* 48.23, *De Popularibus Actionibus*, and *Basilika* 60.32 (V, p. 627), *Peri dêmotikôn agôgôn*, especially *Basilika* 60.32.5—the translation into Greek as *dêmotikê agôgê* of the jurist Julius Paulus' definition at *Digest* 47.23.1 of a "popular action" (*popularis actio*)—and 60.32.11 for the term *popoularia agôgê*.

Zonaras' obvious interest in these synonyms probably stems from issues he addressed as a canonist. In his commentary on Basil the Great's letter to Diodorus concerning the propriety of marriage to a deceased wife's sister (*Ep.* 160, especially 160.5, [ed. Courtonne II, pp. 88–92, especially p. 92.3–6; trans. Deferrari II, pp. 398–411, especially p. 408]), Zonaras raises the question of how to refer to the issue of such a union: "And how do the children call one another? Brothers, as having come from one father, or *anepsioi*, that is, *exadelphoi*, and having come to be from two fathers? And often in the ancients *exadelphoi* are found called by the name *anepsioi*. For both appellations, they say—the one manifestly of brothers, and the one of *anepsioi*— attach to them through the mixture of kinship relationship" (R-P IV, p. 267). This theme appears again in Zonaras' *De Matr. Sobr.*, especially 432C-434A and 436B-C = R-P I, pp. 592–597, especially pp. 593–594 and 596. The propensity of the Comnenian dynasty to grant governmental positions on the basis of familial ties to the emperor may also have contributed to a more precise attention to kinship terms and relationships. See, for example, *TA ΠΡΑΚΤΙΚΑ ΤΗΣ ΕΝ ΚΩΝΣΤΑΝΤΙΝΟΥΠΟΛΕΙ ΣΥΝΟΔΟΥ ΤΟΥ 1166* [*The Acts of the Synod of Constantinople of 1166*] 4.1–3 and 5.2–4, ed. S. N. Sakkos, "Ο ΠΑΤΗΡ ΜΟΥ ΜΕΙΖΩΝ ΜΟΥ ΕΣΤΙΝ ["My Father is Greater than Ι"]," *ΣΠΟΥΔΑΣΤΗΕΡΙΟΝ ΕΚΚΛΕΣΙΑΣΤΙΚΗΣ ΓΡΑΜΜΑΤΟΛΟΓΙΑΣ* 8 (Thessalonike, 1968), pp. 141.30–142.12 and 153.22–154.11.

3   On the famous jurist Domitius Ulpianus (*PIR*² D 169), prefect by December 1, 222, Zonaras follows Xiphil. 355.9–11 and 355.24– 356.2, pp. 729–730. These passages had long seemed to modern scholars to set Ulpian's death *ca.* 228. However, on the basis of *Pap. Ox.* 2565 of AD 224, which names M. Aurelius Epagathus as praetorian prefect, Ulpian must have died *ca.* 223/224. Zos. I.11 names Flavianus (*PIR*² F 180) and Chrestus (*PIR*² G 144) as two of the good men appointed at the beginning of Alexander's reign and links Ulpian's fate to their deposition, a connection tacit at best in Zonaras. Xiphil. 356.3–6, p. 720/Dio LXXX.2.4 implicates Epagathus (*PIR*² E 67) in Ulpian's death and has the former sent to Egypt by Alexander for execution in order to avoid potential problems with the Praetorian Guard in Rome.

4   Zonaras here reflects Herodian VI.1.9–10. John of Antioch probably drew directly from Herodian and, allowing for abridgement of John by the compilers of the *EH* and of *Excerpta* entries by the compilers of the *Suda*, it is reasonable to assume that for Alexander's

reign John's own text was even closer to that of Herodian than are John's fragments. *Cf.* John *fr.* 218.1–23 Roberto p. 384 = *fr.* 138 Müller *FHG* IV, p. 592 = *EV* 44 (I, pp. 192.28–193.15), and, in part, *Suda* A 1124 (I, pp. 103.32–104.2); *fr.* 218.24–37 Roberto, p. 386 = *fr.* 139 *FHG* IV, pp. 592–593 = *EI* 54, pp. 99.25–100.21; *fr.* 219 Roberto p. 386 = *fr.* 140 *FHG* IV, p. 593 = *EV* 45 (I, p. 193.16–27) and *Suda* A 1124 (I, p. 103.22–32); and *fr.* 220 Roberto, pp. 388–392 = *fr.* 141 *FHG* IV, pp. 593–594 = *EI* 55, pp. 100.22–102.34.

Ca. 225 Alexander granted the title Caesar to the senator L. Seius Herennius Sallustius (*PIR*² S 58) and about the same time married his daughter, Gnaea Seia Herennia Sallustia Orba Barbia Orbiana (*PIR*² S 252). By August 30, 227, she was styled Augusta, thereby incurring Mamaea's wrath.

5   Zonaras' account of the rise of the Sasanians (*ODB* III.1845–1846) for the most part reflects Herodian VI.2. However, his reference to "three battles" comes from Xiphil. 356.11, p. 730. For further sources and commentary, see D-L, pp. 9–17, 275–280, and 314–315.

Artaxerxes is Ardashir, first of the Sasanian shahs (r. 224–240), Chosroes/Khusrau II "The Victorious" (r. 590–628) the last of the great Sasanian rulers. Zonaras' notice of Chosroes may reflect the indirect influence of a Persian view of the Sasanian dynasty formalized in the reign of Yazdgird III (*ca.* 632–651) in the so-called *Book of Lords*, itself no longer extant but reflected in a range of sources, *e.g.* Agath. IV.30.2–5. The Arsacid dynasty of Parthia, which began with Arsacides I's break from the Seleucid kingdom in *ca.* 238 BC, ended with Artaxerxes' defeat of Artabanus at the Battle of Hormizdagan, the location and precise date of which are unknown.

Armenia had long been a bone of contention between Parthia and Rome, and powerful Armenian nobles had formed close ties with the contending powers. At the time of Artaxerxes' rebellion, Parthia held the upper hand in Armenia. In Media, too, Parthian rulers had forged close ties with the native elite. Thus initial Armenian and Median opposition to Artaxerxes is no surprise.

Artaxerxes' pledge, if historical, linked the Sasanians to the great Persian dynasty of the Achaemenids (559–330 BC), which began with Cyrus II and ended with the murder of Darius III.

6   *Ca.* 230. Herodian does not mention Cappadocia and Nisibis, and Dio's *History* ends *ca.* 239. Note that Syncellus p. 437.21–22, however, does name these locations as Persian targets.

7   *Cf.* Herodian VI.4.4–6. The incident probably dates to 231, while Alexander was in Antioch.

8   Zonaras' description of events between Alexander's departure from Antioch in 232 and his return to that city in 233 reflects Herodian VI.5–6.3. Alexander would later stage a triumph in Rome (September 25, 233) to celebrate his ill-fated expedition. Indeed, epigraphic, numismatic, and some literary evidence present the operation as a success. See D-L, pp. 26–28 and 31–32, and Whittaker's n. 3 on Herodian VI.7.5.

9   *Cf.* Herodian VI.7.2–10 on Alexander's German campaigns of 234–235.

10   *Cf.* Herodian VI.8–9.7. Alexander and Mamaea died at Mogontiacum (Mainz), in February or March of 235.

11   *Cf.* Eus. *HE* VI.21.2–4, p. 568.3–12; Syncellus p. 439.3–6; and Orosius VII.18.6, who calls Mamaea a Christian. Alex. Mon. 4048C also connects Mamaea to a lull in the persecution of Christians. On Origen, see *EEC* II, pp. 619–623.

12   Rather than Sardianus, Zon. XII.11 (III, p. 559.8) correctly gives Gordius as bishop of Jerusalem. Eus. *HE* VI.10.1, p. 540.16, too, has Gordius; Alex. Mon. 4048B Gordias, Syncellus p. 438.3 Gordianus. Syncellus p. 438.7–9 closely parallels Zonaras on Hippolytus (*EEC* I, pp. 383–385). Sardianus, then, may be a copyist's mistake.

13   Alexander's reign lasted almost precisely thirteen years. Since Eus. *HE* VI.28, p. 582.1–2 ("three and ten"), Syncellus p. 438.3 ("13"), and Alex. Mon. 4048B ("three and ten") give that duration—Herodian VII.1 gives "fourteen"— it is likely that Zonaras himself either used a deficient manuscript or misread his source or his incorrect "ten" appeared during manuscript transmission. Between January 7 and May 16, 236, Maximinus (*PIR*² I 619) proclaimed his son, C. Julius Verus Maximinus (*PIR*² I 620), Caesar.

14   Zonaras' assertion that Maximinus targeted Christian leaders and that he was angered at the number of Christians in Alexander's household transposes the same information in Eus. *HE* VI.28, p. 528, though Eusebius does not comment on the timing of the persecution. *SHA Alex. Sev.* 29.2 records that Alexander had a statue of Jesus among

images of deities and holy men, that he wished to "to build a temple to Christ and to admit him among the gods" (44.6–7, with which *cf.* 49.6), and that he did not persecute Christians (22.4).

Parallels again suggest Zonaras' dependence on an intermediate source rather than his direct consultation of Herodian and Eusebius, the ultimate sources of much of the information he transmits.

| Sym. 74, pp. 98–99: Maximinus reigned 6 years. A shepherd and afterwards a soldier, then, thus, general of Alexandria [*sic*], by the populace and senate he was put forward as sovereign on account of his manliness and intelligence, and afterwards was slaughtered treacherously by Maximus (*PIR*² C 1179) and Balbinus (*PIR*² C 126), having gained an end worthy of his impious intent. Maximinus, in hatred toward Alexander for supporting and honoring many Christians, aroused a great persecution against Christians. | Ced. p. 450.13–20: Maximinus reigned 6 years. A shepherd, then, a soldier and thus afterwards a general of Alexander, on account of manliness of body and savvy and intelligence, by the populace and senate he was chosen sovereign. In hatred toward Alexander, who was supporting and honoring many Christians, he aroused a great persecution against Christians. He met an end worthy of his impious intent, being treacherously slaughtered by Maximus and Balbinus. |

Scut. pp. 35.19–36.11:

Maximinus, three years. After he had received the sovereignty, he then revealed the baseness of his soul, outraging all with total savagery, consulting informers, lusting for riches, unjustly perpetrating murders, and, with all cowed, even venting his wrath on those who had made him sovereign. For he was of the excessively worthless and ignoble, and, solely on account of physical manliness, was advanced by Alexander to the generalship. The Romans in Libya recognized Gordianus (*PIR*² A 833) and his son of the same name (*PIR*² A 834) as sovereigns and they sent ambassadors to Rome. The senate, having learned this, was secretly awaiting the sovereigns' arrival. And Maximinus, in hatred for Alexander and Mamaea, aroused a great persecution against Christians and tyrannized many holy men. And the senate, since the sovereigns had not yet arrived from Libya [36] because of the impassability of the sea, appointed generals men from the council with experience of generalship, Balbinus and Maximus, who, when they had taken control of the roads to Rome, were ready for an uprising. After this had been announced to Maximinus and those deployed to stand guard had repulsed him, when he had launched an attack together with the Moors for the purpose of a preemptive occupation of Aculia [*i.e.* Aquileia] and when there had been a conference, both he himself and his son were slaughtered in the war and his head was borne to Rome. And while the sovereigns were still being delayed through the force of the wintry weather, Maximinus maintained power with Galbius [*i.e.* Balbinus] for three months, and he was slain in the palace, being in his sixtieth year.

Material that once stood in the lacuna between Malal. XII.24 and 25/ 295.16 and 17, p. 225—the reigns of Macrinus (*PIR*² O 108) through Aemilianus (*PIR*² A 330), *i.e.* April 11, 217–September/ October 253—is perhaps linked in some fashion to the tradition from which Zonaras draws. Even if this is so, Zonaras' direct use of Malalas does not necessarily follow.

15   The story of Ambrose (*EEC* I, p. 28) and Origen appears at Eus. *HE* VI.23, pp. 568–570, Syncellus p. 438.17–21, George the Monk, pp. 454.20–455.5; and Ced. p. 444.7–14. Eus. *HE* VI.28, p. 582, deals with Ambrose and Protoctetus (*EEC* I, p. 547, *s.v.* Maximinus Thrax) and notes that it was to them that Origen dedicated his *Exhoration to Martyrdom* (ed. P. Koetschau *Origenes Werke, GCS* 2, I, pp. 1–47; trans. J. O'Meara, *Ancient Christian Writers* 19, pp. 141–196).

16   A broad range of sources, Herodian among them, damn Maximinus for reasons that range from social, senatorial, and religious biases, a tendency to alternate "good" and "bad" emperors, and, so far as we can judge, some very real, frightening patterns of behavior on Maximinus' part. John of Antioch, in turn, copied much of Herodian's assessment. *Cf. fr.* 221 Roberto, p. 393 = *fr.* 142 Müller *FHG* IV, p. 594 = *EV* 46 (I, p. 194.1–9) = *Suda* M 172 (III, p. 321.13–17) and Herodian VII.1.1–2; *fr.* 223 Roberto, p. 394 = *fr.* 144 Müller *FHG* IV, p. 594 = *EV* 47 (I, p. 194.13–16) = Herodian VII.1.12; and *fr.* 224.1–16 Roberto, pp. 394–396 = *fr.* 145 Müller *FHG* IV, pp. 594–595 = *EV* 48 (I, pp. 194.17–195.8) = Herodian VII.3. On the other hand, Alexander the Monk 4048C, Syncellus, Symeon, Cedrenus, and Scutariotes are, as is Zonaras, quite succinct. In addition, Syncellus p. 442.10, too, alleges that Maximinus murdered his wife, which suggests that some intermediate source not only stands between Zonaras and Herodian but also between Zonaras and John.

The alleged victim, whose name is known only through epigraphic and numismatic evidence, was Caecilia Paulina (*PIR*² C 91).

17   Herodian VII.2 treats Maximinus' German campaigns of 235–237/238.

18   The evidence for the reigns of the Gordians is notoriously problematic. Much of Zonaras' account of Gordianus I reflects Herodian VII.4–6 = John of Antioch *fr.* 224.16–64 Roberto, pp. 396–398 = *fr.* 146.1–5 Müller *FHG* IV, p. 595 = *EI* 57, pp. 103.6–104.31. *SHA Three Gordians* 2.1 = Dexippus *FgrH*100 F 16, says that both Arrianus [*i.e.* Herodian] and Dexippus dealt with the Gordians "even if briefly, yet conscientiously." See, too, *SHA Three Gordians* 9.6 = Dexippus *FgrH* 100 F 15). January 238 probably saw Gordianus I's acclamation and death.

19   Zonaras' claim that rebellion against Maximinus began in Rome before the arrival of the embassy bearing news of the events in Africa seems to be the result of garbled transmission or a misunderstanding of Herodian VII.7.2–10.1. Herodian describes the defeat of Gordianus II at the hands of Maximinus' legate Capellianus (*PIR*² C 404) and the subsequent suicide of Gordianus I. Zos. I.14 explicitly places the senatorial appointment of Maximus and Balbinus (Zonaras' Albinus) after the envoys' arrival. *SHA Max.* 19–20 and *Three Gordianus* 15–16 and 22 has Gordianus II die in Africa in battle, Gordianus I commit suicide, and the senate, after having been informed of these events, choose Maximus and Balbinus as Augusti. According to *SHA Maximus and Balbinus* 16.6, Dexippus (*FgrH* 100 F 18d) gave this sequence. For Scutariotes' testimony, see above, n. 14. Zonaras' closing notice of alternative versions of the careers of Maximus and Balbinus probably came from his immediate source rather than from autopsy of variant accounts. See further, n. 21 below.

20   The murders of Maximinus and his son occurred *ca.* mid-April 238. He reigned three years and a few months. Zonaras' "six" (*hex* in Greek) is probably his or a copyist's error, perhaps influenced by the identical initial syllable of the nearby "sixty." Apart from Zonaras, only *CP* p. 501.3 gives Maximinus' age at the time of his death.

   The incorrect identification of Aquileia with Venice may be Zonaras' gloss. If so, it is his lone mention of the city, which, as a result of Venetian naval victories in the Adriatic over the forces of the Norman Robert Guiscard (*ODB* III, p. 1799), had in his own time become a critical factor in the relationship of Constantinople with the West. These successes benefited Alexius Comnenus and resulted in a sort of most favored nation status for Venetian ships in Byzantine ports. See *CMH* ² IV.1, pp. 212–216 and 250–274.

21   The source tradition or traditions that Zonaras reflects are both confused and confusing. As a result, his exposition is best understood in light of the parallels assembled below. Though awkward, variant spellings, even when identifications are transparent, have been retained, the proper identities of the rulers referred to therein are given in brackets. Names of consuls in the *CP* are as printed in Bekker's edition, and these should be compared with those in Mommsen's *fasti*, *MGH.AA* XIII, pp. 513–514. Note that Symeon's testimony represents a single strand of the traditions about the Gordians, while George the Monk, Cedrenus, *CP*, and Scutariotes display the combination of elements of that tradition with the alternative versions noted by Zonaras.

George the Monk p. 461.1–19:	Sym. 75.1–2, p. 99:	Ced. p. 450.21–452.3:
29. About Balbinus [Albinus]	Maximus and Balbinus [Albinus]	Maximus, Balbinus [Albinus], and Gordianus [III] two months. Gordianus had previously become Caesar against Maximinus. Philippus, the prefect, prevented the distribution of grain [451] to the army. He was father of the blessed martyr Eugenia. Under this man the blessed Babylas [*EEC* I, p. 106] was bishop of Antioch, and the blessed Laurentius and Cyprianus [*EEC* I, pp. 211–212] were martyred, and Eugenius became bishop of Byzantium for 25 years.
And after Maximinus, Balbinus [Albinus] reigned 2 months and was slain in the war.	Maximus and Balbinus [Albinus] reigned 22 days. In the same fashion, they were slaughtered by the troops. And similarly Gordianus [III, *PIR*² A 835], who had become Caesar against Maximinus and had himself become sovereign, was killed, since Philippus the prefect [*PIR*² I 461] had prevented the distribution of grain to the army. And this Philippus was father of the blessed martyr Eugenia. 2. Under Maximus and Gordianus [III], Africanus the historian [*EEC* I, p. 460] was noteworthy.	

30. About Pouplianus [Maximus]

And after Balbinus [Albinus], Pouplianus [Maximus] reigned 2 months and was slain in the war.

31. About Jounor [Gordianus III]

And after Pouplianus [Maximus], Jounor [Gordianus III] reigned 3 months, he who first formed Candidates and Protectors and, having organized the detachment of the *Scholarii*, he called it "Jounor" in his own name.

32. About Gordianus [III]

And after Jounor [Gordianus III], Gordianus [Gordianus III], his son, reigned 4 years, and, in the war, after he had fallen with his horse and broken his thigh, he [Gordianus III] died.

33. About Ounior [Gordianus III]

And after Gordianus, Ounior [Gordianus III], his son, reigned 2 years, and, after he had

[*Apparatus criticus* 75.7, p. 99:

Gordianus [[III]]

Gordianus [[III]], having become Caesar perhaps around the age of 13 years, was declared ruler for 6 years and received the realm of Romans, then, when he had been plotted against by Philippus, a prefect, died.]

After Balbinus [Albinus], Puplianus [Maximus] reigned 2 months, and was killed in war.

After him, Junior [Gordianus III] reigned three months, he who first formed Candidates and Protectors, and, having organized the detachment of the *Scholarii*, he called it the "Juniors," in his own name.

After him, Gordianus [Gordianus III], his son, reigned 4 years. And in a war, after he had fallen with his horse and broken his thigh, he [Gordianus III] died.

After Gordianus [III], Unior [Gordianus III], his son, reigned two years and, after he had developed dropsy, died. Under him, Sabellius the archpriest was noteworthy.

After him, Marcus 3 years.

After Marcus, Hustilianus two years. And, when he had opened a vien, while asleep, he poured forth

developed dropsy, died.
Under him, Sabellius
the archpriest [*EEC* II,
pp. 748–749] was
noteworthy.

his blood and, after he
had lost consciousness,
died.

34. About Marcus

And after Ounior
[Gordianus III], Marcus
[*PIR*² M 271] reigned 2
years.

35. About Ioustillianus

And after Marcus,
Ioustillianus [*PIR* V 8]
reigned 2 years and,
when he had opened a
vien, poured forth his
blood while asleep, and,
after he had lost
consciousness, died.

36. About Philippus

And after Ioustilianus,
Philippus [*PIR*² I 461]
reigned 6 years and,
having founded a city
in Europe and having
called it Philippopolis,
he was killed in the
palace.

Sym. 76, p. 99:

Philippus

Philippus reigned five
years, he who was a
devotee of the faith of
the Christians, having
been adorned with
understanding and
fairness, and he sprang
from Bostra of Europe,
and there he founded a
city, having named it
Philippoupolis. 2. He
began to make peace
treaties with Sapor,
sovereign of Persians,
who used to cause
amazement by the size
of his body. For up to
that time no such man
had been seen. 3.
Philippus was killed
together with his son
by Decius, battling on
behalf of Christians.

After him, Philippus
reigned 7 years, he who
was a devotee of the
faith of the Christians,
having been adorned
with understanding and
fairness. He sprang
from Bostra of Europe,
and there he founded a
city, having named it
Philippoupolis. He
began to make peace
treaties with Sapor,
sovereign of Persians,
who used to cause
amazement [452] by
the size of his body. For
up to that time no such
man had been seen.
He was killed together
with his son battling
against Decius on
behalf of Christians.

CP pp. 501.3–504.6:

Balbinus [Albinus] reigned 3 months and was slain. And Pouplius [Maximus] reigned one hundred days and was slain. 24th of Romans, Gordianus Senior [Gordianus III] reigned 6 years.

In all 5,753 [years].

Indiction 2 [AD 241]. [Year] 1. Consuls: Gordianus [III] Augustus, for the 2nd time, and Pompeianus [*PIR*² C 1177].

Olympiad 255

Indiction 3 [AD 242]. [Year] 2. Consuls: Atticus [*PIR* V 322] and Praetextatus [*PIR*² A 1230].

Indiction 4 [AD 243]. [Year] 3. Consuls: Aurelianus [*sic*, *PIR*² A 635] and Pappus [*PIR*² C 684].

Gordianus [III] Augustus made a unit of those called Candidates, having elevated them by selection as mature, strong, and of magnificent appearance, from the formation of those called *Scholarii*, having called the school of the same unit "Seniors" in his own name. These are those of the Sixth School.

Indiction 5 [AD 244]. [Year] 4. Consuls: Peregrinus [*PIR*² A 1059] and Aemilianus [*PIR*² F 529].

Indiction 6 [AD 245]. [Year] 5. Consuls: Philippus [*PIR*² I 461] and Tatianus [*PIR*² M 82].

[502] Olympiad 256

Indiction 7 [AD 246]. [Year] 6. Consuls. Praesentus [*sic*, *PIR*² B 167] and Albinus [*PIR*² A 1059].

Under these consuls, when he had been stricken by disease, Gordianus [III] Senior died, being 79 years old.

25th of Romans, Philippus Junior reigned together with Philippus, his son, 6 years.

In all, 5,759 [years].

Indiction 8 [AD 247]. [Year] 1. Consuls: Philippus Augustus, for the 2nd time, and Philippus [*PIR*² I 462], his son.

Indiction 9 [AD 248]. [Year] 2. Consuls: Philippus Augustus, for the 3rd time, and Philippus, his son, the 2nd time.

Indiction 10 [AD 249]. [Year] 3. Consuls: Aemilianus [*PIR*² F 529], the 2nd time, and Aqulinus [*PIR*² N 6].

Olympiad 257

Indiction 11 [AD 250]. [Year] 4. Consuls: Decius [*PIR*² M 520] and Gratianus [*sic*, *PIR*² V 328].

The sovereign Philippus, together with his son Philippus, constituted a unit of those called Candidates, elevating chosen young men from the *Scholarii*, having called the school of the formation they constituted "Juniors," by the name of Philippus, the father. These are those of the Sixth School.

Indiction 12 [AD 251. The consuls given are those of 252. See below, Indiction 14, for the correct consuls.]. [Year] 4. Consuls: Gallus [*PIR* V 403] and Bolusianus [Volusianus, *PIR* V 376].

[503] Indiction 13 [AD 252. The consuls given are those of 253. Philippus died in 249. See below, n. 25]. [Year] 6. Consuls: Bolusianus [Volusianus], the 2nd time, and Maximus [*PIR* V 121].

Pilippus Junior, having engaged in many wars, fared well. And so, in a war with the Gepids, his horse stumbled and, when he had fallen with it, he suffered a fractured thigh. And after he had come to Rome, he died from the same fracture, being 45 years old.

26 of Romans, Decius reigned 1 year.

In all, 5,760 [years].

Indiction 14 [AD 253, but the consuls are those of 251 and Decius' reign commenced in 249, *CP*'s Indiction 10]. [Year] 1. Consuls: Decius Caesar [*PIR*² M 520] and Decius, his son [*PIR*² H 106].

In the beginning of Decius' reign, when a persecution against Christians had begun, Flavianus [*EEC* I, p. 315, *s.v.* Fabian], bishop of Rome, was martyred. After him, Cornelius [*EEC* I, p. 202] received the bishopric for three years. And similarly, too, Babylas, bishop of Antioch, concluded the race of martyrdom. After him, 13th of Antioch, Fabius [*EEC* I, p. 314] presided 3 years. And many others, both in the East and in other provinces, having risen on behalf of faith in Christ, were killed. According to tradition, this too reached us about the holy Babylas, as the blessed Leontius, the bishop of Antioch, declared to our predecessors. This Decius killed the holy Babylas, not only because he was a Christian, but also because he dared to keep the sovereign Philippus' wife and Philippus himself, being Christians, [504] from entering the church, since Philippus had committed a crime. And the crime was of this sort. Philippus Junior, being a prefect under Gordianus [III?], the sovereign who had preceded him, took as a ward from Gordianus his son. And when Gordianus had died, after he had slain the boy, Philippus reigned.

Scut. pp. 36.9–37.19:

While the sovereigns [the Gordians I and II] were still being delayed by the force of the wintry weather, Maximinus [Maximus] maintained control with Galbius [Albinus] for three months, and he was slain in the palace, being sixty years old.

Pompianus [Maximus], 2 months: And he too was slain.

Pouplius Galbinus [Albinus], 3 months, and he was slain, the sovereign Gordianus the Elder having apprehended him on arrival from Libya, and he reigned only twenty-two days, and, when he had become ill from the lengthy voyage, died, being 70 and nine years old. Gordianus [III], his son, 6 years. In the war against Persia, after he had tumbled from his horse and crushed his thigh, when he had returned to Rome, he died as a result, being fifty years old.

Gordianus the Third, six years: gentle and esteemed, dizzied by the rule, he appointed Timisocles [*PIR*[2] F 581], his own relative-by-marriage, prefect of the court for the sake of domestic security, a man famous for every sort of refinement. And as long as he [Timisocles] was among the living, he maintained affairs of state in firmness and stability and was administering them nobly. And when Timisocles had died, the one after him, Philippus, successor of the prefecture, was turned toward desire of the sovereignty and, after he had won over those in the army disposed to revolution, while the sovereign was staying in Nisibis, when he had reduced the rations of the soldiers, he himself became a cause of insurrection. For the army went over to him with the ruinous result of the shortage of food as a reason, and straightway they killed him [Gordianus III], being 28 years old. And the council in Rome [37] chose Marcus, a certain philosopher, and he died suddenly in the palace, being 43 years old. And Oustilianus [Hostlianus], also [known as] Severus, who, after he had become ill and been bled, died, being 46 years old, assumed control of the realm.

Philippus, six years and 6 months: Against him, Decius, together with his army, rebelled. After he had advanced toward him with a weighty army and joined battle, Philippus was beaten and after a bit fled toward Rome. And when a civil war had occurred in Rome, Philippus was removed with his children as he was emerging from the palace toward them. And immediately the senate made sovereign a certain Marius, styled "the Frugal," and he ruled . . . months.

Report holds that this Philippus was most pious and gentle and respectful of Christians' things. He certainly was not the father of Saint Eugenia, as some through forgetfulness recorded in chronologies. For, holding the prefecture of Egypt, he was not a sovereign, but was a martyr with his daughter. And the sovereign Pilippus died being 63 years old. And in the fourth year of his sovereignty, when a thousand years had been filled from Romulus' foundation, the Romans celebrated an immense array of spectacles.

22   The brief reigns of Maximus and Albinus probably fell in January 238. Zonaras' "Germans" were auxiliary troops probably familiar with Maximus as a result of his service as a legate (of Alexander?) in their territory. *Cf.* Herodian VIII.7.8. *Chron. 354*, p. 147.28–29, states that "Two Gordians ruled 20 days. They died in Africa. Pupenius and Balbinus [Albinus], ruled 99 days. . . . They were killed at Rome." The alternative figures of "twenty-two days" and "not quite three months" may result from some sources listing Maximus and Albinus as emperors during the twenty-day period allotted to the Gordians and then adding as a separate unit the remaining seventy-nine days or "just under three months."

23   Pompeianus is Maximus (M. Clodius Pupienus Maximus [*PIR*[2] C 1179]); Publius Balbinus is Zonaras' Albinus. *SHA Maximus and Balbinus* 17.7 comments that the majority of Latin writers known to him referred to Maximus as Pupienus and *Maximus and Balbinus* 18 that Greek writers employed Maximus rather than Pupienus. If trustworthy, *SHA Maximus and Balbinus* 15.5 reveals that the Greek writer Dexippus distinguished Maximus from Pupienus. *SHA Maximus and Balbinus* 1.2 implies likewise. Jacoby does not print either passage as a fragment, though he notes both at *FgrH* 100 after his F 18. See now J. McInerney, *BNJ* 100 F 18a–d, with commentary.

Gordians I and II had, of course, already died in Africa. Zonaras' son of Gordianus is actually Gordianus III, grandson of Gordianus

II through that Gordianus' daughter. Zonaras' confusion seems to have originated in part through a misunderstanding—perhaps by Eusebius—of the source reflected at Eutr. IX.2.2, where, immediately after discussing the connections of the Gordians, Eutropius (fourth c., *ODB* II, p. 758) states: "And so, when they [Not the Gordians, but Maximus and Balbinus.] had come to Rome, Balbinus and Pupienus were killed in the palace." Jerome, too, plays a role, for *Chron.* p. 216[i], presumably reflecting pre-Eutropian material from Eusebius, records: "When Gordianus had entered Rome, Pupienus and <B>albinus, who had seized power, were killed in the palace." Though Eusebius/Jerome must mean Gordianus III, others could easily have misunderstood, and then extrapolated from, the entry. A parallel, and eventually intersecting, influence, too, could have been propagandistic: the belief that the tale would legitimate Gordianus III, whose senior colleagues in imperial power were, as Herodian VII.8 relates, actually victims of praetorian guardsmen who subsequently acclaimed Gordianus III. Herodian's *History* ends with Gordianus III's elevation to Augustus.

24   So Herodian VIII.9.7–9. Note, too, Amm. Marc. XXVI.6.20, which also specifies Gordianus I's suicide by the rope. See further, n. 19 above.

25   Gordianus III departed Italy for the East in 242 and campaigned against Persia through 243 until his death between January 13 and March 14, 244. To this version of Gordianus III's death, which appears only in Zonaras and George the Monk, *cf.* Cedrenus, *CP* (seventh c., *ODB* I, p. 447, *s.v. Chronicon Paschale*), and Scutariotes in the parallels in n. 21 above. It is, of course, not irreconcilable with Gordianus III's death in battle as recorded, *e.g.* in Sapor I's trilingual *Res Gestae* (Greek Section) 6–8 (trans. D-L, pp. 35–36). *CP* (n. 21, above), perhaps confused, as were George and Cedrenus, by its source's use of Junior with reference both to Gordianus III and Philippus I, tells the story of the latter but sets it in a campaign against the Gepids rather than the Persians and—impossibly because Philippus died in 249—during the year of the consuls of 253.

SHA Three Gordians 31.2 and Zos. I.19.1—both specifically with reference to Gordianus III—label the alternative tradition preserved by Zonaras, George, Cedrenus, *CP*, and Scutariotes in which a Gordianus succumbs to disease misinformation spread by Philippus I to cover his treachery.

26   At Eus. *HE* VI.23, pp. 568–570, this material directly follows the story of Ambrose's patronage of Origen, drawn upon earlier by Zonaras at XII.16 (II, pp. 575.19–576.4).

27   AD 236. *Cf.* Eus. *HE* VI.29, pp. 582–583, but for Eusebius' correct Fabianus Zonaras, his source, or a copyist wrote Flavianus and omitted Eusebius' notice of the Alexandrian succession of Demetrius, Heraclas, and Dionysius (*EEC* I, pp. 225, 374, and 238, respectively). At various points elsewhere, however, Zonaras does mention every bishop of Alexandria named by Eusebius.

28   Zonaras reflects Eus. *HE* VI.29.4–31.1, pp. 584–586 on Zebinus (d. *ca*. 240), Gregory (*EEC* I, p. 368), Athenodorus (*EEC* I, p. 59), and Africanus, broadly synchronized by Eusebius with the beginning of Fabianus' episcopacy and set under Gordianus [III]. Sym. 75.2, p. 99, translated above n. 21, also notices the chronographer Sextus Julianus Africanus (d. *ca*. 240) in association with the same emperor. *Cf.*:

Ced. p. 441.8–10 and 17–21: And Africanus the chronographer says that under him [Commodus] Clement the writer of a miscellany in Alexandria was noteworthy. . . . Under this one [Pertinax], as Eusebius says, was Symmachus, one of the translators of the scripture of the Hebrews, Ebionaean with respect to sect. But also Porphyry the philosopher, the one having written against Christians, and Africanus the chronographer. Under this one, Leonides, the father of evil-minded Origen, was martyred.	Scut. p. 33.10–12: Under him [Septimius Severus] was the Wonderworker Gregory, and Origen—and the father of Origen, Leonides, was martyred in Rome—and Hippolytus the Roman historian. Then, too, Africanus the historian was noteworthy.

Zon. XII.11 (II, p. 556.12–16) likewise places Leonides' martyrdom under Septimius. Clearly, at some point in a strand of the transmission of this information, the *floruit* of Africanus gave way to the synchronism of his death with the starts of the episcopacies of Fabianus and, *ca*. 240, Babylas.

29   Syncellus p. 443.4–9 closely parallels Zonaras.

30   See above, n. 25.

31   Gordianus died between mid-January and mid-March 244. See above, n. 21, for parallels that describe Philippus' supposed scheme, and n. 25.

32   George the Monk, p. 465.2; Ced. p. 451.16; Scut. pp. 36.31– 37.2—all translated above, n. 21—; *LIM* p. 436.12, and Zonaras provide the only mentions of this alleged emperor. Indeed, existence of Marcus, to whom *LIM* allots a reign of six years, seems to be the result of misunderstanding references by *praenomen* to Marcus Philippus I and II, the lengths of whose reigns approximate those assigned to "Marcus."

33   With Zonaras, *cf.* George the Monk p. 465.4–6; Ced. p. 451.17– 19; Scut. p. 37.2–4, all translated above, n. 21. All four situate him in the immediate aftermath of Marcus' death, and Zonaras and Scutariotes both call him Severus Hostilianus. He may, in fact, be a mistake for Gaius Valens Hostilianus Messius Quintus (*PIR* V 8), Decius' son, who was proclaimed Caesar *ca.* September 250 and, after his adoption by Trebonianus Gallus (*PIR* V 403), became Augustus in June 251. He was dead—according to *Epit. de Caes.* 30.2 a victim of plague—by *ca.* mid-July 251. Note that the six-year reign assigned by *LIM* to its "Marcus" would yield a date of *ca.* 250. See further Zon. XII.21 with n. 50 below.

34   Philippus the Arab (*PIR²* I 461) became Augustus sometime between January 13 and March 14, 244 and reached Rome sometime in the summer of 244. The earliest attestations of Philippus II (*PIR²* I 462) as Caesar fall between July 23 and August 15, 244, his earliest attestation as Augustus only between July 11 and August 30, 247. For Philippus' eastern policies, see D-L pp. 45–48. With Zonaras' description of Sapor's physique, *cf.* Ced. p. 451.23–452.2 and Sym. 76.2, p. 99, translated above, n. 21.

35   *Cf.* Eus. *HE* VI.34, pp. 588–589, Syncellus pp. 443.21–444.2, and *CP* pp. 503.18–504.6, the last translated above, n. 21. The parallels between Zonaras, Eusebius, and Syncellus again militate against Zonaras' direct use of Eusebius. With the confused two Gordians of *CP*, *cf. SHA Three Gordians* 29.3–30, which describes Philippus' guardianship and elimination of Gordianus III.

36   Zonaras here opposes the mistaken identification of Philippus the emperor with Eugenia's father as it appears in Sym. 75, p. 99, and Ced.

p. 451.1–4, both translated above, n. 21, and which stems from the *Martyrdom of Eugenia* itself (*PG* 116, cols 609–652). Zonaras' agreement on this matter with Scut. p. 37.12–16 (translated above, n. 21) probably derives from their sources rather than from their own independent application of critical acumen. On the Greek versions of Eugenia's martyrdom, see *BHG* I, pp. 184–185.

37   Zos. I.20 and John of Antioch *fr.* 226 Roberto, p. 408 = *fr.* 148 Müller *FHG* IV, 598 (translated below, n. 39), are the only other literary witnesses to Philippus' western campaigns of 246–247, for which he celebrated a triumph upon his return to Rome in 247. However, though he does not mention Philippus, Evagrius Scholasticus *HE* V.24, p. 219.2–7, notes that Dexippus (*FgrH* 100 T 6) treated the incursions of the Carpi.

38   Marinus' acclamation probably dates to about April of 248. Much of Zosimus I.21–22 closely parallels Zonaras, and these two provide the sole literary attestations of Marinus' existence. The dominant tradition, hostile to Decius, has him conspire to gain the throne. *Cf.*, *e.g.*, Aur. Vict. *Caes.* 29.1, Orosius VII.21.1, and John of Antioch *fr.* 226, Roberto, p. 408 = *fr.* 148 Müller *FHG* IV, p. 598 (translated below, n. 39). Sym. 76.3, p. 99, and Ced. p. 452.2–5, translated above, n. 21, impart to the conflict a religious motive and, in so doing, reflect a tradition that inverts Decius' rise and his initiation of the persecution of Christians as found in Eus. *HE* VI.39.1, p. 594, and Jerome *Chron.* p. 218ᵈ.

As noted above, n. 21, Scut. p. 37.10–11 records: "And immediately [after Philippus' death] the senate made sovereign a certain Marius, known as 'the Frugal,' and he ruled . . . months." Malal. XII, p. 227, xvi.b = *EI* 21, p. 159.31–32, seems to provide further details about this mysterious Marius: "As he was sleeping, his wife murdered Marius the sovereign, who was not proclaimed by the senate, because the army, having had power over the senate, made him sovereign." However, because George the Monk p. 466.17–18 attributes an identical death to the future emperor Trebonianus Gallus, who, like Malalas' Marius, was proclaimed emperor by the troops rather than the senate, it seems likely that the "Marius" of the *EI* reflects a misreading of "Gallus" for "Marius" or the not-uncommon apathy of the excerptor, for whom "Marius" or "Gallus" served equally well to make the point of the quotation. Indeed, the preceding excerpt, *EI* 20, p. 159.29–30 = Malal. XII, p. 227, xv.b, deals with Gallus' acclamation and death. This hypothesis, while it removes the need to explain the obvious contradiction between Malalas and Scutariotes with respect to the impetus behind Marius' acclamation, leaves open the question of the identity of the Marius of Scutariotes.

39   Philippus died in September or October of 249 perhaps at Verona or alternatively at Macedonian or Thracian Beroe. *Pace* Zonaras, Sym. 76.3, p. 99, and Ced. p. 452.2–3, the latter two translated above, n. 21, Philippus' son was probably killed in Rome. Aur. Vict. *Caes.* 28.11 and *Chron. 354*, p. 147.33, place the younger Philippus' death at the praetorian camp in Rome. John of Antioch *fr.* 226, Roberto, p. 408 = *fr.* 148 Müller *FHG* IV, p. 598 = *EI* 59, p. 109.20–32, distinguishes the locations of their deaths and recounts circumstances far different than those described in the tradition from which Zonaras drew:

> Philippus, after he had become sovereign and conquered the Scythians, began to advance against Byzantium. And when he had arrived at Perinthus, as it was announced to him that there had occurred in Rome civil disturbances, which Decius one of the consuls and prefect of the city had fomented, he sent capable men to check what was being done and to frustrate Decius' uprising. And he [Decius], with his sons, began to make offers to comply. As soon as the men whom Philippus dispatched to Rome had been won over by both gifts and flatteries of the people and the senate, they both renounced Philippus and, with the Romans, declared Decius emperor [With the last clause, *cf.* the unattributed *Suda* entry A 2866 (I, p. 259.1–2), probably adapted from John]. When these things had been announced to Philippus, [who was] fleeing to Beroe . . . and they killed him with daggers hidden under robes, after he had directed affairs for five years. And in Rome the soldiers of the city killed his son.

Scut. p. 37.8–10, perhaps confusing the father and son, has Philippus I eliminated in Rome "with his children, emerging from the palace toward them." See further, n. 32 above. On the confused version of Philippus' death at *CP* p. 503.2–5, see above, n. 25.

Malalas *EI* 19, p. 159.22–28, = Malal. XII, p. 227, xii.c, from the missing section of the *Chronographia*, contains unique though not necessarily accurate, detail:

During the reign of Philippus, the sovereign of Romans, when a civil war had arisen in Rome among the soldiers because *Brutides* had committed adultery and, when many had engaged in slaughter, Philippus emerged from the palace among his own sons to stop them, and the soldiers from one side set upon him and slaughtered him among his own children, and he died being 63.

The term *Brutides* is unusual. *Suda* B 560 (I, p. 498.3–4) glosses it as a synonym of "Sibyl" and goes on to state that all women in a state of possession used to be called Sibyls. The unhelpful opening of this *Suda* entry also appears in the *Lexicon* attributed to Zonaras (*Ioannis Zonarae Lexicon*, ed. Tittmann, I, p. 406.13). Since some have posited a connection between Malalas and Zonaras, it is worth noting that they diverge on the deaths of the Philippi and that, if the *Lexicon* is indeed by Zonaras, the entry here in question patently derives from the *Suda* rather than from Malalas.

40   With Zonaras on Bostra and the foundation of Philippoupolis, *cf.* George the Monk p. 465.8–10, Sym. 71.1, p. 99, and Ced. p. 451.21–23, all translated above in n. 21. Though Bostra and Philippopolis are in the Trachones area of Syria, they are hardly identical.

Aur. Vict. *Caes.* 28.1 calls Philippus "an Arab from Traconitis" and mentions the foundation of Philippopolis, which Jerome *Chron.* p. 217[g] mistakes for Philip II of Macedon's Thracian Philippopolis. Cedrenus reflects a tradition that took Philippus' foundation for the Thracian city and then created a nonexistent "Bostra of Europe." In Zonaras' day, Anna Comnena *Alexiad* XIV.8.2, p. 454, took pains to specify Thracian Philippopolis as the city of the Roman Philippus and then compounded her mistake by associating it with Crenides, the location of what later became Philippi—all this despite her having spent time in Thracian Philippopolis with her father Alexius.

41   In George the Monk pp. 465.11–467.8, *LIM* p. 436.14–17, and Ced. pp. 452.4–454.2 the confused sequence of rulers after Philippus is Valerianus, Gallus, Decius, and Aemilianus rather than the correct Decius, Gallus, Aemilianus, and Valerianus found in Zonaras, Sym. 77–80, pp. 100–101, and Scut. pp. 37.23–38.14. *Cf.*:

George the Monk pp. 466.19–467.5 (after Valerianus and Gallus):	Sym. 77, p. 100:	Ced. p. 453.6–23:
[39. About Decius]	Decius	
And after Gallus, Decius ruled one year and was killed in the war. He mandated in Rome that the Christian women not go out with the head covered, thinking through this shameful legislation to draw them toward idolatry. But they went out more eagerly, considering that which seemed a dishonor among men a glory on behalf of Christ. Whence, to the present, observant Christian [467] women go out uncovered, but the Jews and unfaithful cover themselves. And under him, too, Babylas of Antioch and Flavianus of Rome, and Alexander of Jerusalem, and Dionysius of Alexandria were martyred, and Navatus [*EEC* II, p. 603–604] left the church, and Helcesaeus, the high priest, was noteworthy.	Decius reigned two years, he who tortured and gave over to death many holy men. And he was killed by Scythians by instructions of Gallus and Volousianus, having suffocated in a marsh with his own son, having chanced upon a punishment worthy of their own beastliness, as neither their bodies were discovered nor any part of them. 2. Under him lived Clement [*EEC* I, pp. 179–181], the author of *Miscellanies*, and Africanus and Gregory the Wonderworker. Under Decius, Navatus, being an elder, split from the church, he who was not receiving those who had burned incense and repented. Under him, Cyprianus the holy was martyred, and the seven boys in Ephesus, and a multitude of holy ones.	Decius reigned 2 years. This man tortured and gave over to death many holy men. And the holy Cyprianus and the holy Justina were martyred, and the seven boys in Ephesus, and a great multitude of holy ones. He mandated in Rome that the Christian women not go out with the head covered, thinking through this shameful legislation to draw them toward idolatry. But with uncovered heads they went out more eagerly, considering that which seemed a dishonor among men a glory on behalf of Christ. Whence, to the present, observant Christian women go out uncovered, but the Jews and unfaithful cover themselves. Under him, too, Babylas of Antioch and Flavianus of Rome and Alexander of Jerusalem and Dionysius of Alexandria were martyred. And Novatus, an elder, left the church, he who was not receiving those repenting who had burned incense in the persecution. Then Helcesaeus, a high priest, was noteworthy.

> And Decius was killed by the Scythians by the instructions of Gallus, having suffocated in a marsh with his own son, having found, as their bodies were not discovered, a death worthy of their beastliness.

Scut. p. 37.19–30:

> Now Decius, when he had conquered the barbarians in the war, when he had appointed one of his familiars, Olousianus [*sic*] Gallus, over those there, went up to Rome and was sovereign.
>
> Decius, one year, nine months: He was harsh and aroused a great persecution and tortured many of the holy, and the seven holy children in Ephesus he enclosed alive in a certain cave, having sealed it, and he worked myriad horrors. And Gallus, the one also [called] Lousianus, having contrived a plot against him, wrote to him to fall upon Persia posthaste, and, when he [Decius] had occupied a very wet and swampy spot, Gallus, attacking him, slew him, being in his fifty-sixth year.

42   Decius reached Rome in the fall of 249. Zos. I.14.1 says that the consular and future emperor Valerianus—here "Balerianus," "Valerianus" elsewhere in the *Epitome*—was an advocate of the Gordians upon their acclamation in Africa and *SHA Three Gordians* 9.7 has Valerianus, as *princeps senatus*, receive the embassy from Africa announcing the Gordians' recognition there. He would, then, have been an important potential ally. However, there is no evidence to support Zonaras' unparalleled claim that Decius granted Valerianus any formal power, an assertion perhaps motivated by the desire of Christians to lump together emperors viewed by them as persecutors *par excellence*. By early June of 350, Decius had proclaimed his eldest son, Q. Herennius Etruscus Messius Decius (*PIR*² H 106), Caesar. By late September of the same year, Quintus' brother, C. Valens Hostilianus Messius Quintus (*PIR* V 8), received the same honor. When Decius and his elder son departed Rome for their fatal Gothic campaign of 250–251, Gaius remained in the city.

43   The Decian persecution probably began late in 249. A string of Christian testimony—*e.g.* Eus. *HE* VI.39.1, p. 594; Jerome *Chron.* p. 218[d], Orosius VII.21.2; and Jord. *Rom.* p. 37.7–8—makes Decius' hatred of Christians his motive for the elimination of Philippus. Eusebius and Syncellus p. 444.19–20 closely parallel Zonaras. On Babylas, martyred probably on January 24, 251, see *EEC* I, p. 106 and below, n. 111.

   CP pp. 503.18–504.2 (translated above, n. 21), in an odd twist, presents Babylas' martyrdom as recompense for his effrontery towards Philippus and his wife. Yet another version, preserved in Philostorgius and in the *Passion of St. Artemius* attributed to John of Rhodes, very likely reflects the contents of a now-lost Arian historiographer. Unfortunately, the brevity of Zonaras, Symeon, and Cedrenus on this point makes it impossible to judge the relationship of the tradition from which they drew and this hypothetical work.

Philost. *HE* VII.8, pp. 89.2–91.2: He [Philostorgius] says, moreover, that the holy Babylas was martyred together with three boys, youths and by birth brothers, and that the martyrdom arose from the following cause. Babylas was bishop of Antioch. In truth, as the result of some demon, a plan lit on Numerianus the Romans' sovereign, or as others say, Decius, to enter the church when it was full. But the high priest of God, standing at the entrance [90] of the temple, blocked the entrance, saying that as much as he was able, at any rate, he would not allow a wolf to penetrate the flock. And he, on the one hand, immediately desisted from his effort, either suspecting a riot or even altering his plans for another reason. But he first accused the bishop of insolence and afterwards commanded the pious fellow to sacrifice to the demons, for this means alone was capable of freeing him from the charge and of being a guarantor of both honor and glory afterwards. And after he had battled nobly against [91] each of these propositions, he won the crown of martyrdom.

Art. Pass. 54, pp. 89.15–91.10 = *PG* 96, col. 1301A-B: For, in truth, this Babylas is said to have been bishop of Antioch. And it is said that he, having stood before the doors, prevented Numerianus, the sovereign, who was planning to enter the church of the Christians, in truth, during some festival, from entering the temple, [90] declaring that, as far as it was in his power, he would not allow a wolf to enter into the flock. And he, on the one hand, straightway checked his entrance, either suspecting a riot, or even for another reason having changed his mind. However, having borne the opposition of the bishop harshly, as soon as he had returned to the palace, he commanded that he be brought before the tribunal in order to defend himself and, in truth, when he was present, first he charged him with the outrage of the obstruction, then, moreover, he ordered him, if he really wished to escape the punishment for the charge, to sacrifice to the demons. But he defended himself against the accusation and evaded the indictment, having said, on the one hand, that it was fitting for himself, being a shepherd, [91] to be willing to do anything for the flock, and, on the other hand, that he would not, after he had deserted the truly existing God, choose to sacrifice to the falsely named destroyers, demons. Then, as he saw him unpersuaded, he ordered him, after he had been bound in chains and shackles, to suffer the penalty of death by decapitation. But as he was being led away to die, having taken up these words of the psalm, he began to sing: "Return, my soul, to your rest, for the Lord has been kind to you" [*Psalms* 114/116.7].

44   With Zonaras, *cf.* Eus. *HE* VI.39.1–4, p. 594, and Syncellus p. 445.4–21, the former with Fabianus and Fabius as the bishops of Rome and Antioch, respectively, the latter Fabianus for both. Zonaras here and in his commentary on the Synod of Carthage (R-P III, p. 1; *EEC* I, p. 146) follows the mistaken tradition preserved in Sym. 77.2, p. 100, Ced. p. 453.7–8, and Syncellus p. 460.9–16 that had Cyprianus (*EEC* I, pp. 21–212) die a martyr under Decius. In fact, Cyprianus met his end under Valerianus, traditionally on September 14, 258. See further, n. 57 below.

45   On the torture of Origen and his failure to achieve martyrdom, *cf.* Eus. *HE* VI.39.5, p. 594–596, and Syncellus p. 445.22–446.2, the latter again very close to Zonaras.

46   This diatribe against Origen appears to be Zonaras' own contribution.

47   *Cf.* Eus. *HE* VI.39.1–4, p. 594, and 6.43.1–4, pp. 612–614, and Syncellus p. 453.5–12, the latter the closer to Zonaras. After the martyrdom of Fabianus (*EEC* I, p. 315, *s.v.* Fabian [Zonaras' Flavianus]), probably on January 20, 250, Novatianus (*EEC* II, pp. 603–604, *s.vv.* Novatian [Zonaras' Navatus] and Novatianists) was interim head of the Christian community of Rome until the election of Cornelius (I, *EEC* I, p. 202) in March of 251. Once bishop, Cornelius addressed the strict stance of Novatianus with regard to the lapsed. Novatianus was excommunicated in the same year and formed his own schismatic church with himself as a sort of antipope.

In his commentary on the Council(s) of Carthage (R-P III, pp. 1–2), Zonaras says:

> And when Cornelius, having then assumed direction of the church of Rome, with the bishops under him, when he had investigated the matter under consideration [*i.e.* a second baptism for the lapsed], decreed that even those who had sacrificed be received into repentance; and Navatus [Novatianus] was not abandoning his personal opposition; they excised and banished him from the church as a "brotherhater."

See further below, n. 57.

48   *Cf.* Eus. *HE* VI.44.2–6, pp. 624–626, and Syncellus p. 457.2–21.

49   Decius and Q. Herennius perished in very early June 251 near Abritus in what is now Bulgaria. With Zonaras and the testimony quoted in n. 41 above, *cf. Epit. de Caes.* 29.3–4: "On foreign soil, among disordered troops, he drowned in the waters of a swamp, so that his corpse could not be found. His son, in fact, was killed in the war. He lived fifty years." Malal. XII, p. 227, xvii.e = *EI* 22, p. 159.34–36— "After he had departed, in a war of the Franks, Decius, as he was withdrawing, was killed with his son by one of the prefects in Adytus, being 60 years old."—and *CP* p. 505.4–6 —"And the same Decius, after he had departed for a war against Franks, as he withdrew was killed with his son by some of the prefects in Abyrtus, being 60 years old."— both label Decius' adversaries Franks and specify the killers of the emperor and his son as one or more Roman commanders.

Zosimus and Syncellus, the latter dependent on Dexippus, provide more detail:

> Zos. I.23 (ed. Bekker, pp. 24.16–25.14): After he had advanced and conquered them [the Scythians] in all the battles and also had seized part of the plunder they had taken, Decius was attempting to cut off their homeward withdrawal, planning to annihilate them totally so they might not, when they had regrouped, ever attack again. In truth, when he had positioned Gallus on the bank of the Tanaïs with a suitable force, he himself attacked with those who remained. With matters unfolding according to plan, Gallus, after he had turned toward revolution, sent a message

to the barbarians, inviting them to share in the plot against Decius. When they had most readily accepted the proposal, while Gallus kept guard on the bank of the Tanaïs, the barbarians, when they had moved forward in three groups, deployed the first portion in a certain spot before a marsh. When Decius had destroyed most of these men, the second formation assaulted him. When this one, too, had withdrawn, a few men from the third formation appeared near the marsh. And when Gallus had signaled to Decius to advance against them through the marsh, after he had advanced thoughtlessly in ignorance of the terrain, had been caught in the muck together with the force with him, and was bombarded with missiles on all sides by the barbarians, he perished with those who accompanied him, no one having been able to escape.

Syncellus p. 459.5–19 = Dexippus *FgrH* 100 F 22: Scythians, those called Goths, when they had crossed the Ister River in very great numbers under Decius, began occupying the dominion of Rome. They surrounded the Mysians, who were fleeing toward Nicopolis. Decius, after he had attacked them, as Dexippus records, and had killed thirty thousand, was beaten in battle, with the result that Philippopolis, when it had been taken by them, was sacked and many Thracians were killed. And the same Decius, the fighter against God, when he had attacked Scythians who were returning to their own territory, was killed very piteously in Abrytus, the place called Forum Thembronium, with his son, and the Scythians returned with a great number of captives and much booty. The encamped armies acclaimed sovereign a certain Gallus, who had once been a consul, together with Decius' son Volusianus. And according to Dexippus, they too reigned for 18 months, having done nothing noteworthy, but according to some 3 years, and according to others 2 years. And they were slain, after they had been betrayed by their own forces, in the market of Flaminius, victims of the same maliciousness as Decius, as the blessed Dionysius, Alexandria's bishop, somewhere says, writing to Hermammon . . .

50   Trebonianus Gallus (*PIR* V 403) became Augustus about mid-June 251. At that time or slightly later he seems to have bestowed the

title of Caesar on Volusianus, his son (*PIR* V 376). Around the same time, according to Zos. I.25.1, Gallus adopted and made Augustus Decius' son Hostilianus (*PIR* V 8), who by mid-July had succumbed to plague in Rome. *Epit. de Caes.* 30.2 agrees on the circumstances of his death, but states that the senate, not Gallus, proclaimed him Augustus. Pol. Sil. I.41, p. 521 calls Hostilianus with Volusianus Caesars. Aur. Vict. *Caes.* 30.2 mistakenly makes Hostilianus the victim of plague. *Cf.* Aur. Vict. *Caes.* 30.1, Eutr. IX.5, Orosius VII.21.4, and Scut. p.37.20–30, translated above, n. 41, and pp. 37.31–38.1, translated below, n. 53.

51   Gallus arrived in Rome in the fall of 251, about the same time as Volusianus began to be styled Augustus rather than Caesar. On the pact with the barbarians, see Zos. I.24–25.

52   Zonaras' Teridates—Trdat or Tiridates II (r. 217–252; *PIR* T 181), an Arsacid—fled *ca.* 252 in the face of Shapur I's invasion, made possible by the diminution of Roman power in the East after Gordianus' defeat and the Decius' death.
    With regard to the plague, Salmasian John, Symeon, and Cedrenus clearly depend on a common tradition:

Salmasian John *fr.* 228 Roberto, p. 410 = John of Antioch *fr.* 151 Müller *FHG* IV p. 598:	Sym. 78, pp. 100–101: Gallus and Volousianus	Ced. pp. 452.13–453.5:
After Gallus became sovereign, a plague held sway for 15 years, having spread from Ethiopia as far as the West. And it was transmitted from clothing and simply on sight. And the Scythians, when they had crossed the Ister, took 500 cities. They say that women who wish to become pregnant drink from the Strymon River and conceive.	Gallus and Volousianus reigned 2 years and 8 months. And there was in those days a plague, having spread from the East as far as to the West, and not one was found free of this threat. And it was in force 11 years, beginning from the autumn and abating at the rising of the Dog Star. And this pestilence was transmitted both from clothing and simply on sight. And the Scythians, when they	And after Valerianus, Gallus and Volousianus reigned 2 years, 8 months. And in those days the plague held sway, having spread from Ethiopia as far as the West, with the result that not any city remained free of it. And often it even attacked the city twice, and it held sway 15 years, beginning from autumn and abating at the rising of the Dog Star. And this same pestilence was

had crossed the Ister, plundered all the West and Italy and East and Asia and twice occupied Ilium alone and Cyzicus. 2. And Gallus and Volousianus were killed by the troops, and Aemilianus was acclaimed sovereign by them. Under Gallus and Volousianus began the Sabellian heresy.

transmitted both from clothing and simply on sight. For there was not a home in which there was not a fatality. And some, in fear of contracting the disease, left the dead unburied, but the more pious, heedlessly tending to the sick, directed the disease toward themselves, and with them or after them they quit life. At this time the Scythians, when they had crossed the Ister, plundered all the West and Italy and the East and Asia and twice occupied Ilium alone and Cyzicus. And Volusianus was Gallus' son. And Gallus, on the one hand, was killed in his sleep by his own wife, but Volusianus by soldiers.

See also Eutr./Paean. IX.5; Jerome *Chron.* p. 219[a]; Jord. *Get.* 104, pp. 84.19–85.4, and Orosius VII.21.5, the last of whom presents the disease as divine retribution for the persecution of Christians. Malalas *EI* 20, p. 159.29–30 = Malal. XII, p. 227, xv.b—"Gallus was acclaimed sovereign by the troops and immediately after he had come to Rome was murdered, being 60 years old."—does not necessarily contradict the version of Cedrenus.

For the erroneous account of the murder of Gallus by his wife (Afinia Gemina Baebiana, *PIR*[2] A 439, had predeceased him), see above, n. 38, and George the Monk p. 466.17–18: "After Valerianus, Gallus, his son, ruled one month and was killed in his sleep by his own wife."

53   For Symeon and Cedrenus on the Scythian eruption, see above n. 52. It is impossible to decide if Symeon's claim that Aemilianus had the support of an army in Libya reflects reality or a garbling of sources.

George the Monk p. 467.6–8:	Sym. 79, p. 101:	Ced. p. 454.1–2:
[40. About Aemilianus]	Aemilianus	Aemilianus reigned one year and was slain in the palace by the troops.
And after Decius, Aemilianus reigned 1 year and was slain in the palace.	Aemilianus reigned 4 months, and he commanded the army in Mysia, also having a Libyan corps, with which, after he had battled [78] and conquered the Scythians, he was inflated by good fortune and staged an insurrection. 2. And he too was killed by the troops.	

Scut. pp. 37.31–38.8:

Gallus Lousianus, two years, three months: He killed the children [38] of Decius. And a certain Aemilianus, being in command of Paeonians, emboldening the troops under him and having attacked the barbarians there, destroyed many and was recognized sovereign by the troops there. And he launched the forces with him against Italy. Gallus, when he had learned that this had happened to Aemilianus, when they had joined battle, was beaten. And the troops killed Gallus and his son and, with Aemilianus, occupied Rome.

With Zonaras' unique story of Aemilianus' promise to his troops, *cf.* Jord. *Get.* 105, p. 85, which has Aemilianus and his troops plundering Moesia after the example of the Goths rather than recovering through victory the bribes paid to the invaders.

54   As Aemilianus entered Italy with an army of uncertain size and proceeded southward along the Flaminian Way, the emperors Gallus and Volusianus moved against him. The opposing sides met at Interamna Nahars, near the southern terminus of the eastern branch of the Flaminian Way, with Aemilianus emerging the victor. In the aftermath, Gallus and Volusianus apparently retreated northward up the western branch of the same road, only to be murdered at the Forum Flaminii by their own men, who then went over to Aemilianus. John

of Antioch refers to the killers as men "of the household," perhaps *domestici, i.e.* either members of a regiment of imperial guards or simply officials or retainers:

> *Fr.* 229 Roberto, p. 410 = *fr.* 150 Müller *FGH* IV, p. 598 = *EI* 60, p. 110.1–11: Under Gallus and Volusianus, Aemilianus, the prefect of Mysia, thought to revolt, both striving to link the sovereignty to himself from his ancestors and making the gravest charges against the Romans' senate. The champions of the might of Romans, when they had sallied forth against him with a force most great, after being betrayed by their household [troops?], were destroyed, not yet having completed a third year in the leadership of the public affairs, and having achieved nothing illustrious or worthy of sovereignty and having been among the sovereigns only in memory. At any rate, having jumped at the command against the Scythians' territory and eager to depart from Rome, in the fourth month of his usurpation Aemilianus both met premature ruin and vanished from among men.

55   *Fr.* 2 Müller *FHG* IV, pp. 190–199 = *ES* 158, p. 264, of the so-called Anonymous Continuator of Cassius Dio, perhaps Peter the Patrician, reflects this same tradition: "After he had been acclaimed sovereign, Aemilianus wrote to the senate: 'I leave the realm to you and strive in every way as your general.'"

56   Epigraphic and papyrological evidence set Aemilianus' death between late July and mid-September of 253. Scut. p. 38.9–14 closely parallels Zonaras: "Aemilianus, 4 months. Valerianus, general of those beyond the Alps, rebelled against him and moved with a force upon Rome, planning to attack Aemilianus. And the army, seeing Aemilianus weaker militarily and Valerianus more a leader in affairs of state, killed Aemilianus, who happened to be forty years old, and gave the power to Valerianus."

   Zos. I.28.3 unconvincingly alleges that Gallus and Volusianus had dispatched Valerianus from Rome to bring to their aid legions from Gaul and Germany. More likely, Valerianus was already in command of those forces (perhaps being readied for an eastern campaign), began to move toward Italy after learning of Aemilianus' elevation, and resolved to battle Aemilianus for imperial power after the deaths of Gallus and Volusianus. This seems the most reasonable explanation for Valerianus' clash with Aemilianus about a month after the latter's victory over Gallus. For additional Greek accounts of Aemilianus' death, see above, nn. 53–54. Aur. Vict. *Caes.* 31.3 has Aemilinaus succumb to disease.

57   *Cf.* Eus. *HE* VII.2–3, pp. 636–638, and Syncellus pp. 458.31–32 and 460.22–25. Eusebius gives Lucius a tenure of "not eight whole months ['years' in Zonaras])," Syncellus of 2 years. Unlike Zonaras, both Eusebius and Syncellus only mention and quote from letters of Dionysius of Alexandria to Stephanus (*EEC* II, p. 794, *s.v.* Steven I) on the subject of those previously baptized by heretics. Perhaps Zonaras or his source inferred from Eus. *HE* VII.3 the existence of Stephanus' "directive" in response to a series of African synods on this matter in 255–256. On the other hand, Zonaras' somewhat opaque "is recorded" may refer to Cyprianus *Ep.* 74, p. 799–809; trans. Clarke, IV, pp. 69–78, with annotation, pp. 233–246, which explicitly describes the receipt of Stephenus' correspondence and proceeds to describe its contents.

When Zonaras produced his commentary on the Council(s) of Carthage he seems to have thought on the basis of Eus. *HE* that Cyprianus had died during the Decian persecution. *Cf.* Sym. 77.2, p. 100, and Ced. p. 453.7–8 (trans. above, n. 41), Zon. XII.20, and R-P III, p. 1. *CP* pp. 506.20–507.2 sets his death 18 days before the Kalends of October, in the consulship of Tuscus and Bassus (September 14, AD 258). Indeed, apparently in possession of no record of the dates of the three gatherings in Carthage—autumn 255, spring 256, and September 256—and with no idea that there had been multiple meetings, Zonaras sought to establish the priority of "the Synod of Carthage" to the Synod of Antioch—actually convened in 268 but erroneously associated with Aurelianus, whose reign began in 270—by using Cyprianus' alleged martyrdom under Decius as a *terminus ante quem* for the gathering in Africa and then pointing out that "many sovereigns" intervened between Decius and Aurelianus. Stephanus' now-lost letter to Cyprianus was prompted by the former's notification of the findings of the council of spring 256, which had maintained the necessity of rebaptism. See further *EEC* I, p. 146.

58   *Cf.* Eus. *HE* VII.5–6, pp. 638–642, and Syncellus pp. 461.17–19 and 462.7–9. Xystus is Sixtus II (*EEC* II, p. 784). In Eusebius and Syncellus, notice of Ptolemais appears in the quoted text of a letter of Dionysius of Alexandria. Sym. 78.2, pp. 100–101, translated n. 52 above, notes the Sabellian heresy at the end of his treatment of Gallus

and Volusianus. Sabellius' views of the nature of the trinity had been condemned *ca.* 230. See *EEC* II, pp. 748–749, *s.vv.* "Sabellius" and "Sabellianism."

59   Valerianus had been styled Augustus since perhaps as early as June 253. Upon his arrival in Rome in late September or early October of that year the senate granted Gallienus, his son, the title of Caesar. Zonaras here reflects Eus. *HE* VII.10.1 and 11.1, pp. 648 and 654, respectively, skipping intervening material and summarizing in one sentence the series of martyrdoms recounted by Eusebius. The persecution under Valerianus did not begin until about the summer of 257.

Eus. *HE* VII.21.2–22.10, pp. 674–682, preserves two letters from Dionysius of Alexandria—the first links to local outbreaks of disease the carnage of sectarian violence in Alexandria; the second contrasts Christian and non-Christian behavior during a plague in Valerianus' reign—adapted by the lost source employed by George the Monk and Cedrenus in their misplaced description of a plague during the reign of Valerianus. Both situate their accounts, clearly dependent on a common Christian tradition, between the reigns of Philippus and Gallus.

George the Monk pp. 465.12–466.15:	Ced. p. 452.4–13:
Valerianus one year. And he was slain by his own people. Under him, God having sent forth a great wrath upon all the inhabited world, a pestilential disease began destroying the human race to the point of annihilation. For from the earth and the sea certain vapors arose, and, in addition to these, winds and breezes blew from the rivers and an exhalation from the harbors, so it was deemed that the dew was the effluence of corpses. From this, then, unremitting plagues and grave and incurable diseases afflicted the earth, and limitless and numberless [466] became the destruction of mankind, with the result that the majority of the dead were abandoned unburied. And wailings and lamentations through	Valerianus one year. And he was slain by his own people. Under him, God having sent forth a great wrath upon all the inhabited world, a pestilential disease began destroying the human race. For from the earth and the sea certain vapors arose, and, in addition to these, winds and breezes blew from the rivers and exhalation from the harbors, so it was deemed that the dew was the effluence of corpses. From this, then, unremitting plagues and grave and incurable diseases afflicted the earth, and limitless and numberless became the destruction of mankind, with the result that the majority of the dead were abandoned unburied.

the multitude of those destroyed
arouse everywhere, in no respect
falling short of those concerning the
death of the firstborns of Egypt. For
there was not a household in which
was not one dead and reeking, and
the harsh peoples of the gentiles,
avoiding the transmission of the
sickness and of death, cast people out
unburied or even half-dead, hardly
sparing kinsmen, friends, or any
others, although they most certainly
could not have expected to escape
wrath or death. And most of those
fearing the Lord, heedlessly tending
to the ill and contracting the disease,
ended life with them, and others,
having cared for different people and
achieved the removal of the disease,
departed, having drawn the death of
those to themselves.

Cedrenus, unlike George the Monk, deals with Valerianus again in
his proper chronological spot after Aemilianus, and here his account
has obvious affinities with that of Symeon. At the same time, Symeon
and Cedrenus now diverge from Zonaras and Scutariotes:

Sym. 80.1–2, p. 101:	Ced. p. 454.3–6:	Scut. p. 38.15–19:
Valerianus and Galenus [*sic*]: Valerianus and Galenus, 15 years. 2. Valerianus, when he had warred with Sapor of Persia and been captured in the city Caesarea with 40,000 men, after he had been flayed by Sapor, died.	Valerianus and Gallienus, 15 years. Valerianus, when he had warred with Sapor of Persia and been captured in Caesarea with 20,000 men, after he had been flayed by Sapor, died.	Valerianus, 16 years, with his own son Galienus: He ardently attempted to conduct affairs of state well, but then the tribes from all over began to bedevil the Romans, and the Scythians reduced to slavery and obliterated cities and territories. And after he had been outwitted by the Persians, Valerianus was led off a captive.

It seems clear that some rupture had occurred in the branch of the source tradition known to George the Monk and Cedrenus. The most likely explanation, since their handling of the plague is linked to the wrath of the Christian god, is the chronologically inaccurate insertion of the plague material by a Christian writer into the mainly secular summary of Valerianus and a subsequent expurgation of the secular events of Valerianus' reign from George the Monk's source or by George himself. If so, Symeon represents the secular strand of the tradition, Cedrenus' source and Cedrenus himself reflect that strand augmented with Christian material on the plague, and George the Monk an expurgation of that augmented strand. In any case, with Valerianus it is Syncellus, rather than Symeon, Cedrenus, or Scutariotes, who provides the closest parallels to Zonaras.

60   Syncellus p. 466.1–7 parallels Zonaras almost verbatim. Zos. I.30–36.1, probably following Dexippus, gives more details of the movements of the Scythians, *i.e.* Goths, the precise chronology of which is beyond recovery. On Dexippus' command against and account of the inroads of the Goths, see *SHA Gallieni* 13.8 = *FgrH* 100 T 3 and the references above in nn. 37 and 49. Gregory the Wonderworker (*EEC* I, p. 368) provides first-hand information about one of these Gothic raids in his *Canonical Letter* (*PG* 10, cols. 1019–1022; R-P IV, pp. 45–4; trans. P. Heather and J. Matthews, *The Goths in the Fourth Century*, *TTH* 11 [Liverpool: Liverpool University Press, 1991], pp. 5–11), Zonaras' brief commentary on which survives (*PG* 10, cols. 1023–1026; R-P IV, pp. 46–47). If Zonaras' commentary preceded the *Epitome*, his failure to mention Gregory's testimony here or elsewhere in Book XII suggests that Zonaras viewed relentless attention to the abbreviation of the text in front of him, rather than the interjection of information from other texts, as the proper procedure for him in his role of epitomator. If, on the other hand, the *Epitome* preceded the commentary, it is equally revealing that Zonaras made no use of the material he had incorporated into the *Epitome*.

61   No other literary source links Valerianus' initial defeat in battle to Edessa. The *Res Gestae* of Sapor, however, does make the connection. See lines 19–26 of the Greek version at D-L, p. 57. Whatever the precise circumstances, the emperor was in Sapor's hands by between late spring or early fall of 260. See further, D-L, pp. 57–67.

62 Syncellus' correspondence with Zonaras resumes at p. 466.8–15 of the *Chronographia*. The tradition upon which both depend may have mistaken the Greek *loimos* ("plague") for *limos* ("famine"). See further above, n. 59.

63 This alternative version of Valerianus' capture—similar to Zos. I.36.1–2 and to Pet. Patr. *fr.* 9 Müller *FHG* IV, p. 187 = *ELRG* 1, p. 3.4–9, trans. D-L, p. 62—seems to reflect another variant in which plague and a botched embassy play decisive parts.

64 Agath. IV.23.3–7 assigns Valerianus the same fate. In contrast, at XII.30, Zonaras says it was Numerianus who was flayed. See below, n. 115.

65 The exploits of Demosthenes (PIR^2 D 48) are otherwise unrecorded.

66 Syncellus p. 466.15–23, though fuller, again provides a very close parallel. Manuscripts of Syncellus have both Ballista and Callista (PIR^2 B 41). *SHA Val.* 4.2–3 attributes the capture of Sapor's concubines to Odenathus.

67 See again Syncellus pp. 466.23–467.1. For Zonaras' extended treatment of Odenathus, see XII.24.

68 No other source mentions this detail, perhaps, whether historical or purely literary, intended to recall the supposed service of Amazons in the armies of the Achaemenid kings of Persia.

69 Agath. IV.24.3 tells the same story.

70 Zonaras mirrors but reproduces an abbreviated version of Eus. *HE* VII.14, p. 668. Eusebius' notices of the bishops Gregory the Wonderworker, Athenodorus, and Theotecnus—all with connections to Origen—and the predecessors in their sees have vanished, and either Zonaras, his immediate source, or a later copyist has replaced Eusebius' Fabius with Flavianus. On Fabius/Flavianus, see above, n. 44.

71 The divergence, noted above in n. 59, between Zonaras and George the Monk, Symeon, and Cedrenus continues:

George the Monk p. 467.11–14:	Sym. 80.3, p. 101:	Ced. p. 454.6–10:
And after Aemilianus, Gallienus reigned 3 years and was slain in war. Under him, Artemon and Synepon the archpriests were noteworthy, and Gregory the Wonderworker and disciple of Origen was prominent.	Galenus [*sic*], after him [Valerianus], first established cavalry units. For generally the troops of the Romans were infantry. And he himself also was slain by the troops.	And his [Valerianus'] son Gallienus after this first established cavalry units; for generally the troops of the Romans were infantry. And he also was slain by the troops near Mediolanum. Under this man, Gregory the Wonderworker reached his prime and the archpriests Artemon and Synepon were noteworthy.

Before passing to the circumstances of Galleinus' [*sic*] death—on which, see below, n. 82—Scut. p. 38.20 simply notes that he reigned 9 years. *CP* pp. 507.18–508.3, erroneously has Valerianus killed by the Persians in the consulship of Claudius (the future emperor) and Paternus (4 *PLRE* I, p. 671) in the initial year of the two hundred and sixty-second Olympiad, *i.e.* 262, and succeeded immediately by Claudius. Thereby it omits all mention of Gallienus' sole reign and misdates Claudius and Paternus' consulship from 269.

The precise nature of Gallienus' emphasis on cavalry, if it did in fact occur, and its relationship to a supposed change from a Roman "grand strategy" of preclusive defense to defense-in-depth is much debated.

72   Gallienus seems to have defeated the Alamanni around the fall of 260. Syncellus p. 467.15–26 describes the incursion of the Heruli—Zonaras' Aerouli—and their subsequent defeat by Gallienus. Zos. I.30–34 details some of Gallienus' campaigns. Apart from Zonaras, Aur. Vict. *Caes.* 33.3 alone explicitly names the Franks in connection with Gallienus.

The tradition upon which Zonaras here depends either ignored or did not know a Christian view represented, for example, by Orosius VII.22 .1–9, which saw these barbarian inroads as divine retribution for Valerianus' persecution and which emphasized that Gallienus formally ended the state persecution of Christians.

73   Aur. Vict. *Caes.* 33.2 makes Valerianus' defeat the impetus of Ingenuus' (*PIR*[2] I 23, *PLRE* I, p. 457) acclamation, which *SHA Tyr.*

Trig. 9.1 sets in 258, the consulship of Tuscus and Bassus (*PIR*² N 237 and M 702, respectively). For the mainstream Latin tradition, *cf.* Aur. Vict. *Caes.* 33.2, which has Gallienus destroy an Ingebus at Mursa and soon thereafter a Regelianus (*PLRE* I, p. 762); Eutr. IX.8.1, which has Gallienus kill Ingenuus and Trebellianus (Paean. p. 155.3 names only a Genuus), again at Mursa; and Orosius VII.22.10, which has Genuus die at Mursa. Syncellus p. 467.27 calls Auriolus a "Gallic general," Scut. p. 38.20–21 a "general in Galliae." See further below, nn. 80 and 82.

Several fragments of the Anonymous Continuator of Cassius Dio betray a detailed, probably heavily moralistic, account of this episode:

> *Anon. Cont. fr.* 4 Müller *FHG* IV, pp. 193–194 = Pet. Patr. *ES* 160–161, pp. 264.26–265.3: After he had been dispatched to collect supplies, Memor [*PIR*² M490], a Moor, became desirous of a new state of affairs and was immediately killed by the soldiers. The commanders began to complain that he had been unjustly slain. Theodotus [*PIR* T120; one of Memor's killers and perhaps Aurelius Theodotus *PIR*² A1617], when he had been called upon to give an explanation, said, "Memor was not worthy of much contempt because, possessing the compass and power of such commanders, he undertook the impossible, but because he and those with him failed to achieve their aim through my zeal and through sovereign providence." And the sovereign was pleased with the defense and decreed that no one be prosecuted on Memor's account.
>
> Men who have been poorly raised are not accustomed to guard friendships carefully, but they change them for minor reasons.

> *Fr.* 5.1, Müller *FHG* IV, p. 194 = Pet. Patr. *ES* 162, p. 265.4–12: The wife of the sovereign Gallienus [Cornelia Salonina] was offended by the countenance of Ingenuus, and, when she had summoned Valentinus [*PIR*¹ V10; 1 *PLRE* I, p. 935], said to him, "I know your reputation, and, while I praise the sovereign with respect to your selection, I do not praise him with respect to that of Ingenuus. For he is highly suspect to me. But I am unable to act in opposition to the sovereign. But you keep an eye on the man." Valentinus answered, "Would that Ingenuus be viewed sincere with respect to your service, since, as much as is in me, I could

not be at all neglectful of those who see to the favor of your house."

Fr. 5.2 Müller *FHG* IV, p. 194 = Pet. Patr. *ES* 163, p. 265.13–21: In the war against Ingenuus many children, parents, and siblings perished, to such a degree that a certain fellow brought his own brother before Galienus as a captive and said, "Sovereign, this is my own brother, and I captured him in the war." He considered the matter, resolved that he be pardoned, dismissed and commended him, and undertook to give him many rewards and to absolve the sin of the usurpation. And he said, "It is not proper that a man live who once took up arms against a sovereign!" And he killed him with his sword. Galienus was displeased, but he acquiesced in light of the unexpectedness of the events.

74   The date of Postumus' rebellion, the genesis of the *Imperium Galliarum*, was probably *ca.* 259. Gallienus' son is P. Licinius Cornelius Saloninus (*PIR*² L 183). Zonaras' Scythians are Goths, his Albanus the Silvanus (*PIR* S 520) of Zos. I.38.2. Agrippina is Cologne. *SHA Tyr. Trig.* 3.1 has Saloninus fall out with Postumus, whom it maintains Gallienus had placed in charge of Saloninus.

75   The campaigns against Postumus probably date to *ca.* 262. The siege during which Gallienus was wounded is otherwise unrecorded.

76   *Pap. Ox.* 2710 places the consulship of Macrinus' (*PLRE* I, p. 528, *s.v.* Macrinus 2)) sons (*PLRE* I, p. 528, *s.v.* Macrinus 3, and p. 757, *s.v.* Quietus 1) in 260 and thereby sets the immediate aftermath of Valerianus' defeat as the context of the brief reign of the Macrini. Eus. *HE* VII.10.5–8, p. 652, quotes a letter of Dionysius of Alexandria which mentions Macrianus' [Zonaras' Macrinus] physical infirmity and the elevation at their father's request of his two sons, neither of whom Dionysius names. *Anon. Cont. fr.* 3 Müller *FHG* IV, p. 193 = Pet. Patr. *ES* 159, p. 264.13–20, describes Macrinus:

Macrinus, Count of the Fisc and supervisor of the stock of rations, because he had been crippled in one foot, was not to be found in the battle, but in Samosata he received and revived the troops. Sapor sent Cledonius (1, *PLRE* I, p. 213), a man who ushered litigants before the sovereign. He encouraged Macrinus to come to Valerianus. He would not consent to depart, saying, "Who is so mad willingly to become a slave and captive in place of a free man? Moreover, those who command me to depart are not my lords. For one is an enemy, the other neither his own master nor ours." And he advised Cledonius to stay and not to return to Valerianus. But the latter said that he would not betray the trust of the man who had been his master. And after he had returned, he was held with the captives.

SHA Tyr. Trig. 12.1–12 maintains that collusion between Macrianus and Ballista resulted in the elevation of Macrianus—represented as initially reluctant to become emperor because of his age—and his two sons.

77 The battle probably dates to 261. *SHA Gallieni* 2.5–7 and *SHA Tyr. Trig.* 12.13–14 and 13.3 set the battle "in Illyricum or on the borders of Thrace" and after the elevation *ca.* 268 of Auriolus (*PLRE* I, p. 136, *s.v.* Aureolus). They also name one of Auriolus' commanders, Domitianus (1, *PLRE* I, p. 262), perhaps to be identified with a usurper of the same name mentioned at Zos. I.49.2. Zonaras' story of the standard-bearers is unique.

78 *Anon. Cont. fr.* 8.1 Müller *FHG* IV, p. 195 = Pet. Patr. *ES* 167, p. 266.25–30, also mentions this episode, which dates to 261:

Cyntus [or "Cyetus," *i.e.* Quietus], the son of Macrianus, forthwith established the palace too at Emisa [*sic*]. And Odenathus (*PLRE* I, pp. 638–639) was at hand with multitudes of barbarians and he directed them, "Surrender yourselves or fight." And they said that they were content to abide anything whatsoever than to surrender themselves to a barbarian.

Odenathus' appointment as general occurred in 262.

79 According to Zos. I.39.2, Odenathus was killed in Emesa (*ca.* 266/267) as the result of a conspiracy. *SHA Tyr. Trig.* 17.2 implicates Zenobia (*PLRE* I, pp. 990–991), Odenathus' wife and the stepmother of Herodes, jealous for the position of her two sons, Herennianus and Timolaus. Zonaras' anonymous killer, a son of Septimius Haeranes (*PIR* S 329), was perhaps also named Odenathus.
Syncellus p. 467.7–14, who locates the murder at Pontic Heracleia, simply gives the killer's name too as Odenathus (*PIR*² O 72); *SHA*

Tyr. Trig. 15.5 and 17.1–3 call him Maeonius (*PIR*² M 71) and have the victim's bodyguard slay him. Odenathus' oldest son was Herodes (1, *PLRE* I, p. 426), perhaps identical to Septimus Herodianus (3, *PLRE* I, p. 427). On the latter, see D-L 4.3.4, p. 77. *SHA Tyr. Trig.* 15.2 names two younger sons, Herennianus (*PIR*² H 95; 1 *PLRE* I, p. 421) and Timolaus (*PIR* T 162; *PLRE* I, p. 915). John of Antioch *fr.* 231 Roberto, p. 412 = *fr.* 152.2 Müller *FHG* IV, p. 599 = *EI* 62, p. 110.27–30, trans. D-L, p. 81, makes Odenathus the victim of a conspiracy of Gallienus. The *Anon. Cont. fr.* 7 Müller *FHG* IV, p. 194 = Pet. Patr. *ES* 166, p. 266.10–24, trans. D-L, p. 81, makes a Rufinus (*PIR* R 108) on his own initiative kill Odenathus and then explain his actions to Gallienus.

80 Auriolus' usurpation dates to *ca.* September 268. Zonaras' story of the un-named empress (Cornelia Salonina, *PLRE* I, p. 799) is unique. Salonina appears in literary sources only at *SHA Gallieni* 21.3, Aur. Vict. *Caes.* 33.6, and *Epit. de Caes.* 33.1—in these always in close proximity to that of Pipara (*SHA Gallieni* 21.3), elsewhere Pipa (*PLRE* I, p. 702)—and at Porphyry *Vit. Plot.* 12. She is the unnamed subject of *Anon. Cont. fr.* 5.1, translated above, n. 73.

81 Zonaras' Aurelianus is Gallienus' praetorian prefect Aur[elius] Heraclianus (6, *PLRE* I, p. 417). This confusion in names contributed to variant versions of Gallienus' death (*ca.* September 268), both recounted by Zonaras.

82 There is no parallel to Zonaras' account of this flight and near escape. The sentiment concerning Gallienus' leniency may be connected to anecdotes preserved in *Anon. Cont. frs.* 4 and 5.2, translated above, n. 73.

Parallels between Zosimus, John of Antioch, Scutariotes, and the *SHA* reflect the tradition upon which Zonaras depends and suggest the genesis of several points of divergence from what seems to have been a single account, probably in Greek, of Gallienus' end:

Zos. I.40.2–3:	John of Antioch *fr.* 232 Roberto, p. 415 = *fr.* 152.3 Müller *FHG* IV, p. 599 = *EI* 63, p. 111.1–5:	Scut. p. 38.20–29:
With him [Marcianus] managing the war well, Gallienus, making the journey to Italy, succumbed to a plot of the following sort.	Gallienus, around the city Mediolanum with	Against him [Galeinus [[*sic*]]], Auriolus, the general in Galliae, having meditated insurrection, came to the city Agrippiane—

After he had taken as a collaborator in the venture Claudius (11, *PLRE* I, p. 209), who, after the sovereign, seemed to be in charge of everything, Heracleianus, the praetorian prefect, plotted death for Gallienus. And when he had located a man most ready for such things who was in command of the cavalry detachment of the Dalmatians, he entrusted the act to him. When he had interrupted Gallienus, who was dining, and said that one of the scouts was announcing that Auriolus, together with his force, was approaching, he terrified him with such words. Then he began seeking weapons and, after he had leapt upon a horse, was signaling to the troops to follow with their weapons, and, not even having waited for his bodyguard, he rode off. Then the cavalry commander, when he observed him unarmed, slew him.

his brother Valerianus, after the death of his father, who reigned six years, was cut down by the cavalry commander of the Dalmatians. This was Heracleianus, who, after he had collaborated with Claudius, through one of the most daring [men], at mealtime slaughtered Gallienus.

also [called] Salona— and, finding there Galeinus' son, killed him [After "Agrippiane," *i.e.* Agrippina/Cologne, the text appears corrupt and perhaps originally said: "and finding there both Salonina and Galeinus' son, killed them."] and departed for Italy. And Galeinus himself, too, when he had rushed against Auriolus, was betrayed on the road by his prefect Heracleianus, having as a collaborator Claudius too, a man intelligent and very much a general. At night, then, when he had stood beside Galeinus, who was resting, Heracleianus said that Auriolus was at hand. And the sovereign, thrown into a state of confusion, began seeking his arms. But Heracleianus, finding him exposed and in fear, killed him, being in his fiftieth year.

Lacunose *SHA Gallieni* 14.1–4 and 7–9 has Marcianus (2 *PLRE* I, pp. 553–554) and Heraclianus conspire with "a certain Ceronius or rather Cecropius [1 *PLRE* I, p. 189, *PIR*[2] C595 (The common transcriptional confusion of Greek pi and nu may be behind 'Ceronius.')], commander of the Dalmatians," to kill Gallienus. The future emperor Claudius is named but expressly excluded from the plot. Marcianus and Cecropius inform Gallienus of Aureolus' approach and, as he moves against the latter, have him murdered, "pierced by the spear of Cecropius, the Dalmatian commander, some say near Mediolanum, where his brother Valerianus, too, was at once put to death." On Auriolus, see further n. 73 above.

Testimony about Gallienus' end is especially complex. *Epit. de Caes.* 33.2–3 mentions the bridge "Aureolus," the siege of Mediolanum, Gallienus' death at his own men's hands, and that "he ruled fifteen years, seven with his father, eight alone. He lived fifty years." Syncellus p. 467.26–27, too, names Gallienus' assassin "Auriolus, a Celtic general of Romans." *Epit. de Caes.* 40.3 notes his tomb at Tres Tabernae in connection with the death of Fl. Valerius Severus (30, *PLRE* I, pp. 837–838). Eutr./Paean. IX.11.1 has Gallienus killed, along with his brother Valerianus, at Mediolanum in the ninth year of his reign; Pol. Sil. I.41, p. 148.5 has him slain with his sons Saloninus and Licinius and also mentions Aureolus as a tyrant in Italy; *Chron. 354* p. 148.5 and Orosius VII.22.13 have him killed in Mediolanum, as does Jord. *Rom.* p. 37.20, following Jerome *Chron.* p. 221[h]; Malal. XII.27/298, p. 230, has him die of an illness at Rome at the age of 50. George the Monk p. 467.10–11 comments: "After Aemilianus, Gallienus ruled 3 years and was killed in the war." *LIM* p. 436.19 gives him a 14-year reign; Syncellus p. 465.23 gives Valerianus and Gallienus a joint rule of 15 years. *SHA Gallieni* 19.5 says that Gallienus' reign "exceeded ten years;" *SHA Gallieni* 21.5 that Valerianus and Gallienus ruled fifteen years together and that "some have recorded in writing that Gallienus reigned for nine years, and others, in turn, that it was nearly ten." *SHA Gallieni* 19.3 mentions the Dalmatian city of Salonae, but only in connection with the derivation of the name of Gallienus' son Saloninus. *SHA Gallieni* 21.3, the account of Gallienus' son Saloninus, correctly gives Salonina, *i.e.* Cornelia Salonina Augusta, as the empress' name.

83   Zonaras reflects a conflation in the source tradition of Eus. *HE* VII.27–28, pp. 702–704, and 30.18–19, p. 714, of the beginning of Paul of Samosata's bishopric (*ca.* 260; *EEC* II, p. 663)) and two synods at Antioch (*ca.* 264 and 268), the second of which sought Aurelianus' aid. *Cf.* Syncellus pp. 473.5–478.8, the end of his *Chronographia*.

This confusion is evident, too, in Zonaras' commentary on what transpired at Antioch with respect to Paul:

> There were in Antioch of Syria two synods, the first under Aurelianus, sovereign of Romans, against Paul of Samosata, who became bishop, saying our Lord and God Jesus Christ was a simple human and the Son of God was uttered word.

And many various men were present at this synod, especially the holy Gregory the Wonderworker. And they were gathered in Antioch, of which the Samosatan was bishop. Paul, plainly unconvinced by exhortations and demonstrations from the Scriptures to depart from the blasphemies against the Lord, by common vote they both condemned and anathematized. But he did not vacate the see of the church of Antioch. Hence those of the synod referred this matter to the sovereign Aurelianus, and he ordered the bishop of the church of Rome and the archpriests about him to examine the matters concerning Paul, and, if he was justly condemned, to expel him from the church of the Christians, which happened, too, as Eusebius Pamphyli recounts [R-P III, p. 122].

Zonaras' second synod of Antioch was that "under Constantius, the son of Constantine the Great, after five years from the death of his father [*i.e.* in 341]" (R-P III, p. 122).

84   Claudius' accession and Auriolus' death occurred *ca.* September/ October 268. Parallels to Zonaras are particularly rich:

Sym. 81, p. 102:	Ced. p. 454.11–22:	Scut. pp. 38.30–39.8:
Claudius		Claudius, 8 years: Auriolus, who was immediately killed by the troops as a result of the insurrection, willingly subjugated himself to him. And Claudius [39], being a good man, and affectionate and beneficial to all, having excelled in every virtue, died in Sirmium, having bequeathed to the Romans much longing for him, being in his fifty-sixth year. And hence, through him, they elevated to the sovereignty his brother Qintilianus [*sic*], a man detached
Claudius reigned one year. He was the grandfather of the father of Constantine the Holy. 2. Under him, the Scythians, who had broken through, who had gone off to Athens, took her, and, having gathered all the books, were planning to burn them. But one of them, since he was intelligent, hindered them, when he said, "The Romans, spending their leisure on these, are neglectful of wars." After he [Claudius] had advanced Aurelianus to	Claudius reigned two years. He was the grandfather of the father of Constantine the Holy and Great. Under him, the Scythians, when they had broken through and looted the cities and had also taken Athens, gathered all the books and were planning to burn them, except that one of them, more powerful by far in intelligence than the others, hindered them, saying, "The Romans, spending their leisure on these, are neglectful	

the sovereignty, he died from disease.

[*Apparatus criticus* 81.8, p. 102:

Cyntillus
After Cyntillus, brother of Claudius, had been acclaimed sovereign, reigned a few days, and done nothing worthy of memory, when he understood that Aurelianus was about to assume the rule, took his own life, having cut the vein of his hand with the help of a certain physician, until, after he had lost consciousness, he died.]

of wars." After he had advanced Aurelianus to the sovereignty, he died.

Quintilianus, brother of Claudius, reigned 6 days. For when he understood that Aurelianus was about to assume the rule, he took his own life, having cut the vein of his hand with the help of a certain physician, until, after he had lost consciousness, he died.

and impractical, who, after he had ruled only 17 days, when he heard that Aurelianus had been advanced to the sovereignty, willingly stepped down and, having cut the vein of his hand, after he had survived until evening, died, being in his forty-first year.

Zos. I.41 (ed. Bekker, p. 38.12–16):
Auriolus, who had long since set himself outside the power of Gallienus, immediately sent ambassadors to Claudius and, when he had surrendered himself, was killed by the troops around the sovereign who were enraged on account of the rebellion.

I.47 (p. 42.6–14): And when Quntillus, who was a brother of Claudius, had been proclaimed sovereign and had lived a few months and had accomplished nothing worthy of memory, Aurelianus was raised to the sovereignty when Quntillus, according to certain authors, had been persuaded by his attendants, at the moment when he perceived the realm had been handed over to Aurelianus, to voluntarily abdicate the rule for one far better, which, in fact, he is said to have done by means of one of the physicians, who cut a vein for him and allowed the blood to flow until he was drained dry.

John of Antioch *fr.* 233 Roberto, p. 414 = *fr.* 153 Müller *FHG* IV p. 599 = *EI* 64, p. 111.6–10:

Under Claudius the sovereign, Auriolus, for a long while having set himself outside the power of Gallienus, immediately sent ambassadors to Claudius and, having surrendered himself, was killed by the troops around the sovereign who were enraged on account of the rebellion.

fr. 234 Roberto, p. 414 = *fr.* 154 Müller *FHG* IV p. 599 = *EI* 65, p. 111.11–14):

Quintilius, Claudius' brother, who was sovereign of Romans, at the moment when he recognized that the realm had been handed over to Aurelianus, willingly withdrew from the rule and, when one of the physicians had cut a vein for him and allowed the blood to flow, gradually became unable to speak.

SHA Claud. 5.3 sets Auriolus' death near Milan and has him slain by his own men, while *SHA Aurel.* 16.2–3 records that some sources blamed Claudius, others Aurelianus.

85   The positive portrayal of Claudius' character that dominates the literary tradition seems linked to the favor he found with the senate and, later, to his alleged kinship tie to Constantine, on which see below, n. 95. On this matter, *cf.*, for example, Eutr. IX.11.2, *SHA Gallieni* 15.3, Zos. I.46.2, and Scut. (n. 84, above); with this and the following *bon mot*, *cf. frs.* 9.1 and 9.3–4 of the *Anon. Cont.*, translated below, n. 88. Does the sudden appearance of these sayings reflect the dominance of a new component in the source tradition from which Zonaras drew?

86   In late 268. The victims were, respectively, Marinianus 1 (*PLRE* I, p. 559 = [Licinius Egnatius] Marinianus, *PIR²* L198), then perhaps only three, and P. Licinius Valerianus 14 (*PLRE* I, p. 939).

87   Gothic naval operations probably began in the spring of 268. *Cf.* Zos. I.42–43. Thessalonica (H. Berve *Das Alexanderreich* [Munich: C. H. Beck, 1926], II, pp. 179–180, no. 370) was the daughter of Philip II of Macedon and Nicesipolis. She married Cassander (Berve no. 414), the son of the Antipater, *ca.* 316, during the jockeying for position and power after the death of Alexander the Great. Though various ancient sources—*e.g.* Lucillus Tarrhaeus *fr.* 1 (Müller *FHG* IV, p. 440) —so explain the eponym of the city Thessalonica, only a marginal note in a fifteenth-century manuscript (*Monacensis gr.* 126) of Thucydides at I.61.2 (*Scholia in Thucydidem*, pp. 49.26–50.1: "[Thessalonika] used to be called both Hypate and Emathia.") and Zonaras give Emathia as its prior name.

Dexippus' *History*, which Evagrius says did not go beyond the reign of Claudius, and *Scythica*, "in which the battles and noteworthy deeds of Romans and Scythians against one another are written up by him" (Photius *Bibl. cod.* 82 [I, p. 188.14–17] = *FgrH* 100 T 5) and which refer (*e.g. FgrH* 100 F 28) to events as late as *ca.* 267, likely are the ultimate sources for most of what is said about the Gothic incursions as presented by the source tradition reflected in Zonaras. Immediately after his notice of the terminus of Dexippus' *History* (*HE* V.24, p. 219.2–9), Evagrius does mentions a certain Eusebius, who "having taken up from Octavian, Trajan, and Marcus, came down to the death of Carus" and who is perhaps the same Eusebius who wrote a detailed account of the siege of Thessalonica (Müller *FHG* V.1, p. 21; *FgrH* 101 F 1). However, it is impossible to gauge his relationship to any other source, extant or fragmentary.

88   The Goths probably occupied Athens in 268. With Symeon and Cedrenus (above, n. 84), *cf. Anon. Cont. fr.* 9.1 Müller *FHG* IV, p. 196 = Pet. Patr. *ES* 169, p. 267.7–13:

> During Claudius' reign, when the Scythians had taken Athens and had collected all the books and decided to burn them, one among them considered to be intelligent stopped them, saying, "The Romans, devoting their leisure time to these, neglect war." But how ignorantly he spoke! For, if he had known the virtues of the Athenians and Romans, who were esteemed in words and in wars, he would not have said this.

Note Zonaras' change from "Romans" to "Greeks."

89   *SHA Gallieni* 13.6, the only other mention of Cleodemus, has him deputed with Athenaeus (1, *PLRE* I, p. 121, *PIR*² A 1286), both of whom are said to be from Byzantium, by Gallienus to see to the defenses of unspecified cities against the Goths—Dexippus, mentioned at *SHA Gallieni* 13.8 = *FgrH* 100 T 3, is the probable source. There is a chance that Zonaras or, more probably, his source has mistaken Athenaeus for Cleodemus' patronymic and transferred the episode to Claudius' reign.

90   The vicissitudes of the Goths are the probable context of a trio of fragments of the *Anon. Cont.*:

> *Fr.* 9.2 Müller *FHG* IV, p. 196 = Pet. Patr. *ES* 170, p. 267.14–18: The Scythians were shouting in insult to those who had shut themselves in the cities, "These men do not live a human life but a life of birds who have perched on high in barns," and "Having abandoned the nurturing earth, they choose these barren cities," and, "They had more confidence in inanimate objects than in themselves."

> *Fr.* 9.3 Müller *FHG* IV, p. 196 = *ES* 171, p. 267.19–26: There was a certain Andonnoballus [*cf. PIR*² A 581, *PLRE* I, p. 62, and p. 618, *s.v.* Naulobatus], who fled from the Heruli to the Romans. And he had words with Bibulus . . . [A word such as "eunuch" or "servant" seems to be missing.] to the sovereign of the Romans, for he [Bibulus] was exhorting him to give himself to the emperor. And he

[Andonnoballus] was calling him a despot-loving slave and less than a belly and saying that he traded freedom for food and dress. And he responded to him, "I am a free man. For I am indeed friend of so great a sovereign and no good thing does he deny to me. But you are well off neither in dress nor food."

Fr. 9.4 = ES 172, pp. 267.27–268.4: After the victory over the Scythians, while the sovereign was celebrating and feasting, Andonnoballus came before everyone and said, "I wish at some point to ask a favor of you." And since he thought that at some point he was going to request something great, he granted him a request. And Andonnoballus said, "Give me some fine wine, that I may summon all of my household and celebrate with them." And the sovereign laughed and commanded that wine be given him. And he gave to him many other gifts, too.

See further below, n. 91.

91 Syncellus p. 469.18–21, though not mentioning Sirmium, is a close parallel:

And under him [Claudius], too, the Aelouri faired badly, again having made attacks with a great fleet throughout diverse locations of the territory of Romans, and at one time having succumbed in sea battles, and at another to storms, and at another to a plague, having been seized by which the same Claudius ended his life. After him, Centillius was in control 17 whole days and died.

Claudius died in September 270. Note the agreement between Zonaras, Symeon, and Cedrenus (n. 84 above) about Claudius' choice of Aurelianus as successor. While Aurelianus may have benefited from such a version of events, the testimony of Zonaras and Symeon perhaps derives from the transmission of a misunderstanding of, or an inference from, the circumstances that led to the suicide of Quintilus as set forth by Zosimus, John of Antioch, and Scutariotes (n. 84 above). Another possibility is elaboration at some point in the Christian source tradition of Eusebius' comment at *HE* VII.28.4, p. 704, that: "After he had completed a second year, he [*i.e.* Claudius] gave the leadership to Aurelianus."

92   *SHA Claud.* 12.3–5 and *Aurel.* 17.5 come closest to Zonaras.

93   *Ca.* September 270. The assertion of Scutariotes (above n. 84) that Quintillus was forty-one when he died is unique.

94   *Cf.* Eus. *HE* VII.28.4, p. 704. Syncellus p. 469.16 has Claudius reign one year, but at p. 474.4 gives him a second year of rule. George the Monk p. 467.15 gives two years. With Scutariotes (above, n. 84), *cf.* Malal. XII.28/298–299, p. 230, which has Claudius reign nine years and die on campaign near Sirmium at the age of fifty-six. Eutr. IX.11.2, without specifying a place of death, says "within a two-year reign," which Paean. p. 157.10, rendered "in a second year of rule." Aur. Vict. *Caes.* 34.1 and Jerome *Chron.* p. 221[h] give him a more precise one year and nine months, and *Chron.* p. 222[a] has Claudius killed at Sirmium. *Chron. 354* p. 148.6 gives one year, four months, fourteen days and also locates his death at Sirmium. The one and two year variant results from ignoring or counting as a second year the months beyond Claudius' initial year, the nine year figure from confusion with the nine months.

95   Constas is Constantius Chlorus. On the fictitious link between Claudius and Constantius, *cf.* Symeon and Cedrenus (n. 84 above). Aur. Vict. *Caes.* 34.6–7 and Eutr. IX.22.1/Paean. p. 163.28–29 report it independently, perhaps reflecting a common source, *i.e.* the *Kaisergeschichte* whose existence A. Enmann demonstrated (*Eine Verlorene Geschichte der Römischen Kaiser, Philologus* Supplementband IV [1884], pp. 337–501). Note, too, *SHA Claud.* 13.1–2. The connection is first attested in Latin in 310 in the anonymous *Pan. Lat.* VI (VII) 2.1–2, p. 187.3–9, and, in 310 or 311, V (VIII) 2.5, pp. 175.26–176.4, and in Greek in 355 or 365 in Julian's *Or.* I.5.1–8//6c-d 6 (I.1, p. 16).

96   For Aurelianus, who reigned from September 270 to September or October 275, Zonaras is much fuller than Symeon, Cedrenus, or Scutariotes and has clear affinities with Eusebius, Syncellus, and the Anonymous Continuator of Dio, the last of whom, in turn, exhibits some points of contact with the *SHA*, but differs significantly from Zosimus and the tradition transmitted through Eutropius to John of Antioch.

Sym. 82, pp. 102–103:

Aurelianus

Aurelianus reigned 6 years and was killed by the troops between Heracleia and Byzantium, in the so-called New Castle [Cenophrurium], and was buried there. 2. Aurelianus had a certain informant who conveyed to him everything done and said. After he had been threatened by him once for some offence and become frightened, he imitated the sovereign's hand, [103] having made in writing a list of names of powerful men as if they were going to be sentenced to death. When they had become frightened, they removed him. Also under him the holy Chariton [EEC I, pp. 160–161, s.v. Charito] bore witness. Under Aurelianus, lived Manes the detestable, from whom the name Manichaean became familiar to the masses.

Ced. p. 455.1–14:

Aurelianus reigned 6 years and was killed by the troops between Heracleia and Byzantium, in the so-called New Castle, which, in the vernacular is styled Cenoflorium. For he had a certain informant who conveyed to him everything done and said. Now, after he had been threatened by him once for some offence and become frightened, he imitated the sovereign's hand, and when a register had been made of powerful men as if they were going to be sentenced to death, they, when they had become frightened, removed him. Under him the holy Chariton bore witness, and Paul of Samosata occupied the throne of Antioch. Under him Manes the accursed and thrice-accursed, having fashioned himself Christ and the Holy Spirit, and borrowing whatever was evil from every heresy, slinked from Persia to the land of Romans against the agreement of God.

Scut. p. 39.9–17:

Aurelianus, six years: He rebuilt the walls of Rome, which had fallen into ruin through time and, being noble and very much a general, won many wars and was victorious over not a few peoples, and was slain in Heracleia of Europe. For Eros [PLRE I, p. 283], a reporter of remarks made extra muros, when he had been angered by him and become frightened, forged the sovereign's writing, having composed a register of some powerful individuals in order that they be sentenced to death, and, having become frightened, they killed him, being in his 60th year. The blessed Chariton bore witness.

Anon. Cont. fr. 10.1 Müller *FHG* IV, p. 197 = Pet. Patr. *ES* 173, p. 268.5–12, alone parallels Zonaras' opening anecdote:

> After he had become sovereign and gathered all those in repute in Ravenna as a council, Aurelianus was considering how he ought to rule them. For he was hoping from what he had accomplished after the death of Claudius to appear greater than him. And one from the assemblage said to him, "If you want to rule nobly, fortify yourself with gold and iron, the iron against those who discomfit you, the gold for those who do you service." And he who had recommended this base advice was the first banished.

With regard to this feature of the Aurelianus tradition, *SHA Aurel.* 22.4–23.3 observes that the emperor was as famous for his sayings as for his deeds and goes on to recount the upshot of Aurelianus' declaration that he would not even leave a dog alive after capturing Tyana, a boast paralleled only by *Anon. Cont. fr.* 10.4 Müller *FHG* IV, p. 197 = Pet. Patr, *ES* 176, pp. 268.24–269.1.

97   *Cf.* Eus. *HE* VII.30.20–21, p. 714, and Syncellus p. 470.25–26. For Zonaras' association of Aurelianus with the Council of Antioch, see XII.25 with n. 83 above.

98   Aurelianus' Palmyrene campaign was in 273. Egypt had fallen to Zenobia's general Zabdas (*PLRE* I, p. 990) in 270, at which time Probus, not the later emperor but the prefect of Egypt (Te)nagino Probus (*PLRE* I, p. 740), committed suicide. Syncellus p. 470.2 has Zenobia kill Probus. But this is almost certainly due to his misreading of his source or a subsequent mistaken transcription. *Cf.* Zos. I.44.2, and *SHA Prob.* 9.5 and *Claud.* 2.1–2.

99   Syncellus p. 470.5–7 alleges Zenobia's marriage to "a man of the senate." No other source mentions daughters of Zenobia, let alone Aurelianus' marriage to one of them. Zos. I. 59, among others, has Zenobia die on the way to Rome and speaks only of her son.

100   The destruction of the *Imperium Galliarum* occurred in mid 274, Aurelianus' triumph that same fall.

101   The campaign against the Gauls and Aurelianus' death both date to 275. Aurelianus had reigned from September 270 until September

or October of 275. Cenophorium was on the Via Egnatia between Perinthus and Byzantium. Several sources relate the story of the forged warrant. *Cf., e.g.* Eutr. IX.15.2, Aur. Vict. *Caes.* 35.9 and *SHA Aurel.* 35.5. Zos. I.62 names Eros but is otherwise only superficially close to Zonaras. Eutr. IX.15.2, probably filtered through Capito's translation, closely parallels John of Antioch *fr.* 238 Roberto, p. 418 = *fr.* 156 Müller *FHG* IV, p. 599 = *EI* 66, p. 111.15–27:

> Aurelianus was done away with in the sixth year of leadership, one of the domestics writing in shorthand having arranged his death for him, who, after he had imitated his hand, conveyed to certain corps commanders and to friends of Aurelianus himself a memorandum which bore their marked names, feigning that Aurelianus had written these. And, since they, as a result of the sovereign's quickness with respect to every unwonted and harsh action, estimated the thing credible, they resolved to act before they suffered. And they did way with him as he was going from Byzantium toward Heracleia, about midway in the journey, around the so-called Cenophrurium. To be sure, he did not die unavenged. For his murderers suffered punishment and he was placed by vote among the divine emperors.

102   Tacitus' reign probably began in November or December of 275. Zonaras' evaluation of Tacitus exhibits a pro-senatorial, perhaps Italian, bias evident in other sources. The main narrative of the *SHA Tacitus* describes a formal six-month interregnum between Aurelianus' death and the accession of Tacitus, while Aur. Vict. *Caes.* 36.1, though not mentioning a formal interregnum, notes a six-month gap and stresses in connection with Tacitus' reign a reassertion of senatorial prerogative vis-à-vis the soldiery. This contrast between senate and army appears too at *SHA Tacitus* 7.5, which also asserts that many literary sources placed Tacitus in Campania. Zonaras is the only other extant witness to that location, while his description of Tacitus' appearance before the senate and that of *SHA Tacitus* 7.7 offers another point of contact. If this reflects any historical reality, "army" must refer to the Praetorian Guard.

103   The campaign was probably in the early summer of 276. The Scythians are, of course, the Goths. Lake Maeotis is the Sea of Azov. The future emperor Florianus was perhaps Tacitus' uterine brother.

Zos. I.61.1–2: When Tacitus had donned the regalia of Rome and held the office, Scythians, having made a foray through Lake Maeotis, began to overrun from the Black Sea as far as Cilicia. When he had advanced against them, Tacitus himself, after he had subdued them, killed some of them. When he had delivered the others to Florianus, who had been appointed praetorian prefect, he hastened back toward Europe. There, forthwith, after he had fallen into a plot, he too was killed for the following reason. He gave the rule of Syria to Maximinus, a relative by kinship. Behaving most savagely toward those in office, he brought himself into enmity together with fear. And when these had given birth to hatred, the result culminated in a plot, having made those who had killed Aurelianus accomplices in which, they, on the one hand, when they had attacked Maximinus, slaughtered him and, after he had pursued Tacitus en route toward Europe, killed him.

John of Antioch *fr.* 239 Roberto, p. 420 = *fr.* 157 Müller *FHG* IV, pp. 599–600 = *EI* 67, pp. 111.28–112.6): When Tacitus had received the sovereign affairs of Rome, the Scythians made a foray through Lake Maeotis. After he had subdued them, he hastened back toward Europe. There, forthwith, after he had fallen into a plot, he too was killed for the following reason. He gave the rule of Syria to Maximinus, a relative by kinship. Behaving most savagely toward those in office, he brought the sovereign into enmity coupled with fear. And when these had given birth to hatred, the result culminated in a plot, having made those who had killed Aurelianus accomplices in which, they, on the one hand, after they had attacked Maximinus, slaughtered him and, when they had pursued Tacitus en route toward Europe, killed him, having reigned six whole months.

Sym. 83, p. 103: He [Tacitus] put Maximinus, his kinsman, in charge of Assyria. Because of the injustices which had transpired under him, the soldiers, when they had killed him, frightened lest Tacitus avenge him, killed him too, and Probus and Florianus became sovereigns.

Ced. p. 463.7–10: He put Maximinus, his kinsman, in charge of Assyria. Because of the injustices which had transpired under him, the soldiers, when they had killed him, frightened then lest Tacitus avenge him, killed him too at the instigation of Florianus.

104   Maximinus (1, *PLRE* I, p. 576) is known only in the context of this episode. George the Monk's assertion (p. 476.11), that Florianus (*PLRE* I, p. 367) killed Tacitus (*PLRE* I, p. 873) may simply reflect increasingly minimalist, formulaic entries in the transmission of the tradition. *Cf.*, for example, George pp. 476.13–477.3 on Florianus, Probus, Carus, and Carinus.

Salmasian John *fr.* 239 Roberto, p. 420 = *fr.* 157 Müller *FHG* IV, pp. 599–600, translated above, n. 103—apart from its Maximus for

Maximinus, Aurelius for Aurelianus, and the omission of mention of Florianus—mirrors Zosimus almost exactly and shows either John's use of Zosimus or their common direct or indirect dependence on the same source. The differences are easily explained, for the provenance of John *fr.* 239 is the section of the Constantinian *excerpta* devoted to plots, the compilers of which frequently shortened the forms of some names or omitted what they deemed irrelevant material.

Tacitus probably died in June or July of 276. Syncellus p. 471.2, among others, sets his demise in Pontus. Aur. Vict. *Caes.* 36.2, has him die at Tyana and gives no cause of death; *Epit. de Caes.* 36.1 at Tarsus from a fever. *SHA Tacitus* 13.5, without providing a location, notes two versions of Tacitus' death: one that he was a victim of the troops, the other that he died of disease.

105   Florianus reigned from about June/July to August/September of 276. *SHA Tacitus* 14.1–2 says that he took power without senatorial authorization and was killed after two months at Tarsus by soldiers sent by Probus (3, *PLRE* I, p. 736). John of Antioch *fr.* 240, Roberto, p. 420 = *fr.* 158.1 Müller *FHG* IV p. 600 = *EI* 68–70, p. 112.7–9 gives the same duration and, perhaps in reaction to another tradition or as part of a positive picture of Probus, pointedly says that Probus acted against his will in killing Florianus: "The duo Probus and Florianus reigned together at the same time. And Probus, not by his choice, killed Florianus after he had enjoyed power 2 months and 20 days."

The tradition from which Zonaras' account of Probus derives is clearly identical to that preserved by John and Zosimus, who, just as clearly, was not John's direct source. Zos. I.64.1 virtually mirrors Zonaras' opening remarks; Zos. I.65.1, on Probus' punishment of the killers of Aurelianus and Tacitus, corresponds to Zonaras and contains particulars mentioned by Symeon and Cedrenus (translated below); Zos. I.66, on Saturninus, agrees almost verbatim with Zonaras; and Zos. I.67.1–2, on the rain miracle, approximates Zonaras. Strong parallels also exist with John of Antioch. *Cf.* Zos. I.66.1–2 and John *fr.* 241 Roberto, pp. 420–422 = *fr.* 158.2 Müller *FHG* IV p. 600 = *EI* 69, p. 112.10–22:

During Probus' rule of Rome, Saturninus, by race Moorish, most dear to the sovereign and consequently entrusted with the rule of Syria, after he had betrayed the trust of the sovereign, came to a scheme a rebellion. The troops in the East anticipated Probus, who had heard about this and planned to attend to the matter, extinguishing the usurper before him. And he also suppressed another rebellion in Britain, attended to through Victorinus, Moorish by race. On his recommendation, he had appointed governor of Britain the fellow who had rebelled. And, after he had summoned Victorinus to him and censured him about the advice, he dispatched him to correct the misstep. Having immediately set out to Britain, he killed the usurper by a clever deception.

Cf., too, Zos. I.67.1 and Salmasian John *fr.* 242 Roberto, p. 422 = *fr.* 159 Müller *FHG* IV p. 600: "During Probus' rule, there occurred a rain which brought down grain, which, when collected, they made into great piles. Under Aurelianus bits of silver were borne down."

These parallels, in turn, have significant points of contact with Symeon, Cedrenus, and Scutariotes:

Sym. 84, pp. 103–104:	Ced. pp. 463.11–464.5:	Scut. pp. 39.21–40.5:
Probus and Florianus	Probus and Florianus reigned two years and 4 months. Now Probus, having feigned insanity, killed Florianus. Under him, when there was a rain, much grain mixed with the water was borne down, which, when collected, they made into great piles. Likewise, too, under Aurelianus they say that bits of silver were borne down. And Victorinus, a friend of Probus, requested that a friend of his be sent to Britain; and he, having departed, rebelled. Therefore Victorinus, being shamed because of him, was dispatched to quell the disturbance. Having surmised from his demeanor that he was fleeing the sovereign, he was received as a friend	Probus, 2 years: While he reigned, the soldiers deployed about Europe, proclaimed Florianus the prefect sovereign. And, Probus, on the one hand, ruled Syria and Phoenicia, Palestine and all of Egypt; Florianus, on the other, from Cilicia as far as Italy and all the western parts. But when Florianus had been killed rather quickly by the troops, the entire realm came over to Probus. He was eloquent and wise, and was victorious over many races.
Probus and Florianus reigned two years [*Apparatus criticus* 84.2, p. 103: "and 4 months"]. Now this Probus, having feigned insanity, killed Florianus. Under him, when there was a rain, much grain [*Apparatus criticus* 84.3, p. 103: "mixed with the water"] was borne down, which, when collected, they made into great piles.		
[*Apparatus criticus* 84.3, p. 103: Likewise, too, under Aurelianus they say that bits of silver were borne down. And Victorinus, a friend of Probus, requested that a friend of his be send to Britain; and, after he		Under him, rain mixed with grain was borne down. For, since the Germans were troubling the cities, he was compelled to bring

128

had departed, he rebelled. Therefore Victorinus, shamed because of him, was dispatched to quell the disturbance. Having surmised from his demeanor that he was fleeing the sovereign, he was received as a friend of the rebel and killed him. When he had returned, as he disembarked the ship, after unfastening his belt, he flung it into the sea and, beltless, approached the sovereign. And he, thinking that he had suffered this at another's hands, was enraged. And Victorinus, after he had requested that he no longer be in charge of anything of importance, said that he had done this himself, for every office was full of risks and hazards. And he granted him retirement and many gifts.}

Sym. 82.2, p. 104: And he also killed all those who had killed Tacitus and Aurelianus in Perinthus, having summoned them to a banquet. And he, too, was himself killed by those about him, and Carus and Carinus and Numerianus reigned.

of the rebel and killed him. When he had returned, as he disembarked the ship, after unfastening his belt, he flung it into the sea and, beltless, approached the sovereign. And he, thinking that he had suffered this at another's hands, was enraged. And Victorinus, after he had requested that he no longer be in charge of anything of importance, said that he had done this himself, for every office was full of risks and hazards. And he granted him retirement and many gifts. And he killed all those who had killed Tacitus and Aurelianus, having summoned them to a banquet in Perinthus. And he himself, too, was killed.

aid to them in person. And when the war had arisen and when [40] a famine had befallen those there, an immense downpour also brought down much grain, having stockpiled which, his army both repelled the famine and won the war. He died as a result of a plot of his own men, happening to be in his fiftieth year.

---

106 Probus' defeats of the western usurpers Proculus (1 *PLRE* I, p. 745) and Bonosus (1 *PLRE* I, p. 163) at Agrippina (Cologne) pass unmentioned.

107   Saturninus (*PLRE* I, p. 808), probably a native of Africa, was acclaimed emperor in 281 and killed in the same year at Apamea. Contrary to Zos. I.66, which makes Saturninus a Moor, *SHA Saturninus* 7.1 calls him a Gaul and, at *Saturninus* 11, in a passage suspiciously like John of Antioch's account of Florianus' end (see above, n. 103), twice says that Saturninus' death was not Probus' choice but that troops dispatched by Probus had taken the initiative.

For events under Probus, note the strong parallels between Jerome's *Chronica* and Syncellus translated in n. 110 below. These betray the influence of Eusebius' *Chronici Canones*, on which see R. Burgess, *Studies in Eusebian and Post-Eusebian Chronography, Historia Einzelschriften* 135 (Stuttgart: Franz Steiner Verlag, 1999), p. 76.

108   The tale of Victorinus and the anonymous usurper in Britain does not appear in the Latin sources or in Syncellus. Zonaras' appended comments about Probus' character are reminiscent of Malal. XII.33/302, p. 232.

109   The miracle supposedly occurred during the German campaign of 277–278. Zonaras makes no mention of Probus' campaigns of 279 in Isauria and in Egypt or of his western campaigns of 280–281.

110   Probus (3, *PLRE* I, p. 736) reigned from June 276 to September 282. Malal. XII.33/302, pp. 232–233, with which *cf. CP* p. 509.6, has Probus killed at Sirmium on campaign against the Goths and mentions famine and the discontent of the troops at not being paid as factors in his murder. Malalas gives his age at death at fifty and the duration of his reign at three years and three months. Eus. *HE* VII.30.22, p. 714, sets his reign at about six years. John of Antioch *fr.* 243 Roberto, p. 422 = *fr.* 160 Müller *FHG* IV p. 600 = *EI* 70, p. 112.23–29:

> When Probus had accomplished much and had managed the realm nobly and justly, a rebellion from the West was announced, the forces in Rhaetia and Noricum having conferred the purple on Carus. And when he had dispatched a force to oppose him, some who had been sent deserted to Carus, and others, having turned against Probus, who was destitute of aid, with none opposing them, destroyed him after he had reigned six years, 4 months.

See further Sym. 84.2, p. 105, Scut. p. 40.4–5, both translated above, n. 105, and:

Syncellus
pp. 471.7–473.4: In year 3 of Probus, Anatolius, the bishop of Laodicea, eminent in philosophical studies, was distinguished.

In year 4 of Probus, the perditious destruction of the maniacal Manichaeans was introduced into the life of mankind.

In year 6 of Probus, Saturninus, an army commander, began to build New Antioch, Later, after he had rebelled from the rule of Rome, he was slaughtered in Apamea by his own men. Probus was slaughtered in Sermium [sic].

Jerome *Chron.* p. 223[i]: Anatolius of Laodicea, bishop, erudite in the studies of philosophers, was celebrated in much discourse.

p. 223[l]: The insane heresy of the Manichaeans aroused evils in the commonweal of the human race.

p. 224[c]: Saturninus, an army commander, undertook to fashion a new city of Antioch. Afterward, when he had contrived to assume power, he was killed at Apamea.

111   Carus, Augustus from August 29/September13, 282 to July/August 383, made Carinus and, slightly later, Numerianus Caesars *ca.* November 282. Numerianus is first called Augustus in July/August 283, Carinus between March and mid-May 283. The Persian campaign was in 283.

The common tradition underlying Zonaras, Symeon, Cedrenus, and Scutariotes remains discernable:

Sym. 85, p. 104:	Ced. p. 464.6–13:	Scut. p. 40.6–26: Saros
Carus and Carinus and Numerianus	Carus and Carinus and Numerianus reigned 2 years. Carus captured Persia and Ctesiphon, having suffered this four times: by Trajan, by Verus and Severus, and Carus. When Carus had died of plague and Numerianus [sic] had gone blind, Aper, his father-in-law, killed him and Numerianus, who was *dux* of Mysia, reigned. Under him the holy Babylas suffered martyrdom in Antioch. Diocletian killed him.	[sic], 2 years: He was completely victorious over the Persians and, with plunder and prizes of war, returned toward Rome. After he had departed for war against the Huns, he was killed, being in his 60th year.
Carus and Carinus and Numerianus reigned 2 years. Carus captured Persia and Ctesiphon, which already had been taken four times: by Trajan, by Verus, Severus, and Carus. When Carus had died [*Apparatus criticus* 85.5, p. 104: "of plague"] and Numerianus had gone blind, Aper killed him and Numerianus [*Apparatus criticus*		Numerianus, his son, 2 years: Under him began a great persecution against Christians and many became martyrs, among whom Saint Babylas of Antioch, too. When he had

131

85.5–6, p. 104: "Carinus"] reigned. 2. Under him the holy George [*Apparatus criticus* 85.6–7, p. 104: "Germanus"] suffered martyrdom and the holy Babylas in Antioch. Diocletian, who happened to be *dux* of Mysia, killed him.

campaigned against Persia, he was beaten and fled and, after he had been captured by them, was flayed like a wineskin, being in his 36th year.

Carinus, his brother, 2 years: Under him the physicians Cosmas and Damianus were martyred in Rome, not by the sovereign, but by their teacher. For when the sovereign Carinus had campaigned against Persia for the purpose of avenging his brother, and when he had conquered them and was on his way back, suddenly his face was contorted from behind, and, when all the physicians were unable to heal the sovereign, these holy men healed him through prayer. And hence, when he had glorified God, he sent forth his command throughout his realm that no Christian be harmed. Now to the holy men's teacher, stricken with envy through the wonderworking of the holy men and the sovereign's respect for them, after he had secretly plotted with the household slaves against them, having thrown them from a cliff, killed them. And Carinus, too, was killed by a certain corps commander.

Malal. XII.34/302.20–303.4, p. 233, gives the same sequence as Zonaras and Cedrenus of a campaign against Persia, return toward Rome, and offensive against the Huns, *i.e.* Sarmatians. Malal. XII.35/ 303.8–22, p. 234, and Cedrenus both place Babylas' martyrdom under Numerianus. Zon. XII.20, p. 585, correctly sets it under Decius. Philost. *HE* VII.8, p. 89.2–5, demonstrates knowledge of both versions. See above, n. 43. Malal. XII.36/304.14–306.7, pp. 234–235, gives an account of Cosmas and Damianus slightly more detailed than Scutariotes but clearly connected in some way to it. On these martyrs, see *ODB* II, p. 1151, *s.v.* Kosmas.

112   The story of the trench is unique to Zonaras.

113   Zonaras' source has transposed the Persian campaign of 283 and a victory in the Balkans against the Sarmatians earlier in the same year.

114   *Cf.* Syncellus p. 472.10–14:

> Carus, a brave man of Gaul, subdued the Sarmatians, who had rebelled. Having warred against Persia, he captured Ctesiphon. Camping by the Tigris, all at once, when he had been struck with a thunderbolt, he was destroyed, together with his tent.

115   George the Monk p. 477.5–7, in a doublet of the fate of Valerianus, recounts Numerianus' capture and flaying: "And after Carinus, Numerianus, his brother, reigned one year and, when he had warred against Persia and been captured, they flayed him alive." *Cf.* above, nn. 59 and 64. *CP* p. 472.2–15 attributes this alleged fate of Numerianus to Carinus, whom it has Numerianus succeed.

116   Diocletian defeated Carinus in the spring of 285 near Viminacium, modern Kostalac, Yugoslavia. Diocletian's alleged visit to Rome, where Zon. XII.30, p. 612, has him kill Carinus, could only have occurred in the summer of 285. The corps commander (*chiliarch*) to whom Scutaritotes attributes Carinus' death may reflect the tradition preserved in the *Epit. de Caes.* 38.8—"He [Carinus] was tortured to death chiefly by the hand of his tribune, whose wife he was said to have violated."—and in John of Antioch *fr.* 246 Roberto, pp. 424–426 = *frs.* 162–163 Müller *FGH* IV, p. 601 = *EI* 51, pp. 195.22–196.2 and 71, pp. 112.30–113.10:

Carinus, the son of Carus, having become sovereign, performed no act bearing on the common advantage and, having given his own affairs over to a wanton and luxurious style of life, was making a byproduct of wantonness murders of men who had done no injustice who had been considered in some respect to have rubbed him the wrong way. And while everyone was being oppressed by bitter tyranny compounded with youthful caprice he was doing everything discordantly and contrary to calculation, when Numerianus' death had been announced to those in Italy, angered against Carinus' general carelessness and cruelty, those who commanded the garrisons there, after they had bestowed the regal mantle on Sabinus Julianus [*cf. PLRE* I, p. 474, *s.v.* M. Aurelius Sabinus Julianus 24, and p. 480, *s.v.* Sabinus Iulianus 38], who held the prefectural office, decided to battle Carinus with him. Having learned of the rebellion, Carinus was on his way toward Italy. At that very moment, the troops, having persuaded those who had returned from Persia to conspire with them, led against Italy Diocletian, who already donned the purple at Nicomedia. And while he was still on the road, after he had engaged the troops of Sabinus Julianus and routed them in the battle, when some of those with him had attacked him, Carinus was unexpectedly killed, one of the corps commanders, whose wife he happened to have corrupted, having slain him.

117   *Cf.* Eus. *HE* VII.31, p. 716, and Ced. p. 455.10–13, translated in n. 96.

118   *Cf.* Eus. *HE* VII.30.23, p. 714, on Dionysius and Felix, and 32.1, p. 716, on Eutychianus and his successors. For the dates of their tenures, see *Chronologies of the Ancient World*, ed. W. Eder and J. Renger, *BNP, Supplement* I (Brill: Leiden, 2007), p. 317. In Eusebius, the invective against Manes separates these passages.

119   An abridgement by Zonaras' source of Eus. *HE* VII.32.2–4, pp. 716–718, and 32.29–31, pp. 728–730, omitting Eusebius' comments on Socrates, Eusebius (*EEC* I, p. 301), Anatolius (*EEC* I, p. 37), Stephanus, and Theodotus (*EEC* II, p. 830) of Laodicea, on Theotecnus (*EEC* II, p. 832), Agapius, and Pampilius (*EEC* II, p. 638) of Caesarea, and on Hymenaeus (*EEC* I, p. 400), Zabdas, and Hermon of Jerusalem. For the dates of their tenures, see *Chronologies of the Ancient World*, pp. 324 (Alexandria), 326 (Antioch), 330 (Jerusalem), and 334–335.

120   Diocletian's reign marks a significant shift in the dynamics of the tradition upon which Symeon, Cedrenus, Scutariotes, and Zonaras drew. At this point parallels between Eutropius, via a Greek translation, and Theophanes the Confessor (*ca.* 760–817, *ODB* III, pp. 2063) become far stronger than those between Zonaras and Symeon, Cedrenus, and Scutariotes. This remains true for Eutropius through the end of the *Breviarium*, which concludes in 364, and for Theophanes up to the reign of Leo the Armenian (813). Syncellus p. 472.17–26 is uniformly positive about Diocletian. *Cf.*:

Sym. 86, pp. 104–105:	Ced. p. 464.14–21:	Scut. pp. 40.27–41.8:
Diocletian reigned 20 years, by race a Dalmatian. And when he had failed to gain control of affairs of state, he appointed sovereign Maximianus Herculius, an in-law and his friend. Under them a great persecution against Christians was set in motion.	Diocletian reigned 22 years, by race a Dalmatian. And when he had gained control of the affairs of state, he appointed Maximianus Herculius, an in-law and his friend. Under them a great persecution against Christians was set in motion. For they decreed, on the one hand, that throughout city and countryside the assembly places of Christ be destroyed and that their divine scriptures burned, and, on the other hand, that the Christians who were discovered be compelled to sacrifice to the demons. And hence many donned the crown of the struggle, among whom were	Diocletian, 20 years: in the fourth year of his sovereignty, he chose Maximianus Herculius sovereign, and they— men most abominable and despicable, having beaten all their predecessors with regard to idolatry and cruelty—roused a most serious persecution against Christians and consecrated many holy men martyrs.

121   Diocletian was acclaimed Augustus at Nicomedia on November 20, 284. Eutr./Paean. IX.19.2: "most believe that he was a son of a copyist, some a freedman of Anullinus [Paean.: 'Anulinus;' *PLRE* I, p. 78], a senator."

122   So *SHA Carus* 13.1—"then commanding the *domestici*"—and Aur. Vict. *Caes.* 39.1. *Cf. Suda* Δ 1350 (Ader III, p. 126.3–4) = Zonaras

Lexicon (I, p. 559.7): "*Domestici*: The cavalry of the Romans. Or among Romans, household troops." The origin of the *domestici* is obscure. Certainly by Diocletian's day the term sometimes referred to a sort of cadet corps which often traveled with an emperor's retinue.

123   *Cf.* Eutr./Paean. IX.20.1 and *SHA Carus* 13.1–3 on Aper's death. Diocletian's alleged visit to Rome could only have occurred in the summer of 285.

124   Zonaras confuses the specifics of the elevations of Maximianus, who became Caesar on July 21, 285, in Diocletian's second year as Augustus, and Augustus on April 1, 286, the third rather than fourth year of Diocletian's reign. The odd "fourth year" also appears in Scut. p. 40.27 and suggests a common source tradition. Symeon and Cedrenus (translated above, n. 120) imply the same motive behind the selection of a colleague as that stated by Zonaras. *Cf.*, too, Theoph. *AM* 5780, p. 6.18–19.

125   Zonaras indirectly echoes Eus. *HE* VIII.2.4–3.1, p. 742, where events are explicitly set in the nineteenth year of Diocletian's reign, when the so-called "great persecution" began (February 23, 303). Notice of a persecution at this point in the narrative appears too in Symeon, Cedrenus, and Scutariotes (translated above, n. 120) and reflects confusion in a common source due to Eusebius' brief notice of the persecution at *HE* VII.30.22, p. 714, immediately after a mention of Diocletian's accession. *Cf.* Theoph. *AM* 5787 (294/5), p. 7.15–19, with explicit mention of Eusebius.

126   *Cf.* Theoph. *AM* 5782, p. 6.23–25, John of Antioch *fr.* 248 Roberto, translated below, n. 127, and Ced. p. 467.19–21: "And in their 7th year, Busiris and Coptos, cities in Thebes of Egypt which had rebelled from the rule of the Romans, they razed to the ground."

127   With Zonaras and Ced. p. 470.3–5—"And in his [Diocletian's] 10th year, when Alexandria with Egypt had rebelled under Achilles, most perished in the Romans' assault."— *cf.* Eutr./Paean. IX.22.1 and IX.23, Theoph. *AM* 5786, p. 7.10–13 and 5788, p. 8.15, and John of Antioch *fr.* 248 Roberto, p. 428 = *fr.* 165 Müller *FHG* IV, pp. 601–602 = *EV* 52 (I p. 196.3–10) and *Suda* Δ 1156 (II, p. 104.18–25):

Diocletian [*Suda*: "This silly and Christ-hating man], in remembrance and rage about those who had rebelled concerning the rule of Egypt, was content with ruling neither moderately nor mildly, but, defiling by proscriptions and murders of the illustrious, he assaulted Egypt. And indeed, after he had closely examined the books which had been written by their men of old about the chemistry of silver and gold, he burned them in order that wealth from such a skill no longer be at the Egyptians' disposal and lest they, emboldened by an abundance of wealth, subsequently rise up against Rome.

128   The Caesars assumed their titles on March 1, 293. Zonaras more fully parallels Eutr./Paean. IX.22.1 and Theoph. *AM* 5785, p. 7.1–6. *Cf.*:

Sym. 86.1, pp. 104–105: And in their own realms they appointed Constantius and Gallerius Caesars and made them in-laws, having persuaded them, when they had divorced their own wives, to take their daughters. And Theodora [1, *PLRE* I, p. 895] [105] was Constantius' and Valleria [*PLRE* I, p. 937, *s.v.* Valeria] Gallerius'.	Ced. pp. 469.20–470.2: And in the 9th and 10th year of his sovereignty they made Caesars Constantius, the one called Chlorus because of the paleness of his face, and Maximianus Gallerius, having persuaded them, after they had divorced their own wives, to take their daughters. [470] Theodora was Constantius' and Valleria, the daughter of Diocletian, in truth, Galerius'.	Scut. p. 41.1–8: They appointed in turn two others Caesars, Diocletian, on the one hand, Maximianus Gallerius, Herculius Maximianus, on the other, Constans Chlorus, the son of the daughter of Claudius who had previously been sovereign, having also made him husband of his own daughter Theodora.

Therefore, when they had become Caesars, both set aside the women whom they used to hold previously as wives for the sake of goodwill and close kinship to the sovereigns. |

129   Amandus' (*PLRE* I, p. 50) rebellion was in 285–286. Only in 297 did Maximianus defeat this group of Berber tribes, which had troubled the Romans throughout the 280s. Eutr./Paean. IX.20.3–23 and Theoph. *AM* 5788, pp. 7.30–8.4, treat Amandus, Carausius (*PLRE* I, pp. 180–181) = Crassus, Crasus in Theophanes), Achilles (*PLRE* I,

p. 9, *s.v.* Aurelius Achilleus 1), and the Quinquegentiani. A careless reading of Paean. IX.22.2 may explain Zonaras' claim that Asclepiodotus (3, *PLRE* I, pp. 115–116) eliminated Carausius rather than Allectus (*PLRE* I, p. 45). *Cf.* the final portion of John of Antioch *fr.* 247.11–13 Roberto, p. 428 = *fr.* 164 Müller *FHG* IV, p. 601 = *EI* 72, p. 113.21–26:

> Now when he [Carausius] had been ordered killed by Heraclius, he donned the purple and seized Britain. And after he had done this, and when the prevailing state of affairs had been thrown into turmoil, Achilles both launched a rebellion in Egypt and Africa and battled with "5 Men called Gentianii [*i.e.* Quinquegentiani]."

130   Closely paralleled by Eutr./Paean. IX.23, which sets the incident in the territory of the Lingones, modern Langres, and Theoph. *AM* 5788 (295/6), p. 8.4–13. The date is uncertain, though 302 is a good possibility.

131   With Zonaras' fuller account, *cf.* Eutr./Paean. IX.24–25.1, Theoph. *AM* 5793, p. 9.1–15, and:

Sym. 86.2, p. 105: 2. Of these Gallerius, after he had implored Diocletian, was dispatched toward the Persians to war against them. When he had conquered them in battle, he took both the royal insignia and the wife of Sapor . . .	Ced. p. 470.15–18: In the 16th year, Gallerius Maximianus, when he had marched against Narses, the king of the Persians, pursued him and, after he had captured his wife and many of his possessions, having made a great slaughter, marched back toward Diocletian, . . .

132   Pet. Patr. *frs.* 13–14 Müller *FHG* IV, pp. 188–189 = *ELGR* 12, pp. 393.10–394.17, and *ELRG* 3 pp. 3.22–4.20, translated D-L, pp. 131–133.

133   *Cf.* Eutr./Paean. IX.25.2 and Theoph. *AM* 5793, p. 9.15–16. Zonaras' claim that the tetrarchs "expanded the boundaries of the realm" may be a misunderstanding of Paeanius' "the Roman land was made full."

134 *Cf.*:

Sym. 86.2, p. 105: . . . having bags filled full of precious stones and pearls from which Diocletian first used clothing and shoes adorned with precious stones and gold. And he [Diocletian] ordered him [Galerius] to kneel before him contrary to immemorial usage, . . .	Ced. p. 470.18–22: . . . having bags filled full of precious stones and pearls, too, from which Diocletian first used clothing and shoes adorned with precious stones and gold, and he ordered himself to be revered contrary to immemorial usage . . .

See, too, Eutr./Paean. IX.26, Theoph. *AM* 5793, p. 9.17–20, and the second half of John of Antioch *fr.* 248.8–12 Roberto, p. 428 = *fr.* 165 Müller *FHG* IV, pp. 601–602 = *EV* 52 (I, p. 196.11–16) = *Suda* Δ 1156 (II, p. 104.25–30):

> On the one hand, Diocletian [*Suda*: "his character"] was a bit fickle and villainous, but truly by the sagaciousness and sharpness of his intelligence he often yielded to the baser features of his personality, attributing every harsh act to others. But he was careful and quick to do what needed done and, contrary to the established Roman traditions, altered many of the components of the royal ceremonial in the direction of over-presumptuousness.

Zonaras levels the same criticisms against Constantine. See Zon. XIII.4, p. 25, with commentary, n. 42.

135 Zonaras, Symeon, and Cedrenus often exhibit the same confusions about Diocletian's reign, though not necessarily in the same sequence. In addition, Cedrenus gives two accounts of Diocletian's death, the first, p. 469.4–19, the culmination of notices of Galerius' campaign of 298 against the Persians in Armenia, Diocletian's initial edict of persecution in 299, and a contingent plague (Ced. pp. 467.21–469.4):

> And not long after, the tyrants themselves, too, garnered the wages worthy of their impiety, as if garnering then down payments of the punishments they were going to receive after death. For Diocletian, when he had succumbed to a most terrible disease after the abdication of the sovereignty, was racked through all his flesh with acute pains, and his insides were being destroyed by the most violent inflammation,

while all his flesh was melting like wax. And with these, the wretch went blind and sank into senility. And thereafter, piteously wasting and terribly rotting away, he spouted a mass of worms from his throat together with his rotted tongue. He exuded such a stench that he was indistinguishable from the corpses decomposed in graves. And the tyrant, inhaling these, after a groan, called upon death and, breathing his last, said, "Woe to me, piteous and worthy of lamentations! The punishment I suffer is worthy of the impieties undertaken by me against Christians." But these things happed to the sinful man later.

For the second version of Diocletian's death, see below, n. 147.

136 *Cf.* Eus. *HE* VIII.2.2–4, p. 742.8–16, *Exc. Hist. Eccl.*, ed. Cramer II, p. 90.17–19, Theoph. *AM* 5795, p. 10.5–9, and Ced. p. 470.14: "In the 13th year, they [Diocletian and Maximianus] expelled the Christians in the army."

137 The joint resignation was on May 1, 305. With Zonaras, *cf.* Symeon, Cedrenus, and Scutariotes (these three translated in n. 147 below), Eutr./Paean. IX.27.1, Theoph. *AM* 5796, p. 10.11–14, Salmasian John *fr.* 251.2 Roberto, p. 432 = *fr.* 167.2 Müller *FHG* IV, p. 602

Diocletian and Maximianus, having been unable to overcome Christianity and having gone mad, resigned the sovereignty. And Diocletian, when he held the first position for twenty years, died. But Maximianus, after he had plotted to assume the sovereignty again and had failed, hanged himself.

Ced. p. 464.14, in contrast to p. 472.1–2, and others, *e.g.* George the Monk p. 477.9–10, perhaps misled by their premature twentieth anniversary celebration or *vicennalia* at Rome (November 20, 303), have Diocletian and Maximianus rule 22 years.

138 With n. 133 above, *cf.* Eutr./Paean. IX.27.2 and Theoph. *AM* 5796, p. 10.14–17. The "triumph" was probably part of the *vicennalia*.

139 Zonaras is fuller than Symeon, Cedrenus, and Scutariotes:

Sym. 86, p. 105: . . . and he carried out a triumph (and it was named "triumph" either because of the so-called rapture [*thriasis*], that is to say, madness, of the poets or because the leaves of the fig are named *thria*. And in the twentieth year of his sovereignty, Diocletian and Maximianus resigned the sovereignty on a single day.

Ced. pp. 470.22–471.3: . . . and he carried out a triumph. And it is named "triumph" from the poems [471] to Dionysus. For they call the madness of the poets rapture (*thriasis*). Or from *thria*, the leaves of the fig being dedicated to Dionysus.

With these, *cf*.:

John of Antioch *fr.* 250 Roberto, p. 430 = *Suda* A 494 (II, p. 729.9–22): "Triumph" is named from the first verses which had been written about Dionysus as he returned from India on a chariot of tigers. For they call the madness of poets *thriasis*. Or from the *thria*, the leaves of the fig dedicated to Dionysus. And because, before masks were devised, they first covered all their faces with fig leaves and jested in iambs. And the soldiers, too, imitating those on stage, covering their faces in fig leaves in the act of ridicule, used to scoff at those participating in triumphs.

Salmasian John, *apparatus* to *fr.* 250 Roberto, p. 430 = *fr.* 167.1 Müller *FHG* IV, p. 602: "Triumph" is named from the first of the verses to Dionysus. For they call the madness of the poets *thriasis*. Or from the *thria*, the leaves of the fig dedicated to Dionysus. For before masks were devised, they covered their faces with fig leaves and jested in iambs. And the soldiers used to do this too, and used to jest at those parading.

Zon. VII.21 (I, pp. 76.19–79.9, trans. E. Cary, *Dio's Roman History*, I, pp. 193–201), from a lost book of Dio, is the most detailed extant description of a triumph.

Two fragments of the Anonymous Continuator of Cassius Dio, both dealing with Diocletian's reign, perhaps reflect the tradition drawn upon by Zonaras.

Fr. 13.5 Müller *FHG* IV, p. 198 = *ES* 185, p. 270: Lucius Octavius, who had been summoned to a dinner from a triumph and called away, responded that he would not attend the banquet unless the finest portions possible were sent to him [*Cf.* Plut. *Quaest. Rom.* 80/*Mor.* 283A and Val. Max. II.8.6].

Fr. 13.6 Müller *FHG* IV, p. 198 = *ES* 186, p. 270: Because some sort of apparition had repeatedly troubled him in his dreams to entrust the realm to precisely whom the apparition signified by name, Diocletian suspected this to be the result of witchcraft, and one day he summoned him and to him alone said, "Take the empire that you seek from me every night and do not begrudge the emperor the nourishment from rest."

140   *Cf. Etymologicum Gudianum* θ p. 265.14 and T, p. 534.45.

141   With Zonaras, *cf.* Ced. p. 470.12–13—"In the 12th year, Maximianus Herculius gained control of Gaul and Britain, Constantius of Alania and Africa."—and Scut. p. 41.8–11—"Therefore, when he had displayed many trophies, Diocletian, after he had been victorious over both the Persians and the remaining races and persuaded them to be peaceful, in the twentieth year, having, with Herculius, resigned the sovereignty, . . ."— *cf.* Eutr./Paean. X.1.1, X.2.3 (with mention of the praetorians), and Theoph. *AM* 5796, p. 11.4–8. Paeanius writes Gallerius but not Maximinus and has Constantius rather than Constans and without Chlorus. The date was October 28, 306. Zos. II.9 gives a far more detailed account of Maxentius' elevation.

142   Zonaras' assessment of Constantius through the end of XII.32 is a sometimes-jumbled conflation and slightly augmented version of Eus. *HE* VIII.13.12–14.9, pp. 776.3–782.7. *Cf.* Symeon on Constantius, n. 151 below. Maximinus is Maximinus Daia though Zonaras, misunderstanding his source, may mean Galerius. In late April 311, Galerius ended his persecution, which Daia renewed by November of the same year.

143   *Cf.* Eus. *HE* VIII.14.2, pp. 778.19–780.3, said there of Maxentius rather than Maximinus Daia. In connection with the persecution by Diocletian and Maximianus, both Symeon and Cedrenus relate the story of Adauctus told at Eus. *HE* VIII.11.1, p. 764:

Sym. 86.4, p. 105: Under Diocletian Adauctus, a teacher, suffered martyrdom. When his wife and two daughters were being sought, having resorted to flight, lest their chastity	Ced. p. 470.6–11: And in the 11th year [*i.e.* 298], when they had roused a horrible persecution against Christians, they made many thousands martyrs. This year was the

be ruined, she threw herself with her daughters in the river. As for them, let one seek if they are reckoned martyrs.	5787th of the universe. And Eusebius says, "Adauctus, a teacher, suffered martyrdom. When his wife and daughters were being sought, lest their chastity be ruined, they threw themselves in the river. Let one seek, then, if they are counted for martyrs."

144   *Cf.* Eus. *HE* VIII.14.8–9, p. 782.1–7, there with reference to Daia's persecution of 311. At this point, Symeon and Cedrenus both mention a magician, Theotecnus (2, *PLRE* I, p. 908), associated at Eus. *HE* IX.2–5, pp. 806–810, with Daia:

Sym. 86.5, p. 105: A certain Theotecnus, a magician, when at Maximianus' suggestion he had fabricated what actually had been done by Pilate to Christ, sent memoirs full of every blasphemy to city and countryside, Maximianus having ordered the teachers of grammar to teach the children this in order that our mystery be mocked.	Ced. p. 471.13–19: In the 18th year of Diocletian [*i.e.* 303], Galerius, persuaded by Theotecnus, a magician, roused a persecution against the Christians. When he had fabricated what had actually been done by Pilate to Christ, this Theotecnus sent memoirs full of every blasphemy to city and countryside, Maximianus having ordered the teachers of grammar to teach the children this in order that our mystery be mocked.

145   Zonaras or his source seems to conflate Eusebius' indictments of Maxentius and Maximinus (Daia) at *HE* VIII.14.1–16, pp. 778.11–786.2. It is unclear whether Zonaras realized that Eusebius' Maximinus was Daia rather than Galerius. *Cf. Exc. Hist. Eccl.*, ed. Cramer II, p. 91.1–7, Theoph. *AM* 5797, p. 12.5–7, and *GVC* 74r-v, pp. 320.14–321.2, trans. L-M, p. 116.

146   Eus. *HE* VIII.14.16–18, p. 786.2–20.

147   *HE* VIII Appendix 3, p. 796.14–16. The date of Diocletian's death is uncertain, through probably 311 or 312 and perhaps precisely on December 3, 311. The same is true of Maximianus', probably between *ca.* July 310 and near the end of 311. *Cf. Exc. Hist. Eccl.*, ed. Cramer II, p. 90.27–30, Theoph. *AM* 5796, p. 11.13–17, and *GVC* 74, p. 319.20–30, trans. L-M, p. 116. *Cf.*:

| Sym. 86.3, p. 105: In the twentieth year of their sovereignty, Diocletian and Maximianus resigned the sovereignty on the same day. Diocletian, on the one hand, lived for twelve years in retirement, and, after his tongue had rotted, with his throat having spouted a mass of worms, expired. On the other hand, Herculius, after he had plotted to regain sovereignty and failed, hanged himself. | Ced. p. 472.1–8: In the 20th year of his sovereignty, Diocletian and Maximianus Herculius out of desperation resigned the sovereignty on the same day, having established in their place as sovereigns of the East, on the one hand, Gallerius Maximianus, the son-in-law of Diocletian, and of the West, on the other, Constantius, the son-in-law of Herculius. And Diocletian, on the one hand, after he had lived in retirement for 12 years, when his tongue had rotted, with his throat, too, having spouted a mass of worms, expired. On the other hand, Herculius, after he had plotted to regain sovereignty and failed, hanged himself. | Scut. p. 41.11–14: . . . both chose a private habit and life, so word reports, through the inability to do away with Christianity which daily was ever advancing, and they ended their lives wretchedly. |

For Cedrenus' first account of Diocletian's death, see above, n. 135.

148   George the Monk p. 481.18–19 = *Suda* Δ 1156 (II, p. 104.17–18) = *EV* 14 (I, p. 146.24–25), says, "And the one [Diocletian] was slain by the senate, the other [Maximianus] hanged himself." The tradition that had the senate kill both Diocletian and Maximianus because they had decided to emerge from retirement may have originated with the *Ecclesiastical History* of Gelasius of Caesarea (*ca*. 395). *Cf*. Gel. *Epit. HE* p. 158.7–8 = Cramer II, p. 91.12–18, Theoph. *AM* 5796, p. 11.17–19 = Gelasius *fr*. 4, pp. 348–349, and *GVC* 74r, p. 320.1–3, trans. L-M, pp. 115–116, the last two explicitly naming Gelasius. Note, too:

John of Antioch *fr.* 251.1 Roberto p. 432 = *Suda* Δ 1156 (II, pp. 104.31–105.2): Diocletian and Maximianus, when they had resigned the sovereignty, lived in retirement. One went to Salona, an Illyrian city, the other to the city of Leucane. And while Maximianus, in longing for rule, became regretful, Diocletian aged in peace for three years, having demonstrated surpassing virtue and not having completely renounced the Hellenic worship.

Salmasian John *fr.* 251.2 Roberto, p. 432 = *fr.* 167.2 Müller *FHG* IV, p. 602: Diocletian and Maximianus, when they had been unable to overcome Christianity and become furious, resigned the sovereignty. And while Diocletian, after he had lived 12 years in retirement first, died, Maximianus, after he had resolved to assume the sovereignty again and failed, hanged himself.

The first passage came to the *Suda* from a now-lost volume of the Constantinian *EH*. Its positive assessment of Diocletian and his faithfulness to "Hellenic worship" suggests Eunapius rather than John of Antioch as its ultimate source. With it, *cf.* Eutr. IX.27–28, Zos. II.8 and II.10.3, and Theoph. *AM* 5796, p. 10.11–14. With the second entry, *cf.* Theoph. *AM* 5796, p. 11.13–17, explicitly citing Eusebius.

149 At Carnuntum in November 308. *Cf.* Eutr./Paean. X.2.3–4.

150 Zonaras' account resembles in many respects Eutr./Paean. X.2.3–3.2, though the latter does not say that Maximianus hanged himself. See too John of Antioch *fr.* 253 Roberto, p. 436 = *fr.* 169 Müller *FHG* IV, pp. 602–603 = *EI* 73, pp. 113.27–114.19, especially 2–19, and Theoph. *AM* 5796, p. 11.4–13. *Cf.* Eus. *HE* VIII.13.5, p. 778.7–9, and VIII Appendix 3, p. 796.15–16.

151 *Cf.* Eus. *HE* VIII.13.12, p. 776.3–7 and VIII Appendices 4–5, pp. 796.19–797.8. Constantius died in York on July 25, 306. Constantine was born in 272 or 273. With Zonaras' assessment of Constantius, *cf.* Sym. 87.2, p. 106:

> Constantius was pious and raised his son Constantine similarly, and in the persecution against us he in nowise participated, but even permitted those under him to practice Christianity without fear and unhindered. After he had designated Constantine Augustus and sovereign in Rome, Maximinus in the East did many terrible things against Christians, likewise, too, Maxentius in Rome.

152   Zonaras, his source, or a careless copyist perhaps has replaced Dalmatius (6, *PLRE* I, pp. 240–241), the eldest of Constantius and Theodora's three sons, with Constantinus. On the other hand, Constantinus may be a doublet of Chlorus' son Julius Constantius (7, *PLRE* I, p. 226). Theoph. *AM* 5796, p. 10.30, says that Hanaballianus was also called Dalmatius.

153   Eus. *HE* VIII.16.2, p. 788.20–22, also speaks of the workings of providence, though with no mention of Constantius' vision. *GVC* p. 312 notes Constantius' disappointment with his sons by Theodora.

154   *Orig. Const.* 2.3, pp. 1.17–2.1, notes the exploit against the Sarmatians.

155   Maximinus = Galerius (*PLRE* I, pp. 574–575, *s.v.* Maximianus 9). Licinius (3, *PLRE* I, p. 509) became Augustus on November 11, 308. Paralleled by Eutr./Paean. X.4.1 and X.5, both using Galerius rather than Maximinus. Licinius did not wed Constantia (1, *PLRE* I, p. 221) until 313. Note that Sym. 86.3, p. 105 (translated below, n. 158), also mistakenly has Galerius select Licinius as his colleague. See, too, Zon. XIII.2, with accompanying n. 8.

156   Unlike Eutr./Paean., Zonaras' chronology and principles are confused. Probably in the first half of 307, Galerius dispatched Fl. Valerius Severus (30, *PLRE* I, pp. 837–838) against Maxentius (5, *PLRE* I, 571), then an Augustus, with the immediate result here described by Zonaras. Severus subsequently withdrew to Ravenna and abdicated. Shortly thereafter, he either was killed or died by his own hand. Galerius died in late April or early May of 311. Licinius, between his elevation and Galerius' death, did campaign with success against the Sarmatians.

157   Licinius' adversary actually was Maximinus Daia (*PLRE* I, 579, *s.v.* Maximinus 12), the Augustus, whose defeat near Heracleia and subsequent death near Tarsus date to 313. *Cf.* Alex. Mon. 4056B-D and Theoph. *AM* 5806–5807, p. 15.4–26. Eutr./Paean. X.4.4 gives the correct antagonists.

158   Closely paralleled by Eus. *HE* VIII.16.2–5. Galerius died in late April or early May 311. *Epit. de Caes.* 40.4 says: "After his genitals had been consumed, Galerius Maximianus died." *Cf.* Sym. 86.3, p. 105— "And Gallerius, when he had become food for worms, having taken

Licinius as a colleague in the sovereignty in the East, expired."—and Ced. p. 472.9—"And Gallerius, when he had become food for worms, expired."

159   Eus. *HE* VIII Appendix 1, p. 796.2–3, mentions Galerius' recovery but not the alleged renewal of persecution. Alex. Mon. 4049D-4053A and Theoph. *AM* 5797, p. 13.9–19, recount Galerius' recovery, his renewal of persecution, and attendant natural disasters.

160   The absence of this excursus on bishops from two thirteenth-century manuscripts of the *Epitome*—*Codd. Regiae* 1714 and 1717 (formerly *Cod. Colberteus*)—has led to the reasonable suspicion that this material is not Zonaras' work.

Whatever the case, the lists for the most part parallel information preserved in Theophanes, including the shared incorrect durations of the tenures of Marcellinus, who was bishop of Rome from June 30, 296 to October 25, 304, and Anastasius, who was bishop of Rome from November 24, 496 to November 22, 498, along with the omission of Acacius, bishop of Antioch from 458–459. Absent from [Zonaras'] lists, but present in Theophanes', are for Rome Silvester's successor Marcus (*AM* 5821, p. 28.21), Liberius' successor Felix (*AM* 5844, p. 41.7), Siricius' successor Anastasius (*AM* 5888, p. 74.25), Boniface's successor John II (*AM* 6025, p. 186.6), and Gregory's predecessor Benedict (*AM* 6062, p. 243.15), with whom Theophanes' list of Bishops of Rome ends; for Antioch absent from [Zonaras] but present in Theophanes are Eustathius' successor Eulalius (*AM* 5825, p. 29.26), Maximus' successor Basil (*AM* 5946, p. 108.1), Stephanus' possible successor Stephanus II (*AM* 5973, p. 128.14), and Severus' successor Paul (*AM* 6012, p.166.16). [Zonaras'] Antiochene bishop Arrianus is an error for Anianus (*AM* 5861, p. 57.23) and the four years assigned by [Zonaras] to Maximus, the nine years to Martyrius, and the ten years to Euphraimius were actually three (*AM* 5942, p. 101.26), thirteen (*AM* 5948, p. 109.16), and eighteen (*AM* 6020, p. 174.8), respectively. Copyists' mistakes can explain all these errors, omissions, and discrepancies. The termination of the Antiochene list with the tenth year of Ephraimius, bishop from 527–545, reflects the disruption caused by the Persian invasion of Syria in 540, on which see G. Greatrex and S. Lieu, *The Roman Eastern Frontier and the Persian Wars. Part II, A.D. 363–630* (Routledge: London and New York, 2002), pp. 102–114.

See *Chronologies of the Ancient World*, pp. 313–343, for lists of bishops and dates of their tenures.

BOOK XIII.1–19

1

[1] Now then, as has been said, thus did Constantine the Great, celebrated among sovereigns and most distinguished among the orthodox, become successor of his father's realm. He was born to his father from the blessed Helen, about whom the writers disagree and are discordant and among them there is no consensus as regards her. For some say that she dwelt with Constans by ordinance of marriage, but was sent away when Maximianus Herculius, as has previously been said, betrothed to him his daughter Theodora and appointed him Caesar. Others have recorded that she was not Constans' legitimate spouse, but a diversion of his erotic desires, and that it was actually from that that Constantine was conceived.[1]

[2] When he had succeeded to his father's realm, he ruled Britain and the Alps, and in addition Gaul, still leaning toward the religion of the Hellenes and opposing the Christians, enticed by his wife Fausta toward ardor in the worship of the idols. Fausta was the daughter of Maximianus. He and his father dwelt with two sisters.[2]

There being three sovereigns, Constantine himself, Licinius, and Maxentius, who was in control in Rome and in Italy, Maxentius behaved not as a sovereign, but as an outright tyrant, inflicting on those whom he tyrannized, as I have already described, a host of horrifying and disgusting things. The people of Rome, unable to endure, dispatched messengers to Constantine, begging that he rid them of Maxentius' tyranny. Thereupon he rose up to depose him, launched a campaign, and advanced toward Rome.[3] Maxentius, for his part, stayed put for a long time within the walls, not taking the field against those besieging him, [3] with the additional result that gibes were made against him by some. After some length of time, he marshaled his forces, after he had employed magical practices, both engaging in divination by means of the dissection of infants and doing other illicit things which instilled dread in Constantine. Then indeed, as he agonized as a result of these things, through a star there appeared to him at midday an image of a cross in heaven and writing about the star in Roman letters, these emblazoned by means of stars and declaring, "Through this conquer!" So then he immediately designed out of gold a cross in accordance with the image that had appeared to him, commanded that this precede his army, and engaged and overwhelmed Maxentius' men, with the result that the greater part of those serving under him were killed and the remainder looked toward flight. Maxentius fled with them and, while he was on the bridge over the Tiber which is called Mulvian, lost his footing and, with his horse, fell into the river and perished. Thus was he destroyed.[4] The Romans, for their part, released from his tyranny, after they had thrown open the gates of [4] Rome, welcomed Constantine magnificently, praised and glorified him as liberator of the city, and voted to raise at public expense a monument to him in the forum of Rome. He ordered that his monument be fashioned grasping the sign of the cross. He also issued directives that those revering Christ as a god not be punished on account of their worship.[5]

When both Italy and Rome herself had been added thus to his realm, he and Licinius, his sister's husband, remained as sovereigns. For Licinius executed both the son and daughter of Maximinus and from that time on each of them suspected the other. For each thought that, with the other removed, he alone would be monarch, there being no one to dispute with him about the empire.[6]

Now some say that Licinius came thus into control of Gallerius' share, having been chosen colleague by him, as has been said. Others say, after the sister of Constantine had been joined by him in marriage to him, that the soldiers, favoring Constantine, proclaimed him Caesar; that he was dispatched by him to array himself against Maximinus; that, after he had been victorious and had routed him, he ceded his realm to him;[7] [5] and that, after he had commanded him not to trouble the Christians, he did not observe his injunctions, however, but raged against the Christians no less than had his predecessors, if not even more. For they say that he surpassed every degree of savagery, and that, in addition to the other causes of the differences between them, there was this, too.[8]

Therefore, when he had mobilized the army against Licinius and had often clashed with him, Constantine was at last victorious. Then he made a truce with him on account of his sister, and did not deprive him of his office, but conceded it to him according to their pacts.[9] Being faithless, he did not maintain the agreements. Hence, Constantine again warred against him and, when victorious, took both Byzantium and Chrysopolis.[10] Licinius, for his part, fled toward Nicomedia and, when Constantine's sister had approached him, she pleaded on her husband's behalf that his office be preserved for him. As she did not bring her brother to agree to this, she introduced the plea about his safety. And she convinced her sibling. Licinius came to him in common dress and was ordered to reside in Thessalonica [6] as a private citizen. There he lived.[11] But the soldiers, for their part, faulted the sparing of Licinius' life because he had often shown himself faithless and a transgressor of pacts. Hence, the decision about this matter was referred to the senate by means of a letter of the sovereign. Now some relate that the senate granted to the soldiers to act with regard to Licinius as seemed fit to them and that they killed him in Thessalonica or near Serrae, as he was trying to escape somewhere. Others say that he was not quiescent while residing in Thessalonica, but was contemplating usurpation. And that, when he found this out, the sovereign Constantine dispatched men to kill him.[12]

It is said that in the battles against him or in those against Maxentius Constantine beheld an armed horseman who was bearing the image of the cross instead of a standard and was advancing before his formation. Again at Adrianople he saw two youths slashing the enemies' ranks. Near Byzantium by night, when all slept, a light was seen by him flashing around the rampart of his [7] army. As a result, then, it began to enter his mind that his success and victories had come to him from a god.[13]

2

When Constantine had thus become sole ruler he was named Flavius (and thus, I suppose, was styled Flavius Constantine), and resided in Rome, not having abandoned the worship of the idols but being initiated into and already accepting Christian teachings.[14] Since he happened to have a body that was diseased and produced many rashes as a result of an unhealthy state of the humors and of corrupt matter, when these were called a contagion by the doctors and likened to leprosy, and their treatment abandoned, he discovered that the priests of Zeus on the Capitoline were saying that he would in no wise effect a cure unless he bathed in the still-steaming blood of young children. Accordingly, from all the territory under him the infants were gathered forthwith and the day of the slaughter was fixed. The sovereign then set off toward the Capitoline in order to bathe in the children's blood. Their [8] mothers, as he proceeded, began to emit mournful cries and to wail. When he heard these, he asked, "What is the cause of the lamentation?" When he learned that the babies' mothers were mourning, just as if he had come to from drunkenness, he said, "The impiety of the deed is manifest; the result, however, unclear. And even if it were beyond doubt, better that I suffer beset with diseases than to decree the destruction of so many infants and skewer their mothers' souls with a scimitar of sorrow." When he had said this, he turned about, after he had commanded that the children be returned to their mothers and that riches be bestowed on them in order that they have equivalent or even double joy because they had recovered their offspring alive and in addition received riches, too, besides.[15]

After he had done this, two men saying they were Peter and Paul the apostles of Christ seemed to be standing beside him by night, and they were saying, "If you wish to gain bodily and spiritual health, summon the bishop Silvester [9] and he will cure for you the corruption of your flesh and will deign to grant you life indestructible." Whereupon, awaking from his sleep, the sovereign sent men to summon the bishop respectfully. When the sacred Silvester had arrived, he said to him, "Tell me, bishop, are gods named Peter and Paul worshipped among you?" He replied, "One God is known to us, and Peter and Paul are his attendants and servants." In turn, then, the sovereign detailed to him the dream, and by him was initiated into our mystery and baptized. He emerged from the all-holy font entirely healthy, and immediately proclaimed amnesty for the Christians, threw open the churches for them, and allowed new ones to be built. Contrariwise, he closed the precincts of the false gods, and decreed that those who wished join the faith of Christ with impunity. For he used to say that he wished no one to be forced, but that he accepted those who were willingly submitting themselves to Christ be received.[16]

Thus, then, he came to the faith of Christ. The gospel was spreading and freedom of speech was being granted to Christians. [10] Then Jews approached the sovereign's mother, saying that the sovereign had been deceived and had confused a deed hateful to God with a deed dear to God, calling the destruction of the idols dear to God, but faith in Christ hateful to God. For they said that the sole true god was the one worshipped by them. The abominable ones disparaged Jesus as a human criminal and a wizard. His mother reported these things to her sovereign and son. He judged it necessary that in his presence and in the presence of the select of the senate the Jews who were saying this debate with the bishop of Rome Silvester and with his adherents, in order that he understand what the allegations from the Jews were. The debate took place. The words of the holy Silvester seemed stronger. The Jews kept saying that Silvester prevailed as a result of his dialectical power, kept seeking a display of signs. Even more, a certain man among them, a wizard named Zambres requested a bull be brought in, saying that through this he was going to reveal the power of his own god. The bull was led forward. Zambres drew near it, whispered something to it in its ear. After it had bellowed out something loud and mournful and had spun about, with a shudder, [11] it collapsed and died.

The Jews began boasting about this, saying that he who heard their god's name could not endure it. "Why then," said Silvester, "does he who is saying this into the animal's ear not hear what is being said? How, then, does he not die, too?" Zambres said, "Now there is no need of twisting and persuasiveness of words, bishop, but of actions." Silvester said, "If then I myself, by the name of Christ, revive this bull that has been killed by you, shall I not seem to do something greater and shall I not demonstrate that the power of Christ is great?" He vowed and forthwith swore by the emperor's health, if he saw the bull recalled to life, to acknowledge Christ as God. Silvester, when he had gazed toward heaven and invoked the Lord, stood near the bull, raised his voice, and cried, "If Christ, whom I preach, is true God, awake, bull, and stand on your feet." Then indeed the bull immediately stirred and sprang up. Those present exclaimed, "Great is Silvester's god." And the Jews, dumbstruck by the marvel, fell at the holy man's feet and implored that God be gracious to them and judge them worthy of divine baptism. The sovereign's celebrated mother, too, being uninitiated, [12] asked to be initiated and baptized.[17] So then, when she had gained her request and recognized the true God, she desired to look upon the places which Christ's beautiful feet had traveled as he preached the gospel of peace. She took with her the marvelous Silvester and arrived in Jerusalem, and she venerated the Lord's tomb, discovered the divine cross to which our God was bodily affixed, and, after she had built many lavish places of worship, returned to her son and sovereign.[18]

From Fausta, the daughter of Maximianus, the sovereign produced three sons—Constantine, Constantius, and Constans—and a daughter Helen, who later married Julian. By a concubine he also had another son, called Crispus, older than his other sons, who distinguished himself often in the war against Licinius.[19] His stepmother [13]

Fausta, being erotically obsessed with him, since she did not find him compliant, denounced him to his father as being in love with her and as having often attempted to use force against her. Hence, Crispus was condemned to death by his father, who had been persuaded by his spouse. When the emperor later realized the truth, he chastened his wife both because of her unchasteness and on account of the murder of his son. For after she had been led into an exceedingly hot bath, there she violently ended her life.[20]

When the Sarmatians and Goths had bestirred themselves against territory of Romans and were plundering the Thracian sector, Constantine the Most Great took the field against them. When he had occupied Thrace, he joined battle with the barbarians and set up a most glorious trophy over them.[21]

3

When, on the basis of a divine oracle, he had resolved to build a city so he might call it after his own name, he first proposed to establish it in Serdica, then in Sigaeum (this is the promontory of the Troad), and there they say he laid foundations. Thereafter, in Chalcedon he began to erect the city. It is said [14] that eagles swooped down and seized the builders' ropes; that, crossing the intervening strait, they threw them down on Byzantium. Then indeed, when this had happened often, it was reported to the sovereign. It did not seem that what had happened had happened by chance, but rather that the divinity was trying to indicate something through it. Then indeed the emperor himself turned his attention to Byzantium, was pleased examining the place, changed his purpose, transferred the workmen there from Chalcedon, lavishly constructed the city, called it Constantinople after his own name, and dedicated it to the Virgin and Mother of God.[22]

With the city already completed, on the eleventh day of the month of May, he celebrated its birthday or dedication, at the beginning of the year 5838.[23] Then, as some have written in their histories, he summoned the astronomer Valens, of those who then occupied themselves in this skill the most precise, and commanded him to cast for the city's birthday [15] a horoscope, in order that he know how many years it was going to endure. He foretold that it would last 696 years, and these already have long since passed. Then either one must in fact suspect Valens' prophecy was false and that his skill failed or one must reckon that he spoke of the years in which the qualities of the constitution were preserved, the status quo and senate honored, its citizens flourished and authority was legitimate, that is, sovereign power, to be sure, but not an outright tyranny, with those in control reckoning public things private and using them for their own pleasures, and some of these not innocent, and making gifts from the treasury to whom they wished, not comporting themselves to their subjects in the fashion of shepherds, shearing the excess of wool and making sparing use of the milk, but in the fashion of brigands, sacrificing the sheep themselves and taking their fill of the meat or sucking out the marrow itself.[24]

Now the city was constructed thus by this pious sovereign on the site of the ancient Byzantium. The city Byzantium, even before this, happened to be neither among the inglorious nor among the obscure, but was flourishing in an abundance of citizens, in wealth [16] and in well-breeding of men and in strength of walls, and so much so that they were besieged by the Romans for three years, under Severus, who had reigned in the old Rome, and withstood much from those besieging them, as has previously been related by me in my treatment of Severus.[25]

Concerning the power of Byzantium and the strength of its walls, Dio says the following in his treatment of Severus:

> Byzantium used to have very mighty walls. For their breastwork was constructed with thick rectangular stones connected with bronze plates, and on the inside they were fortified with earthworks and buildings, with the result that the whole thing seemed to be one thick wall. There were many towers, large and offset, and they had closely spaced openings all around. The landward walls rose to a great height, the seaward ones were less lofty, and the harbors within the wall both were able to be closed by chains, and their breakwaters bore towers which extended far in both directions. There were 500 ships for the Byzantines, [17] most uniremes, and also those which are biremes, and in some of these rudders were fitted from the prow and the stern, and they had two sets of helmsmen and sailors, in order to attack and withdraw without turning about and to frustrate their adversaries both in attack and retreat.

In addition to these things, Dio mentions that seven towers had been situated between the Thracian Gates and the sea. If anyone approached another of these, it was quiet, but if, in fact, he shouted to or even tossed a stone at the first, it emitted a noise from some sort of device and transmitted to the second to do the same, and thus it advanced alike through all, and they did not disquiet one another, but all in turn, each from the one preceding it, took up the cry and wail.[26]

Now such was the ancient city of Byzantium. The celebrated Constantine made it many times larger. [18] Churches were consecrated by him therein and many things were done for its adornment, above all the circular porphyry column, which, the story goes, was conveyed from Rome and set up in the marketplace which was covered with paving stones from which it derived its name "The Plaza." On it he consecrated a bronze cult statue, a marvel to behold on account of its craftsmanship and size. For it was gigantic, and it exhibited the precision of an ancient hand, almost fashioning things actually animant. It is said that the cult statue was a monument of Apollo which had been transferred from the city of Ilium in Phrygia. That most divine emperor erected the statue in his own name, having fastened to its head some of the nails which fastened the body of our Lord to the salvific cross. It stayed standing on the column until our own day. It fell while Alexius Comnenus was reigning, when a powerful and mighty wind blew. It was itself smashed and smashed many of those who happened to be there. He also transferred the Palladium from Troy and erected it in this Plaza marketplace.[27]

[19] Now the great Constantine adorned the city in many other ways and by elevating Byzantium, which previously was a bishopric of Thracian Heracleia, since it had been subjected to Perinthus by Severus after its capture (as is related in my treatment of Severus), to the patriarchal rank, having preserved seniority for the senior Rome on account of its senior birth and on account of his transference of the sovereignty hither from there.[28] Metrophanes the most sacred, who was the son of Dometius, brother of the sovereign Probus, was then bishop of Byzantium. Indeed, it was this Dometius, after he had crossed from faithlessness to faith and had on this account left Rome, who had arrived at Byzantium and was elevated to the summit of the bishopric. After him, another Probus, his son, he whom his brother Metrophanes succeeded, was consecrated for the archpriestly throne.[29]

4

Under this emperor, Arius, a priest of the church of Alexandria, became notorious, having dared to say that the Son of God was a creation, a word, of another essence, and not co-eternal with the

Father, not himself being the originator of this heresy.[30] For first, [20] in addition to many other corrupt opinions, Origen importuned that the only begotten Son of God was a creation, other than his paternal essence, and unable to see his Father, and adduced that the Son himself was invisible to the Spirit, vomiting forth from the vile strongbox of his heart these slanderous things—but they had been set down in letters alone, had been kept secret, and had not yet become public.[31] Arius brought these to prominence, proclaimed them from the rooftops, caused many to stagger toward impiety, and filled the churches full of disturbances and schisms. When the most pious sovereign recognized this, he ordered the bishops of the prefectures to convene in Nicaea of Bithynia and, after there had been gathered 318 of the holy fathers, among whom were some priests, deacons, and moreover, monks, too, and when the great Athanasius, still enrolled in the contingent of deacons, was present there, and the most Christian sovereign himself arrived at Nicaea and, after he had taken a seat with the sacred fathers, left it to them to discuss the matters spoken of by Arius and to investigate if these deviated at all from the orthodox opinion. After they had investigated and done a careful examination, they declared [21] the Son the same essence and co-eternal with the Father, and they also banished from the company of the orthodox Arius and those of the same mind with him.[32]

Of those representing Arius' positions, there was also Eusebius Pamphili, who was bishop of Caesarea in Palestine. He is said to have apostatized subsequently from the opinion of Arius, to have agreed with those who declared the Son co-eternal and of the same essence with the Father, and to have been received by the divine fathers into communion. Now, this is found related by some.[33] But he himself casts these matters in doubt through the things which he is found to have written in his *Ecclesiastical History*. For often in the aforementioned composition he is caught Arianizing, immediately, at just about the beginning of the book—introducing David, who says, "He himself spoke, and they came into being. He himself commanded, and they were created."—, he says that the Father and Maker is to be thought of as supervisory maker, prescribing with a regal nod, and that the Divine Word is a subsidiary of this, performing its paternal injunctions. [22] And a bit later he says that this, as if it exists as the Father's power and wisdom, has been entrusted with the subsidiary affairs of the realm and rule of all things. Again, after a bit, also that there is some sort of pre-cosmic essence, living and subsisting, the thing acting in service to the

Father and God of all things for the purpose of the making of things that come into being, and Solomon says in the persona of God's wisdom, "The Lord created me ruler of his ways," and so forth. After many other things, he says, ". . . in addition to all these, just as God's Word, pre-existing and existing as an essence prior to all ages, having received the very august honor from the Father, to be venerated as a god."[34] These and other things reveal Eusebius in agreement with the Arianizing dogma, unless someone shows that he wrote these things before his reversal. For he is found in the *Acts of the First Synod* championing the right dogma.[35]

Now the holy synod, when it had ordained the "of the same essence" and "co-eternal" about [23] the Son, immediately set out a pledge of the faith, having theologized in it about the Father and the Son as far as ". . . of whose reign there is no end," having made this the end. For the theology about the Holy Spirit thereafter was added in the second synod, which was convened against Macedonius when was an inquiry about this.[36]

The emperor, equal to the apostles, was pleased about the unanimity of the fathers and acknowledged them. Since some bore on their bodies the wounds of their pledge on behalf of the Savior, he kissed their crippled limbs and members and blessed them on account of their disfigurements.[37] When charges had been given to him against some bishops, he neither read these nor brought them to an inquiry, but in front of all reduced them to ashes in a fire, saying, "Even if I had been an eyewitness of some archpriest committing a sin, I would have sheltered him in my purple."[38] When he had transferred those divine fathers thence to the regal city which he had founded, had judged it worthy of their blessing, and had prepared the sacred Alexander to be selected second patriarch therein [24] (for the celebrated Metrophanes had quit his life), he permitted each to depart to his own dwelling place after he had favored them with honors and gifts.[39]

When the sovereign's mother, the blessed Helen, had reached a very old age (for it is said that she lived eighty years), she, whom her son regally interred, departed for the celestial abodes.[40] Campaigning against the Persians, he was conveyed by triremes to Soteropolis, which now is called Pythia. After he had there made use of the hot springs, where it is also said he drank a noxious drug concocted for him by his half-brothers, he arrived at Nicomedia. This is where he died, after being ill a considerable time, at the age of sixty-five and having reigned two months short of thirty-two of these. His son Constantius, when he arrived from Antioch (for he was there

157

fighting against the Persians), found him still alive, tended to him in the fashion befitting his greatness, and lay him in the Church of the Holy Apostles, [25] moreover, in a particular stoa which he himself had constructed for the purpose of his father's burial.[41]

The celebrated emperor is recorded to have expended riches zealously and more zealously to have procured them for himself, so his profligacy with respect to extravagances is not to be condemned, but contrariwise judged magnificence befitting a great man—but let me not say anything mean about that divine man! Hence the accursed Julian, in his discourse *Concerning the Caesars*, jeering just so at this most pious sovereign because of his excessive extravagance, introduces Hermes, who converses with him and asks what is the distinguishing feature of a good sovereign, and him saying in response to the question that the emperor ought to have acquired much and expended much.[42] It is said that he was not unacquainted with words but even to have been no less keen about these than about arms. Therefore, it is said that his tongue was honed for discourse and that there were certain charms in it which enchanted his listeners' ears. It has also been recorded that he despised evil and regularly remarked that it was necessary that the man in control spare nothing at all, [26] not even his own limbs themselves, to ensure the stability of public affairs. Being humanely disposed toward those converting from evil, he used to say that one must amputate the diseased and rotted limb lest it also infect the healthy, not, however, that which already happened to be healthy or was becoming healthy.[43]

5

The thrice-blessed sovereign was transferred to the everlasting abodes. The leadership of the Romans was apportioned among his three sons, as some have related, divided among them by their father, but according to others, when they distributed it among themselves after their father's demise. The division among them is recorded to have proceeded thus: to Constans was allotted Italy, Rome herself, both Africa and Sicily, the rest of the islands, but moreover Illyricum, Macedonia, and, with Greece, the Peloponnese; to Constantine were distributed the Cottian [27] Alps, together with Gaul (the Cottians were named from Cottius, who had been sovereign of these places), and the Pyrenean incline as far as the Moors, who have been separated by the ocean's strait; Constantius' share was as much as was subject to Romans in the eastern portion and, in addition to this, Thrace, together with the city of his father.[44]

When the apportionment of the empire had proceeded in this fashion, Constantius departed for the East, marching against the Persians. For after Sapor, their leader, had learned of the death of the great Constantine, he incessantly attacked and plundered those paying taxes under the Romans.[45] Constantine, faulting the division of the territories and either demanding that he concede parts of the empire to him or seeking that both redistribute their realms, kept pestering Constans. Because he adhered to the existing distribution of the empire, was clinging to what had been allotted to him, and was not the least bit accommodating to his brother, Constantine took up arms against him and invaded Constans' share. He was abroad in Dacia and, when he learned of Constantine's action, [28] he dispatched against him an army and generals, having himself promised to attack almost immediately with a larger army. Then indeed, when those who had been dispatched had come near Constantine, they set ambuscades and, after they had joined in battle with him, pretended to flee. When Constantine's men pursued them, the men placed in ambush, who were now in their rear, set upon them from behind and, after those in flight had turned about, trapped them in between. Much of Constantine's army and he, too, were destroyed. For when his horse had been wounded and, as a result of the wound, had thrashed about and bucked, Constantine fell from his seat and was killed after he had received many wounds, having failed to attain his desire and forfeited his life itself besides, and because he had been the instigator of injustices, also having lost his portion of the empire. Control of the western portion, too, came under one sovereign, Constans.[46] Then, after he had plunged into depraved loves and a perverted mode of life, he was plotted against and wretchedly destroyed by Magnentius—Magnentius, whom he had saved when he was in jeopardy stemming from a military disturbance, his soldiers [29] having already drawn their swords and having rushed forward to slay him.[47]

Constantius, staying in the East, was battling the Persians, Sapor, as has been said, being sovereign of the race. He was a son of Narses, however, not from a noteworthy wife. For from the foremost of his wives three sons were born to Narses, Adarnarses, Hormisdas, and a third one. After Narses died, the eldest of these three, Adarnarses was the heir of his empire. Since he happened to be inordinately cruel and hard and, as a result, was hated by the Persians, he was deposed from his sovereignty.[48]

Let there be told, too, a typical example of his proverbial cruelty. Once a tent very ornately fashioned for his father from indigenous hides was brought from Babylon. As soon as he saw it unfolded, Narses asked Adarnarses, who was still a boy, if the tent satisfied him. He replied that, if he gained control of the realm, he would make one better than this from hides of humans. Thus, from childhood he exhibited his cruelty.[49]

[30] So then, after he had been deposed from his sovereignty in this fashion, Sapor, in turn, entered into the office. Forthwith he blinded the one of his brothers, but arrested Hormisdas and kept him under guard. The latter's mother and his wife bribed the guards with money and were permitted to visit him. After they had entered, they furnished him with a file, in order to cut through his iron chains with it, and they also set forth what he must do after this, having readied for him horses and men who would accompany him in his flight. Then his consort served a lavish dinner to the guards. When they had taken their fill of food and had quaffed wine stronger-than-strong, they were seized by a heavy sleep. While they slept, Hormisdas cut through the chains with his file, escaped from the prison, got away, ran off to the Romans, and was most honorably received. Sapor seemed pleased at his flight, since he no longer had anything to fear on his account. For not only did he not seek that the fugitive be returned to him, but he also honorably dispatched his wife to him. Hormisdas was very strong and expert with the javelin, so much that, [31] while aiming a javelin at someone, he could predict where it would strike the enemy.[50] So then, when he had been appointed to command a large detachment of cavalry, he campaigned with Constantius against his countrymen. The sovereign Constantius, having often attacked the Persians, came up short and lost many of his own men. Of the Persians, very many fell and Sapor himself was wounded.[51]

6

Now then, when the wars against the Persians had ended thus for the sovereign Constantius, Magnentius, who had been born from a British father and then was serving in the *protectores* and was named *comes* of two Roman units, learned this and, lately desiring to usurp power, then applied himself more to his objective, because he heard that Constantius was experiencing ill-fortune against the Persians and because he judged that time a suitable opportunity for attempting usurpation. After he had pretended to celebrate his birthday ceremonies in the city Augustulum, he called together the leading men of the city to participate in his symposium, some [32] who knew along with him of the plan and others who had no part of his scheme. He extended the drinking until evening. After he had risen suddenly from the symposium, he ran into his bedroom and emerged from it after a brief moment in a sovereign's attire with many guardsmen, which threw into confusion those who did not share with him knowledge of the business. After he had addressed those present, he convinced some to join him, but others, indeed, he also compelled. He took them with him, set out immediately for the palace, made distributions of money and set guards for the gates of the city with instructions to admit those entering but to permit no one to exit, lest the enterprise be proclaimed too soon.[52] He immediately sent men to kill Constans before he learned of the enterprise. He was occupied with a hunt. For he was mad about the chase though fighting constant arthritis, which he suffered as a result of an excess of pleasures, living intemperately. On the pretext of a hunt he was even accustomed to go deep into the woods with the boys and young men who accompanied him, who were collected and brought into proximity with him on account of their beauty, were made up with special care and were a hotbed of licentiousness for lustful eyes, and were for him, so it is said, catamites. [33] At least he used to pass an excessive amount of time in the woods, shunning intercourse with decent men.[53] So then, by the Rhone River men who had been dispatched by Magnentius murdered Constans, who was sleeping after the hunt, and also killed some of the few who were with him. Some say that his death did not happen in this fashion, but that, after he had learned of the rebellion against him and had been abandoned, since those about him had deserted him, he fled to a shrine. And they say that there he stripped off the regalia of his sovereignty and, after he had been expelled from there, was killed, having completed his seventeenth year in office and already having passed thirty years of age. It is said that at the moment he was born his father had entrusted astrologers to cast a horoscope about his birth, and that they, in addition to other things which they predicted about him, said this, too, that he would be killed in the embrace of his grandmother.[54] When she died, Constans made fun of this. But the matter proved in actuality to be so and the prediction of the astrologers did not miss the mark, even if it was oblique. For it was in a small hamlet [34] called Helena after the name of that empress that Constans was killed.[55]

After he had lived so licentiously, thus was he piteously deprived of life. While his attempt at usurpation was flowing smoothly for him, Magnentius was eager that the most notable of those who held offices be put out of the way. [56] He fabricated letters sent to them as if from Constans, supposedly summoning them to him, lay in wait along their route, and killed most of them, sparing not even his own conspirators, but destroying them, too.

Such were the things in which he was involved, strengthening the usurpation for himself. For Constantius, when he had learned of his brother's death, was of two minds, as he considered whether to opt for resistance to the Persians, who were ravaging places subject to Romans, or, at least for the present, to ignore them and move against the usurper in order to avenge the murder of his kinsman and gain the West for himself. [35]

7

While Constantius was contemplating these things and continuing to vacillate, Sapor, to whom what had come to pass for Constans also had become known, used the opportunity and, with a weighty army attacked both the territories and cities subject to Romans. [57] He plundered much territory, but, moreover, captured garrisons and ultimately besieged Nisibis, which of old belonged to the realm of the Armenians, but which under Mithridates, who was a relative-by-marriage of Tigranes, then ruler of Armenia, and had received the city from him, was taken by Romans in a siege. [58] For after he arrived there Sapor enlisted every device to take the city for himself. For he set rams to the walls and made underground passages, but all these the besieged nobly resisted. He diverted the river which flows through the middle of the city, in order that, oppressed by thirst, the city's inhabitants might betray the city to him. But there was an abundance of water for them from wells and springs. [59] Since his plans produced nothing efficacious for him, he devised an alternative. [36] Returning up the river, which, as has been said, flowed through the city, and having come to ravines where the terrain through which it flowed narrowed, he dammed the spot and checked its flow. After the water had backed up, he all at once removed the material which was blocking the water's passage and unleashed the flood against the city. Since the water had risen to such a great depth and had struck the wall with extreme force, it collapsed part of it. The barbarian did not immediately enter the city, but, as if it had already been captured and because the time was approaching evening, delayed taking possession of the city until morning so as not to meet any resistance. The people in the city were in turmoil on account of the breaching of the wall, but, since they saw the Persians delaying their entry, they passed the night without sleep and, with much effort, fortified the spot, having raised another wall within. When Sapor saw this at dawn, he attributed the setback to his own carelessness. But not even under these circumstances did he abandon the siege. After he had devised many things against the city and had thrown away most of his own men (for it is said that over 20,000 of the Persian army were imperiled while Nisibis was under siege), he withdrew in disgrace. For already [37] the Massagetae had attacked Persia and were inflicting indignities on her.[60] Constantius the sovereign secured Nisibis and reinstated her citizens, and he himself, since, at the Persians' initiative, there already was a truce in the East, hastened toward the West.[61] It was reported to him that Vetranio had acted in common with Magnentius. For this man, when he happened to be commander of the troops in Illyricum and had learned of Magnentius' rebellion and the murder of Constans, did not yield to the usurper, but he too, for his part, had attempted usurpation. He wrote a letter to Constantius saying that he was resisting the usurper and urging him to press on toward his destruction. Then Vetranio and Magnentius, who had concluded a truce with one another under specified conditions, both in common sent ambassadors to Constantius, demanding that he lay down his arms and retain the first rank. Then indeed, the ambassadors, meeting the emperor near Heracleia of Thrace, delivered their messages to him. As a result, he became worried and, when it was night, he saw a dream of the following sort. It seemed that his father [38] was standing next to him, holding his son Constans firmly by the hand and saying to him, "Constantius, behold Constans, your brother, kinsman of many sovereigns, who was destroyed by a usurper. You must avenge him, you must not overlook the empire being sundered or the state being overturned, you must hasten to quash the usurpation, and not leave your brother with justice undone." After this, when Constantius awoke, he took the ambassadors into custody and sent them to jail.[62] Straightway, with no hesitation, he arrived at Serdica. Vetranio cowered at Constantius' unexpected arrival and received him as one receives a master, having both abandoned his formed plans and jettisoned his agreements with Magnentius. Constantius accepted him warmly and made him a companion at his table. For, after he had stripped off the marks of sovereignty, Vetranio, in the garb of a commoner, embraced the sovereign's feet. And he embraced Vetranio, called him "father," and, offering his hand to him and supporting him, since he was elderly, made him his dinner companion. [39] Then Prusa (this is a city in Bithynia) was assigned to him for a residence and the countryside allotted to him for supplying of provisions. Living there in luxury for about six years, he measured out his life.[63]

8

When matters with regard to Vetranio had reached such an end, emperor Constantius hastened against Magnentius. He was staying in Mediolanum, having proclaimed his brother Decentius Caesar and having dispatched him to guard Gaul. While this was happening, Sapor, in turn, since he was free of fear, despoiled the eastern regions and, after he had taken booty and many captives, returned home. Then the sovereign, encircled on all sides by the concerns of war, honored his cousin Gallus with the rank of Caesar and, after he had wed to him his own sister Constantia, sent him to the East to check the Persian inroads.[64]

Now Gallus, when he had been appointed in this fashion, departed to the East, taking his wife, too. Constantius, for his part, [40] departed for the war against Magnentius. In order that the Romans not defile one another in internecine battles and mutual slaughters, he judged it necessary to summon the usurper to negotiations. So then he sent to him men of the notables and inscribed a letter to him, granting pardon for the undertaking, if he should abstain from arms, and conceding Gaul to him, in order that he rule this and be bounded by it. But he, having nothing moderate in mind, did not accept what had been offered to him without trouble by Constantius, but chose war.[65] Moreover, he advanced toward this with haste, because Silvanus, one of his unit commanders, along with a multitude of infantry, had deserted him and surrendered to Constantius, the emperor. When they had already drawn near and encamped opposite one another, Constantius aroused his own soldiers to valor in speeches and Magnentius implored his men to show themselves loyal and good, promising them many things. When they had deployed themselves opposite one another, they spent most of the day inactive, since no one advanced upon the opposing formation.[66] Magnentius also employed enchantments. For a certain female magician advised him to slaughter a maiden [41], to mix her blood with wine, and to give it to the soldiers to taste of, while she, in addition to this, recited some spells and invoked the aid of demons.[67] Just when the day had almost passed, the armies engaged one another and, after the battle had many reversals, in the end victory smiled on Constantius, and until deep into the night Magnentius' men were being cut to pieces and destroyed. Since the upshot of the war had turned out thus for the usurper, he looked to flight. Lest he be conspicuous fleeing in the imperial regalia, he set these aside and donned common dress, and, after he had put the regalia on the royal horse, released it to run free, in order that it be reckoned by those who saw the horse running riderless that he had been killed and that he not be closely pursued by anyone. Now thus he escaped. But at dawn Constantius ascended a hill, and viewing the adjacent plain—but, moreover, the river flowing beside it, too—filled with corpses, openly shed tears, not so much pleased on account of his victory as much as stung by the destruction of those who had fallen. For it is said that from [42] his men, who numbered altogether about 80,000, about 30,000 fell, and from those of Magnentius, who were 36,000, 24,000 were destroyed. So then he immediately ordered that all the dead among the fallen have the honor of burial, his own men or the enemy not being distinguished, and that those still breathing receive care and medical treatment.[68]

After he had escaped, as has been said, Magnentius both gathered from his own men those who had survived and summoned others, and was trying to compose himself. He sent a man of senatorial rank to Constantius to negotiate, who, suspecting that he was going to spy under the guise of an embassy and meddle with his affairs, restricted his movements. Magnentius then used bishops for a delegation, seeking to be pardoned in order that he serve with the sovereign in a soldier's role. But Constantius made no reply to this delegation and dismissed the ambassadors to depart with nothing accomplished. After he had put his army in motion, he set off, [43] and many of those under Magnentius went over to him, putting into his hands both themselves and their bases. Since he despaired of gaining pardon, Magnentius prepared for war and, remaining in Gaul, gathered great numbers.[69] In order to throw the emperor into worry and to divert him from himself toward other things, he sent one of those close to him to Antioch for the purpose of killing Gallus. The man who had been sent, in order to avoid suspicion, lodged in an old woman's hut, which had been built by the Orontes River (which earlier was called Ophites, as some relate, then was dubbed Orontes, since the son of the Persians' king Cambyses, who was called Orontes, had fallen into it). Then indeed, when, sent by Magnentius, he had already organized the plot against Gallus and had won over many of the infantry there, while dining one evening with some of his conspirators in the old woman's hut, he began discussing rather freely with them the things which they were planning, giving little thought of the old woman on the grounds that, on account of her old age, she was uninvolved and did not even comprehend what was being said. She, so it seems, happening to be of a rather clever nature, [44] appeared to hear none of what was being said, but to herself carefully noted everything. When her guest, who had become drunk, dozed off, she secretly left the house, came to the city, and reported everything to the Caesar. Men dispatched by him arrested the plotter against him, who, under compulsion, disclosed the whole affair. Thus did Gallus escape the plot, having punished the plotter and those conspiring with him.[70]

9

After these affairs had ended thus, Magnentius again readied for battle and, when he had engaged Constantius' men, was beaten and fled. Then indeed, the soldiers who had fled with him, since they saw no hope of salvation left for them from any quarter and judging it pointless to risk danger on behalf of a desperate man, planned to surrender him to the emperor. They surrounded his dwelling, where he was lying, and, in the fashion of guards, kept watch on him, lest he escape them unseen. When Magnentius realized their intent and that he had been caught in a place from which there was no escape, he performed, so the story goes, the deed of a madman, having killed all those with him, both kinsmen and friends, and then having struck Desiderius, [45] his brother, many blows with a sword (however, not one of these was fatal). After he had done this, he killed himself, lest he be surrendered to Constantius the emperor by those who had guarded him and endure a more protracted punishment. His brother Decentius, whom he had chosen Caesar, being in Gaul and preparing to come to his brother as an ally, fell into despair when he learned of his destruction and used the noose. After he had received blows from Magnentius, his sibling Desiderius, when he had eluded death and recovered from the blows, willingly went over to Constantius. When Magnentius' usurpation had been so dissolved, as much as he controlled also became subject to Constantius and he became the only one in control of his father's entire realm.[71]

Now the West subsequently maintained peace, but the affairs of the East were in turmoil. For Gallus, buoyed by his good fortune, after his arrival in Antioch behaved brutally to those under him, wronged in multiform fashion by him, while his consort, too, urged him on.[72] As a result, Constantius, alarmed [46] lest those being wronged by him be stirred to rebellion and there be need of a civil war for him, selected Domitianus, a man both distinguished and senior, prefect of the praetorians, and, after he had enjoined him in secret to ingratiate himself somehow to Gallus and to convince him to come to him, dispatched him to Antioch. After he had arrived in Antioch, he handled the matter very unskillfully, having openly ordered the Caesar to proceed to the emperor and threatened to withhold the grain allowances to those under him if he did not obey. Provoked to anger by these things and being in general easily moved to rage, he put the prefect under restrictions and assigned soldiers to him as guards. When Montius the *quaestor* objected to the action and said that this was tantamount to outright usurpation, the Caesar was further enraged—but also being incited to anger by his wife on the grounds that he was being treated with contempt —, put the *quaestor* himself in chains and also turned the pair over to the soldiers. They bound both men together, dragged them through the marketplace, tortured them, and, in the end, tossed them in the river and destroyed them.[73]

When Constantius had learned of these things, he dispatched men to bring [47] Gallus to him. But he sent his wife ahead for the purpose of propitiating her brother, yet while she was en route the end of life came upon her as the result of an illness. Then, after Constantius had learned of his sister's death, sending orders, he immediately stripped Gallus of his rank and exiled him. Then, when he had been urged to do so by his retinue, he also sent men to kill him. Then he changed his mind and sent others to prevent the execution. Those who hated Gallus, especially the eunuch Eusebius, who occupied the office of *praepositus* and was very influential with Constantius, convinced them not to announce the imperial change of mind to those who had been commanded to execute Gallus until they knew the man had been killed.

He, then, was killed.[74] Since the barbarians beyond the Rhine were threatening Gaul, to check their raids he dispatched Silvanus, a man who was a most able commander and outstanding with regard to matters of war. The sovereign believed slanders against him (for he had ears attentive to slanders) and began contemplating terrible things against the man. When he learned of this, he turned to rebellion and dressed himself in the attire [48] of a Caesar. He did not indulge in rebellion for long. For Ursicinus was sent there, corrupted some of his soldiers with wealth, and through them killed Silvanus and quashed the rebellion.[75]

Now then, ambassadors from Persia who had been sent by Sapor, who was demanding that Mesopotamia and Armenia be ceded to

Persia in order that the Persians thus cease hostilities against the Romans, met with Constantius near Sirmium as he was moving from the West and returning to Byzantium. For from the remote days of their ancestors these territories had belonged to them. If he did not agree, he made it clear to the emperor that the pursuit of the discussion would be made under Ares as adjudicator. To this, Constantius responded to him that he was amazed that, if he had forgotten, Persians were slaves to the Macedonians and that, since Macedonians were subordinate to Romans, those who were slaves to them were also subjects to Romans. Sapor was enraged by this and looked toward war. Again he settled himself down to a siege of Nisibis. Since he was making no headway against it, he withdrew and made trial of other places. Because he was repulsed from these, too, he arrived at Amida and captured it.[76] [49]

10

Constantius, unable to administer the whole empire alone, it being of such size as to stretch almost from one end of the earth to the other, summoned from Athens Gallus' sibling Julian, pronounced him Caesar, and gave to him in marriage his own sister Helen. It is said that a dream came to his mother while she was carrying him and that she seemed to give birth to Achilles. When she had awaked and described the dream to her husband, she gave birth to him, feeling almost no pain while she was in labor and giving birth almost before she realized she was about to give birth. Then, since they had great hopes for him, his parents entrusted him to Eusebius of Nicomedia in order that he be initiated by him into the divine scripture.[77] Having proclaimed him Caesar, the emperor Constantius dispatched him to Gaul with very few soldiers, so there was suspicion that Constantius had not chosen Julian as a colleague of his office, but that, as a pretense for [50] plotting against him, had clad him in the regalia of the Caesar, in order that he be destroyed by the enemy, not having a force sufficient for the war against them.[78] When he had departed and experienced good fortune, he met the enemy and unexpectedly was victorious. Again, after the enemy had recovered themselves, he engaged them and, after many had been killed, many destroyed in the river flowing adjacent, and no fewer captured alive, erected a victory monument. They say that, when the enemy had been beaten, 11,000 Roman prisoners were then released from the bonds of captivity. He then warred against the Alamanni, experienced good fortune against them, and, after they had implored him, made peace with the people, who had freed from slavery the Romans among them who had been taken in war.[79]

Then the Caesar Julian, having become conceited and haughty because of these successes, and, as some have recorded, also because he feared Constantius, who was envious of him due to his successes, lest, as he had done with his brother Gallus, he surreptitiously deprive him, too, of life, contemplated rebellion [51] and, when he had won over some of the unit commanders under him, through them he incited the army, and it united and acclaimed him Augustus. Then, drawing their swords and pressing about him, since he pretended he was not going to accept their acclamation, they began to threaten to kill him if he did not comply. Thus, perhaps actually against his will, he yielded to the impetus of the soldierly multitude and accepted the office. When a diadem was sought in order that he be immediately crowned with it, he swore he did not have one. When some began searching for some women's jewelry in order that a diadem be fashioned from it, Julian prevented this on the grounds that it was an unpropitious omen. Since one of the unit commanders was wearing a golden torque which held stones set in gold, they took this and fit it to his head.[80] He dispatched Pentadius, *magister* of the imperial units, with others to Constantius, and wrote him, defending himself on the grounds that he was brought forward against his will to the proclamation of sovereignty and had been forced by the soldiers, who were not willing to campaign under a Caesar but under a sovereign [52] and in order that they be able to demand from him recompense worthy of their labors, asking that the collegiality of the office be accepted for the benefit it would be to the state, and also promising to send to him the racehorses from Spain, as was customary, and the picked men from Gaul. When he had written these things in the letter, in the signature he did not style himself sovereign, but Caesar, lest Constantius take offense at the signature and dismiss the letter.[81] When this had been delivered to the sovereign Constantius, who was staying at Caesarea in Cappadocia, out of anger he made no response. But he announced to the soldiers the campaign against the Persians and he sent Leonas the *quaestor* to Julian, having written a letter to him and faulting him because he had not awaited his judgment, attributing to his outrageous behavior rather than to his own the fact that he had received the title of Augustus not by the judgment of the holder or authority but at the hands of a disorderly mob of soldiers, and advising him to distance himself [53] from what had improperly occurred and to return to his earlier rank, which he had received from him. Now then, he entrusted the *quaestor* to remove from authority those who were obtaining offices there and to appoint to office both the prefect of the praetorians himself and others whom he had named for each position.[82] Therefore, the *quaestor* departed to Julian and reported Constantius' words to him. They were: "You must keep in mind how indebted you are to me, not only because I proclaimed you Caesar, but also because, when you became an orphan at a young age, I raised you, taking charge myself." But he interrupted and said to the *quaestor*, "My good fellow, who imposed orphanhood on me at such an age? Or was it not, in point of fact, my parents' murderer? Does he not see, then, that reminding me of these things, he is scratching the wound and making it worse?" When he had come to the note to him, Julian, in reference to the advice of setting aside the imperial dress and reassuming the rank of a Caesar, said to the *quaestor*, "I shall do this, but at the behest of the armies." For his part, the *quaestor* was terrified, since, if Julian revealed this to the soldiers, being present, [54] he would be ripped apart by them on the spot, and begged him not to share any of these things with the military mob. Now then, having abandoned hope that he would be able to accomplish any of the things assigned to him, he returned with a letter of the usurper which openly reviled the emperor, reproached him as having committed the greatest wrongs against his kin, and threatened that he would become an avenger of those who had unjustly suffered.[83]

11

He departed for Constantius. The usurper, knowing that many among those close to him sympathized with Constantius, expelled them all from there and began readying himself for civil war. At this time, his wife died, as some say, giving birth to a child by him, as others say, after she had been cast out.[84] He assembled the soldiers, provoked them to the civil war, and advised that it was necessary that they move against Constantius and not wait for him to come against them.[85] He already had disowned the Christian faith and, on account of this, was wary of the soldiers, knowing that almost all were Christians. Hence, shadowing his own baseness, he ordered each to worship as he wished. He himself, when the day of our Savior's birthday celebration [55] had arrived, entered the church and, after he had knelt in order to seem to the soldiers to be of the same belief, departed.[86] He also appointed to offices those whom he wished, and thus advanced toward civil war. He kept saying that he was not moving against Constantius, but that he wished to bring together as one the Eastern and Western armies, in order that, when they were together, they select the one who would be their sovereign.[87] He also was boasting that he had foreknowledge of the day on which Constantius would die, having been shown it in a dream through verses which declared the following:

> When Zeus the broad boundary of the Water-Pourer
>   renowned doth reach,
> And Cronos upon the Virgin's twenty-fifth degree doth
>   tread,
> Sovereign Constantius of Asia's land, of his dear life,
> Will a baneful, biting boundary hold.[88]

And Constantius died when he had abandoned Persian matters (since their sovereign had returned home) and was moving against the usurper. For he was burdened by many cares and, consequently, [56] after he had been overcome by a constant fever and had vomited up black bile, he died in Mopsucrene (this is situated along the foothills of the Taurus), having, so it is said, faulted himself for three things: the murder of his kinsmen (for he killed not only Gallus, as has already been stated, but also the brothers of his own father); the elevation of Julian; and innovation of the faith.[89]

This emperor was kindly disposed to his subjects, aligned with justness with regard to his verdicts, controlled with regard to his regimen, aiming at propriety in the disposition of positions of leadership and honors, appointing no one to the senate who did not have a share of culture or who was not trained in speaking and who knew how to write both in verse and in prose.[90] But with regard to the faith, he was not pure. For he did not keep in line with the piety of his father, but sided with those who Arianized through the eagerness of Eusebius, foremost of the royal eunuchs.[91] As a result, he compelled the divine Alexander, who had, after the divine Metrophanes, been chosen patriarch of the New Rome, to receive Arius in communion, but he did not assent. Hence, the sovereign commanded that a synod be organized. Then a day for the synod was marked out. [57] On that evening, Alexander went to the sanctuary, threw himself face down, begged God not to allow the wolf, that is to say Arius, to enter among his flock, and said "or release me first from my life!" With tears he passionately entreated this. Then, at dawn, just as the synod was being convened, Arius set out with high hopes. As he went, he felt an urge in his belly to empty his bowels and bladder. He turned from the road and sat down to void the waste. There also streamed out with the excrement the innards of the wretch, who brought his life to a violent end.[92]

Now then, after the patriarch Alexander had served as archpriest for twenty-three years, he departed life and Paul the Confessor was introduced by the orthodox in his stead to the throne of Constantinople. When Constantius had returned from Antioch, he removed him from the throne and set in his place Eusebius of Nicomedia, who happened to be a partisan of Arius. Blessed Paul had gone to Julius, Pope of Rome, and, after he had been established by him on the throne of Constantinople, was persecuted again by Constantius, and, sent into exile, [58] was killed by the Arians.[93] When Eusebius died, there was elevated by the Arians to the throne of the New Rome Macedonius, who became haughty and transferred the most sacred body of the sainted Constantine from the Church of the Holy Apostles to the divine precinct of the sainted martyr Acacius. As a result, Constantius became enraged, returned to the city of his father, and deposed from the throne and exiled Macedonius the Spirit-fighter, who had served one year, and placed on it Eudoxius, who, representing Arius' faction, served ten years as archpriest. He again transferred his own father's body to the Church of the Holy Apostles.[94]

Then, to be sure, with the help of Artemius, the *dux* of Alexandria and later also a triumphant martyr, Constantius brought back to the city of his father the most sacred bodies of the holy apostles Andrew and Luke and deposited them inside of the altar of the Church of the Holy Apostles.[95]

His wife was Eusebia, who was renowned for her beauty. But she was unlucky in her spouse, who was impotent and, [59] from both sickness and nature, very languid in matters aphrodisiac. For this reason, gradually wasting away, she predeceased Constantius, having remained childless through life. As some say, also having succumbed to hysteria, she died. It is said that Constantius was expert at horsemanship and the javelin, and was acquainted with literature to the degree that he was able to compose verse.[96]

12

After Constantius' death had been announced to Julian, the army acclaimed him Augustus and, having removed the imperial and donned mourning garb, he looked downcast. According to custom, he performed public mourning for the deceased sovereign.[97] He then hurried to Byzantium. The senate and people met him and, to the accompaniment of propitious cheers, he advanced toward the palace and took in hand the management of affairs of state. The army which had been with him and its commanders conveyed Constantius' body to Constantinople on a carriage. Julian met and accompanied it, having removed the diadem from his head. The corpse [60] of the deceased emperor was laid to rest in the Church of the Holy Apostles.[98]

Julian executed many of those connected with the palace, and others he exiled and deprived of their possessions.[99] To the rest of the administrative duties of sovereignty, he added adjudication. Then indeed, once while hearing the case of a man who had been accused of having stolen public funds and who was denying the theft, when the prosecutor said, "Who, O sovereign, will pay the penalty for his crime, if those prosecuted benefit from denial?", he replied, "And who will be acquitted, if prosecutors without proofs are believed?" He also negotiated with embassies which had been sent from various peoples to Constantius. The armies he inspected and reviewed, and the majority of the palace staff he dismissed. He asked for a barber and, when Constantius' barber approached him attired very lavishly, he said he was looking for a barber, not a senator, and dismissed him. Also, when he noticed one of the palace cooks in garb more resplendent than his station, he sent for his own cook, who was dressed like a cook, and asked those present which of them they thought to be a cook. When they [61] said the one attired inexpensively, he excused the other. He was doing these things pursuing esteem as a result of seeming to be without affectation and a genuine philosopher. After he had distributed money to the soldiers, he began to prepare for the war against the Persians.[100]

When he had become emperor and had gained control of the empire for himself, he immediately broke forth into manifest Hellenism. For, as has been stated, although he had earlier forsworn Christians' things, he did not allow the birth pang of impiety to burst into the open. For it is said that, while he was nurturing a desire of sovereignty and hiding this in his soul as under a heap of ashes, he approached seers and sorcerers, inquiring whether he would gain power, and by them he was corrupted and diverted to Hellenism.[101] After he had gained power, by the inaccessible decrees of God, he produced many martyrs. For he so raged against Christians that he even prevented them from partaking of Hellenic teachings, saying that those who styled these things myths and traduced them must not enjoy the benefit of their assistance nor be armed by them against them. Wherefore, since the children of Christians were being made to abandon the poets, Apolinarius [62] is said to have hastened to his paraphrase of the Psalter, and Gregory, great in theology, to the composition of verses, in order that, studying these instead of Hellenic teachings, the young be Hellenized in their speech and be instructed in metrics.[102]

He also permitted the Jews to rebuild the temple in Jerusalem. When, with much zeal and great expenditures, they had begun the construction and were endeavoring to dig the earth for the setting of foundations, it is said that fire suddenly burst forth from the trenches and consumed the diggers, so they were compelled to abandon the construction.[103] He killed Eusebius the eunuch, who was made away with on the grounds that he was the murderer of his brother Gallus, and all the other eunuchs he expelled from the palace.[104] Once, when the transgressor was passing by Chalcedon, the bishop Maris began calling him "Avenging Spirit" and "Christ-denier." He feigned patience and said, "Be off, wretch, [63] and bewail the blindness of your eyes." (For he was suffering from a cataract.) He retorted, "I give thanks to my savior Christ because he made provision that I not see your shameless and most impious face!"[105]

He set his army in motion against the Persians and arrived at Tarsus, a famous city of Cilicia. When he had arrived there, Artemius, the priest of Asclepius, approached him—for in Aegae (this, too, a city of Cilicia) there was a renowned temple of Asclepius—and requested that he restore again to the temple of Asclepius the columns which the archpriest of the people of the Christians had removed and upon which he had built his church. The transgressor straightway commanded that this be done at the bishop's expense. Then the Hellenes, when they, with much labor and with the greatest cost, had barely taken down one of the columns and moved it with machines as far as the threshold of the door of the church, even after a great length of time were unable to get it outside. They abandoned it and departed. And after Julian had died, the bishop easily righted it again and returned it to its spot.[106]

[64] When Julian had arrived in Antioch and began constantly visiting the district of Daphne, in which was located a cult statue of Apollo, a work marvelous for its artistry, the Antiochenes jeered at him and began saying that a sacrificer, not an emperor, was in residence among them. Because he had grown his beard long, they dubbed him "Billy Goat" and the same people began saying that he was ideal for the braiding of ropes. In return, he ridiculed them for their laziness, softness, and effeminacy, and said that he would not offer his beard

to the Antiochenes for the braiding of ropes, lest their hands become worn by its roughness. To them he also wrote a speech, which is titled "Antiochene" or "Beard-hater."[107] He burnt entire hecatombs to Daphnian Apollo, seeking an oracle from him. Since the image was mute, the temple attendants, being asked the cause of its silence, said that the cult statue was silent because of corpses interred there. For the remains of other martyrs and of the holy martyr Babylas had been interred there. So then Julian commanded that all these be removed from there. After they had been removed, a thunderbolt struck Daphne [65] by night and reduced the temple and the cult statue to ashes. Therefore, thinking that the conflagration was the result of a plot of Christians, the "Avenging spirit," in a rage, even closed the churches of the faithful.[108] The great Artemius was punished by him as a Christian and the murder of Gallus was a charge laid upon him; and the presbyters Eugenius and Macarius were punished by him and were deemed worthy of the crowns of martyrs; and also Manuel, Sabel, and Ishmael, who had been sent to him from Persia for the purpose of an embassy, and many others.[109]

13

When he had invaded Persia, at first he fared well, captured some cities, killed many men, took possession of much booty and many prisoners, and began to besiege Ctesiphon. After matters suddenly deteriorated for him, he and the majority of his army were destroyed. For the Persians were desperate and clearly willing to hurl themselves toward destruction to cause the Romans some suffering.[110] Then indeed two men in the guise of deserters stole toward the sovereign and promised him victory against Persia, if he followed them. For [66] they advised him to leave the river, to burn the triremes which he was bringing with him and the other supply ships, lest the enemy use them, and, with them guiding the way, to lead the army through other routes, safely and swiftly take possession of the interior of Persia, and effortlessly master her. The sinner insanely obeyed them and, although many, including Hormisdas himself, kept telling him that the business was a deception, he set fire to the ships and burned all except twelve. There were 700 triremes and 400 supply ships. When they already had been reduced to ashes, since many of the unit commanders kept objecting that what the deserters were saying was an ambush and deception, he only just, I suppose, gave his assent that the false deserters be interrogated. After they had been interrogated under torture, they revealed their secret.[111]

Now some state that Julian was deceived thus, while others say that, after he had abandoned the siege of Ctesiphon due to its great strength and also because necessities for the army failed, he took thought of withdrawal.[112] They say that the Persians appeared to them from behind as they were withdrawing [67] and that they threw those in the rear into disorder; that the Gauls, who comprised the rear guard, arrayed themselves against the enemy very nobly and killed many of them, not just ordinary people, but the distinguished among them, too. The Romans were severely beset by a lack of supplies. Julian, at a loss of what had to be done and whence he ought to continue to withdraw, chose to make his line of march through the hill-country. The Persians observed this, massed in the same spot, and attacked the Romans. On the left wing, the Romans were winning, but on the right they were, in fact, losing. When Julian had learned this, he was in haste to aid those being beaten. He happened, on account of its weight and the searing heat of the sun (for the season was summer), to have removed his breastplate. Then, when he had come in the midst of the enemy, he was struck about the side with a spear. It is said that because the wind had been blowing strongly, a thick cloud spread over the air there. For the masses of the soldiers were stirring up much dust, so that they neither knew where they were nor what they were doing. For it was unclear whence the spear that struck him had been thrown at him, whether by an enemy, by one of his own men, or from a power more divine, [68] for this, too, is sung. Hence, they state that, when he had taken in cupped hand some of the blood flowing from his wound and scattered it in the air, he said, "Have your fill, Nazarene!"[113]

Thus did he who had lived impiously violently spew forth his soul, having reigned two years. The army conveyed his body to Tarsus and buried it in a suburb of the city. On his grave was inscribed this epigram:

> By Cydnus silver-flowing, when from Euphrates' stream,
> Out of Persia's land, with task undone,
> An army he had moved, obtain this tomb did Julian,
> Both sovereign good and spearman strong.

Later he was brought back to the Queen of Cities.[114]

He was aflutter about reputation and wanted to be praised about every little thing, but, being set straight by his friends about those things on which he slipped up, [69] he did not become upset. He also had a share of every sort of wisdom, and especially the very esoteric; with regard to regimen, he was disciplined, with the result that he even avoided these natural things, belches and expectoration. He used to say that a philosopher ought, if possible, not even breathe.[115] They state that while at Antioch he saw a dream, a youth with blond hair, who said to him, "It is necessary that you die in Phrygia." Then, when he was wounded, he asked those present what the place was called. When he heard that it was called Phrygia, he cried out, "O Helios, you have destroyed Julian!"[116] It is said that on the day in which he died, his death was known in Antioch. For one of those of the judicial order there—and that man a Hellene and of the same religion as the Transgressor—, passing the night standing watch over the senate house, beheld a composition of stars in heaven emblazoning letters which said, "Today in Persia Julian is being killed." Then, since the day had been noted, it was recognized after this that he was killed on that day. Having lived thirty-one years, [70] thus, as has been described, did he cease life. The man who had been taught through the stars beforehand about his death, held the spectacle to be an inducement toward belief.[117]

14

After Julian had died, Jovian, then a corps commander, a pious man, son of Varonianus, who had born the title *comes*, was selected by common vote for the rule.[118] He was loath to accept the sovereignty. When asked the reason, he cried out that he was a Christian and was not content to reign while the army was practicing Hellenism. Immediately, with one voice, as from a prearranged signal, all cried out that they were Christians.[119] When he had received the empire thus, he made peace with the Persians, having from necessity made a treaty not suitable for Romans, for he ceded to them possession of Nisisbis and Singara, famous cities, after he had resettled the cities' inhabitants, by whom, in their lamentations, he was violently cursed, too. But he also yielded many rural areas to them and rights accruing from the first to Romans. When hostages had been given on both sides, the treaty had thus been confirmed. Afterwards, as the Romans were on the march, they were beleaguered by a shortage of supplies, so as not even to have enough water.[120] [71] Then indeed, as soon as he had arrived in Antioch of Coele Syria, priests of the Christians who, under Constantius and the Transgressor, had been expelled from their churches, he returned to them, and before the others the great Athanasius to Alexandria. After he had come from Antioch to Tarsus and had decorated Julian's memorial, he returned.[121] After he had come to Ancyra of Galatia, he departed from there, advanced one day's march, halted in Dadastana, and suddenly died, as some have written, after he had eaten fresh mushrooms that were poisonous (for he was simple with regard to his diet), as others have written, since it was winter, he went to sleep in a home that had recently been plastered and, on account of the excessive cold, after coals had been lit inside, much vapor arose from the plaster as it was affected by the fire, he suffocated as a result of this, asleep and unaware of his choking, being heavy in the head from wine. For it is said that he had imbibed much straight.[122] His wife is said not to have seen him, although she, together with her son Varonianus, had arrived with regal pomp prior to this for a meeting.[123]

Now then, after Jovian had died, his dejected soldiers came down to Nicaea and, when they had arrived, began deliberating about a sovereign. [72] Some named one man, others another. The majority agreed upon Salustius, who happened to be prefect of the praetorians. After he had put forward his old age for an excuse, he declined. When they requested his son, he did not consent, having judged him unsuitable for such office on account of his youth and naiveté. Hence, Salustius, with the others, voted Valentinian sovereign, even though he was not present.[124]

Now then, Jovian was pious with regard to dogma and a man of goodwill. He had a weakness for wine and sex. With respect to the height of his body, he happened to be tall and was not ignorant of letters.[125] While a corps commander, he was once marching in a steep place behind Julian, who was leading the way, and stepped on the hem of his purple. Julian, whether he inferred from this or recognized from some prophecy that Jovian was his successor, said, "So be it, even if a man . . . ."[126] He did not rule eight whole months. Now then, his corpse was conveyed to Byzantium and buried in the Church of the Holy Apostles, where, subsequently, [73] his wife Charito also was buried with him. Jovian died in the course of his thirty-third year of age.[127]

15

Now as has been said, Valentinian thus was elected sovereign. When he had been brought forth and acclaimed, he donned the emblems of sovereignty. Salustius, because he demonstrated eagerness that he be acclaimed, requested as a reward to be released from the concerns of the prefecture. The sovereign said, "Have you loaded me with the weight of such great affairs for this, in order that you yourself not be burdened even by this one?"[128] Valentinian came from Paeonia. He was pious in matters concerning God. As a result, Julian condemned him to exile, then, after he had been recalled, made him *tribunus* of a unit. He was most noble in strength and most just in judgment. As a result, he punished as unjust many of those then claiming offices, saying that the ruler was obliged, before all others, to take thought of justice.[129]

He took his brother Valens as a colleague in his sovereignty and, having entrusted to him the eastern portion, he himself [74] stayed in the west, organized wars against barbarians, and erected many monuments of victory against them. He had, before his reign, a son named Gratian, who was born to him from his wife Severa. He proclaimed him emperor. He also married a second wife, while the earlier one, too, was still alive. The second wife was Justina, from whom he also begot the young Valentinian and daughters, Justa, Grata, and Galla.[130]

During his reign, when Eudoxius of evil opinion, archpriest of the New Rome, had died, Demophilus, who happened to be of the same opinion as his predecessor, was introduced in his stead. He controlled the church for about twelve years. This sovereign also selected Ambrose the Great as bishop of the city of Mediolanum. When he learned that his brother Valens was espousing the Arian heresy and was forcing all to agree to it, he rebuked him via letters and advised him to abandon the heresy. But he did not abandon it of his own volition and became even more savage against the orthodox.[131]

A certain Rhodanus, a *praepositus*, had great influence over Valentinian. Against him, a certain woman called Bernice came [75] to the sovereign Valentinian, charging the *praepositus* with injustice. Then indeed, after the emperor had investigated and learned that the woman was not lying, he summoned the *praepositus* and ordered him to make amends for the injustice to the woman. Confident in his license toward the sovereign, he took no account of the wronged woman. Then the woman again approached the sovereign. When he learned that the *praepositus* had not taken any thought of the woman, he immediately stripped him of office and ordered him bound and led about in the theater during an equestrian contest, while heralds went before him proclaiming his injustice to the woman and his disregard of sovereign command. And he ordered that, after the circumambulation and the proclamation, he be burned there straightway. Such was the end he met. Through sovereign writ, his entire fortune was given to the woman.[132]

This sovereign died while residing in Gaul, after he had enjoyed a long span of life. For he lived to eighty-four years, having reigned eleven of these and having left his son Gratian as successor of his sovereignty in the West.[133]

16

Valens, championing the Arianizers, since he was like-minded to them, persecuted the orthodox and inflicted upon them many [76] terrors, heeding his own spouse Domnica.[134] Once, while he was staying in Nicomedia, there approached him in a delegation from the body of the orthodox eighty priestly men, all of whom, together with the boat on which they were traveling, he ordered burned. All were incinerated in mid-sea, along with their boat, which lasted as far as Dacibyze. Gregory, the one great in theology, has memorialized them, saying, "maritime conflagrations of presbyters."[135] Not only did he punish the orthodox, but he also assigned to the Arians all their churches, banishing from these their orthodox bishops. Then indeed, it is said that those of the correct dogma who had been exiled from the catholic church in Nicaea approached Basil the Great, and that he went on a delegation to Valens about this, that he was not won over, and that Basil the Great said, "O Sovereign, your verdict about this must be entrusted [77] to God, let the church be securely locked, and let those of Arius' faction pray to God while they stand outside. If the church spontaneously opens to them, let them have it! But if it does not open, we must also be permitted to pray to God! And if the doors are spontaneously thrown open, it must be concluded that God has allotted the divine precinct to us. But if the temple does not open for us either, in this case, too, let it be yielded to the Arianizers." This was pleasing to the sovereign and he permitted that it be so done. Therefore, the church in Nicaea was completely closed. The Arianizers kept praying and prattling for a sufficiently long time, and the church did not open. After a lengthy duration, once the heretics had withdrawn, the orthodox, with Basil the Great leading them, began their entreaty. Immediately the bars and the bolts burst asunder and the doors stood apart from one another and granted entrance for the faithful.[136]

This sovereign allowed the Hellenes to make sacrifices and was solicitous to Jews. To the orthodox alone he was opposed.[137] When Scythians were ravaging the Thracian and Macedonian territory, he set out with the intention of meeting them in battle. It was then when the great father [78] Isaacius chanced to meet him as he passed by on horseback and said, "Restore the churches to the orthodox, O sovereign, and know that you will return victorious. But if you wage war against God, thence you will not return." The most impious sovereign was upset about these words and ordered that the holy man be placed under guard until he came back. And he said, "If you return, God has not spoken in me."[138] And in a dream Valens beheld a man saying to him:

Fast off with you, wretch, to Mimas the Great
Where there waits to seize you a horrible fate.

Then, when he had awakened, he asked who Mimas was. One of those who have devoted themselves to words (for such men used to accompany and reside with emperors, would that it be so now, too!) said to him that Mimas was a mountain in Asia, situated by the sea. He also said that Homer made mention of this in the *Odyssey*, saying, "by windy Mimas." He said, "What need is there for me to go to this mountain and there to die?" Then he campaigned against the Scythians, engaged them around Thrace, was disgracefully beaten, and, fleeing, was hidden in a building, beside which chaff had been swept. Then, after the sovereign's defeat, when the Scythians [79] were plundering that area and also setting homes ablaze, they burned that building to the ground and Valens perished within. Now then, holy Isaacius, while imprisoned, knew in his spirit of Valens' incineration and said to those who happened to be there, "At this moment Valens is dying by fire." Since the day was noted, it was later recognized that the holy man did not err. After the withdrawal of the barbarians from there, when some men were searching for the sovereign's body, a tombstone was discovered in the house in which he had been burned, having an epigram of a man of yore:

Here lies Mimas, a Macedonian, a Commander.[139]

Procopius, the cousin of Julian, rebelled against this sovereign and gained control of Byzantium. When he had been betrayed by his own men and bound from his legs to two trees which had been forcibly bent down, the wretch was ripped in half when the trees were let up. Then, too, the walls of the city of Chalcedon were dismantled, since its citizens sided with Procopius. While they were being dismantled, in their foundation was discovered a tablet which had the following written on it: [80]

> But when, indeed, Nymphs, delighting in dance,
> Throughout the Holy City, about her fortressed ways, will stand,
> And a wall a safeguard mournful for baths will be,
> Then, indeed, countless tribes of men dispersed,
> Savage, mad, in vile prowess clad,
> Having Cimmerian Ister's ford with spear traversed,
> Will Scythic range and Mysian land destroy.
> And having trod with frenzied hopes on Thrace,
> There life's end and destiny would face.[140]

Now Valens used the material of Chalcedon's wall for construction of an aqueduct, which popular parlance terms "conduit," by which he caused water to be brought to the city, in order that there be in it an abundance of water for other use and for bathing, and he named it "Valens." The prefect of the city outfitted a Nymphaeum in the so-called Taurus, thereby demonstrating the benefits from the aqueduct. The incursion of the barbarians who took Thrace and also remained afterwards throughout it, occurred after this, as had been written [81] on the tablet.[141]

In truth, during Valens' reign, it is said that, seeking to know who would reign after Valens, Libanius the sophist and Iamblichus, Proclus' teacher, performed a rooster-divination. This, as word has it, is of this sort. In dust the twenty-four letters are written, and upon each of them a kernel of wheat or barley is placed. Then, as some spells are chanted over them, a rooster is released and it is observed from what letters he takes kernels. It is thought that these, being put together, make a revelation of what is being sought. So then they did this and saw that the rooster took the kernel on the theta, the kernel on the epsilon, the one on the omicron, and the one on the delta. Therefore, what was being revealed seemed ambiguous. For it seemed to reveal either "Theodorus," or "Theodosius," or "Theodotus." When he had learned of this, Valens was suspicious of many called by such names and executed them. He also began to seek the men who had made the divination. As a result, in fear of his cruelty, Iamblichus drank a poison, [82] so some have recorded, and betook himself from life. For Valens was inexorable in his rages. As a result, he used to say, "He who swiftly sets aside rage, could as soon set aside justice." He had reigned thirteen years and four months and perished in a way worthy of his impiety.[142]

17

Valentinian's son Gratian and the young Valentinian, his brother, gained control of the Roman empire. For Gratian alone was proclaimed by his father, just as has already been recorded. When Valentinian died, he was not present at his father's death. Then indeed, under these circumstances the army proclaimed sovereign the young Valentinian, who happened then to be four years old. After he had returned from his absence, Gratian accorded the soldiers his malediction and some of them even maltreatment, having punished the ringleaders of his brother's proclamation because they had acclaimed another without the current sovereign's permission. He did not reject having his brother rule with him, but accepted him as colleague in his sovereignty.[143] This sovereign rivaled his father [83] in regard to piety. As a result, he did not provide military cooperation to his uncle Valens, who had once requested it from him against the Scythians, having written to him that, "One must not cooperate with God's enemy." To the pastors who had been driven from their own churches, he allowed by decree their return to them.[144]

When, after Valens' defeat, the Scythians were swelled with arrogance, were ravaging Thrace and its environs, and were out of control, Theodosius, a man both most noble and pious he summoned from Hispania (the Hispania of European Iberia is the most distinguished city of those in it). Then, after he had appointed him general, he dispatched him with an army against the barbarians. He attacked them, was victorious, and raised a victory monument, a vast Scythian multitude having been slaughtered in battle and the rest after they had turned to flight, some of them killed while being captured, others killed by one another in their flight. So then, when almost all of those barbarians had perished, Theodosius left the army there and himself went, his own messenger of victory, to Gratian, [84] who was staying in Paeonia. After he had announced his victory to the sovereign and proclaimed the good news of the barbarians' destruction, he was doubted on account of the speed of his achievement and the invincibility of the Scythians. When the emperor had recognized the truth and had been informed of the barbarians' ruin, he both marveled at the man on account of his swiftness and prowess and praised him. Since Valens' portion had, after his ruin, already been attached to him, he surveyed the near limitlessness of the empire, saw, at the same time, that he alone would not be able to guide an empire so great, and acclaimed

Theodosius sovereign of the New Rome, at the same time rewarding him for his valor and judging that no man would be better than he for a sharing of the empire. Then indeed, he entrusted to him all the East and Thrace, and to himself allotted the West.[145] After he had arrived in Gaul, he was killed treacherously by Andragathius, his general, after he had reigned six years from the time of his father's death.[146]

18

After Gratian had died, there remained as sovereign emperor [85] of the West the young Valentinian, who was not yet an adolescent. Because his Arianizing mother Justina had corrupted him, he was in agreement with the dogma of the Arians and opposed the orthodox. Therefore, after Maximus had rebelled against him and made an attempt at usurpation, and had prevailed in battles, he, seeking a military alliance, wrote the sovereign Theodosius what had happened. The latter wrote back to him that there was no need for amazement if a slave rebelled and prevailed over a master when the latter was denying his own Master, calling the Creator a creation, a slave, and the same substance and same rank as the Father. After he had departed to assist him, he captured and killed Maximus and the general Andragathius, who had deceitfully murdered Gratian.[147]

Then, in turn, Eugenius rebelled against the young Valentinian and made an attempt at usurpation. Therefore, Valentinian, seized with fear, betook himself from life by hanging. Learning of Eugenius' usurpation, Theodosius marched out against him.[148] After he had reached Thessalonica with his army, he was insulted [86] by the Thessalonicans and the prefect was murdered, the populace having rioted as a result of certain grievances. Now the sovereign then seemed to exhibit forbearance toward the populace's action. But subsequently he announced an equestrian contest and, when the populace had gathered in the theater, the army surrounded them and with arrows and javelins shot the populace down, with the result that of them almost 15,000 died. After he had sated his anger in this fashion, Theodosius departed and went to the city of Mediolanum. There he was censured by Ambrose the Great and not allowed to enter the church. He did not permit him entrance to the divine precinct unless he enacted a law that capital sentences not be enforced until thirty days should elapse after the sentence. This he did on account of the sovereign's predisposition toward anger, in order that, his anger being spread through the thirty days, he re-examine his sentences dispassionately and confirm the lawful but annul those that had perhaps been promulgated through rage.[149] After [87] he had engaged the usurper Eugenius in battle in Gaul, Theodosius defeated, captured, and killed him.[150]

While a private citizen, he had a pious, modest, and charitable wife, Placilla, from whom were born to him Honorius and Arcadius. Her, too, he made Augusta. After he became sovereign, when she died he married Galla, the daughter of Valentinian the Great.[151]

While the sovereign was absent in the West, the Jews, who had warmly welcomed Honoratus, the prefect of the city, built a lavish synagogue in Chalcopratii after he had given them permission, for he was serving the interests of the Hellenes. The populace of the city was annoyed about this and abused the prefect. But he paid no heed to the abuse. Then the populace, unable to endure this, set a fire in the synagogue by night and burned it. The prefect therefore wrote about this to Theodosius. He sentenced those who had dared the conflagration of the synagogue to payment of the expenditure on it and commanded that it be rebuilt. [88] After Ambrose the Great had learned this, when the sovereign was residing in the city of Mediolanum and had come to the church for one of the dominical celebrations, he began to speak:

> Why, Sovereign, do you outrage Him who made you sovereign from a private citizen and entrusted to you his own flock—which He won with his own blood—and who crowned your recently squalid head, regarding those who deny Him more worthy than those who acknowledge Him, exacting judgments on Christians in behalf of Jews, and, in the middle of this city where Christ is preached and the cross revered, forcing them to build a synagogue for the Christ-killers?

The sovereign was shamed by his reproach and said, "Bishop, shall we grant to the populace to do in unseemly and shameless fashion whatever they wish in well-regulated cities?" "But this is what one must not grant:" retorted the sacred Ambrose, "Jews to possess synagogues in the midst of a pious city and to send up blasphemous prayers in the hearing of the god-fearing! You, of all people, most orthodox Augustus, must not sanction this!" [89] Theodosius was mollified by this, revoked the penalty for the Byzantines, and forbade the Jews to possess a synagogue within the Queen of Cities.[152]

When new taxes had been imposed on the Antiochenes, the populace, having been aroused to anger as a result of the novelty of the exaction, toppled statues of the former wife of the sovereign which were standing in their city's marketplace and dragged them into the public thoroughfares. Enraged on account of this, he abrogated the city's legal rights, subjugated it to its neighbor Laodicea, and threatened to punish its citizens. He would have brought this to pass, if Flavianus, then archpriest of Antioch, had not come to the sovereign, engaged in negotiations, and made him relinquish his anger.[153] This was when the great father John Chrysostom, who happened to be presbyter of the church in Antioch, composed the speeches titled *The Statues*.[154]

19

Then Gregory, the mighty in theology, of late instructing the orthodox in secret in the church of Holy Anastasia [90] on account of the impudence and audacity of the heretics, after the sovereign Theodosius made the churches available to the orthodox and expelled the Arianizers, in forthrightness proclaimed the Son to be the same substance as the Father, and the Holy Spirit God, jointly reverenced and jointly honored with both. For Macedonius, who, as has been stated, also had briefly been Patriarch of Constantinople, did not allow It to be called God, nor equal in strength to the Father and to the Son, nor, for that matter, of the same substance. As a result, a second synod had then been organized, after the sovereign had issued the order, and, when there had been assembled in the reigning of the cities one-hundred fifty fathers possessed of God—of whom Gregory the Theologian, and the great Gregory, bishop of Nyssa, and the holy Amphilochius, who was in charge of the church of Iconium, took the lead in the disputations—, they decreed the Holy Spirit God, both of the same substance and same power as the Father and the Son, they excommunicated from the catholic church Macedonius and those who held the same opinion as he, they added to the holy creed the clause about the Holy Spirit from "and in the Holy Spirit" to the conclusion, and what had been decreed in the first synod [91] they confirmed. It was then when some of the bishops who envied the Theologian on account of the throne of Constantinople said that he had ascended the throne irregularly, since it had previously been offered to another. As a result, the holy one composed his *Farewell*, read it in public, vacated the throne, and returned to Nazianzus, his own native land. Nectarius, a man of the senatorial order and one who had held public offices, was selected Constantinople's patriarch. [155] At that time the throne of the New Rome was allotted second rank, having been placed after the elder Rome but preferred before the others. [156]

But then, too, Amphilochius the Great began requesting that the sovereign drive the Arians from the city, inasmuch as they were blaspheming the Son of God, or, in the interim, to forbid conventicles. Since he saw that Theodosius was hesitant toward this, he watched for the right moment and, when Arcadius was deliberating with his father, he entered, rendered the appropriate salutation and obeisance to the sovereign, and to Arcadius nonchalantly spoke thus, "Hello to you, too, little boy." When the sovereign became upset about his slight [92] of his son, the holy man then said, "You, being human, did not meekly bear the slighting of your son. Do you think that God does not abominate and despise those who blaspheme his only begotten son and become angry at those who allow them to consort with the orthodox and to destroy many?" Then, astonished at the holy man's method, the sovereign terminated by ordinance the conventicles of the heretics. [157]

Upon the sovereign who had destroyed Eugenius, the recent usurper, devolved the entire empire of the Romans, and he proclaimed his two sons sovereigns. [158] Since he wished them to have a share of education both in words and in ethics, he brought from Rome Arsenius the Great, who was a deacon of the church there, famous both for wisdom and for virtue. To him he delivered his sons, after he had enjoined him to behave toward them not as to sovereigns but as to private individuals and ordinary people, to flog them if he saw them being careless or deviating one bit from propriety, and to deal with them as with his own sons. He deemed Arsenius worthy of great honor and greatly enriched him with wealth. After he had taken charge of the boys, [93] he used to seat them on thrones while he himself stood and filled them with his teaching. Once the sovereign unexpectedly surprised them and, when he saw them sitting and Arsenius standing, became upset, roused the boys from their thrones, seated Arsenius, and ordered him to teach them thus. Thereafter, they used to stand beside their teacher while the teacher was sitting. Well now, once the teacher was laying lashes on Arcadius, who had made an error. Wroth with him as a result, he devised a plot against him, began diligently practicing to kill the man, and was planning the slaughter. When he had learned what was being rehearsed, Arsenius secretly retired from the palace and, after he had retreated to Scetis, adopted the solitary life and became like an angel. Although the sovereign Theodosius made a massive search for him, he did not know where on earth he was.[159]

This sovereign became ill in Mediolanum and quit his life after he had guided the realm eighteen years, having apportioned it to his two sons, to Arcadius having assigned the New Rome and the eastern portions, to [94] Honorius having allotted the elder Rome and the western.[160]

COMMENTARY ON
BOOK XIII.1–19

1   Constantine likely was born on February 27, 272 or 273.
Constantius was wed to Theodora by April 21, 289. Constantine had
had an earlier wife, Minervina (*PLRE* I, pp. 602–603). He married
Fausta *ca.* September 307. *CP* p. 517.6–7 labels Constantine a bastard.
Theoph. *AM* 5814, p. 18.8–9, attributes the story of Constantine's
illegitimacy to Arians and Hellenes, *i.e.* pagans. Zos. II.8.2, following
Eunapius, is an example of one pagan version. George the Monk
pp. 484.23–485.1 says: "Some who say that he [Constantine] was
the product of fornication are openly accused by various exegetes of
being liars and gossips." Ced. p. 476.5–15 comments on the story in
the context of objections to the claim that Eusebius of Nicomedia, who
was regularly associated with the theology of Arius, had baptized
Constantine:

> Those who say that [Constantine] was baptized in Nicomedia
> at the time of his death by Eusebius of Nicomedia, the Arian,
> lie. For they say that he delayed the baptism through the hope
> he would be baptized in the Jordan. For what, indeed, was
> impeding him, campaigning against Gallerius in the East and
> advancing toward Persia again a second time, from going off
> and being baptized in the Jordan? Furthermore, slandering
> him as a bastard, too, is utter malice. For his lineage was royal
> even prior to Diocletian. In fact, his father Constantius was
> son of the daughter of Claudius the sovereign, and from Helen,
> his first wife, he had Constantine the Great, as has been said.

See further, n. 15 below.

2   It is uncertain whether Theodora and Fausta were full- or half-
sisters. *Cf.* Scut. p. 44.22–25: "And the devil, despiser of good, when

he saw his [Constantine's] faith reach the boiling point, entered into and stirred to zeal for the ancestral religion his wife Fausta, who also deluded her husband to increased sacrifice to the idols."

3   Constantine left Trier for Rome in 312.

4   The engagement at the Milvian Bridge occurred on October 28, 312. On the battle, *cf.*:

George the Monk pp. 487.21–488.5: After this, when he had heard the harsh and disgusting things which had happened in Rome under Maxentius, about which he also had received an embassy from the Romans, he campaigned against him, and when he had beheld the sign of the cross in the heaven luminously bearing the inscription [488] "In This Conquer," having immediately modeled it in stones inlaid with gold and attached it to a spear, he commanded that it go before his army. After he had, through this, driven Maxentius to flight in the river, he entered and gained control of Rome, Maxentius having drowned in the river while being pursued.

Ced. pp. 474.6–475.2: And Maxentius perpetrated horrible evils on the Romans; for he was carrying off their wealth and wives and daughters and killing them in various ways and, following the demons, performing sacrifices without measure. As a result, too, the Romans, when they had made an embassy to Constantine against the impious Maxentius, stirred him to action. And Maxentius, after he had bridged the river flowing beside the city, marshaled his forces against Constantine the Great. And he, dreading the witchcrafts of Maxentius, was in much agony. Then there appeared to him in the sixth hour of the day the precious cross, bearing an inscription fashioned from light via stars, "Through This Conquer." And in a vision during the night the Lord stood beside him, "Employ the sign which has been revealed to you and conquer!" Then, when he had improvised a cross of gold which exists even now, he gave the command to advance to the battle; and, when the encounter had begun, those about Maxentius were beaten and, when the multitude had been killed, Maxentius, fleeing with the rest, began to cross the bridge, which, shattered by a divine power, plunged all into the river. And the Romans, delivered from the tyranny of the wicked Maxentius, after bedecking the city with crowns, welcomed [475] with joy the

Sym. 87.2.9–11: When he had consecrated Constantine Augustus and sovereign in Rome, Maximinus did many terrible things against Christians, as, too, did Maxentius in Rome. Therefore, the divine Constantine turned his attention to the dissolution of the tyrants, and Maxentius, on the one hand, was killed by him in Rome, when, too, God supplied him the sign of the cross as an ally.

victorious Constantine along with the victory-making cross, hailing him savior.

Scut. p. 42.4–21: And Constantine, having yielded to the entreaty of the Romans, gathered an army and moved against Maxentius. For everyone hated him on account of his cruelty and licentiousness. And that is when, in the eighth hour of the day, there appeared in the heaven both to him and to the whole army the revered cross, formed from light, bearing an inscription made of stars, "In This Conquer." But also on that night the Lord stood next to him in a vision saying, "Use what has been shown to you for your insignia and conquer. And you will build a city for my mother." When he had awakened from sleep, after he had prepared a cross from gold similar to the one which had been shown, Constantine commanded it to be put in the vanguard of his household army in the war. And when the symbol had been made, Maxentius was beaten and, fleeing with the survivors, began to cross the bridge of the river in Rome, which collapsed by divine power and plunged both him and the men with him into the water. And the Romans, delivered from the tyranny of the villain, with rejoicing also crowned the victor Constantine with the divine cross and welcomed him.

5   Constantine entered Rome on October 29. For the monument and Constantine's directives, see Eus. *HE* IX.9.10–12, p. 832.5–20. Note that Eusebius credits both Constantine and Licinius for the order of protection of Christians, which he says they sent to Maximinus Daia. Gel. Cyz. *HE* I.81–2, p. 11.5–17, approximates Zonaras.

6   Licinius and Constantia married in February 313. Probably in the same year, Licinius killed Maximinus' son—perhaps named Maximus (see Lactant. *De Mort. Pers.* 50.3, pp. 75 and 124, n. 5)—

and Maximinus' anonymous daughter. At XII.34, p. 624, Zonaras calls
Galerius Maximinus. For the mistaken view noted by Zonaras, see Sym.
86.3.22–23, p. 105: "And Gallerius, when he had been devoured by
worms, expired, having beforehand taken Licinius as colleague in the
East."

7 Licinius actually had been proclaimed Augustus on Nov. 11, 308,
at the so-called Conference at Carnuntum. See Lactant. *De Mort. Pers.,*
p. 109, n. 2, on 29.1–2. Licinius defeated Maximinus Daia at
Adrianople on April 30, 313. Zonaras' "ceded" is misleading, as
Maximinus fled to Nicomedia and beyond, and died, probably by his
own hand, at Tarsus *ca.* July 313. See further, n. 8 below.

8 It is Constantine whom Zonaras says commanded Licinius to
allow Christians freedom of worship. Constantine's propaganda and
his *post eventum* glorification in Christian sources at the expense of,
and through the demonization of, Licinius grossly misrepresent the
latter's complicated and evolving policies with regard to Christians,
which never seem to have involved outright persecution. *Cf.* the
compressed remarks of Ced. pp. 477.21–478.2: "In the 12th year, after
he had demanded assurances that he would do Christians no harm,
[Constantine] proclaimed Licinius a sovereign and, when he had marked
it off, gave him a portion of Rome's territory. Then the persecution
against Christians was, [478] by God's grace, ceased. Under Licinius
was martyred the holy Theodorus [2, *PLRE* I, p. 896]."

9 This seems to be a reference to Constantia's later intervention on
Licinius' behalf, for which see below, n. 11. Multiple notices of the
war between Constantine and Licinius in the source tradition are
the probable cause of the doublet. *Cf.* Ced.:

p. 495.12–15: In the 14th and 15th year, Licinius set in motion a persecution against Christians, having forgotten about the previous pacts. Constantine, admonishing him through letters, failed to persuade him to desist from the wickedness.	p. 497.3–16: In the 19th year, Constantine the Great, observing Licinius more insanely indulging in the persecution against Christians and practicing intrigue against his benefactor, took up arms against him on land and sea. And when the war between Constantine and Licinius has lasted eleven and eight months, as war was wrought throughout Bithynia, the sinner was captured alive in Chrysopolis and dispatched

to Thessalonica to be kept under guard, previously, however, having warred, too, in Philippopolis and been beaten. As he was sent into Thessalonica and there, again hiring barbarians, was fomenting rebellion, the sovereign commanded that he be cut down by sword. And so, at last, he expelled the troubles from total tranquility.

See, too, Sym. 88.2–3, p. 107:

After he had made Licinius a relative by marriage by his sister, he appointed him sovereign. And certain men who had deserted Constantine for Licinius for the purpose of rebellion, when sought by him, were not delivered, and Constantine, having marched against Licinius, drove him toward Paeonia. And there he beheld the sign of the cross bearing the inscription "In This Conquer." And when he made this sign of gold and hung it upon a spear, he routed the enemy. And Licinius, after being routed, fled to Thrace, and thence, when he had been besieged in Philippopolis, having been brilliantly and famously beaten, sought peace. Then, having again proven himself an enemy, he was besieged in Adrianople and beaten, and, after he had come to Byzantium, he fled to Chrysopolis, and, when beaten again there, fled to Nicomedia. And when Constantine's sister had come to him and beseeched him, it was granted to her husband to live in private dress, and, when Licinius had chosen to depart to Thessalonica, he had there created unrest, he was killed by the army. Under Licinius, too, the holy Theodorus was martyred, in the eighteenth year of the war which had risen between Licinius and Constantine.

10 The struggle for Byzantium occurred between July and September of 324. Chrysopolis fell on September 18 of that year, at which time Licinius already seems to have been at Nicomedia.

11 Licinius' resigned on September 19, 324. Sym. 88.3, p. 107.16–19, too, recounts Constantia's intervention: "And when Constantine's sister had come to him and beseeched him, it was granted to her husband to live in private dress, and, after Licinius had chosen

to depart to Thessalonica, he had there made commotions, he was killed by the army." With this, *cf. Orig. Const.* 28, p. 8.4–9, translated by Jane Stevenson, L-M, p. 47.

12   Licinius was executed in the spring of 325. *Cf.* Gel. Caes. *Excerpta HE* p. 159.13–14 = Cramer II, p. 91.23–25—"He [Constantine] ordered him [Licinius] to dwell in peace in Thessalonica, but commanded that he, again fomenting revolution and being about to take-up arms, be killed."—and Gel. Cyz. *HE* I.12.3–4, p. 21.11–15:

> For a brief time he seemed to be peaceful, but after this, summoning some barbarians and considering with them ways to renew hostilities, he began to pursue the worse. When he had learned this, the most pious sovereign commanded the God-hater to be killed, and the usurper of Christ and of his servant was killed.

Soc. *HE* I.4, p. 4, and Theoph. *AM* 5815, p. 20.5–8, represent Zonaras' alternative version.

13   Only Zonaras mentions the celestial phenomena allegedly seen at Byzantium. Naz. *Pan. Lat.* IV (X).14.1–4, pp. 155.21–156.5, says that armies appeared in the heavens before the Battle of the Milvian Bridge. Zonaras' apparitions have biblical parallels: *2 Maccabees* 3.24–25 (a single horseman) and 26 (two young men) and 10.28–31 (five horsemen).

14   It is difficult to see the rationale for Zonaras' parenthetical comment about the *praenomen* Flavius. The subsequent account of Constantine's conversion and baptism is, of course, unhistorical.

15   Zonaras, Cedrenus, and Scutariotes all reflect complex biographical and hagiographical traditions that begin with Eusebius *Life of Constantine* and the lost work of Praxagoras (*FgrH* 219). However, rather than these biographies, it is some of the content of the so-called Opitz and Guida *Lives*, as distinct from these specific *Lives* themselves, that provides the greatest number of significant points of contact with Zonaras. Foremost among these parallels are the tales of Constantine's conversion in Rome and his baptism by Silvester (*EEC* II, p. 802), both key components of the *Acts* and *Lives* of the bishop.

The Greek Orthodox saint Nicodemus Hagiorites (1748–1809) compiled a collection of saints' lives, *The Synaxaristes of the Twelve Months of the Year*, in which he noted:

> In the Great Complex and in the Holy Monastery of the Iberians [For which see, *ODB* II, pp. 1025–1026, *s.v.* Iveron Monastery.] is preserved one account about the sainted Silvester, the beginning of which is: 'The revered and God-seeing apostles . . . .' It is a composition of John Zonaras ("Il testo greco del ΒΙΟΣ di S. Silvestro attribuito al Metafraste," *Roma e l'Oriente* 6 [1913], p. 334).

Nicodemus' quotation agrees with the opening of the *Life of Silvester* as it appears in two Vatican codices (*Vat. gr.* 816 and 1190, the bases of the anonymously edited ΒΙΟΣ ΚΑΙ ΠΟΛΙΤΕΙΑ ΤΟΥ ΕΝ ΑΓΙΟΙΣ ΠΑΤΡΟΣ ΗΜΩΝ ΣΙΛΒΕΣΤΡΟΥ ΠΑΠΑ ΡΩΜΗΣ, *Roma e l'Oriente* 6 [1913], pp. 340–367). However, since neither manuscript names an author, Nicodemus' adscription may be conjecture rather than a reflection of his autopsy of a manuscript which actually bore Zonaras' name. Even if Zonaras did write this *Life of Silvester* and, if so, whether it antedates or postdates the *Epitome of Histories*, note-worthy correspondences between the works are so few that in the context of an appreciation of the *Epitome* they merit no more than passing notice. For the purpose at hand, the relationship between Zonaras, Symeon, Cedrenus, and Scutariotes takes precedence.

This said, with Zonaras *cf.*:

Ced. p. 475.3–17: In the 7th year of his sovereignty the great Constantine, having gained control of Rome, before all else consigned the remains of the Blessed Martyrs to pious burial and recalled those in exile. And by Silvester the most pious pope of Rome he is baptized and freed from leprosy in the following fashion: Having come to Rome after the victory against Maxentius, he seeks physicians to be cured of the disease. And some Jews come, saying that he needs to make a bath from blood of infants at the breast and, having washed in it, to be purified. Therefore, the infants are gathered	Scut. pp. 44.26–45.10: And the good and philanthropic god brought this man to himself in the following fashion: Having fallen into the disgrace of leprosy, he was seeking one who could heal him. And indeed certain Magi and Jews came forward and ordered that a bath be made on the Capitoline and be filled with human blood of uncorrupt children, having descended into which, he, having washed himself, would become healthy. [45] Accordingly, they gathered a multitude of infants from the provinces, and on the appointed day, while the sovereign was headed there, the infants'

with their mothers. And what need is there to relate the lamentations of the mothers and the rending of hair and the other sorts of things which characterize those mourning from the soul? And seeing these things and joining in their weeping, he said: "It is a fine thing that I alone, rather than these infants, die a vile death. But, too, who knows the manner of his end?" After he had said these things and favored the mothers with gifts, he dismissed them in peace [Cf. Ced. p. 476.5–15, trans. above, n. 1].

mothers, wailing and plucking out their hair encountered him. The sovereign, when he had seen these things and become tearful, said, "I prefer the salvation of the infants to my own health." O imitation of Christ! O cry! O blessed and sovereign soul! Forthwith, indeed, he turned back to the palace and commanded that the infants be restored to the mothers, having honored them with gifts most great and commanded that each go to their own.

16   With Sym. 88.1, p. 107.2–3—"In Rome, after he had been baptized by Silvester, he [Constantine] became a Christian."—*cf*.:

Ced. pp. 475.17–476.4: At this point, he also saw in a dream the two great apostles Peter and Paul encouraging him to seek Sylvester, the bishop of the city: "And he himself will reveal to you the bath through which you will be cured of the diseases of the soul and of the body." Then Sylvester came, serving in exile through the impending persecutions, and, after he had given him catechism, baptized him. Then immediately, as Constantine emerged from the divine bath, just like scales they fell from his body and he was purified and became totally healthy, like a little boy. And when they had observed this, the people were baptized in unlimited numbers, even Crispus, the son of Constantine.

Scut. pp. 45.10–46.11: And on this night he saw while asleep the holy apostles who hold pride of place, Peter and Paul the holy, urging him to seek Sylvester, the bishop of Rome. "For he," they said, "will show you the bath through which you may heal the diseases of both soul and body." Then, when Sylvester had been found and approached and advised the sovereign about our divine faith, he immediately commanded that the temples of the idols be closed, and, having trusted from his whole heart in our Lord Jesus Christ, he was baptized in the name of the Father, and of the Son, and of the Holy Spirit. And while being baptized, a sort of gleam of light glowed and dimmed, just like a skillet heated by a fire, and he emerged from the bath healthy, and the waters of the bath were full of leprous scabs. And the sovereign kept saying, "While in the waters, I saw that a hand sent forth from heaven touched me." And after donning a white robe, straightway he shouted thus, "He who dares blaspheme our Lord Jesus Christ or wrong a

Christian, I command that half of his resources be forfeit to the treasury." [46] And wishing to demonstrate to all his personal piety, when he had taken a mattock in his own hands, he, first, began to dig, having ordered that there be a church in the name of our Lord God Jesus Christ. And there were baptized both all his kinsmen and many of the senate, and of those in office around 12,000, and Crispus his son, whom he had had not from Fausta but from another, unlawfully known to him. Then, too, the names of the hebdomad of days were changed from Ares', Hermes', Aphrodite's, Cronos', Zeus's, Selene's, and the Sun's to the Second, and Third, and Fourth, Fifth, Preparation, Sabbath, and the Lord's.

17   Ced. pp. 478.13–494.22 features a long exegetical agon between Silvester and a series of learned Jews, the story of Zambres, and an appreciation of Helen. With Zonaras, *cf.*:

Ced. pp. 494.5–495.11: Then Zambres vowed, "If Silvester resurrects the dead bull, we all, having abandoned the Judaic law, shall desert to the faith of the Christians." And the blessed Silvester, after he had stretched his hands heavenward, and, in the midst of tears, prayed, when he had withdrawn toward the bull, said in a loud voice, "My Lord Jesus Christ, on all occasions I evoke your all-holy name, in order that this people learn that the devil's name killed the bull, but by the evocation of your vivifying and most illustrious name he was brought to life." And when he had approached the bull, he said with a loud shout, "In the name of Jesus Christ, whom the lawless Judaeans crucified under Pontius Pilate, arise with solemnity." And immediately the bull stirred himself and arose.

Scut. p. 46.12–20: And after she had been persuaded by some Jews who were giving her accurate instruction in the law, Helen, the holy and mother of the sovereign, being with her son, constrained him to draw closer to the Jewish faith. Moreover, some Magi, producing monstrous portents, were opposing themselves to the holy Sylvester, all of whom, with the blessed Helen, when he had won them over by wonders and the power of the Spirit, he converted to the Christian faith and thus baptized. And the orthodox faith was increasing and all were praising the sovereign, who had become the cause of such fine things for them.

And when he had loosed his bonds,
the holy Silvester released him,
saying, "Depart whence you came,
having wronged none along the way."
When they had witnessed this great
wonder and been much amazed,
straightway all the Judaeans fell at
the feet of the holy Silvester,
beseeching holy baptism. But the
most blessed empress Helen, too,
having fallen at the blessed Silvester's
feet, appealed that a place of
repentance be granted to her. [495]
And when this had happened, the
Christ-loving sovereign and the most
blessed Augusta and the entire
multitude of the people rejoiced
greatly, so that for two hours all
shouted, "Great is the God of the
Christians." And thus were the God
of the Christians and His attendant,
the holy Silvester, revered by all. In
the same hour, many possessed were
cured through the holy pope's
prayers, and many other maladies and
diseases were purified by the power of
our Lord Jesus Christ, glorified
among his saints. And when the
multitude of the Judaeans had been
baptized, there was great rejoicing in
Rome and her environs.

18   Though Helen had lived in Rome since sometime after
Constantine's victory at the Milvian Bridge, there is no reason to believe
Zonaras' story of her journey with Silvester. Helen traveled from Rome
to Jerusalem in the fall of 326. She died in Nicomedia, where
Constantine then resided, *ca*. 330. For her foundations and activities,
see *PLRE* I, pp. 410–411. *Cf*. Scut. p. 52.19–31:

> And after he had adorned Helen, his blessed mother, with
> a royal diadem, he sends her to Jerusalem in quest of the
> precious cross of the Lord, which, too, she discovered, by
> the grace of Christ the God who had been affixed to it, and
> with it the nails by which he was nailed to it. And to the
> poor there she distributed many resources and built shrines

conspicuous for beauty and size. And after she had taken a part of the life-making cross of the Lord and the nails and secured all the remainder in a solid silver chest and committed it to Macarius, the bishop there, she joyfully returned to her son and sovereign. And, having lived piously and illuminated her life by charitable acts and good deeds, she died, being eighty years old. And she is buried beside the sovereign and her son in the shrine of the Holy Apostles.

19   Constantine, Constantius, and Constans were born *ca.* August 7, 316, August 7, 317, and in 320 or 323, respectively. Helen's birthdate is unknown. Zonaras omits Constantia, wife of Gallus. Constantine's first wife Minervina bore Crispus *ca.* 305. *Anon. Cont. fr.* 14.2 = *ES* 188, p. 270 = Müller *FHG* IV, p. 199, notes Crispus' victories over Licinius:

> The momentous achievements of Crispus, Constantine's son, were patent. And Licinius, often beaten by him, was annoyed and uttered these Homeric lines: "Old man, for certain it is that young warriors distress you, / and your strength has been destroyed, and dire senility pursues you [*Il.* 8.102–103]."

The war in question began in October 316 and peace terms were ratified on March 1, 317.

20   Crispus and Fausta died in 326. *Cf.* Scut. p. 48.10–24:

> It is said that [Constantine], when his wife Fausta, who was mad for her stepson Crispus and, because he resisted her advances, had brought an accusation to his father that she had been violated by him, by his command had him, a Caesar, killed, and, after he had discovered later that she had lied, also executed her, having three sons with him, Constans, Constantius, and Constantine, whom he also proclaimed Caesars.

21   Constantine's Sarmatian campaigns were in the summer of 323 and in 334, the Gothic campaign in 332. With Zonaras, *Orig. Const.* 31–32 and 34, pp. 9.4–10.3, trans. Jane Stevenson, L-M, p. 48, and Theoph. *AM* 5818, pp. 27.31–28.2, *cf.*:

Ced. p. 517.16–23: In the 22nd year Constantine the most pious, when he had campaigned against Germans, Sarmatians, and Goths, won a mighty victory through the power of the cross and brought them to the utmost servitude. And after he had refounded Drepana in Nicomedia to honor Lucianus, who had been martyred there, he called it Helenopolis because of his mother. And in the 23rd and 4th and 5th year, he began to build in Antioch the octagonal church. And when he had crossed the Danube, he made a stone bridge on it and subjected the Scythians.

Scut. p. 44.1–22: After the destruction and suppression of those profane and impious usurpers, when a major war had been initiated in Thrace by various peoples and he had gone against them from Rome and been beaten, despondency seized him and the encampment around him. Then, tearfully praying toward heaven and begging to be delivered from such a predicament, when he had been drawn to sleep, he saw in a vision in the heaven the esteemed cross, on which had been written, "In This Conquer." And having immediately awakened, he began to ponder what he had seen. And after he had again gone to sleep, someone stood beside him grasping a staff and bringing it near his nostrils, so that the sovereign screamed and thought he had been struck. And as a result he took the linen lying by his head, placed it upon his nostrils, and returned to sleep. And when he arose at dawn, he saw on the linen an image of the esteemed cross, formed from his blood. And immediately he made a cross and he commanded that this lead the way into battle, saying to the army, "Through this we conquer our enemies." And to all he described his vision and the power of the cross, and he kept saying, "This is the sign of the God of the Christians." And after he had subsequently triumphed over all the peoples, he returned to Rome.

22 Constantinople was founded in 324. With Zonaras and Theoph. *AM* 5816, p. 23.22–27, *cf*.:

Sym. 88.12, p. 110: To the sovereign who had lately begun to establish a city in his own name in the [plain] before Ilium, above the

Ced. pp. 495.22–496.17: In those days, he remembered when, near Rome, a directive by the Lord had come to him in his sleep

Scut. p. 46.21–29: Having become mindful of the voice of the Lord saying to him while he was sleeping, "You will raise a city to grave of Ajax, God, in a dream, commanded the sovereign to establish in Byzantium what now is Constantinople.

[496] saying, "I shall reveal to you where to build a city to the Mother of God." And ultimately, after he had investigated various locations and places, he came to Thessalonica and, pleased with the spot, remained there for two years. And when he had constructed wondrous temples and baths and aqueducts, because he saw plague setting in, he abandoned this spot and came as far as Chalcedon of Bithynia. Finding it razed by the Persians, he began to rebuild. And eagles immediately snatched stones from the wall and stole off to Byzantium. When this had happened often, becoming a matter of concern for all, one of the attendants called Euphratas clarified to the sovereign that it was dear to God to found a city of His mother there. Therefore, after he had immediately crossed over and examined and approved the spot, he left Euphratas with a weighty force and much wealth as the supervisor of the work.

my mother in a spot which I shall reveal to you," after he had investigated many locations, he came upon Chalcedon in Bithynia, and, finding that this had been razed by the Persians, he began to build. But eagles, snatching the stones of the walls, carrying them toward Byzantium, kept dropping them. When this had happened often, one of the sovereign's top advisors, Euphrates by name, made it clear that it was dear to God for his mother's city to be built there.

23   AD 330.

24   D. Pingree, "The Horoscope of Constantinople," *ΠΡΙΣΜΑΤΑ: Naturwissenschaftsgeschichtliche Studien*, edited by Y. Maeyama and W. G. Saltzer (Wiesbaden: Franz Steiner, 1977), pp. 305–315, argues

convincingly that the Byzantine astrologer Demophilus interpreted a horoscope of Constantinople that he had cast around 990 on the basis of rules set down by his second-century predecessor Vettius Valens (*PIR* V 343). If Pingree is correct, and if neither Cedrenus nor Zonaras copied from the other, their common error almost certainly derives from a source written after 990.

25   Zonaras here follows John Xiphilinus' epitome of Dio (*cf.* Xiphil. 310.6–8 and Dio LXXV.12.1, pp. 691 and 336.5–7, respectively), both of whom err about the length of the siege, which actually lasted from around the fall of 193 until around the end of 195. The attack was in response the Byzantium's support of Asellius Aemilianus (*PIR²* A1211), who had backed Pescinnius Niger (*PIR²* P185) against Severus.

26   Zonaras, again drawing from Xiphilinus (Xiphil. 299.25–303.18 = Dio LXXV.10–14, pp. 690–693 and 334.7–338.22, respectively), is fuller here than in his treatment of the siege in the context of his account of Severus at XII.8 (II, pp. 548.9–549.11).

27   The digression that drew him to Xiphilinus now completed, Zonaras returns to the tradition he shares with Symeon, Cedrenus, and Scutariotes.

Sym. 88.7, p. 109: And he built a palace and horse track and the two delightful rostra and the forum, in which he erected a column, monolithic and completely of porphyry, which he had brought from Rome, having bound it by means of inscribed bronze belts, having dedicated atop it a statue in his name, having inscribed: "Through the Radiance in Him, Constantine, Shining Like the Sun." It was a work of Pheidias, and was brought from Athens.	Ced. p. 518.1–6: . . . And he established the forum right between the two great rostra, and in the forum itself he erected a column, monolithic and completely of porphyry, which he had brought from Rome, having bound it by means of inscribed bronze belts. And atop it he dedicated a statue in his name, on which was written "Constantine." It glowed like the sun, was a work of Pheidias, and was brought from Athens.	Scut. pp. 47.28–48.4: Then the sovereign built Constantinople, in beauty and size surpassing all the cities on earth, and like an eye of the inhabited world. For, through the aforementioned Euphratas, he significantly broadened the wall of Byzantium, [48] and established the royal quarters and the horse track, and the two rostra, and the forum, and the very exquisite masterpiece of the senate, and placed his own monument upon the porphyry column in the forum.

Malal. XIII.7/320, pp. 245–246, *CP* pp. 527.18–529.7, and George the Monk pp. 499.15–500.13 provide further parallels, though in each case framed by details divergent in important respects from the tradition reflected by Zonaras and sometimes from one another. The statue fell on April 5, 1100 or 1101. Anna Comnena *Alexiad* XII.4.5, p. 370, describes the event.

28   *Cf.* Zon. XII.8 (II, p. 549.3–7). Constantinople became independent of the bishopric of Heracleia either in 330 or 381. Zonaras' comments here reflect views on the primacy of the see of Rome expressed in his commentary on Canon 3 of the Second Ecumenical Council of Nicaea of 787 (*ODB* II, p. 146):

> The prior canon having been constituted about the other patriarchal sees, this one is concerned only with the see of Constantinople, and it ordained that it have the priorities of honor, whether the first rank or singular, as New Rome and Queen of Cities, after the bishop of Rome. Now some have supposed that the preposition "after" does not indicate diminution of honor but the temporal posteriority of this arrangement. For the ancient city was Byzantium, also self-administering. But under Severus, emperor of Rome, it was besieged by the Romans, and after it had withstood the war for three years, was afterwards conquered, when necessities had run out for the inhabitants. And its walls were razed, and also its political rights abolished, and it was subjugated to Perinthus. And Heracleia is Perinthus, whence the selection of the patriarch, too, has been assigned to Heracleia, the bishop of Byzantium thus being confirmed by him. And subsequently this great city was built by Constantine the Great, and was called in his name, and was named New Rome; hence some said that the preposition "after" was a temporal designation, and not a reduction of honor in relationship to the elder Rome.
>
> [R-P II, p. 173]

29   *Cf.* Sym. 88.11, p. 110: "And sainted Metrophanes [*EEC* I, p. 21] was bishop of Byzantium before Alexander [*EEC* I, p. 21]." Scut. p. 49.20–27:

> Domitianus, the brother of Probus the sovereign, 28 years. Probus, son of Dometius, 12 years. Metrophanes, son of

Domitius, ten years. Under him, as we said, Constantine the Great sojourned in the city, and Constantinople was consecrated, and the holy first synod by sovereign command was convened in Nicaea against Arius, and the throne of Constantinople was elevated to the apex of the patriarchate.

30   *Cf.* Zonaras' introduction to his commentary on the canons of the synod, convened early in June of 325 (*EEC* II, p. 595):

> The Holy and First Ecumenical Council took place during the reign of Constantine the Great, when three-hundred and eighteen holy fathers were gathered in Nicaea of Bithynia, against Arius, who had become a priest of a church at Alexandria, who was blaspheming against the Son of God, our Lord Jesus Christ, saying he was not "of the same essence" as the God and Father, and that he was a creation, and that there was a time when he was not. And this Holy Council condemned and anathematized him along with those of the same mind with him. And it decreed the Son to be "the same essence" as the Father, and true God, and Ruler, and Lord, and Creator of all creators, but not a creation, and certainly, moreover, not a piece of workmanship.
>
> [R-P I, p, 112]

Arius (*EEC* I, pp. 76–78) had actually been priest of the congregation at Baucalis, near Alexandria's harbor. His theology clashed with that of Alexander (*EEC* I, p. 20), bishop of the city, who, *ca.* 320, convened a council of bishops of Egypt and Libya which condemned Arius' position and excommunicated those who maintained it.

31   Zonaras restates in abbreviated form his earlier condemnation of Origen at XII.20 (II, pp. 586–587). For the relationship between the theologies of Origen and Arius, see *EEC* I, pp. 76–77 and n. 34, below. Zonaras' commentary on the Fifth Ecumenical Council, held in 553 at Constantinople (*EEC* I, p. 197), notes that the synod "anathematized Origen and his impious writings" (R-P I, p. 292).

32   Zonaras' focus on Arius' person and theology hardly reflects the agenda of the Council of Nicaea, for which see *EEC* II, p. 595. Sym. 88.6–7, pp. 108–109, gives but a perfunctory nod to the Council: "In the twentieth year of his reign, occurred the first synod in Nicaea, against Arius. From there, he came to Byzantium, having taken the

holy and illustrious fathers with him for [109] the city which he founded to be blessed by them." Cedrenus includes several distinct accounts of the gathering, one of which reflects that of Scutariotes.

Ced. p. 495.16–19: In the 16th and 17th and 18th year, measures were taken against the impious Arius, and there occurred the first holy and ecumenical synod in Nicaea of three hundred and eighteen holy and God-inspired fathers, which anathematized Arius and those in agreement with him.

pp. 499.21–500.6: In the 20th year occurred the holy and ecumenical first synod in Nicaea, 318 fathers having convened. Legates of Sylvester, pope of Rome—presbyters Vito and Vicentius—, [500] Metrophanes of Byzantium, Alexander of Alexandria [*EEC* I, p. 20], Eustathius of Antioch [*EEC* I, p. 303], Macarius of Jerusalem [*EEC* I, p. 514] led it against Arius, who had become presbyter of Alexandria, blaspheming that God, the Word, was a creation and of another essence than the Father, and having opined that there was a time when It was not. Having deposed him, it anathematized him, along with those in agreement with him.

Scut. pp. 49.28–50.12: And the holy and first ecumenical synod in Nicaea was convened against Arius the presbyter of the church in Alexandria, who was blaspheming the son of God, our Lord Jesus Christ, and saying that He was a creation and not the same in essence [50] to the God and Father. But the holy synod, having confuted him, stated clearly that the Son was the same in essence to the Father, since, too, every son is the same in essence to the father who has begotten him, having decreed: ". . . light from light, and true God from true God, and maker of all things visible and invisible with his Father who is without beginning, and judge of living and dead." And the moderators of the synod and those through whom the synod was organized were Sylvester's, the pope of Rome's, through the legates Vito and Vicentius, both presbyters, Hosius of Corduba [*EEC* I, p. 626, *s.v.* Ossius], Alexander of Constantinople [*EEC* I, p. 21], Alexander of Alexandria, with Athanasius the Great, who was then still enrolled in the deacons, Eustathius of Antioch, and Macarius of Jerusalem.

33   For the tradition of the recantation of Eusebius of Caesarea (*EEC* I, pp. 299–301), pupil of Pamphylus (*EEC* II, p. 638, *s.v.* Pamphilus), see, for example, Soc. *HE* I.14, pp. 33–34.

34   *Cf.* Eus. *HE* I.2.5, p. 12.18, quoting *Psalms* 32(33).9; I.2.11, p. 16.12–14, and 14–15, pp. 18.12–20.4, quoting *Proverbs* 8.22; and I.3.19, pp. 36.25–38.1. Eusebius did, in fact, complete the *HE* long before the Council of Nicaea, Book I in its original form probably before 300. Eusebius produced a revised and expanded edition of the *HE ca.*

315. Soc. *HE* II.21, pp. 85–87, uses passages from Eusebius' *Ecclesiastical Theology*, including *Proverbs* 8.22, in the same manner as those Zonaras employed from the *HE*, but to vindicate Eusebius of the charge of Arianism. Note, too, that at the end of his examination of Eusebius' theology, Socrates links him to what he represents as the benign influence of Origen. In short, whatever its origin, Zonaras' consideration of Eusebius reads like an inversion of Socrates, whose notice of Origen may explain the attention given him by Zonaras in connection with Arius, for which see n. 31, above.

35 No formal acts of the Council of Nicaea survive. Zonaras perhaps refers to Gelasius of Cyzicus' account of what transpired at Nicaea— mentioned by Photius *Bibl. Cod.* 15 (I, p. 12)—which employs precisely the same words as Zonaras. *Cf.* Gel. Cyz. *Comm.* II.18–19 and 26, *PG* 85, cols. 1265B-1284A and 1307B-1310B.

36 The name of Macedonius (*EEC* II, p. 516) had come to be applied to those who denied the divinity of the Holy Spirit (*EEC* II, p. 516 and 2, p. 700, *s.v. Pneumatomachi*). The synod in question is the Council of Constantinople of 381 (*EEC* I, pp. 195–196), particularly Canon I, on which Zonaras provided a substantial gloss (R-P II, pp. 165–167). See, too, Ced. p. 553.6–15.

37 Soc. *HE* I.11, p. 29, focuses on Constantine's homage to Paphnutius (*EEC* II, p. 646), who had lost an eye in the persecutions. Ced. pp. 503.23–504.1 also mentions Paphnutius. Elsewhere Cedrenus and George the Monk, in words identical to one another, tell the story related by Zonaras.

George the Monk, p. 504.11–17:	Ced. pp. 500.22–501.3: And when
And when he had beheld some who had lost their right eyes and had learned they had suffered this by Diocletian and Maximianus through allegiance to Christ, embracing them, he applied his lips to their wounds, believing that he could thence attract a blessing by his kiss.	he had beheld some who had lost their right eyes and [501] learned they had suffered this by Diocletian and Maximianus through allegiance to Christ, embracing them, he applied his lips to their wounds, believing that he could thence attract a blessing by his kiss.

38 *Cf.* Gel. Cyz. *HE* II.81–4, p. 42.10–30 = Gel. Caes. *fr.* 11, p. 350; Theod. *HE* I.10.4–6, p. 47.9–24; and George the Monk p. 508.4–16 with:

Ced. p. 504.10–21: Quarrelsome men subsequently gave to the sovereign written charges against certain bishops. And when he had received these and bound them shut and sealed them with his ring, he ordered them to be put under guard. Then, after he had reconciled them to peace and understanding, these he burned in the presence of all, having satisfied them by a pledge that he had read none of what had been written in them. For he used to say that it was not right that the faults of priests become evident to the masses, lest they, having taking from them a justification of scandal, shamelessly sin. And "I, if I witnessed a bishop furrowing another's wife, would cover the crime with this purple of mine, so the sight would not harm those who beheld what was being done."

Scut. p. 50.15–22: And also when the synod was concluded, some brought charges against bishops, which the Christ-imitating sovereign, without having retired to read them, consigned to oblivion through fire, having added that statement ever-memorable and admirable and of goodness and sympathy of God: "I, even if I had caught a priest in the act of committing adultery, I would cover him with the wing of my cloak, so the abomination not be known, in order that God might also cover my transgressions."

39   Constantinople was not dedicated until 330. Alexander (*EEC* I, p. 21) had been bishop of Byzantium from 314, the year of Metrophanes' death, and was bishop of Constantinople from 330–337. With Zonaras, *cf.* Scut. p. 52.11–16:

And the sovereign, after he had elected through them the most godly Alexander patriarch of Constantinople—the most pious Metrophanes already having met his end—, all via the public horse and at public expense he discharged to their own sees, having praised God, who had graced mankind with such a Christ-loving and orthodox sovereign.

40   Helen died *ca.* 330 in Nicomedia.

41   Constantine died on May 22, 337. Zonaras alone places Constantius in Antioch. He errs in attributing to Constantius the construction of Constantine's resting place. *Cf.* Soc. *HE* I.40, pp. 62–63 Soz. *HE* II.34.5–6, p. 2–12, and:

Sym 88.8, p. 109:
Then, when he moved against Persia, he arrived from Nicomedia at the hot springs in Pythia and, after he had become ill and gone from there through Helenopolis to the camp, when a violent fever had seized him, he died in the ninth year after the foundation and dedication of Constantinople. And his remains were conveyed to the Church of the Holy Apostles and deposited in the sepulcher, which was built by him for burial of sovereigns . . . .

Ced. p. 519.16–24: In the 33rd year of his reign, the great Constantine died. For when he had moved against Persia from Nicomedia, he arrived at the hot springs in Pythia. And after he had become ill and gone from there through Helenopolis to the camp, after a violent fever had seized him, he died, in the 9th year from the foundation and dedication of Constantinople. And he was buried in a porphyry or Roman sarcophagus, both him and his mother Helen, who had died twelve years before his death, and his wife Fausta, daughter of Maximianus Herculius . . .

Scut. p. 54.6–9: And Constantine the Great died in the month May on the twenty-first and was buried with his mother in the Church of the Holy Apostles in the sepulcher which he himself built, in a porphyry sarcophagus.

42   *Epit. de Caes.* 41.14, p. 167.15–16—"The royal garb he adorned with gems, and his head, at all times, with a diadem."—and 41.16, p. 167.24–27—"He was a mocker rather than a flatterer. From this he was called after Trachala in the folktale, for ten years a most excellent man, for the following twelve a brigand, for the last, on account of his unrestrained prodigality, a ward irresponsible for his own actions."—are among a range of sources which fault Constantine on this point. *Cf.* Ced. pp. 472.23–473.1—"In stature Constantine the Great was middling, his shoulders rather broad and neck thick, whence, too, Trachela he [473] was named, . . ."—and 517.7–9—"And they say that he first of all the sovereigns used a diadem and adorned himself too elaborately in pearls and other stones." However, here Zonaras or his source seems to be reacting specifically to Julian's portrayal of Constantine at *Caesares* 36/335b (II.2, p. 69).

43   Only Zonaras attributes this sentiment to Constantine. *Mark* 9.43–47 may have provided inspiration.

44   Zonaras is the only source to note the existence of two traditions. In 335 Constantine certainly had assigned portions of the empire to Constantine, Constans, Constantius, and Dalmatius. After Constantine the Great's death, a purge eliminated Fl. Julius Dalmatius 7 (*PLRE* I, p. 241), his brother Hannibalianus 2 (*PLRE* I, p. 407), and Julius Constantius 7 (*PLRE* I, p. 226, the father of Gallus and Julian). The brothers evidently met in Pannonia in the early fall and, by the date of their formal acclamation as Augusti on September 9, had worked out among themselves a division of the empire and some order of precedence that seems to have recognized Constantine's pre-eminence in the college of rulers.

The specifics in Zonaras reflect this division of 337, with Dalmatius' former holdings of Thrace, Macedonia, and Achaea divided between Constantius and Constans. The designation of "King of Kings and of the Pontic Peoples" granted in 335 by Constantine to Hannibalianus disappeared with the latter's death. Zonaras' two traditions, then, seem to result from his or the source tradition's confusion between Constantine's arrangement of 335 and that reached among the brothers in 337. It seems more likely that Zonaras found in his source or sources a notice, or what he took as a notice, of the two traditions than that he came to an independent judgment about their existence on the basis of his consideration of what appeared to him to be two discrete versions of the division of the empire among Constantine's sons. Ced. p. 519.13–15 comments: "in the 29th year [of Constantine's reign] Dalmatius was proclaimed Caesar. Calocaerus [*PLRE* I, p. 177], who had usurped power in Tarsus of Cilicia was burned alive by Dalmatius." *Cf.* further:

| Sym. 88.8, p. 109: . . . having left behind three sons, Constantius, Constantine, and Constans, having assigned Constantius to hold the areas of Thrace and the East, Constantine the western areas toward Ocean, and Constans Crete, Africa, and Illyricum † of these. | Ced. p. 519.24–520.4: . . . having left behind in sovereignty three [520] sons, Constantius, Constantine, and Constans, having assigned Constantius to hold the areas of Thrace and the East, Constantine the western areas toward Ocean, and Constans Crete, Africa, and Illyricum. | Scut. p. 53.18–23: Indeed, the most godly sovereign, having piously and devoutly reached the end of his life, having left his three sons as successors of the realm—Constans in Italy and Rome, Constantius in Constantinople, and Constantine in the Gauls and the provinces beyond the Alps— departed for the immortal realm. |

Epit. de Caes. 41.19–20, pp. 167.30–168.7: Thus rule of the Roman world was returned to three men, Constantine, Constantius, and Constans, the sons of Constantine. 20. These individually held these areas as their realms: Constantine the Younger, everything beyond the Alps; Constantius, from the Strait of the Propontis, Asia, and Oriens; Constans, Illyricum and Italy and Africa; Delmatius, Thrace and Macedonia and Achaea; Hannibalianus, brother of Delmatius Caesar, Armenia and neighboring, allied nations.

Zos. II.39 (ed. Bekker, p. 105.7–23): After he had oppressed the state in all these fashions, Constantine died by disease. His sons, being three, when they had received the realm—these were not born from Fausta, the daughter of Maximianus Herculius, but from another, whom, after he had introduced a charge of promiscuity, he killed—, they took charge of affairs, submitting to youthful impulse rather than to the benefit of public affairs. For first they divided the peoples: Constantine, the eldest, at the same time to Constans, the youngest, was allotted all the peoples beyond the Alps, and Italy and Illyricum as well as these, and, further, the peoples around the Euxine Sea and Libya below Carthage; and to Constantius had been entrusted the peoples about Asia, and the East, and Egypt. And, in a fashion, Dalmatius, who had been made Caesar by Constantine, and further Constantius, who was his brother, and Hannibalianus were sharing in the rule, having employed the purple and gold-embroidered garb, having achieved out of respect of kinship the rank of the so-called *nobilissimus*.

45 It is generally thought that Sapor was attempting to take advantage of what he perceived to be a period of confusion and, therefore, an opportunity after Constantine's death to redress the balance that had tilted in Rome's favor as a result of the terms agreed upon by Narses in 298 or 299. Of course, his forces would already have been prepared to counter the offensive Constantine was poised to set in motion. For sources, see D-L, pp. 131–134 and 164–210.

46 *Ca.* 338 Constans had moved to the Danube frontier of the Balkans to campaign against the Sarmatians. Constantine invaded Italy in the spring of 340, which prompted Constans' return and led to Constantine's defeat and death at Aquileia. Zonaras provides the most detailed extant account of the battle. Philost. *HE* III.1, pp. 29.1–30.3, makes a plot by Constans against Constantine's life the *casus belli*. Cf.:

Sym. 89.1, p. 111: Constantius reigned 24 years, Constans 17 years. Constantine died swiftly. And he died in the following fashion: having communicated with his brother Constantius, he began approaching certain locations with much strength and power, which induced Constantius to consternation lest he was advancing toward him for the purpose of attempting a rebellion. And when he had attained base counsels which induced him more toward action and fear and, through these, toward war, than disabused him of such calculations, he moved against him. And when the war had begun, when he had been discovered among the last of those fleeing, Constantine was killed, being the third brother, and Constantius came into control of the entire West.

Ced. p. 520.15–23: Constantius reigned 24 years, Constans 17 years. Constantine died swiftly in the following fashion: after he had communicated with his brother Constantius, he began approaching certain locations with much strength and power, which induced Constantius to consternation lest he was advancing toward him for the purpose of attempting a rebellion. And when he had attained counsels which were base and inciting him toward war, he moved against him. And when the war had erupted, when he had been discovered among the last of those fleeing, Constantine was killed, being the third brother, and Constantius came into control of the entire West.

Scut. pp. 53.24–54.3: Constantine, unwilling to be satisfied with his father's arrangement, but having begun a war against his brother Constans, himself died in the war, while Constans both gained control of his realm and began to reside in the old Rome.

47   This is the first of two treatments of Constans' death—the second at XIII.6—each of which appears to derive from separate strands of the tradition upon which Zonaras depends. Here Zonaras alone mentions Constans' foiling of an attempt on Magnentius' life. Constans died sometime in January 350, since Magnentius was proclaimed Augustus on January 18 of that year. *Cf.* Eutr. X.9.3, p. 176.10–11, "depraved friends," "grave vices;" Aur. Vict. *Caes.* 41.24, p. 127.9–12, on Constans' purchase of young barbarian hostages to satisfy homosexual desires; Zos. II.42.1, alleging license granted by Constans to attractive barbarians in return for their sexual favors; and John of

Rhodes *Pass. Art.* 10, p. 49.23–25/*PG* 96, col. 1261A: "Constans, having taken his ease in revelries and drunken carousals and unnatural erotic dalliances, gambled the whole empire without a care, dancing away the majesty of the realm."

48   Adarnarses (*PLRE* I, p. 12, *s.v.* Adanarses) was the son of Hormisdas II. Adarnarses, who succeeded his father upon the latter's death in 309, was quickly deposed and killed by a faction of the Persian nobility. An older brother, Hormisdas 2 (*PLRE* I, p. 443), escaped and surfaced at the Roman court.

49   Salmasian John *fr.* 266 Roberto, p. 450 = *fr.* 178.1 Müller *FHG* IV, p. 605, recounts the same tale:

> Adarnarses, while still a child, was asked by his own father Narses, King of Persia, if the tent which had been brought to him made from Babylonian skins was beautiful. He said that, if he too would rule the realm, he would make one more beautiful than this from human skins.

Zos. II.27, provides as a context a birthday celebration at which Hormisdas, rather than Adarnarses, threatens with Marsyas' fate Persian nobles who have not shown him due respect.

50   *Suda* M 230 (III, p. 331.11–20), probably from Eunapius' *History*, though not included in any of the standard collections of its fragments, and Salmasian John *fr.* 266 Roberto, p. 450 = *fr.* 178.1 Müller *FHG* IV, p. 605, provide closed parallels:

Suda: And a story circulates concerning Hormisdas the Persian, who deserted to Constantine the Great [*sic*]. For he, when he had gone out to the hunt and returned to the palace, when those who had been invited to dinner had not risen according to the established custom, threatened to inflict the death of Marsyas on them. Those of the Persians who had learned what this meant from someone who had heard proclaimed the younger [*i.e.* Adarnarses] king after the death of his father, and he [Hormisdas] they shut	John: He [Shapur] held Hormisdas under guard. His mother, with his wife as an accomplice, having fashioned by some artifice iron bonds, filled them with pearls and, after she had implored the favor of the guards, removed the former chains on the grounds that they were heavy and replaced them with those, so he would, if he were able to escape, bear wealth without weight. And his wife also gave him a file and, having provided dinner for the guards, made them sleep. And when he found the right moment, he broke the bonds

in a cell and fettered in irons. His wife, having brought him a file through the device of the fish, got him out, and, after he had fled, he came as a suppliant to Constantine. The story is well known.

and escaped, and, having employed horses at intervals, dressed as a slave he was honorably received by Licinius. Such a javelin-thrower was he that it is said that he alone had a spear unstained with blood, which he was subsequently depicted holding in a painting.

The version here attributed to Eunapius appears, too, in Zos. II.27.2–3. Amm. Marc. XVI.10.16 alludes to his description of Hormisdas' flight, which he had dealt with in a now-lost portion of the *Res Gestae*.

51 At Singara in 343 or 343. Zonaras alone alleges the wounding of Sapor. For sources, see D-L, pp. 181–190.

52 Zonaras' Augustulum is wrong, either his own error, that of his sources, or perhaps the fault of a copyist. Zos. II.41.4 gives the correct Augustodunum, modern Autun. The date of Magnentius' acclamation was January 18, 350. *Epit. de Caes.* 41.22 and Zos. II.42.3 maintain that Marcellinus 8 (*PLRE* I, p. 546) had organized a birthday party for his own son as a cover for Magnentius' plot.

53 Eutr. X.9.3 and *Epit. de Caes.* 41.24 refer to his ill health. For Constans' alleged immorality, see above, n. 47.

54 Zonaras alone mentions the prophecy.

55 Constans' death came shortly after Magnentius' acclamation. *Epit. de Caes.* 41.23 names Gaeso (*PLRE* I, p. 380, *s.v.* Gaiso) as the killer; Eutr. X.9.4 and Jer. *Chron.* 237ᶜ give the place as Helena; Zos. II.42.5 specifies both Gaiso and Helena. Sym. 89.2, p. 111.11–12: "In the 17th year of his reign, Magnentius, a usurper, when he had been acclaimed in the Gauls, killed Constans in his sleep after a hunt."

56 By February 27, 350, Rome had a new urban prefect, Fabius Titianus (6, *PLRE* I, pp. 918–919). However, contrary to the tradition followed by Zonaras, Titianus had formerly held a series of prestigious offices under Constans.

57 This campaign and the third siege of Nisibis occurred in 350 and lasted for about four months, beginning around mid April. For

sources with translation and commentary, see D-L, pp. 193–210. Ced. p. 524.1–4, is highly compressed:

> In the 13th year, Sapor, a Persian, after he had artfully invested the city Nisibis and channeled the river against the city and made all types of siege devices, was defeated and withdrew in flight toward his homeland, having lost most of his people.

58   Tigranes II became King of Armenia in 96 or 95 BC and at that time allied himself with Mithridates VI of Pontus through his marriage to Mithridates' daughter Cleopatra (*BNP* 3, p. 446, *s.v.* Cleopatra II.16). As part of this alliance, Mithridates received Nisibis, which, in turn, was captured by L. Licinius Lucullus (*OCD*[3], p. 859, *s.v.* Licinius Lucullus 2, Lucius) in 68 BC during the Third Mithridatic War. It is impossible to tell if Zonaras knew the precise kinship bond between Mithridates and Tigranes or the particulars of the Roman capture of Nisibis.

59   The Mygdonius (modern Jaghjaghah) River.

60   Zonaras may mention the Massagetae at XI.24 (II, p. 519.2), where some manuscripts give "They are Massagetae according to Dio." as a gloss on "Albani." The area inhabited by the ancient Albani was roughly in the northern portion of modern Azerbaijan and Dagjestan. "Massagetae," which appears in Herodotus, is an example of Zonaras' use of anachronistic ethnic designations. His mention of the Massagetae in the context of the siege of Nisibis is unique.

61   Constantius arrived in Nisibis around September 350.

62   Pet. Patr. *fr.* 16 Müller *FHG* IV, p. 190 (marred by a serious printer's error) = *ELGR* 14, p. 395.1–32, offers a detailed account of the embassy:

> Magnentius and Vetranio send ambassadors to Constantius. Rufinus [Vulcacius Rufinus 25, *PLRE* I, pp. 782–783] and Marcellinus [9, *PLRE* I, p. 546] were sent, one being a praetorian prefect, the other a commander, and Nunechius [*PLRE* I, p. 635], head of the senate, and, in addition to them, Maximus, in order to suggest to Constantius that he lay aside arms and assume first rank in the realm. And

through them Magnentius was promising moreover to give
his own daughter to Constantius as a wife and that he would
take Constantia, the sister of Constantius. The sovereign,
then, received the ambassadors of Vetranio and Magnentius,
among whom Rufinus, employing his personal rank, often
reminded Constantius of the current state of affairs, saying
that there was no need for him, when he had already labored
in wars, to summon to war against him two sovereigns
experienced in military science and of like mind with one
another and still fresh; the quality and quantity of these men
who, unless he agreed to a peace, would be arrayed against
him in the course of a civil war, whether one was alone or
both together were at hand, he [Rufinus] did not wish him
to learn from anywhere other than their previous accomplishments, when, by their engagements, on his and his family's
behalf, triumphs were achieved. And Nucherius straightway began saying in his opening remarks that Magnentius
sought peace. When he had heard this embassy, the sovereign
was deeply perplexed, and, after he had gone to sleep, saw
a vision—that his father, as if descending from the heavens
and holding by the hand Constans, whom Magnentius
had killed, bringing him to him, seemed to utter these
words: "Constantius, behold Constans, the progeny of many
sovereigns, my son and your brother, treacherously slain.
Therefore, neither suffer to look upon a realm sundered and
a constitution overturned nor continence threats, but pay
heed to the glory of every enterprise that will henceforth
come to be for you and do not see your brother unavenged."
After this vision, when he had awakened, Constantius, when
all the ambassadors save Rufinus had been placed under
arrest . . .

Peter's notice is the sole mention of any child of Magnentius.

63   Philost. *HE* III.22, pp. 49.12–50.6, *Soc. HE* II.28, pp. 99–100,
and Soz. *HE* IV.4.2–4, p. 142.5–18, give more detailed accounts of
Vetranio's meeting with Constantius late in 350 and its aftermath.
Vetranio's six years in Prusa is unique to Zonaras.

64   The elevation of Decentius occurred in July or August of 350,
of Gallus on March 15, 351, in Sirmium. Zonaras' Constantia is actually
Constantina 2 (*PLRE* I, p. 222).

65   With Zonaras, *cf.* Zos. II.46–48.1, many of the details of whose account are unique.

66   The army of Constantius, who himself was actually at Sirmium, faced Magnentius and Silvanus (2, *PLRE* I, pp. 840–841) at Siscia on the Save, in present-day Croatia. This would have been late in the summer, perhaps in September, of 351.

67   The story is unique to Zonaras, though the theme is common. The tale likely reflects contemporary *ex post facto* embellishment of the sort common in panegyric. Magnentius was a Christian, not that that in itself would rule out recourse to magic.

68   Zos. II.50.4–51 and Zonaras are the fullest accounts of the battle of Mursa, on the Drave shortly above its confluence with the Danube, fought on September 28, 351. On Magnentius' near capture, see, too, John of Antioch *fr.* 260 Roberto = *fr.* 174 Müller, n. 75, below. Again, contrary to Zonaras, Constantius was probably still at Sirmium rather than on the field at Mursa.

69   Magnentius withdrew first to Aquileia and then, sometime after late July 352 and in the face of an offensive by Constantius' forces, to Gaul. Constantius retired to the Balkans to campaign against the Sarmatians. With Constantius' treatment of this unknown senatorial legate, *cf.* Zonaras XIII.7 and n. 62, above. In 350, Magnentius had used the bishops Servatius of Tongres and Maximus as ambassadors to Constantius. So, *e.g.*, Athanasius *Apologia ad Constantium Imperatorem* 9, *PG* 25 605B.

70   Amm. Marc. XIV.7.4 may provide a parallel:

> . . . his [Gallus'] propensity for doing harm was inflamed and incited by a worthless woman, who, on being admitted to the palace (as she had demanded) had betrayed a plot that was secretly being made against him by some soldiers of the lowest condition. Whereupon Constantina, exulting as if the safety of her husband were now assured, gave her a reward, and, seating her in a carriage, dispatched her through the palace gates into the public streets, in order that by such inducements she might tempt others to reveal similar or greater conspiracies.

Zonaras' account may reflect rhetorical elaboration rather than access to informed sources, while that of Ammianus seems to mirror public knowledge of the incident as the result of the presentation of the informant to the populace of Antioch. There is no need to posit any common literary source. At any rate, the incident seems to fall soon after Gallus' arrival in Antioch, when the assassination could divert Constantius and, if the *magister equitum* Ursicinus (2, *PLRE* I, pp. 985–986) was then active in Palestine, Gallus would perhaps have been more vulnerable to attack.

71 *Cf. Soc. HE* II.32, pp. 105–106; Soz. *HE* IV.7.6–7, pp. 146.31–147.6; Theod. Lect. *Epit.* 89, p. 43.10–14; and Theoph. *AM* 5849, p. 44.12–18. Constantius' victory was in the late summer of 353 near Mons Seleucus. Magnentius, who had fled to Lugdunum (Lyons), killed himself on August 10 or 11. Decentius took his own life on August 18 at Sens.

| Sym. 89.2–3, pp. 111.15–112.4: And Gallus [*sic*] overcame Magnentius and then also became hostile to Constantius; Constantius, when he had mastered him by praise and flattery, kills him. | Ced. p. 524.16–17: In the 15th year, Gallus, having exercised a tyranny, killed Dometianus, prefect of the East, and Magnus, a *quaestor*. | Scut. p. 56.5–8: Since his [Constantius'] wife Eusebia did not bear him a son, he adopted his cousin Gallus, and, having appointed him Caesar, dispatched him to administer affairs around Rome and the Gauls. When he [Gallus] had been deceitfully slain there, . . . |

72 Gallus reached Antioch on May 7, 351.

73 Amm. Marc. XIV is by far the most detailed account of Gallus' tenure as Caesar. Amm. Marc. XIV.1.10 condemns the praetorian prefect Thalassius for his failure to check Gallus' alleged violent streak, but allows that he did keep Constantius secretly informed of the Caesar's behavior. Upon Thalassius' death by natural causes in 353, Constantius appointed Domitianus to replace him and sent him to Gallus' court at Antioch. According to Amm. Marc. XIV.7.9, Constantius began to reduce the number of troops actually with Gallus.
John of Rhodes *Pass. Art.* 12–13, pp. 53.19–55.16/*PG* 96 1264A-B, had Constantius, jealous of Gallus' great success against Sapor,

dispatch Domitianus to prevent the Caesar's triumphal entry into Antioch. The haughty Domitianus then enraged Gallus, who ordered Montius to see to Domitianus' death. When Montius objected that Domitianus' execution would exceed the bounds of Gallus' authority, Constantina "dragged down Montius from his judgement-seat with her own hands" and, with Gallus' consent, both Montius and Domitianus were slaughtered. Theoph. *AM* 5846, p. 41.12–15, perhaps reflects popular perception or propaganda in accusing Gallus of plotting a coup and then murdering Domitianus and Montius, both of whom allegedly had revealed Gallus' plan.

74   Constantius learned of the trials at Antioch in the spring of 354, while at Valentia. It was only after Constantius had concluded a peace with the Alamanni and withdrawn to his winter quarters at Milan that affairs came to a head. Zos. II.55 connects Gallus' fate to the desire of court sycophants for position and personal gain, indicting by name Dynamius (2, *PLRE* I, p. 275), Picentius (*PLRE* I, p. 701), and Lampadius (properly C. Ceionius Rufius Volusianus 5, *PLRE* I, pp. 978–980). Amm. Marc. XIV.11.1–5 describes secret meetings at which the emperor discussed with his confidants how to destroy Gallus. Flavius Arbitio (2 *PLRE* I, pp. 94–95), Constantius' *magister equitum*, and the *praepositus cubiculi*, the eunuch Eusebius (11, *PLRE* I, pp. 302–303), he maintains, argued against summoning Gallus before Ursicinus, whom they charged had designs on the throne, had been brought to the West. They argued that agents of Ursicinus had incited Gallus in the hope that his resultant unpopularity would open the way to the throne for the sons of the *magister equitum* himself. Whether this is an accurate picture or not, Constantius called Ursicinus to Milan on the pretext of planning for a campaign against the Persians and then sent him to the East as an interim commander with the title *dux*, replacing him with his vicar Prosper (*PLRE* I, p. 751).

After Constantina died of a fever at Caeni Gallicani in Bithynia and Gallus hesitated in Antioch, the *tribunus scutariorum* Scudilo (*PLRE* I, pp. 810–811) enticed him with news that Constantius planned to raise him to the rank of Augustus and to enlist his aid in some future campaign. En route, Gallus, apparently in a formal *adventus*, entered Constantinople, staged horse races, and crowned a champion charioteer. Letters from Constantius eventually caused him to continue west to Petobio in Noricum, where picked troops led by Barbatio (*PLRE* I, pp. 146–147), accompanied by the *agens in rebis* Apodemius (1, *PLRE* I, p. 82), surrounded his palace. Barbatio, whom Amm. Marc. XIV.11.24 accuses of contriving charges against

Gallus before Constantius, stripped Gallus of his imperial robes, assured him that no harm would come to him, and transferred him under guard to Pola. There Eusebius, Pentadius (2, *PLRE* I, p. 687), and Mallubaudes (*PLRE* I, p. 539) interrogated him about the treason trials at Antioch. Ammianus alleges that in response Gallus attempted to place on Constantina the responsibility for the deaths of those executed. This, Ammianus relates, so enraged Constantius that he dispatched Serenianus (2, *PLRE* I, p. 825), who, together with Pentadius and Apodemius, informed Gallus that he had been sentenced to death. The precise date of Gallus' death is unknown and only Zonaras gives his age at the time.

75   Silvanus, who had been a commander under Magnentius, deserted the latter for Constantius shortly before the battle of Mursa. From 352/353 to 355 he served as Constantius *magister peditum* in Gaul. In early August of 355 he took the title of Caesar and, after 28 days, was murdered on September 7, 355 at Colonia Agrippina. John of Antioch *fr.* 260 Roberto, p. 444 = *fr.* 174 Müller *FHG* IV, p. 604 = *EI* 74, p. 114.20–115.10, comments:

> For in fact, on the twenty-eighth day after the revolt, when he [Nepotianus] had been captured by Magnentius' commanders, he was beheaded; this, lifted on a pole, his captors carried through the whole city. Subsequently, there were in fact hefty payments of money and murders of the most prominent Romans through suspicion of complicity with Nepotianus. Not very much later, in truth, Magnentius, near the city Mursa, when he had been driven from the ranks at the hands of Constantius' men and also barely avoided falling into the hands of the enemy, fled, much that was Roman having been destroyed on each side in this battle, which would, when deployed, have sufficed for both foreign and civil wars and stood as an agent of many victory parades and security for those of the same race. And Constantius turned toward civil war. After which, indeed, Magnentius, defeated in numerous battles, removed himself from life by suicide around the city Lugdunum, having killed his mother beforehand, in the fourth year and seventh month of his reign. And his brother shared death with him, having been appointed Caesar for defense of Gaul.
>
> About these very times, in truth, by Gallus, the Caesar— a man savage by nature and who was intending to establish

a tyranny as the government, if it had resulted for the Preeminent Ruler to assign the hegemony to him—, after many unfitting actions, was killed by Constantius the sovereign. And a certain Silvanus, engaging in revolutionary activities throughout Gaul, inside of thirty days was disposed of.

76 Zonaras' Persian embassy is probably that dispatched by Sapor in 357 and which had arrived in Constantinople—here called Byzantium by Zonaras—on February 23, 358. Pet. Patr. *fr.* 17, *FHG* IV, p. 190 = *ELGR* 15, pp. 395.33–396.2, provides the name of its leader:

> Under Constantius, ambassadors came from Persia. And the head of the embassy, Narses (*PLRE* I, p. 617. *s.v.* Narseus), after he had combined the harshness of the letters which he was carrying with the mildness of his own manners, delivered them for a reading.

Zonaras is correct that Constantius was then in Sirmium. Amm. Marc. XVII.5 quotes the purported contents of Sapor's letter and Constantius' response. Ammianus' version, contrary to Zonaras', contains no reference to the Macedonian conquest, if, indeed, Zonaras actually means that these comments he attributes to Constantius were part of the emperor's formal, written response to Sapor. Likewise, Ammianus gives by far the most detailed account of the diplomatic wrangling and jockeying of forces that preceded the broad Persian offensive of 359. Amida fell in 359 after a seventy-three-day siege, after which the campaigning season ended with Sapor's withdrawal to Persia. For Amida, see Amm. Marc.XVIII.6–19.9; for chronology and additional sources, D-L, pp. 211–230.

77 Julian's parents, Julius Constantius (*PLRE* I, p. 226, *s.v.* Constantius 7) and Basilina (*PLRE* I, p. 148), married sometime after the death of Constantius' former wife and the mother of Julian's half-brother Gallus, Galla (2, *PLRE* I, p. 382), an event for which Gallus' birth in 325/326 provides a *terminus post quem*, and a date of about nine months before Julian's birth in May or June of 332, a *terminus ante quem*. Basilina died shortly after Julian's birth. Since his father had been a victim of the purge of 337 following the death of Constantine, Zonaras' assertion that Julius and Basilina committed their son to Eusebius is incorrect.

Constantius summoned Julian to his court before Gallus' execution. Thereafter, at the intercession of Eusebia, Constantius permitted him to go to Athens to study. He soon was called to Milan and proclaimed Caesar on November 6, 355, at which time he and Helen married. The story of Basilina's dream is without parallel.

78   Eun. *VS* 7.3.7/476 attributes the identical motive to Constantius. Zos. III.1.2–3 has Eusebia plant this seed in Constantius' mind, though mainly to counter the emperor's alleged suspicions of his relatives and to smooth the way for Julian's command in Gaul. Amm. Marc. XVI.11.13 says that a rumor current among the troops in Gaul after Julian's arrival attributed this purpose to Constantius, and Amm. Marc. XXII.3.7 treats this as fact. *Cf.* Libanius *Or.* 12.42–43 and 18.36–37 and Soc. *HE* III.1, p. 138, which takes pains to counter the story.

79   The campaigning seasons for 356–360 saw Julian victorious in a major battle at Strasbourg in 357, when many of the enemy perished in the Rhine. After Strasbourg Julian crossed the Rhine to attack the Alamanni. The following year, he returned to complete the job that the onset of winter had forced him to leave undone. The year 359 saw further action against the Alamanni, among others. The return of Roman prisoners was one of the conditions of a subsequent peace. Among the sources that mention the return of prisoners are Julian *Ep. ad Athen.* 8/280C (I.1, p. 227); Eun. *Hist. fr.* 19 Blockley *FCH* II = *fr.* 13 Müller = *ELGR* 2, p. 593.20–31; Amm. Marc. XVIII.2.19; and Zos. III.4.4–7.

80   Julian's elevation to Augustus probably dates to February of 360. With Zonaras' version, *cf.* Julian *Ep. ad Athen.* 10–11/282B–285D (I.1, pp. 229–233), Libanius *Or.* 18.90–105; Amm. Marc. XX.4—which, at XX.4.17–18, contains an account of the diadem incident; Zos. III.8–9; and John of Antioch *fr.* 264 Roberto, pp. 446–448 = *fr.* 177 Müller *FHG* IV, p. 605 = *EI* 75, p. 115.11–31:

> For a time, Julian the Transgressor, saying he was second, continued to serve the emperor. But when Constantius, stirred to envy of what was being accomplished by him, began to compel the so-called Germanic unit, assigned from the most distant past to protect Galatia [*sic*], to leave their traditional mission so that Julian, isolated, could be more easily attacked by him and the barbarians, with approval

of the soldiers who were aware of Constantius' intent, he [Julian] presented himself as emperor and, when he had remained there for a year, stabilized Galatia. But, when he had won over the army, he neither marched on Italy nor openly hastened toward civil war, but again attacked the barbarians. When he had come to and crossed the river, he began to advance on the so-called Hercynian forest. And there, after he had built ships for the river and boarded the strongest element of the army, he began to convey it along the riverbank so he could escape notice. And he accomplished much. When Constantius observed this, he turned with rage toward civil war. It was not, however, granted to him to meet Julian in battle, God having presided over the war and Constantius having met his end in the midst of his march near the city Mopsuestia, situated on the boundaries of Cilicia and Syria, in the 45th year of his life, in the 38th of his reign.

81 With Zonaras' version, *cf.* Julian *Ep. ad Athen.* 12/285D-286D (I.1, pp. 233–234), Amm. Marc. XX.8.2–19—close to Zonaras, though sometimes fuller, as, *e.g.*, in naming Eutherius (*PLRE* I, pp. 314–315) along with Pentadius—and Zos. III.9.3–4.

82 Amm. Marc. XX.9.1–5 closely mirrors Zonaras. Ammianus names Nebridius (1, *PLRE* I, p. 619) as the new prefect of the Gauls and adds that Constantius made Felix (3, *PLRE* I, p. 332) *magister officiorum*. All this occurred in 360.

83 Leonas found Julian at Paris. Zonaras is again close to Amm. Marc. XX.9.6–8, though there is divergence in the treatment of common themes. For example, Ammianus has Julian actually read aloud Constantius' directive to retain the title Caesar and makes Leonas withdraw in the face of the ugly reaction of the attendant assemblage.

84 The precise cause and date of Helen's death are uncertain. Amm. Marc. XVI.10.19 records a miscarriage, though he does not link it to Helen's demise. She was alive at the time of Julian's acclamation as Augustus but dead by the time of Julian's celebration of quinquennial games in early November 360 in Vienna (modern Vienne), at which time Amm. Marc. XXI.1.5 says Julian had her remains interred at a villa of his near Rome on the Via Nomentana. Ced. p. 532.15–18

reflects the alternative tradition of Julian's rejection of Helen noted by Zonaras: "And he [Julian] also went after the remaining eunuchs of the palace on account of the rejection of his wife, whom Constantius, her brother, joined to him." See, further, n. 104 below.

85　Amm. Marc. XXI.5.1–10 describes these events in greater detail.

86　Amm. Marc. XXI.2.5 parallels Zonaras.

87　Amm. Marc. XXI.8.1 details the appointments. No other source mentions the motive of uniting Roman forces in order to allow them to choose their emperor.

88　Amm. Marc. XXI.1.6–12 mentions portents of Constantius' death and considers divination in general, while Amm. Marc. XXI.2.2 and Zos. III.9 quote the verses that appear in Zonaras, the celestial positions in which do, in fact, correlate with the date of Constantius' death, November 3, 361. Gregory of Nazianzus *Or.* 4.47.12–15, pp. 148–150, with which *cf.* Libanius *Or.* 18.105, presents such predictions as part of a partisan version of events. Gregory clearly inspired Soz. *HE* V.1.8, p. 189.18–21: "Hellenes tell tales that even before he departed from Galatia prophecy and demons stirred him to this campaign, having indicated in advance the death of Constantius and the change of affairs of state."

89　Amm. Marc. XXI.15.2, among others, describes the fever without mentioning bile. For Constantius' regrets, see, *e.g.*, Theoph. *AM* 5853 p. 47.2–4.

90　See n. 96 below.

91　For Eusebius' (11, *PLRE* I, pp. 302–303) influence on Constantius with respect to Arianism, *cf.* Soc. *HE* II.2, p. 65, and Soz. *HE* III.1.4, p. 101.16–19.

92　It was actually Constantine who forced Alexander of Constantinople's (*EEC* I, p. 21) resignation in July 336. The synod is the Council of Constantinople, which, at that same time, approved Arius' participation in communion. Arius' death prevented this. Tradition may have embellished his sordid end to bring it in line with that attributed by Christian legend to Judas.

Ced. pp. 518.15–519.7: In his [Constantine's] 28th year, the impious Arius, after he had been deposed, having bewitched the ears of the most serene sovereign by feigned repentance and deceitful words—having taken two books (having written the one containing his own perverted opinion in his own hand, he held in secret; having written the other in accordance with the creed set forth in Nicaea through another hand), and having given the latter to the sovereign—and, in truth, solemnly swearing that he so believed just as he had actually also written, he so ensnared the sovereign by his deceitfulness that he [Constantine] commanded he be received forthwith by Alexander the bishop into communion in the church. [519] Accordingly, the bishop, as was to be expected, after he had resisted and entreated God through the whole night, made him an accomplishment of prayer. For, on the next day, the unholy one, advancing with pomp and circumstance toward the church, when he was in the forum near the so-called senate, after he had withdrawn to the latrines nearby when his stomach had spurred him, was hauled down by an angelic hand, when both his body cavity and innards had burst forth with his soul and been discharged in the latrines.

Scut. pp. 54.10–56.5: Constantius, his son, 24 years. After he had become enamored of the Arian heresy, he imposed the greatest terrors on the orthodox and on the holy churches of God. For the moment he obtained the sovereignty, he, urged by the counsels of Eusebius the *praepositus* [11, *PLRE* I, pp. 302–303], began compelling the godly Alexander of Constantinople to receive Arius in the church. And Alexander did not assent to effect this, saying: "The man condemned and anathematized for so great a transgression and impiety by so many holy fathers and exiled by your father and sovereign I am unable to receive." And the sovereign said, "Take heed, bishop, lest you receive him even unwilling." And the patriarch, saying, "Let the will of the Lord come to pass!", after he had entered the godly shrine, threw himself beneath the holy altar, and with lamentations and tears began shouting to God, "Lord, do not grant to the shameless wolf entry into your holy flock. But if you command that Arius be introduced, first release me from the present life." And after he had remained six days in such prayer, he continued without food. And indeed, when the Lord's Day was at hand, at dawn Arius, with the prefect with sovereign powers, was departing for the church. And on the road, when his stomach had spurred him, he was turning aside to a certain spot for this purpose, where, after he had sat down, with the excrement he also discharged all his innards, and so sundered his [55] wretched life, with the patriarch still persevering in earnest prayer. And Alexander lived until the sixth year of the reign of Constantius, having completed twenty-three in the high-priestly throne, but in the years of his life 67. And after his death, while the

sovereign was residing in Antioch,
the confessor Paul was chosen by the
Orthodox on Metrophanes' advice.
But Constantius, when he had
returned, deposed Paul from the
throne as Orthodox, and Eusebius of
Nicomedia as Arian sat on the throne
of Constantinople. However, when
the confessor Paul had fled to Julian,
the bishop of Rome, and through
him had recovered his proper throne
and been conspicuous in this for
three years, after he was both deposed
again and exiled to Cucusus by
Constantius and then killed by the
Arians, after the death of Eusebius,
the spirit fighter Macedonius from
the Arians and also Constantius
illegitimately controlled the church
one year. He too, indeed, stalking
about in madness, transferred the
holy body of the equal of the apostles
Constantine from the Church of the
Holy Apostles to that of the martyr
Acacius, and this gave him
satisfaction in return for the
sovereign's opposition to him. On
which count, too, when he had
occupied the city, he deposed him
from the throne and sent him into
exile and in his place chose as
Patriarch of Constantinople Eudoxius
the Arian, who also served as bishop
ten years.

Moreover, the great Athanasius, the
champion and teacher of the
Orthodox, he often expelled from the
church and exiled. But also the holy
Eustathius, Patriarch of Antioch, who
had brought down Arius in the synod
and had proclaimed the *homoousios*,
through Eusebius, the one who had
impiously served as bishop, he drove
from the church, and all the churches
of God he delivered to the enemies of
the Son of God.

[56] Constantius also returned the
remains of the blessed holy apostles

Andrew the First-Called and Luke
the Evangelist from Achaea through
the great martyr Artemius and
deposited them in the Church of the
Holy Apostles.

93   Alexander had been bishop of Constantinople from 314 and died
shortly after his deposition. Paul's (*EEC* II, pp. 662–663) initial tenure
began in the summer or fall of 337, immediately after Constantine's
death, but without the customary ratification by bishops of nearby sees.
Constantius' arrival from Antioch probably dates to September 337.
Eusebius died in late in 341 and Julius I's (*EEC* I, p. 460) directive
was written under the cover of the Synod of Rome, held the same year.
However, and contrary to Zonaras, a group of bishops assembled as a
synod in Antioch rejected Julius' position, and Paul, it seems, did not
regain his throne, which had been filled by the Arian Macedonius.
Subsequent rioting brought Constantius from Antioch to Constantinople. He again expelled Paul, who traveled to the court of Constans
at Trier. The Council of Serdica (343) appears to have reinstated him,
and he returned to Constantinople where he replaced Macedonius,
though without Constantius' sanction. This, in turn, led Constantius
to order Paul's expulsion and Macedonius' restoration. Constantius'
officials compelled Paul to remove himself to Constans' territory.
By July 344 at the earliest, he was in Thessalonica. He then surfaced
at the court of Constans, with whose help he regained the see of
Constantinople in 346. The year 349 saw his final deposition, subsequent arrest and deportation. He was murdered in 350 at Cucusus
in Armenia. For a detailed exposition of the evidence and its interpretation, see T. D. Barnes, *Athanasius and Constantius* (Cambridge MA:
Harvard University Press, 1993), pp. 212–217.

94   *Soc. HE* II. 38, pp. 120–121, says that structural problems with
the Church of the Holy Apostles had, in Macedonius' view, rendered
the site too dangerous to house Constantine's remains. The rioting that
their removal in 359 caused was an important factor in Macedonius'
fall from imperial favor, and a year later a council of about seventy
bishops that met at Constantinople saw to the bishop's deposition and
the elevation of Eudoxius (January 27, 360). Eudoxius (*EEC* I,
pp. 295–296) did retain the bishopric until his death in 370.
Socrates'—and by extension Zonaras'— Church of St Acacius may be
an anachronism. Whatever the case, its location and the identity of its
namesake are problematic. On all this, see D. Woods, "The Church

of 'St.' Acacius at Constantinople," *Vigiliae Christianae* 55 (2001), pp. 201–207.

95   *Cf.* John of Rhodes *Pass. Art.* 16–17, pp. 156.7–157.4 and 31–32 (not in Bidez' Philostorgius)/*PG* 96, cols. 1265–1268 and 1280–1282, according to which Constantius, while at Adrianople, learned the relics were in Achaea, to which he dispatched Artemius. Artemius' supposed reward for the completion of his mission was an appointment as *dux Aegypti*. The episode's likely date is late 359.

96   Amm. Marc. XXI.6.4 notes Eusebia's beauty; XXI.16.4 Constantius' regimen, health, and extreme chasteness; and XXI.16.7 his skill at verse composition, with the javelin, and as a horseman. In marked contrast is the estimation of *Epit. de Caes.* 42.18–20. Philost. *HE* IV.7, p. 61.9–16, which says that Constantius recalled from exile the bishop Theophilus the Indian (*EEC* II, p. 832), who, by a laying-on of hands, cured the empress of hysteria, perhaps reflects the alternative tradition about Eusebia's death. Unmentioned in the tradition followed by Zonaras is Faustina (*PLRE* I, p. 326), whom Constantius married in 361 shortly after Eusebia's death and who bore to him a daughter, Constantia 2 (*PLRE* I, p. 221).

97   *Cf.* Philost. *HE* VI.6, p. 74.3–5—"When Constantius was being escorted to burial, Julian, when he had arrived, after he had removed the diadem from his [Julian's] head, was marching before the bier and honoring the corpse of the man whose life he was campaigning to take."—and John of Rhodes *Pass. Art.* 21, p. 74.19–21/*PG* 96, cols. 1269–1272—"When the corpse was being escorted to the Church of the Apostles, because they were going to place him near his father, after he had removed the diadem from his head, he [Julian] preceded the litter." Both Amm. Marc. XXI.16.20 and Ced. p. 531.10–13— "Jovian, the one afterward sovereign, then a *protector*, escorted his body and placed it near his father's in the shrine with Eusebia, his first wife."—use Constantius' funeral procession as an opportunity to anticipate Jovian's reign. Ammianus, too, labels Jovian a *protector*.

98   Julian entered Constantinople on December 11, 361.

99   Amm. Marc. XXII.3 details the trials at Chalcedon to which Zonaras alludes.

100   Eun. *Hist. fr.* 25 Blockley *FCH* II, p. 36 = *fr.* 16 Müller *FHG* IV, p. 21 = *Suda* I 437 (II, p. 643.7–20), stresses Julian's excellence

as a judge. Salmasian John *fr.* 268 Roberto p. 452 = *fr.* 178.3 Müller *FHG* IV, p. 605, alone parallels the purported exchange between Julian and a defendant:

> Numerianus was accused by someone of stealing public funds. He denied it. And the accuser, having no evidence to the contrary, said, "Who of those accused would be subject to justice, if denial alone suffices for acquittal?" Julian said, "Who will be acquitted, if the accuser is to be believed without proof?"

For Julian's reign, verbatim correspondence between sections of Symeon, Cedrenus, Scutariotes, Socrates, Sozomenus, Theodoret, and Theodore Lector point strongly to the last as the filter through which material from Socrates, Sozomenus, and Theodoret reached Symeon, Cedrenus, and Scutariotes. Zonaras, on the other hand, here depends on some parallel tradition that antedated and in places influenced Socrates, Sozomenus, Theodoret, and Theodore Lector.

For the positions that Zonaras says Julian targeted, *cf.* Amm. Marc. XXII.4 and n. 104 below.

101   Zonaras alludes to a tradition reflected in Soz. *HE* V.2, especially V.2.15–18, pp. 193.25–194.20, and Theod. *HE* III.3.1–5, pp. 177.18–178.19. *Cf.* Scut. pp. 56.23–57.2:

> Julian the Transgressor, 2 years, six months. This most polluted man, nurtured from youth in piety and educated in divine words, so that he held the title of a cleric of the metropolis of Nicomedia and in it read the divine books, and desiring to come to be in control of the realm, found men who deceived him, and, after he had washed away divine baptism with human blood, received the devil as his associate, and having openly begun to practice Hellenism after the sovereignty, surpassed all the tyrants and impious before him in inhumanity and savageness, and [57] produced many martyrs who were not persuaded to heed his impiety, among whom was Artemius, great among the martyrs of Christ.

See, too, incidents treated by Eun. *VS* 7.3.8/476 and 21.1.4/498 = Eun. *Hist. fr.* 21.1–2 Blockley *FCH* II, p. 32, though there is no need to go beyond the ecclesiastical historians to understand Zonaras' point.

102 For this aspect of Julian's legislation on education and the reaction it inspired, *cf*. Soc. *HE* III.16, pp. 156–158; Soz. *HE* V.18.1–8, pp. 222.2–223.11; Theod. *HE* III.8, p. 185.7–15; Theoph. *AM* 5854 pp. 48.18–49.9 (especially close to Cedrenus, below); and:

Theod. Lect. *Epit*. 131, p. 58.13–17: Julian legislated that Christians not partake of Hellenic teachings. And Apolinarius made a display of every sort of discipline of a professor, maintaining the Holy Scripture in substance, but having imitated the idioms of all the ancients. And he wrote a discourse against Julian himself, or rather against Hellenes, which he titled *About Truth*.	Sym. 90.5, p. 114: And the same man [Julian] legislated that Christians not partake of Hellenic teachings. And Apollinarius, while maintaining the Holy Scripture in substance, having imitated the idioms of the poets, wrote to bring culture to Christians through these.	Ced. p. 533.20–23: And in the second year, the impious Julian made a law that Christians not partake of Hellenic teachings. And Apollinarius, having maintained the Holy Scripture in substance, imitating the idioms of the poets, wrote to bring culture to Christians.

For the Apollinarii, see *EEC* I, pp. 58–59, *s.v.* Apollinaris, senior, and Apollinaris of Laodicea.

103 Zonaras' notice is too brief to justify detailed discussion of its relationship to the numerous accounts of Julian's directive and the abandonment of the project. Zonaras is not alone among Christian accounts in failing to link explicitly to divine causation the disasters that halted the reconstruction. From among the ecclesiastical historians and chronicles, *cf*., for example, Philost. *HE* VII.9, pp. 95.1–96.7; John of Rhodes *Pass. Art.* 58 and 68, pp. 95.13–96.34/*PG* 96, cols. 1305 and 1315–1317; Rufinus *HE* X.39–40, p. 998.3–24; Soc. *HE* III.20, pp. 160–162; Soz. *HE* V.22, pp. 229.19–232.6; Theod. *HE* III.20, pp. 198.15–200.6; Theod. Lect. *Epit*. 145, p. 61.4–7; Theoph. *AM* 5855, pp. 51.27–52.4; George the Monk pp. 543.8–544.8; and Ced. p. 537.9–14:

And in his third year, after he had punished many and made martyrs, he also commanded that the temple of the Jews be built. And when the work had been undertaken, initially a furious storm carried away the lime—more than twenty thousand units of it—and, when the Jews persisted with the work, a fire, having issued the foundations, incinerated them, and thus did they cease from the work.

Amm. Marc. XXIII.1.3 occurs in the context of a series of omens boding ill for Julian's invasion of Persia.

104   *Cf.* Amm. Marc. XXII.3.12; John of Rhodes *Pass. Art.* 21 p. 74.17–20 /*PG* 96, col. 1271A; and Soc. *HE* III.1, p. 140:

Theod. Lect. *Epit.* 124, p. 57.3–9: And Eusebius, the first of the court eunuchs, he killed, on the grounds, I suppose, that he was unjust, seeking to receive the reputation of the just. And he also was going after eunuchs of the palace on account of the rejection of his wife, whom—his own sister, Constantia by name—Constantius had joined to him, after cooks, for the sake of simple regimen, he says, and after barbers, because one sufficed for many, as he used to say. And from the public conveyance he barred the camels and asses and mules; horses alone he allowed to render service to the public conveyance.	Sym. 90.4, p. 114: He killed Eusebius, the first of the court eunuchs, on the grounds that he was unjust, pursuing, I suppose, the reputation of the just. And he also was going after both all eunuchs of the palace on account of the rejection of his wife because she was Constantius' sister, because of hatred toward him, and also after cooks and barbers, and from the public conveyance camels, cattle, asses, and mules. And he allowed horses alone to render service to the public conveyance.	Ced. p. 532.15–22: And Eusebius, the first of the court eunuchs, he killed, on the grounds, I suppose, that he was unjust. And he also went after the remaining eunuchs of the palace on account of the rejection of his wife, whom Constantius, her brother, joined to him. Similarly, too, after cooks, for the sake of simple regimen, and after barbers, because one sufficed for many, as he used to say. And from the public conveyance he cut the camels and asses and mules, having allowed horses alone to render service through much greed, of which he was a slave.

105   With Soc. *HE* III.12, pp. 152–153, *cf.*:

Theod. Lect. *Epit.* 127, p. 58.1–3: Maris of Chalcedon applied many insults to Julian to his face as he was sacrificing at the dwelling of Fortune.	Ced. pp. 535.17–536.3: And when Julian arrived at the city Chalcedon, Maris, her bishop, applied many insults to Julian to his face as he was sacrificing in the temple of Fortune, calling him transgressor and avenging spirit and alien from the

glory of God. And seeing that he fashioned himself a philosopher, he reviled Maris in this one statement, saying, "Begone, wretch, and lament your blindness." For Maris had suffered from cataract. And he said to the transgressor, [536] "I thank my Lord Christ, who had granted me this, lest I behold your most shameless and most impious face."

106   Zonaras is the sole witness for this incident. However, Salmasian John *fr.* 268 Roberto, p. 452 = *fr.* 178.2 Müller *FHG* IV, p. 605, does mention an encounter at Tarsus between Julian and a priest of Asclepius: "When he had come to Tarsus, when a certain Eudaimon, a one-eyed priest of Aesclepius, was ashamed to be seen by him because of his blindness, he [Julian] examined his unfortunate eye and, in front of all, kissed it."

107   Julian reached Antioch in June or July of 362. The extant *Misopogon* or *Beard-hater* (II.2, pp. 156–199) probably dates to February 363. The insults recorded by Zonaras appear in a number of sources. *Cf.*, for example, Amm. Marc. XXII.14.2–3 ("sacrificer," "Billy Goat") and Soc. *HE* III.17, p. 159 ("sacrificer," "Billy Goat," ropes from Julian's beard), both of which give to Julian's composition the alternative titles *Antiochenes* and *Beard-hater*. Note, too, Theod. Lect. *Epit.* 140, p. 60.3–6:

As he prepared for the war against Persia, Julian dunned the Christians much wealth. When he was in Antioch of Syria, on the pretense of goods for sale, his behavior was especially outrageous. And then, in fact, he composed the speech the *Beard-hater* or *Antiochene* for a defense.

108   *Cf., inter alia*, Soc. *HE* III.17–19, pp. 158–160; Soz. *HE* V.19–20, pp. 223.12–227.13; John of Rhodes *Pass. Art.* 51–56 pp. 86.27–94.7/*PG* 96, cols.1297–1304; and:

Theod. Lect. *Epit.* 140–141, p. 60.6–13: In this [the *Beard-hater*] he commanded that the tomb of the remains of Babylas [*EEC* I, p. 106]. the martyr in Daphne be moved.

Ced. pp. 536.9–537.3: And Julian, continuing to Antioch, and continually going up to Daphne and worshipping the idol of Apollo (for there was the most wondrous work

Reviled about this by the faithful in song, he tormented a certain youth, Theodorus, with cruel tortures on the grounds that he [Theodorus] had been an instigator of the outrages against him.

Gallus, the brother of Julian, when, holding the office of Caesar, was staying in Antioch, wishing to cast into the shadows the unlawful activities which he learned were taking place in Daphne, himself built in Daphne a shrine of Babylas the martyr and placed his body in it. And Julian destroyed the shrine and moved the remains.

of the sculptor Bryxis, which no one else was able to imitate), was seeking an oracle from it, but he chanced on no reply. When he concluded that it was silent because the remains of the holy blessed martyr Babylas were interred in Daphne, he ordered all these to be transferred. When this had been done, all at once fire came down out of the heaven on that night and burned down both the temple and the statue of Apollo, so that not even a trace of it was visible. Then the accursed one, shocked about it and having concluded that it was the result of a Christian plot, interrogated the priests. And when he had exacted retribution in every sort of way, so as even to kill some of them, he heard this alone from them, "Neither by Christians nor another human plot, but, when it had descended from the heaven, fire immolated both the temple and the statue." Then, angered, the transgressor and fighter against God closed the great church of Antioch and [537] plundered all the sacred things. When, after they had been dismissed, the counts Felix [3, *PLRE* I, p. 332] and Julianus, his [Julian's] uncle [12, *PLRE* I, pp. 470–471], said, "We considered the force which hindered us was something providential," the accursed one jeered at them.

The destruction of the shrine and the removal of Babylas' remains preceded the composition of the *Beard-hater* (*Misopogon* 33/361B–C, II.2, p. 187).

109   On the martyrdoms of Artemius (2, *PLRE* I, p. 112; *EEC* I, p. 83, *s.v.* Arthemius), Eugenius, and Macarius, *cf.* John of Rhodes *Pass. Art.* 21–23, pp. 74.15–75.25/*PG* 96, cols. 1269D-1271D, and 25–40 (not in Bidez's Philostorgius)/cols 1273B-1289A, and Ced. p. 537.4–8:

And Artemius, *dux* of Alexandria, since he had displayed much zeal in Alexandria against the idolaters, when he had been decapitated after many tortures on account of his Christian faith, was put on public display. And similarly, too, two presbyters, Eugenius and Macarius.

Also Scut. pp. 56.30–57.2 above, n. 101; and Nicephorus Callistus Xanthopoulus *HE* X.11, *PG* 146, 472B-C:

And Artemius, the noble champion of piety, who was *dux* and an *Augustalis* of Antioch, was punished by him [Julian]. In truth, because, burning with divine zeal, while serving Constantius he ruined and razed many precincts of the idols and because he brought the bones of the divine apostles, Andrew, Luke, and Timothy, from Patris, Achaea, and Ephesus to the city of Constantine, but explicitly on the charge that he had concocted the murder of his brother Gallus. For, after he had stripped the martyr of all his possessions and dismissed him from office, after many unbearable tortures, he finally beheaded him. And besides him, having no regard for the dignity of an embassy, he also punished the ambassadors from Persia who had come to Chalcedon—Manuel, Sabel, and Ishmael—because they had represented the interests of Christians.

Only the *Passio* and Callistus agree with Zonaras about the association of Artemius with Gallus' death.

Manuel, Sabel, and Ismael appear in two factually problematic accounts of the topography of Constantinople: "... the land wall descends as far as the old port of the Prodromus and the monastery of Dius and those of Icasia and goes as far as the [the cistern of] Bonus and toward Saint Manuel, Sabel, and Ismael (in which spot the Saints were executed) ..." (*Scriptores Originum Constantinopolitinarum* 1.53, p. 142.2–6); "The Church of Manuel, Sabel, and Ismael: after they had been burned by Julian the Transgressor, Theodosius the Great erected the church at the land wall and deposited the saints' bodies there ..." (*Scriptores Originum Constantinopolitinarum* 3.190, p. 275.8–12).

110   Julian's army left Antioch on March 5. Amm. Marc. XXIV.1–5 and Zos. III.12–24 describe the army's progress and initial victories, Amm. Marc. XXIV.6 and Zos. III.25 deal with actions near

Ctesiphon. For the chronology and translations of the sources for the expedition, see D-L, pp. 231–274.

111   Zos. III.26.1–3 does not mention the alleged Persian "deserters" and has Julian himself decide to burn the fleet. Amm. Marc. XXIV.7.1–6 corresponds to Zonaras. However, a large lacuna between Amm. Marc. XXIV.7.2 and 3 renders impossible a precise verdict on the extent of their agreement. No other source agrees with Zonaras on the breakdown of the types of ships in Julian's fleet, though the 1,100 total of Zonaras' figures matches that of Amm. Marc. XXIII.3.9—1,000 supply ships, 50 warships, and 50 ships to be used in the construction of bridges. No other source mentions Hormisdas in this connection. The Roman withdrawal began on June 16.

112   No other source gives this combination of strategic and logistical motives for a withdrawal. Indeed, the ancient consensus is that Julian's departure from the environs of Ctesiphon was the result of his wish to bring Sapor to battle. Note Eun. *Hist. fr.* 27.5 Blockley *FCH* II, p. 40 = *fr.* 22.3 Müller *FHG* IV, p. 23 = *ES* 22, p. 80.21–23, who stresses an alleged abundance of supplies around Ctesiphon.

113   Julian died on June 26, 363, probably near modern Samarra. With the sources on Julian's death assembled in D-L, pp. 238–274, *cf.*:

Sym. 90.3 and 6, pp. 113–114: 3. For when he had campaigned against Persia, he was enticed by deserters to burn the ships. Then, after he had marched a sufficient distance through desert and rugged areas, when all the supplies and necessities had been expended, and when those with him had suffered much, when opportunity for war and battle arrived, having turned to flight, he was wounded by a lance,	Ced. pp. 538.6–539.2: And Julian, after he had considered prophecies and sacrifices and incantations of demons and deceptions, as Agathias says [There is no parallel in Agathias], campaigned against Persia, when, too, he received an oracle of this sort: "Now do all we gods hasten to prepare trophies of victory beside a beast that is a river. And of these, I, raging, Ares, raising the war cry, shall take the lead."	Scut. p. 57.4–6: And God, when he had taken pity on his people, by an invisible blow during the war with Persia killed him, having lived thirty years.

[114] and, after he had taken in his hands the blood coming from his nostrils and scattered it to the air, he said, "You have conquered, Christ. Sate yourself, Nazarene," and thus did he cast forth his deceitful spirit. . . . 6. Fortified by prognostications and sacrifices and deceits of demons, he campaigned against Persia, also since, it is said, he received an oracle holding thus: "Now do all we gods hasten to prepare trophies of victory beside a beast that is a river. And of these, I, raging, Ares, raising the war cry, shall take the lead."

And in the course of his advance upon Persia, in the home of a certain Christian woman, there was discovered a small urn standing full of water, which also was changed suddenly into sweet, frothing wine. And this has reasonably been viewed as a sign of the change of affairs to the sweetest through the overthrow of the tyranny shortly thereafter. For when he had campaigned against Persia, he was enticed by some deserters to burn the ships. Then, after he had marched a sufficient distance through desert and rugged areas, when all the supplies and necessities had been expended, and when those with him had suffered much, when an opportunity for war arrived, going about the battlefield and seeing to matters, he was struck by a lance, clandestinely, in the lower chest, so that he cried out. And, after he had taken some blood in his hand, he scattered it to the air, saying, "You have conquered, Christ. Sate yourself, Nazarene." And thus [539] he sundered his accursed life, after he had maligned his own gods, calling them cheats, and imposters, and liars.

Note Zonaras' claim that the blow fatal to Julian was from a weapon thrown as opposed to thrusted. For the alternative exclamation attributed to Julian by Zonaras, see n. 116 below. Zonaras' reference to song may refer to a hexameter poem on Julian's death by Callistius, who credited Julian's death to a *daimon* (*FgrH* 223 F 1 = Soc. *HE* III.21, p. 163, with which *cf.* Nicephorus Callistus *HE* X.34, *PG* 146, p. 549D).

For the Tigris as the subject of the oracle about "a beast that is a river," see Eustathius, *Commentarium in Dionysii periegetae orbis descriptionem*, ed. Carl Müller, *Geographi Graeci Minores*, Vol. II (Paris: Didot, 1861), p. 387.8–13:

> The Tigris is a beast not only far stronger than an elephant but also not very readily comparable in swiftness. And hence a guileful oracle given to Julian maintained that "beside a beast that is a river" he would do what was being discussed, that is to say, beside the Tigris, which is called by the name Beast.

114 Amm. Marc. XXV.9.12 and XXV.10.4, respectively, have Procopius escort Julian's body to Tarsus and Jovian adorn his tomb. The date of the transfer to Constantinople is uncertain. Since two late manuscripts of Symeon (thirteenth and fourteenth centuries) add after "Tarsus" that Julian "was buried near the grave of Maximianus, son of Gallerius, and, in turn, was conveyed and interred in Constantinople—then, too, Jovian's—in a porphyry coffin, cylindrical in shape, with Helen, daughter of Constantine and his wife," the transfer may have occurred between the composition of Symeon's *Chronicle* and that of the common source of Cedrenus, Zonaras, and Scutariotes. See Wahlgren's *apparatus criticus* to Sym. 90.3, p. 114, and Philost. *HE* VIII.1, p. 104.8–10: "Merobaudes and those with him, when they had borne the corpse of Julian to Cilicia, not according to forethought, but by some oversight, placed it opposite the tomb which contained the bones of Maximinus . . . .", this closely paralleled by Nicephorus Callistus *HE* X.43, *PG* 146, p. 585B. *Cf.*:

| Ced. p. 539.3–9: His wretched body was borne to Constantinople and was placed in a porphyry sarcophagus cylindrical in shape, on which was inscribed this elegy: "By Cydnus silver-flowing, when from Euphrates' stream, / Out of Persia's land, with | Scut. p. 57.6–8: And his body was borne to and placed in the Church of the Holy Apostles in the northern part, in its own sepulcher, in a porphyry sarcophagus cylindrical in shape. |

task undone, / An army he had
moved, obtained this tomb did
Julian, / Both sovereign good and
spearman strong."

Zos. III.34.3 and *Greek Anthology* 7.747 (II, p. 396), the latter with
a universally unaccepted attribution to Libanius, give only the last
two lines, the second of these *Il.* 3.179. Julian's hero Alexander the
Great had bathed in the Cydnus. Zonaras' circumstantial details
about troop disposition either contradict Ammianus and Zosimus
or, as in the case of the Gauls acting as a rearguard, for example,
are unparalleled.

115 No such sentiment survives in Julian's writings or in any other
testimony about Julian. However, a connection between being a
philosopher and the negation of breathing appears in the cynic Crates
Ep. 6, p. 208: "Philosophize more often than breath. For living well,
which is the product of philosophy, is to be preferred to living, which
is the product of breathing." Something like this may be the point of
Zonaras' quotation. Whether it is correctly attributed to Julian is
another matter.

116 For the tradition that set Julian's death in Phrygia, *cf.* Amm.
Marc. XXV.3.9. Malal. XIII.19, p. 251.8–14, also recounts this
incident, which it places after a sacrifice to Apollo and says involved
a fair-haired youth who informed Julian of the latter's preordained
death in Asia. However, the manuscript variants Rasia, Rassia, and
Radia in Malalas and in the derivative *CP* p. 551.9 point toward
Phrygia as the spot originally specified by Malalas. See, too,
Eutychianus *FgrH* 226 F 1 = Malal. XIII.23, p. 256.20–39, with
commentary at *BNJ* 226. The story probably began as a *post factum*
validation of pagan prophecy through alleged warnings against the
Persian campaign and predictions of Julian's death, a genesis that would
add significance to Julian's supposed invocation of Helios.

117 In Christian sources, St Basil soon replaced the pious Hellene
of Zonaras' version. *Cf.*, for example, Malal. XIII.25, p. 257.50–64,
paralleled at *CP* p. 552.1–16. Theod. *HE* III.24, pp. 202.25–203.19,
tells a slightly similar story of St Sabbas. The final word of XIII.13
(*eupistia* = "belief") appears nowhere else in Zonaras.

118 Jovian was acclaimed emperor on June 27, 363. Varronianus 1
(*PLRE* I, p. 946) had either resigned or been removed during Julian's

reign from the position of *comes domesticorum*, which he had held under Constantius. Zos. III.30 has Jovian recognized emperor by a common vote of soldiers and officers, names Varronianus, and gives his rank as "*hegemon* of the *domestici*." Amm. Marc. **XXV**.5.4 calls Varronianus *comes* and asserts that initial support of Jovian as emperor was quite limited. Symeon's account of Jovian is given in the reverse order of that in Zonaras.

Theod. Lect. *Epit.* 151, p. 62.1–2: After both consuls and generals had united, they called on Jovian, who until then was a corps commander, to be sovereign.	Sym. 91.1, p. 115: Jovian was chosen sovereign by the whole army due to his being conspicuously pious, mild, and fair.
Ced. p. 539.15–19: Jovian reigned 9 months and 15 days. He was a corps commander, a most mild man and an orthodox Christian, who by the whole army was acclaimed sovereign in the place the transgressor was killed. And he was tall in stature, so that not a single one of the military cloaks fit him.	Scut. p. 57.9–12: Jovian, son Varonianus, 9 months. Being a corps commander, when Julian departed mankind and he [Jovian] had been discovered in the battle, on that very day he was proclaimed sovereign by the entire camp.

119   With Zonaras, Soz. *HE* VI.3.1, p. 239.12–17, and Theod. *HE* IV.1, pp. 210.3–211.14, *cf.*:

Theod. Lect. *Epit.* 151, p. 62.2–4: And he put forward to the army, "I am unable to command an army which used to Hellenize in the times of Julian." All the army confessed to him that they were Christians.	Sym. 91.3, p. 115: He put forward to the army, "I am unable to command an army which used to Hellenize in the times of Julian." All the army confessed to him that they were Christians.
Ced. p. 539.21–24: And he refused the sovereignty, saying that he was unable to command an army which had Hellenized. All shouted to him in one voice, "We are Christians, thrice august emperor."	Scut. p. 57.9–16: And being a most orthodox Christian, in a great voice he shouted, "If you wish me to be your sovereign, I myself also wish that you all be Christians and that the creed approved in Nicaea prevail." And all agreed and praised him.

120   Zonaras' verdict on the terms agreed to by Jovian is similar to Amm. Marc. **XXV**.7.9–14. Other sources are apologetic or, perhaps,

more understanding of the Roman army's dire predicament, *e.g.*
Amm. Marc. **XXV**.7.14, mentioning lack of water and food, and Zos.
III.33.1, noting lack of water and difficulty of terrain. With these and
John of Antioch *fr.* 273.2 Roberto, p. 460.4–5 = *fr.* 181 Müller,
FHG IV, p. 606 = *Suda* I 401 (II, p. 638.29–30, absent from *EV* 63,
pp. 200.22–201.26), *cf.*:

Theod. Lect. *Epit.* 152, p. 62.5–6: Jovian, wishing to save what remained of the army, was forced to cede Nisibis, a very large and populous city, to Persia.	Sym. 91.2, p. 115: When he had made peace treaties with Persia, he died . . .
Ced. p. 539.19–21: And after one engagement of the war, a peace as from God was harmoniously called for both by Romans and Persians, and it was marked out for 30 years.	Scut. p. 57.16–17: And straightway, when he had made peace with the king of Persia and departed from the Persian borders, . . .

121 Not surprisingly, Jovian's restoration of churches and recall of
exiles is a commonplace among the ecclesiastical historians.
Athanasius, in fact, had secretly returned to Alexandria on his own
initiative as soon as he learned of Julian's death. Amm. Marc.
XXV.10.4–5 and Soc. *HE* III.26, p. 172, too, mention Jovian's trip
to Tarsus. *Cf.*:

Theod. Lect. *Epit.* 155, p. 62.14–17: Jovian recalled by a law the bishops in exile. And he wrote to the holy Athanasius to show to him [Jovian] in writing the precision of faultless belief. And Athanasius did just this and wrote a letter to Jovian full of orthodoxy.	Ced. pp. 539.24–540.4: Thereupon, he dispatched laws to all the [540] Roman territory for preservation of the churches of God and recalled the Christians in exile, having written, too, to the holy Athanasius to show to him [Jovian] in writing the precision of faultless belief. When he had done this, he became more devoted to orthodoxy.	Scut. p. 57.17–23: he honorably restored all the orthodox bishops through his divine decree to their own thrones; and before the others the wholly great Athanasius as champion of orthodoxy, but he also dispatched Christian generals and administrators through every province.

122   Jovian died on February 17, 364. Soz. *HE* VI.6.1, p. 243.16–21, closely parallels Zonaras. Philost. *HE* VIII.8, p. 108.2–8, attributes Jovian's death to effusions from newly plastered walls caused by a fire meant to heat the emperor's room. *Epit. de Caes.* 44.4, p. 172.5–8, combines the fresh plaster explanation with that of a stomach ailment: "Hastening from Persia to Constantinople in the middle of a harsh winter, he died suddenly from repletion of the stomach, made more grievous by the plaster of a new building, in about his fortieth year." Amm. Marc. XXV.10.13 gives the same combination. John of Antioch's *fr.* 273.2 Roberto, p. 460.21–22 = *fr.* 181 Müller, *FHG* IV, p. 607 = *Suda* I 401 (II, p. 639.15–17), attributes Jovian's death to a poisoned mushroom. The reference to mushrooms is missing from *EV* 63, p. 201.23–26. *Cf.*:

| Sym. 91.2, p. 115: . . . he died during his return march, after he had eaten poisoned mushrooms. | Ced. p. 540.15–21: And Jovian, hastening from Antioch to Constantinople, when he had reached Ancyra of Galatia, came forward as consul. And when he had come first to a suburb Dadastana, he fell asleep in a small room which had just been plastered, and, when the plaster had given off a heavy vapor, he suddenly died, having been suffocated by the fumes. And as some write, he died after he had eaten a mushroom which had been poisoned. | Scut. p. 57.23–25: For the sovereign, no sooner than he had arrived during the winter in Ancyra of Galatia, when he had been seized by a sudden sickness, died, as they say, after he had eaten a poisoned mushroom . . . |

123   Charito (*PLRE* I, p. 201) was a daughter of Lucillianus 3 (*PLRE* I, pp. 517–518), who had held a high-ranking command position in Illyricum under Constantius, lived in Sirmium as a private citizen after his capture by Julian in 361, and in 363 had been raised by Jovian to the post of *magister equitum and peditum*. He was murdered in Rheims that same year during a military mutiny. *Cf.*:

| Ced. pp. 540.21–22: His wife was Charito, who did not behold him as sovereign. | Scut. p. 57.23–25: He had a wife, Charito, who was scarcely crowned. |

124 Zonaras closely parallels Zos. III.36. Eun. *VS* 7.5.3/479 may allude to Sallustius' refusal, though this could refer to his alleged rejection of the throne after Julian's death, for which, see Amm. Marc. XXV.5.3. Valentinian was at Ancyra when Jovian died.

125 *Cf. Epit. de Caes.* 44.3 and Amm. Marc. XXV.10.14–15, which reflect a common tradition. John of Antioch *fr.* 273.1 Roberto, p. 458.12 = *fr.* 181 Müller, *FHG* IV, p. 606 = *EV* 63, p. 201.7 = *Suda* I 401 (II, p. 638.24), characterizes Jovian as "without a taste of culture."

126 Salmasian John *fr.* 270 Roberto, p. 452 = *fr.* 178.4 Müller *FHG* IV, p. 605:

> Jovian was once following Julian and it so happened that he stepped on his cloak. And he, having turned toward him and just as if expounding the future, said, "Would that, at least, he were a man." And after his death Jovian succeeded him.

The point veiled in Julian's quip—probably part of a verse quotation —seems to be that Jovian was more than a mere man and, *ergo*, suited for the purple. Theod. *HE* V.20.4–8, p. 316.1–26, esp. 15–16, recounts a similar incident, though involving the monk Macedonius and two of Theodosius' officials. *Cf.*:

| Sym. 91.1, p. 115: . . . but he was also close to Julian, with the result that once, when walking behind him, he had stepped on Julian's cloak, Julian, having turned toward him and seeing no one else but him, said, "Would that, at least, he were a man." | Ced. p. 539.10–14: When the Jovian who would reign after him, walking behind the purple robe had misstepped on the slope to descend from a spot, Julian, when he had turned and interpreted from what had occurred that he would rule the realm after him, said, "So be it, at any rate, though he is a man." |

127 Charito's death may have been as late as 380 (*cf. PLRE* I, pp. 201 and 946, *s.vv.* Charito and Varronianus 2, respectively). Scut. p. 57.25–28 also records her burial with Jovian: ". . . and he was 60 years old. And his body was placed in the stoa of the holy apostles, in a porphyry casket, equal in size of Constantine the Great's, in which,

after this, his wife Charito, too, was placed." Zonaras is correct, Scutariotes wrong, about Jovian's age at the time of his death.

128   Valentinian's presentation to and acclamation as Augustus by the army occurred at Nicaea on February 26, 364. *Cf.*:

Theod. Lect. *Epit.* 158, p. 62.25–63.1: And when it had come to Nicaea, the army called upon Valentinian to be sovereign.	Ced. pp. 540.23–541.1: Valentinian, who reigned 13 years, was acclaimed in Nicaea of Bithynia by the army . . .	Scut. p. 58.9–11: And when they had stood him in the center, all said, "No one makes a sovereign of Romans like him." And the entire multitude acclaimed him in Nicaea.

129   With Zonaras *cf.*:

Sym. 92.1, p. 116: Valentinian reigned 13 years. And his harshness through justness was praised and admired. For that harshness was not incurred without reason, but his foremost aim always was justness, being diverted by no one from this nor swayed by anyone from what he once resolved.	Ced. p. 541.1–10: . . . because he had won esteem by his confession as a Christian under Julian and had been exiled. . . . And his harshness through justness was praised and admired. For that harshness was not incurred without reason, but his foremost aim always was justness, being diverted by no one from this nor swayed by anyone from that which he once resolved.	Scut. p. 58.3–15: Then Salustius, along with all, voted for Valentinian as sovereign, whom Julian exiled because he was a Christian, but later, after he had made him a tribune, dispatched to Selubria. He hailed from Cibala in Panonia, bedecked in the noble virtues—not in courage alone, but also in intelligence and moderation and justice—and conspicuous in the size of his body. And he, as soon as he became sovereign, dismissed the prefect Salustius, having commanded those who had been wronged by him to come before him and accuse him, and he did not find anyone. For the man was just. And the

| | sovereign punished many of the administrators who had been convicted. |

130   With Zonaras, *cf.* Soc. *HE* IV.31, pp. 208–209—the fullest account—Theoph. *AM* 5860, p. 56.23–31, and:

| Theod. Lect. *Epit.* 212, p. 74.9–17: Before the sovereignty, Valentinian the Great had as a wife Severa, from whom he had Gratian, whom he presently put forward as sovereign. And while Severa was still living, he also wed Justina on the basis of the testimony of Severa, about whose beauty he testified to her [*sic*], having written a law to make it possible for him who wished to have two legitimate wives. And after he had married Justina, he had from her a child, Valentinian the Younger, whom, after his death, the army acclaimed sovereign, and three daughters, Justa, Grata, and Galla, who also married Theodosius the Great as a second wife, from whom Placida was born to him. For he had Arcadius and Honorius from Placilla, his first spouse. | Scut. p. 58.18–22: He chose his own brother Valens as a colleague of the sovereignty, and, when he had given to him all the East, he himself marched to the West and there remained. And he also recognized his son Gratian, whom he sired prior to the sovereignty from Severa, his spouse. And after he became sovereign he married Justina, too, while Severa was still alive, and Justina also bore a son, Valentinian the Younger, and three daughters, Justa, Grata, and Galla. |

The dates of Valentinian's marriages to Marina Severa (*PLRE* I, p. 828) and Justina (*PLRE* I, pp. 488–489) are unknown, as are the birthdates of Justa, Grata, and Galla 2 (*PLRE* I, pp. 488, 400, and 382, respectively). Gratian was born on April 18, 359, Valentinian (8, *PLRE* I, pp. 934–935) in 371. *CP* pp. 559.4–10 (= Malal. XIII.31, p. 263) and 560.17–18 (= Malal. XIII.32, p. 264, though with Valerian for Gratian) describes Valentinian's exile of Severa in 369 and her recall by Gratian sometime between 376 and 378, so after Valentinian's death (November 17, 375). John of Antioch *fr.* 280.1–11, Roberto pp. 468–470 = *fr.* 187 Müller *FHG* IV, p. 608–609 = *EI* 79, pp. 117.26–118.6:

Under the sovereign Theodosius, the sovereign Valentinian the younger is reported to have been killed as a result of a plot of the following sort: Valentinian, his father, had many wives, contrary to the Romans' established laws. Further, his second wife was, on the one hand, said to have been a daughter of Justus, on the other, to have been wife of Magnentius, who had usurped power in the times of Constantius, and, having had no children on account of her youth, was living apart from him and chastely. When he had fallen in love with her because of her extreme beauty, the sovereign took her by a second marriage. From her was born Valentinian the younger, who reigned with Theodosius, and Galla, who was wed to Theodosius after the death of Flacilla on the occasion when he was conquering Maximus and saving Valentinian . . .

Valentinian's alleged legislation is unknown outside this context.

131 Zonaras is surprisingly wrong about Valentinian and Demophilus (*EEC* I, p. 228), whose champion in 370 was Valens. The tenures of Eudoxius (*EEC* I, pp. 295–296) and Demophilus were 360–370 and 370–380, respectively. Ambrose (*EEC* I, pp. 28–29) became bishop of Milan on December 7, 374. Note Theodore Lector's, Symeon's, and Cedrenus' common error of attributing to Valentinian, who died in 375, the denial of aid to Valens prior to Adrianople (378). If historical at all, this must have issued from Gratian. See further notes 138 and 144 below and *cf.*:

Theod. Lect. *Epit.* 158, p. 63.5–6: However, Valens was an ardent Arian, having been baptized and deceived by Eudoxius.

p. 63.15–17: And Valens, when he had learned this, overturned everything done in Lampsacus and, after he had exiled the bishops who had gathered there, gave over the churches to Eudoxius, who shared their views, and the devotees of the homoousian faith chose a certain Evagrius, whom Eustathius of Antioch, secretly staying in Constantinople, selected, for he had been recalled from exile by Jovian, and, when he had found the sovereign no longer alive, was hiding in the city. And Valens, staying in Nicomedia, after he had learned of

Sym. 92.7–8, pp. 117–118: Valentinian, being most orthodox, appointed bishop in Mediolanum Ambrose, whom they say indicted unjust magistrates before the sovereign. [8] And the Goths were sorely vexing Valens. And he begged the most divine Valentinian to send to him an army for aid. And not only did he not give it but even reproached him, saying that one ought not aid a man who was warring with God.

the selection of Evagrius, sent
soldiers, and exiled Eustathius to
Bizye, and, after he had expelled
Evagrius from the city, rendered to
the Arian Demophilus control of the
churches.

174, p. 66.6–14: When Eudoxius,
who had controlled the see of
Constantinople for eleven years, had
died, the Arians chose Demophilus,
who shared their views.

189, p. 70.11–13: And the people,
when they had set aside their strife
with one another, in one voice voted
for Ambrose. After he had learned
this, Valentinian commanded that
Ambrose be initiated [i.e. baptized]
and appointed.

189, p. 70.17–18: And they say that
Ambrose nobly indicted the
magistrates who were unjust before
the sovereign.

207, p. 73.12–14: And the Goths
were sorely vexing Valens. And he
begged the most divine Valentinian
to send him an army for aid. And he
did not give it, but even reproached
him, saying that one ought not aid a
man who was warring with God.

Ced. p. 541.20–24: Since Valens the
impious was an ardent Arian, he
overturned the acts of the synod in
Lampsacus and banished the bishops
who had gathered there and gave
over the churches of Constantinople
to Edoxius, who shared his views.

p. 545.21–22: In the10th year after
Eudoxius [became bishop of
Constantinople], Ambrose was leader
of the church of Mediolanum, while
Valentinian the sovereign was
passing through there.

Scut. p. 58.24–59.6: When Eudoxius
had died in the fifth year of his reign,
Demophilus, an Arian, was elevated
to the patriarchal throne by Valens—
he, too, being of this heresy—and
controlled the church for twelve
years. And Valentinian the sovereign,
staying in the western parts and
having come to Mediolanum, as a
result of the exhortation of the clergy
and laity, urged that the prefect of
the same city, blessed Ambrose, be
elected bishop. [59] And when he
had heard about his brother Valens—
that, having become champion of

p. 546.20–23: And Valentinian reviled his brother Valens as being of base opinion, having denied to him aid against the Goths which he had requested, but saying, "It is not right to aid a man who is warring with God" (*Cf.* notes 133 and 144 below.). the Arian heresy, he battled the churches of the orthodox and oppressed all the East—, he berated him via letters and advised him to abandon the heresy. And he did not obey his brother's counsel, but was becoming more savage against the orthodox.

132 The story of the otherwise unknown *praepositus* Rhodanus appears in various permutations. With Zonaras, *cf.* Malal. XIII.31/ 339–340, pp. 262–263; *CP* 557.18–559.3; and:

Salmasian John *fr.* 275 Roberto, p. 462 = *fr.* 183 Müller *FHG* IV, p. 607: A widow, robbed of her wealth by Rhodanus, a *praepositus*, approached Valentinian. He appointed Sallustius to judge her, and Rhodanus was sentenced to return what had been stolen. And since he did not obey and the woman kept complaining, the sovereign burned him in the hippodrome.

Suda Σ 64 (IV, pp. 316.33–317.4) = Eun. *Hist. fr.* 30 Müller *FHG* IV, p. 26 (rejected by Blockley): Valentinian assigned the *praepostius* Rhodanus, who had wronged a certain widow Beronice, when she had approached the sovereign, Salustius as a judge. And he found the *praepositus* guilty, and, when the *praepositus* ignored him, consigned him to fire in the hippodrome and gave the entire estate of the top eunuch to the widow.

Sym. 92.4, p. 117: Under him, the wealth of a certain woman was plundered by Rhodanus, the *praepositus*. And the sovereign, having judged them, directed the *praepositus* that her things be returned to her. And he did not obey. And when he had learned this, the sovereign told the woman to come to him. And she came forward in the hippodrome, while the sovereign was there as a spectator. And when she had been questioned and spoken

Ced. p. 544.5–12: A woman named Berenice approached Valentinian, saying that her wealth had been plundered by Rhodanus, the *praepositus*. Having judged them, the sovereign directed that her things be returned to her. And when the *praepositus* did not obey, the woman approached the sovereign in the hippodrome, related the disobedience to the sovereign. The sovereign, therefore, commanded that a pyre be lit in the bend and that the *praepositus* be

Scut. p. 59.6–28: And when a certain women, Beronice by name, after she had approached Valentinian the Great, was bringing charges against the *praepositus* Rhodanus, who was exceedingly wealthy and greatly influential with the sovereign, saying that her wealth had been plundered by him. When the most just sovereign had commanded Salustius to examine the particulars of the matter and he had learned that the woman had been done the greatest injustice by the truth about the *praepositus*—the *praepositus* who had been brought to him with the wealth of both—, he commanded that men who had lit a great pyre in the bend burn him and that all his wealth be given to the woman.

burned with his vestments and that all his wealth be given to the woman.

him, the *praepositus* was commanded to return what he had taken. And having relied on his close relationship with the sovereign and gripped by his avarice, he was as neglectful of what been determined as of things said of naught. And the wronged woman, when she had overcome her fear, while the horse races were in progress, again approached the sovereign and dramatically described the injustice. And the sovereign, shocked by the *praepositus'* disobedience, asked him, standing there with all the senate, whether he had done what had been commanded. And when he had learned the truth, he immediately gave a command and stripped him of his office, and when he had been brought down, stripped and bound, into the hippodrome, he ordered that his injustice to the woman, along with the neglect of the sovereign's order, be proclaimed to all, and that he then be burned in the bend while all looked on. And this was done, and the *praepositus* was consigned to the fire and all his wealth bestowed by divine golden bull on the widow. And all praised the sovereign.

133 Valentinian died on November 17, 375 at Brigetio in Pannonia, modern Hungary, not in Gaul. Scut. p. 60.1–2 simply says that Valentinian died after becoming ill. Soc. *HE* IV.31, pp. 207–208, *e.g.*, Theodore Lector, Symeon, and Cedrenus give the fuller, more famous version:

Theod. Lect. *Epit.* 209, pp. 73.23–74.6:	Sym. 92.6, p. 117: And	Ced. p. 547.1–10: In
Sauromatae rebelled against Valentinian. After they had been defeated, they sent ambassadors requesting peace. When he had observed them, Valentinian asked if all Sauromatae had such physiques. When they had replied that they had dispatched the best among them, he gave a great shout and said that terrible things awaited the Roman empire which had come to him, if Saurmotae, the best of whom were men such as these, dared to war with Romans. As a result of the intensity, when a blood vessel had burst and much blood had been lost, he died in a garrison in Gaul, being in his fifty-fourth year and having reigned 13 years.	when he had warred against the Sauromatae, observing ambassadors who had come from them, he asked if men such as theses were Sauromatae. And after he had learned that the best had come to him, when he had been filled with anger and struck his thigh with the palm of his hand, he said, "Woe to Rome, if such men are worthy to serve as ambassadors." And as a result of his anger, they say that a vein burst and an artery ruptured, and, when much blood had poured out, that the same sovereign, Valentinian, died.	year 11, Valentinian the Great died—having reigned 11 years—in the following fashion. The Sauromatae, beaten by him, sent ambassadors to him seeking peace. When he had asked them if all the Sauromatae were as tall as these, and they had said, "You have here and see the strongest of all," he gave a violent shout and said, "Terrible things await the Roman empire, having been allotted to Valentinian, if Sauromatae, being most lamentable men such as these, rise against Romans." And from the strain and clapping of his hands, when a blood vessel had ruptured and much blood had been lost, he died in a garrison in Gaul.

134 Domnica's (*PLRE* I, p. 265) alleged pivotal role is doubtful. For the tradition, *cf.*:

Theod. Lect. *Epit.* 193, p. 71.11–12: Above all, Domnica, his wife, was diabolically seducing Valens the Arian to Arianize.	Ced. p. 550.11: His wife was Domnica, an ardent Arian.	Scut. p. 60.7–10: He [Valens] had a wife, Empress Domnina [*sic*], an Arian, by whose admonitions he, too, was diverted to such a

heresy, from whom he
produced a son,
Gratian, and daughters
Anastasia and Crossa.

In addition to Anastasia (2, *PLRE* I, p. 58), Crossa (*PLRE* I, p. 182, *s.v.* Carosa), and Gratian, Domnica also bore Galates (*PLRE* I, p. 381).

135 Soc. *HE* IV.16, pp. 188–189, tells the story in detail, but without reference to Gregory. Soz. *HE* VI.14.2–4, p. 255.9–22, gives less detail. Theod. *HE* IV.24.1, p. 262.4–9, incorrectly places the incident at Constantinople and blames "ones of the impious company" (*i.e.* Arians) rather than Valens. For the quotation, see Greg. Naz. *Or.* 43.46, *PG* 36, col. 556C. *Cf.*, too, Theoph. *AM* 5862, p. 58.28–32, and Theod. Lect. *Epit.* 175, p. 66.15–19. Modern Dacibyza is about 45 kilometres/35 miles from Nicaea. The affair occurred in late spring of 370, its context was sectarian strife in Constantinople. There is no certainty that Valens ordered the ship burned. For context and further references, see N. Lenski, *Failure of Empire* (Berkeley CA: University of California Press, 2002), pp. 250–251. Galates (*PLRE* I, p. 381) died in Caesarea *ca.* 370 after Valens rejected Basil's condition that the boy would live provided that the emperor supported a unified church.

Theod. Lect. *Epit.* 175, p. 66.15–19: The orthodox, who thought they would be shown mercy by Valens, dispatched an embassy to him while he was in Nicomedia, having sent eighty holy men, of whom Theodore, Urbasus, and Menedemus were the leaders. He ordered all these to be burned with the ship itself, and all were immolated with the boat, the ship having made it as far as Dacidizae.

Sym. 93.3, pp. 118–119: Valens wrought many terrors against the orthodox, "maritime conflagrations" with ships themselves and drownings at sea and many tortures. Then, after he had plundered every church, [119] he came to Caesarea, having perpetrated against Basil what the Theologian inscribed in the *Epitaph*, at which time Galates, Valens' son, and his partner Domnica were painfully racked by disease.

Epit. 199, p. 72.12–15: After he had plundered every church, Valens came, too, to Caesarea from the East, agitated against Basil. And he did what the Theologian has inscribed in the *Epitaph of Basil* [Greg. Naz. *Or.* 43, *PG* 36, cols. 493–606], at which time Galates, Valens' son, and his partner Domnica were painfully racked by disease, and the son also died.

Ced. p. 544.16–19: And in the 6th year, the orthodox sent an embassy to Valens, 25 holy men. All these Valens ordered to be burned with the ship, and all were immolated with the boat, the ship having made it as far as Dacibyze.

Scut. p. 60.14–26: To this godless sovereign the orthodox sent from Nicomedia as an embassy eighty holy men, all of whom, with the boat, he commanded to be set afire, and they were immolated in the middle of sea, the ship having made it as far as the emporium Dacibyze. And when he had driven the orthodox priests of the churches from all of them, he gave their churches to the Arians. And he also came to Caesarea of Cappadocia in order to drag toward his will Basil the Great, who then occupied the throne of Caesarea, but the wretch was understood as soon as he made contact with the bishop. Then were done the things inscribed in the *Epitaph* of the heaven revealer himself [Basil] pronounced by the Theologian and the things concerning the son of the sovereign, Galates.

136   The story introduced by Zonaras "it is said" is unhistorical. In Greek it appears in much fuller form and with significant differences in detail only in Pseudo-Amphilochius' *Life of St. Basil* 14, ed. R. P. F. Combefis, *Sanctorum patrum Amphilochii Iconiensis, Methodii Patarensis et Andreae Cretensis Opera Omnia* (Paris: S. Piget, 1644), pp. 206–211, for which the mid-ninth-century Latin translation of Anastasius provides a *terminus ante quem*. On the history of the Pseudo-Amphilochius' work and an edition and translation of a Latin version slightly later than that of Anastasius, see J. Nicholson, *The Vita Sancti Basilii of Pseudo-Amphilochius: A Critical Edition with Commentary and English Translation*, M.A. thesis (Athens GA: University of Georgia, 1986). Of course, whether Zonaras drew upon the *Life* or whether both depend on a common tradition is uncertain.

137   Valens' true stance was far more complex. It is difficult to tell whether the tradition here represented is the product of simplification, exaggeration, or stock invective against an "Arian" emperor. With Theoph. *AM* 5863, pp. 58.34–59.3, *cf*.:

Theod. Lect. *Epit.* 180, p. 67.22–24: To the Hellenes Valens gave permission to perform sacrifices and

Ced. p. 544.20–23: And in the 7th year, the accursed Valens gave to the Hellenes permission to perform

festivals and whatever was customary for Hellenes to do. And likewise, too, he comforted and honored Jews. And he was persecuting the champions of the apostolic teaching alone.	sacrifices and festivals. And likewise, too, he honored Jews. And he was terribly persecuting the orthodox alone and what pertained to the apostolic church.

138   Valens left Antioch in the spring of 378. F. Halkin, "Le Synaxaire grec de Christ Church a Oxford," *Analecta Bollandiana* 66 (1948), pp. 59–90, esp. 75–70. The *Life* recounts Isaac's warning but not his announcement of Valens' death as it was happening. Isaac (d. probably after 403) founded the first Orthodox monastery in Constantinople, probably in 382. In addition to the parallels cited in n. 131 above, *cf.* Soz. *HE* VI.40.1, p. 301.1–8; Theod. *HE* IV.34, p. 272.6–18; Theoph. *AM* 5870, p. 65.9–24; and:

Theod. Lect. *Epit.* 216, p. 75.8–14: And the Goths, having again united, were warring with Valens, and so the city uttered angry taunts against him because he did not advance to battle. And when he did depart, Isaacius, the holy monk, grabbed the bridle of his horse and said to him, "Where are you off to, sovereign, campaigning against God and having God as an adversary?" Enraged at him, Valens ordered him to be consigned to the guardhouse, after he had vowed death for him if he should return, as Ahab to Micah.	Ced. pp. 548.23–549.7: And while he was in Antioch, Valens, when he had learned about the Goths, came to Constantinople. And the Byzantines reviled him as a coward and deserter. And when he was departing for the war with the Goths, Isaacius, one of the great monks, grabbed the bridle of Valens' horse and said to him, "Where are you off to, sovereign, campaigning against God and having God as an adversary?" Enraged, Valens consigned him to the guardhouse, after he had promised death should he return.	Scut. pp. 60.27–61.7: When he had approached Valens as he was leaving for the war against the Goths, the monk Isaacius, a man eminent in prophetic gift, who had just moved, not without God, from the desert to Constantinople, grabbed the bridle of the royal horse and said, "Where are you off to, sovereign, campaigning against God?" When the sovereign had replied, "To a war against the Goths," the great Isaacius said, "But you will not return from there, unless you give the churches of God to the orthodox." And Valens, having fallen into a rage, ordered the holy man to be con-signed to a guardhouse until his return. And the holy man said to him, "If you do return, God has not related the future to me."

251

139   Amm. Marc. XXXI.14.8–9 quotes Homer *Od.* 3.172 on Mt Mimas, located on the mainland of Ionia overlooking Chios, and then notes the discovery of a monument that bore an inscription in Greek "indicating that there had been buried a certain ancient man of note, Mimas." The Gothic victory over Valens at Adrianople was on August 9, 378. *Cf.*:

| Theod. Lect. *Epit.* 217, p. 75.8–14: When he had engaged the Goths and been badly defeated, Valens fled with a few men to a dwelling. Observing this, the enemy immolated him, together with those with him and the dwelling itself. | Ced. pp. 549.7–550.7: And before his end, he beheld in a dream some man saying to him: "Fast off with you, wretch, to Mimas the Great / Where there waits to seize you a horrible fate."

Then, having awakened, he asked, "Who is Mimnas?" and summoned one of the wisemen and asked him, "Who is Mimas?" And he said to him, "It is a mountain, lord, greatest of Asia, situated by the sea, near the island of Chios, of which Homer, too, has made some mention, saying in the *Odyssey* "by windy Mimas." And the sovereign said, "What need is there for me to be close to Mount Mimas, in order, after I have arrived, to die? This is a delusion of demons and a dream of deceitful phantoms." And after a bit he departed from Thrace in order to war against the Scythians. And when he had engaged them and been beaten, with all his might he fled to a certain estate, and, after | Scut. p. 61.7–12: And when he had departed and engaged the enemy, he was defeated, and he fleed into a chaff-heap, and there was immolated and incinerated by fire. The divine Isaacius, who had been confined in a guardhouse in Constantinople, perceiving the stench of the fire by purity of soul, announced to those present with a shout, "The wretched Valens at this moment is being incinerated." |

> he had entered, hid in a
> chaff-heap with his
> companions. Then,
> when the Scythians set
> it afire in ignorance of
> those who had hidden,
> they were incinerated.
> And later, after the
> [550] enemies'
> withdrawal, when some
> men were searching for
> the sovereign's body,
> there was discovered in
> the building in which
> he was hiding a
> tombstone of a man of
> old, inscribed thus:
> "Here lies Mimas, a
> Macedonian, a
> Commander." And
> while in the
> guardhouse, the divine
> Isaacius detected the
> stench by the purity of
> his soul and said, "So is
> wretched Valens at this
> moment incinerated."
> Precisely this was
> confirmed through
> those who arrived
> thereafter.

140   The episode of Procopius, given out of temporal sequence with other events of Valens' reign, finds its place within the context of portents. Procopius was acclaimed emperor on September 28, 365, and executed on May 27, 366. According to Amm. Marc. XXVI.9.1–10, the usurper was beheaded on the spot and his betrayers then put to death. Philost. *HE* IX.5, p. 118.2–3, too, has Procopius beheaded. Soc. *HE* IV.5, p. 176; Soz. *HE* VI.8.3, p. 247.11–14; and Theoph. *AM* 5859, p. 55.32–34, record that Valens had Procopius tied to bent trees, which, when released, tore him in half. The date of the destruction of the walls of Chalcedon is uncertain. Soc. *HE* IV.8, pp. 178–179— in chronological sequence—and Amm. Marc. XXXI.1.4—in the chronological position the episode occupies in Zonaras—also reproduce the text of the alleged inscription. *Cf.*:

Theod. Lect. *Epit*.162, p. 64.3–8: A certain Procopius rose against Valens and, after he had gathered a large army, was staying around Nacoleia, a city of Phrygia. When he had learned this, for a brief time Valens ceased persecuting the orthodox. By the treachery of Agelo [*PLRE* I, pp. 28–29] and Gomares [*PLRE* I, pp. 397–398, *s.v.* Gomarius], generals of Procopius, the usurper was betrayed. After he had fastened him by the legs to two bent trees, he had them uncoiled. And the trees sundered Procopius. And he killed Gomares and Agelo, who had betrayed Procopius, having consigned them to flames.

Epit. 163, p. 64.16–18: Valentinian, staying in the West, had a son of the same name. And he had been born to him before the sovereignty, Gratian by name, was proclaimed sovereign by his father.

Sym. 92.5, p. 117: When he had destroyed the city Chalcedon, with its stones he [Valens] built the great aqueduct and brought the water into the city.

Ced. pp. 542.15–543.11: In the third year, Procopius, a cousin of Julian, rose in opposition and, after he had occupied Nacolia and fortified it with a large army, frightened Valens. And he [Valens] relaxed the persecution against the churches for a bit, until his own generals, Angelus and Gomaris betrayed Procopius. And Procopius, who had been bound to two trees, he had violently rended and he burned those who had betrayed him according to the just judgment of God because they were sympathetic to an unworthy man. Then, too, he dismantled what remained of the wall of Chalcedon, since the Chalcedonians had shielded Procopius. While this was being destroyed, this oracle, written upon tablets, was discovered in the foundations: "But when, indeed, Nymphs, delighting in dance, / Throughout the Holy City, about her fortressed ways, will stand, / And a wall a safeguard mournful for baths will be, / Then, indeed, countless tribes of men dispersed, / Savage, mad, in vile prowess clad, / Having Cimmerian Ister's ford with spear traversed, / Will Scythic range and

Mysian land destroy. /
When he has trod with
frenzied hopes on
Thrace, /Here him life's
end and destiny would
face." And, indeed, all
these things came to pass.

141 The barbarians are, of course, the Goths who defeated
Valens at Adrianople. The city in question is Constantinople. Valens
restored the great aqueduct built by Hadrian, which terminated in
the Nymphaeum Maius in the Forum of Taurus, subsequent to its
renovation under Theodosius I often called the Forum of Theodosius
(*e.g.* Soc. *HE* IV.8, p. 179). Because Zonaras regularly uses the name
Forum of Taurus, its appearance here does not necessarily imply a source
that pre-dated the reign of Theodosius. *Cf. ODB* I, p. 45, *s.v.*
Aqueduct, and III, p. 1505, *s.v.* Nymphaeum. The prefect would have
been Clearchus 1 (*PLRE* I, pp. 211–212), whose achievement is noted
by Jer. *Chron.* 247[b] for the year 373.

Theod. Lect. *Epit.* 166, p. 64.19–21: Valens had two daughters, Anastasia and Carosa, in whose names he named two public baths he had founded. And he also founded the aqueduct to the present called "Valentinian."	Ced. p. 543.12–20: And as Valens returned after the victory over Procopius, he graced the city with an abundance of water, having constructed the channel which he named "Valens." And the man then prefect of the city, demonstrating the city's cheer at what had happened, constructing in the Taurus a bath worthy of the city in magnitude, celebrated a holiday, having feted the people in every fashion. And not long after came the tribes from the barbarians, just as the text predicted, having inundated the area of Thrace and subsequently consumed its resources.	Scut. p. 58.22–24: . . . and Justina also bore a son, Valentinian the younger, and three daughters, Justa, Grata, and Galla. The great Valentinian both constructed the aqueduct and brought the water to Constantinople.

142   Early 372. Libanius is, of course, the famous Antiochene sophist (*PLRE* I, pp. 505–507). Any Iamblichus involved in this episode cannot be linked to Proclus. Cf. *PLRE* I, pp. 450–452, *s.v.* Iamblichus 1–3, and *PLRE* II, pp. 915–919, *s.v.* Proclus 4. Though the quotation attributed to Valens is unique, see Amm. Marc. **XXIX**.1.18.

| Theod. Lect. *Epit.* 209, p. 73.20–22: Valens killed many because, on the basis of the letter theta, they had been conjectured from divinations to rule, and foremost a certain Theodorus, the first among patricians. | Sym. 93.5, p. 119: Valens killed many who had been conjectured to rule from the letter theta. | Ced. p. 548.13–23: And Libanius the sophist and Iamblichus the pupil of Proclus made the so-called rooster-divination. For, after they had written the 24 letters in dust and placed upon each letter a kernel of wheat, they released a rooster upon the letters, and the rooster took the kernel on the theta, then the one on the epsilon and omicron and the one on the delta. And their divination became ambiguous. For such are the illusions of things of this sort. When he had learned this, Valens punished without cause many Theodosiuses and Theodotuses and Theodoruses and those similarly connected from their names to these letters. And Iamblichus, when he had become frightened and drunk poison, died. |

143   Zonaras had mentioned Gratian's acclamation at XIII.15. Gratian was at Trier, where he had been left by Valentinian I on the latter's march to Bregetio, when Valentinian II was acclaimed there in absentia by a coterie of troop and commanders on November 22, 375. Philost. *HE* IX.16, p. 123.1–9, affords a close parallel to Zonaras' comments about Gratian's reaction:

After he had reigned twelve years, Valentinian died and left Gratian, his son, heir of the realm. And he also left two other children, Galla, a daughter, and Valentinian, who was about four years old. And immediately his mother Justina and the army in Paeonia made him sovereign. Of course, having learned of the acclamation, Gratian, because this had not happened with his consent, did not approve. But he even punished some of those who had initiated it. Nevertheless, he acquiesced to have his brother reign and filled the position of father for him.

Amm. Marc. XXX.10.6 pointedly denies animosity between Gratian and Valentinian. Theod. Lect. *Epit.* 211, p. 74.7–8, notes: "When Valentinian had died, the troops in Italy on the sixth day after the death proclaimed his son Valentinian sovereign."

144   Gratian's words, as quoted by Zonaras, mirror in part what Theod. *HE* IV.31, pp. 270.21–271.3 reports Valentinian I said to Valens. If the quotation has any historical basis, Valentinian's death in 375 points toward Valens' campaigns of 367–369 as its context. However, Amm. Marc. XXVII.4.1 expressly states that Valens and Valentinian were in consultation and, indeed, that Valentinian was a moving force behind Valens' offensive against the Goths. On the recall of exiles and restoration of churches, *cf.* Theod. *HE* V.2.1, p. 278.15.19; *Cod. Theod.* 16.1.2 and 5.6; and:

John of Antioch *fr.* 278 Roberto, p. 466.1–6 = *fr.* 185 Müller, *FHG* IV, p. 608 = *EV* 66, p. 202.11–18 = *Suda* Γ 427 (I, p. 539.9–15): When Gratian learned of the death of the divine Valens, he immediately passed through Rome as he headed toward the East and, after he had condemned the savagery of the divine Valens concerning Christians, on the one hand, he quickly recalled those

Ced. p. 546.20–23: And Valentinian reviled Valens, his brother, as being of evil opinion, since he had left him in the lurch when he had sought aid against the Goths, saying: "It is not sanctioned to aid one who is fighting against God." (*Cf.* notes 131 and 138 above.)

Scut. p. 61.15–21: After Valens, Gratian, son of Valentinian, ruled alone with his brother, Valentinian the younger, for six years. Having become a champion of the ancestral faith, he wrote a law that those who had been exiled on account of piety be restored to the flocks which had been allotted to them. But he also did not help his paternal uncle Valens, who had requested an who had been exiled by him [Valens], both restoring their property to them and tending to their injuries. And he made it legal for all to gather without fear and without strife in their own churches, but that only Eunomians, Photinians, Manichaeans be excluded from the houses of prayer.

alliance against the Goths, having written to him, "One ought not to make an alliance with an enemy of God." (*Cf.* notes 131 and 138 above.)

145   Theodosius was called from private life in Spain to command operations against the Goths. Gratian appointed Theodosius Augustus at Sirmium on January 19, 379, before he achieved any military victories against the Goths. Zos. IV.24–27, via Eunapius, presents a very different picture of Theodosius. There, in the clearest account of the campaigns immediately following Adrianople, Modares (*PLRE* I, 605) is credited with the Roman successes.

Theodosius, of course, allowed the Goths to settle on territory within the empire and to retain their own leaders in return for a pledge of military service to Rome. Zonaras' tradition is confused. *Cf.* Theod. *HE* V.5, pp. 284.7–285.8, and:

Theod. Lect. *Epit.* 225, p. 76.26–28: Gratian the sovereign took as a colleague in the rule Theodosius, an Iberian by birth, and noble and wondrous. And Theodosius, having immediately warred against the barbarians in Thrace with all his might, was victorious.

Sym. 94.1, p. 119: Gratian, son of Valentinian, reigned three years and with Theodosius three years. For he chose Theodosius the Great for sovereign in Byzantium, having brought him from Spain for the purpose of warring against the Scythians, who were plundering Thrace. And he was staying in Rome.

Ced. p. 550.13–17: Gratian, Valentinan's son, a heretic, reigned alone 3 years and with Theodosius another 3. For ambassadors were sent from Byzantium to Gratian in Panonia as he was returning to request that a sovereign be given to them, and the great Theodosius was given to them, having been

Scut. pp. 61.21–62.9: In the third year of his sovereignty, seeing Thrace being pillaged by Goths and the race of the barbarians confident and most difficult to combat, not seeing anyone else suitable to oppose them, he summoned Theodosius from Spain and, having appointed him general, dispatched him with the existing proclaimed sovereign, and he ruled 17 years, 5 months, 4 days.

p. 552.7–10: Moreover, Theodosius, an Iberian by birth, was from the West, and noble and wonderful with regard to wars. Immediately, being pious and orthodox, he thoroughly defeated the barbarians in Thrace, . . .

.

army to battle the barbarians. And Theodosius, emboldened by the faith of orthodoxy, hastened towards the enemy and, when he had engaged them, slaughtered a limitless multitude, and those who had survived immediately began to flee, and in their disordered flight by one another the majority [62] were trampled and destroyed. And after he had conquered them in this fashion, having left the army there, he himself—messenger of his own triumphs—came to Gratian, who was tarrying in Paeonia. And he, amazed, could not entirely believe in his bravery. But some of the council, too, borne by envy, maintained strongly that he had fled. Then Theodosius asked the sovereign to send these very men and to know the multitude of those who had been slain. And immediately he dispatched them to see if the affairs corresponded to the truths.

146   Gratian was murdered on August 25, 383. See below on XIII.18. *Cf.*:

Theod. Lect. *Epit.* 244, p. 80.3–8: Gratian, the son of Valentinian the Great, was killed by the treachery of Andragathius, the general of Maximus, the one who then was a usurper. For having entered upon a covered carriage, Andragathius dissembled that he was Gratian's spouse, and, when he had thus met him unguarded, killed him by surprise. After this had happened, though Justina was Gratian's stepmother, she nevertheless ended the persecution of Ambrose and the orthodox.

Sym. 94.2–3, pp. 119–120: And a certain Maximus, a Briton, being greatly vexed because Theodosius was deemed worthy of sovereignty while he had gained no honor, roused those in Britain to rebel against Gratian. And he dispatched Andragathius against him. And after he had circulated the story that Gratian's wife had returned from Britain, he boarded a covered litter. Overwhelmed by his love for her, Gratian went to the litter, and, when he had drawn back the cover, saw Andragathius, who, through soldiers who had been prepared for this, immediately slew Gratian. And by Theodosius Gratian was placed in the royal tombs. 3. He shot the bow so accurately and at such a distance that some said [120] Gratian's arrows had minds.

Ced. p. 551.3–13: A certain Maximianus, a Briton, because Gratian made Theodosius a sovereign while he [Maximianus] had gained no honor, roused those in Britain to rebel against Gratian. And he sent Andragathius off against him. And he boarded a covered litter, circulating the story that Gratian's wife had returned from Britain. Gratian, overwhelmed by his love for her, went to the litter. And when he had drawn back the cover, he saw Andragathius, who, through soldiers who had been prepared for this, immediately slew Gratian. He shot the bow so accurately that some said Gratian's arrows had minds. He was placed by Theodosius in the royal tombs.

Scut. p. 66.1–2: Then the sovereign of Rome, Gratian, was treacherously slain by Andragathius, the general, and Maximus usurped power.

147   Magnus Maximus 39 (*PLRE* I, p. 588), *comes Britanniae* since *ca.* 380, was proclaimed Augustus in Britain in the spring of 383 and was killed on August 28, 388, in Aquileia after his defeat and capture. Theodosius had recognized his legitimacy in 384 in return for Maximus' recognition of the legitimacy of Valentinian. However, after Maximus invaded Italy in 387, Theodosius moved against him and joined Valentinian in Thessalonica late in the summer of 387. This was also the occasion of Theodosius' marriage to Galla 2 (*PLRE* I, p. 382), Valentinian's sister. Andragathias 3 (*PLRE* I, pp. 62–63), Maximus' *magister equitum* and commander of his fleet, which had initially moved to the Ionian Sea on the assumption that Valentinian would flee eastward by sea and had remained in position to check any naval forces that Theodosius might dispatch to the West, drowned himself in 388 after learning of Maximus' death. Theod. *HE* V.15, pp. 304.18–305.11, also describes Theodosius' theological reprimand to Valentinian. *Cf.*:

Theod. Lect. *Epit.* 243, pp. 79.32–80.2: Justina, spouse of Valentinian the Great and mother of Valentinian the younger, was an Arian and terribly agitated her son against Ambrose [80] the bishop because he was orthodox, with the result that by his decree Ambrose

Sym. p. 95.2, p. 120: And the usurpers who had killed the kinsmen of Gratian in Rome and Andragathius, who had managed all of them, he delivered to death.

was exiled. And the city, in longing of Ambrose, when it had risen in opposition, hindered the exile.

Ced. pp. 568.21–569.2: In year 11, after he had conquered Maximus, he killed the usurper and Andragathius his general because they had murdered Gratian. [569] And, when he had come to Rome, he crowned his son Honorius sovereign and returned to Constantinople.

Scut. p. 66.1–13: And then the sovereign of Rome, Gratian, was treacherously slain by Andragathius the general, and Maximus usurped power. And Justina, Valentinian the Great's wife, being an Arian, persuaded her son Valentinian to adopt the same heresy. And when she heard about the murder of Gratian and that Maximus had usurped power in Rome—for she was staying in Mediolanum—she fled with her children and prostrated herself, requesting from the sovereign Theodosius that a requital of Gratian be set in motion. And the sovereign did this. And when he had returned to Rome, he killed both Maximus himself and all the murderers and restored the sovereignty to Valentinian and took his sister Galla to wife, seized by love of her beauty.

148 Eugenius (6, *PLRE* I, p. 293) was proclaimed emperor by Arbogast, his *magister militum* (*PLRE* I, pp. 95–97, *s.v.* Arbogastes), on August 22, 392. Valentinian was either executed or committed suicide on May 15, 392. In May of 393, several months after making his son Honorius Augustus (January 23), Theodosius moved against Eugenius.

Ced. p. 568.8–11: When Eugenius had usurped power, Argabastus, too, the one from Gaul, signed on to join with him in the usurpation. And in Rome, Valentinian the younger, son of Valentinian the Great, when he had heard about this, hanged himself. And Theodosius the Great hastened to avenge him.

Scut. p. 66.14–20: But when the sovereign had turned back toward Constantinople, a certain Eugenius usurped power in Rome, having donned the imperial diadem. When he had heard this, Valentinian foolishly hanged himself. And the sovereign Theodosius, after he had settled matters there again, killed the usurper and appointed his own son, Honorius, sovereign of Rome, having joined to him for a wife Placidia, Gratian's daughter.

149 The chronology is confused. The famous riot and massacre at Thessalonica actually occurred around three years earlier, in the spring or summer of 390, while Theodosius was in Milan after the defeat of Maximus. *Cod. Theod.* 9.40.13, issued at Verona and correctly dated to August 18, 390, stipulates a thirty-day interval between sentences "of very severe punishment" and the execution of those sentences. Zonaras' "prefect" was the *magister militum per Illyricum* Buthericus (*PLRE* I, p. 166). Ced. p. 562.11–15, in an uncharacteristic personal observation, explains the extended quotations that distinguish his account of Theodosius' dealings with Ambrose: "I have related these things in detail, having considered it unjust that the forthrightness of the wholly blessed monk be consigned to forgetfulness and having shown that the law which Ambrose the Great exhorted to be written was beneficial." *Cf.* Malal. XIII.42, pp. 268–269, which closely parallels Zonaras, and:

Theod. Lect. *Epit.* 270, p. 84.1–11:	Ced. p. 556.6–21:
Through the killings which had occurred in Thessalonica on the pretence of the charioteer and the son of the prefect and of the anger of the sovereign on account of the prefect's death—from which, also, the unrestrained killings had happened—when Theodosius had come to Mediolanum, Ambrose did not allow him to enter the church until eight months had passed. And on the Savior's birthday, Ambrose terribly abused Rufinus the *magister* [*PLRE* I, pp. 778–781, *s.v.* Flavius Rufinus 18], who was coming to entreat him. And when the sovereign had promulgated a law under Ambrose's guidance that for those condemned to death or also to suffer forfeiture of property an appointed time of thirty days be granted for review, Ambrose admitted him to the church. But he still did not allow him to enter the area of the altar, though he had previously had the traditional power to do so, but rather he suffered the sovereign to stand outside with the people. And from that occasion this practice is maintained.	When he had begrudged this noble act, the demon who despises good concocted something cruel and inhuman. For the sovereign, making a journey from Constantinople to Rome, had arrived in transit in Thessalonica, and, when his soldiers had disturbed the city on account of lodgings, the Thessalonicans rioted, defamed the sovereign, and stoned some of the commanders. And the sovereign, when he learned of these things and was unable to control the force of his anger, left it to the prefect of the city to determine the punishment. When he had received such authority, just like a tyrant who is a law unto himself, he bared unjust swords against all, and the innocent with the guilty he killed, seven thousand (and according to some, fifteen thousand). After he heard of this disaster, Ambrose the Great, bishop of Mediolanum (and this is a city of Italy), when the sovereign had arrived there and wished, as was customary, to enter the church, having stood outside the doors, the holy man prevented the entry, saying forthrightly to him, . . .

557.12–22: Then, when he had submitted to these words, the sovereign withdrew to the palace there, moaning and weeping. And when eight months had passed and the sovereign had not emerged but was vehemently repenting, the birthday festival of our Lord Jesus Christ occurred. And when he had observed that the sovereign did not wish to make the customary procession, Rufinus, the *magister*, said to him, "If you command, master, I shall race off and persuade the archpriest to release you from the bond." And he said, "I know Ambrose's strictness." And when, after he had employed many arguments, Rufinus kept trying to persuade him, he ordered him to depart.

558.17–559.17: And straightaway, when the sovereign had commanded that this [law] be written and had confirmed it with his own hand, Ambrose released the bond and allowed him to enter the church. And when he had entered, having fallen flat upon the floor, he cried with a shout, "My soul is joined to the floor. Revive me according to your word, Lord" [*Psalms* 119.25]. And with his hands he began to tear the hairs from his head, to smite his face, to drench the earth with tears, and [559] to importune God until the hour of communion. Then, when he had arisen and approached the chancel, wishing to enter, he was hindered by Ambrose, who declared to him, "Know, sovereign, that the things within are accessible to priests alone, but to all others inaccessible and not to be touched. Indeed now, depart and share the space with the others. For a purple robe normally makes sovereigns, not priests." And when he heard this, he responded, "I have not done this through presumption, but

I have learned this was the norm in Constantinople. I owe thanks to you, too, for this remedy." Virtue of such a kind and quantity did the archpriest and sovereign radiate! And the sovereign, when he had returned to Constantinople and a festival was taking place, after he had borne the gifts to the holy table, straightaway departed. And when Nectarius, the patriarch at the time, asked the reason, he said, "I have been adequately instructed about the difference between a sovereign and a priest. For I know Ambrose alone is deservedly called 'Bishop.'"

p. 571.2–7: And then occurred Theodosius' slaughter in Thessalonica of 15,000 of the people and the actions performed by the holy Ambrose, bishop of Mediolanum, against the sovereign himself. And hence he publicly exhibited a law for those sentenced to death or forfeiture of property to be granted 30 days for review.

Sym. 95.10, p. 122: As a result of the murders which had occurred in Thessalonica, Theodosius, after he had departed to Mediolanum with the retinue of the prefect and his son, was barred for a long time from the church by Ambrose. Then, when he had eventually been received after much supplication and repentance, Ambrose, having as usual brought forward the customary gifts, after he had given instruction on the character of priests and sovereigns, ordered him to stand outside of the sanctuary. When he had arrived in Constantinople, he used this as a model—sovereigns prior to this having stood within the sanctuary.

Scut. p. 65.15–31: When the sovereign had reached Thessalonica with the army, the city of the Thessalonicans was disturbed on account of lodgings, and they defamed the sovereign and murdered the prefect. And when the sovereign feigned patience and the disturbance had subsided, there was an equestrian spectacle the next morning. And when the entire populace had assembled in the theater, the sovereign commanded the army to shoot down the multitude with arrows. And 1,500 perished. And subsequently, when the sovereign went off to Mediolanum and, as was customary, wished to enter the church, the sainted Ambrose did not permit him to enter within, but he stood outside and reproached him about the atrocity which had occurred and did not allow him to enter, though he was much and often ashamed for many days, until he demonstrated absolute repentance and wrote a law prescribing that the appointed day for those sentenced to death be delayed for thirty days for the purpose of an accurate review after anger had abated, as Ambrose advised.

For sources and critical discussion, especially as they pertain to Ambrose, see N. B. McLynn, *Ambrose of Milan* (Berkeley CA: University of California Press, 1994), pp. 315–330.

150   Theodosius defeated Eugenius and Arbogast at the Frigidus River (Slovenia's Wippach/Vipava and Hubelj, rather than in Gaul) on September 5, 394. Note that Zonaras says nothing of the supposedly miraculous windstorm described by some sources in connection with Theodosius' victory. Eugenius was taken prisoner and executed on September 6; Arbogast took his own life. *Cf.* Scut. p. 66.14–20, translated in n. 148 above, and Theod. Lect. *Epit.* 275–276, p. 85.5–11:

Valentinian the younger, son of Valentinian the Great, killed himself by hanging as a result of a plot of Eugenius, one of the clerks from the grammarians, who had been moved to usurpation with Argabastes, from Galatia Minor. For Eugenius himself also donned the imperial regalia.

151   Zonaras' Placilla is Aelia Flavia Flaccilla (*PLRE* I, pp. 341–342), d. 386, mother of Arcadius (*PLRE* I, p. 99), b. *ca.* 377, and Honorius (3 *PLRE* I, p. 442), b. September 9, 384. On Galla, see above, notes 130, 143, and 147. *Cf.*:

Theod. Lect. *Epit.* 272, p. 84.17–25: Placilla, the spouse of Theodosius, was pious and charitable and personally provided aid to the sick and leprous. And she died before her husband. And what most revealed the affection of the sovereign for her was the anger of the sovereign, which was	Sym. 95.1, p. 120: Theodosius the Great reigned 16 years. He was a Spaniard by race, having a wife by the name Placilla, from whom he had Arcadius and Honorius. When she had died, he wed Galla, sister of Gratian.

roused against Antiochenes, because, agitated due to public burdens the sovereign imposed on the cities by reason of the continuous wars, they shattered and destroyed a bronze stele of the empress Placilla. Then, too, Flavianus the bishop, when he had returned, negotiated in behalf of the Antiochenes. And John Chrysostom, still a presbyter of Antioch and residing in Antioch, delivered wondrous speeches to advise the people in Antioch.

Ced. p. 552.13–15: . . . having a wife named Placilla, from whom he had Arcadius and Honorius. When she had died, he wed Galla, Gratian's sister.

559.18–560.9 (*cf.* Theod. *HE* V.19, pp. 313.21–314.21): And the sovereign also had another inducement of benefit. For his spouse, whose name was Placilla, constantly reminded him of the divine laws. For it was not the sovereign power which motivated her, but the magnitude of the benefaction increased the charm of the benefactor. For to brothers who had become lepers and to those who had otherwise been physically maimed she was providing every kind of attention, [560] becoming personally engaged and on her own offering drinks and serving meals. For, visiting the guest rooms of the churches, she personally cared for the bedridden. And matters which were reckoned the work of slaves and servants, she herself saw to. And she also constantly commented to her spouse, the sovereign, "Husband, it always befits you to reckon who you were, and who you now have become. Therefore, govern this realm lawfully and thereby you will tend to him who has bestowed it." It happened

Scut. p. 66.21–30: This sovereign had as a wife the blessed empress Placilla, whose orthodox faith and many acts of mercy and magnitude of humility and other virtues are also worthy of narratation. For the empress herself personally ministered to the poor and to lepers in all their needs. And she was also accustomed to say to her husband each day, "You should always remember, husband, just who you were formerly, who you happen to be now, and to give thanks to the one who granted you the vantage point of the sovereignty. For in so doing, you will not be ungracious about your benefactor."

that this wondrous and truly praiseworthy empress departed life before her husband.

p. 560.9–22: And after some time, compelled by the incessant wars, the sovereign imposed on the cities a novel impost. And the city of Antioch did not tolerate the new tax. For the populace, viewing those being taxed as being punished, found a cause for disorder and toppled the bronze image of the praiseworthy Placilla and dragged it through much of the city. The sovereign, when he had learned of this and become very angry, rescinded the city's legal privilege and gave the top position to the neighboring city. For Laodicea had long since jealously envied Antioch. And he subsequently threatened to immolate it and to reduce the city to a village. And in fact, before the sovereign knew about the tragedy, the commanders killed some because they had participated in the venture. And the sovereign enjoined all this, but it did not transpire, since the law which Ambrose the Great advised to be enacted was preventing it.

p. 563.5–8: After the dissolution of the tyranny of Eugenius, having taken ill, he apportioned the realm to his sons Arcadius and Honorius, and to the elder, on the one hand, he gave his own hegemony, to the younger, on the other, the scepters of Europe.

pp. 570.17–571.2: In his 15th and 16th year, Theodosius wrote a law which forbade a woman to advance to deaconess unless beyond the age 60 [cf. Cod. Theod. 16.2.27]. In the same year, Placilla, the wife of Theodosius, died, being pious and devoted to the poor, ministering with her own hands to lepers and diseased. The Antiochenes destroyed a statue of her

because of public burdens imposed
by the sovereign as a tax. And then
John [571] Chrysostom, presbyter
of Antioch, delivered wondrous
speeches about this which he titled
The Statues.

152   This story, with its obvious similarities to the famous destruction of a synagogue in Callinicum and the exchange it provoked in
394 between Theodosius and Ambrose, is perhaps a fiction meant to
justify the absence of synagogues from Constantinople. For the affair
at Callinicum, see McLynn, *Ambrose of Milan*, pp. 298–303. No urban
prefect of Constantinople named Honoratus (6, *PLRE* I, p. 439, missing
Cedrenus' testimony) is known apart from Cedrenus and Zonaras, nor
does the quotation attributed to Ambrose find any parallel in his works
or in Paulinus' biography of the bishop. Note, too, Theodosius II's
expulsion of Jews from Chalcopratia, a quarter of Constantinople
that had once been home to many of the city's Jews and where the
Church of the Theotocus was said to have been built upon the site of
their synagogue (*ODB* I, pp. 407–8, *s.v.* Chalcoprateia). The motive
attributed to Honoratus coincides well with *Nov. Theod. 3. Cf.*:

> Ced. p. 571.16–24: While the sovereign Theodosius was in
> Mediolanum, the Jews from Constantinople, by order of
> Honoratus, prefect, built a synagogue of many talents in
> Chalcopratia. When the Christians complained to the prefect,
> he did not pay attention, for he was a Hellene. Then, having
> started a fire during the night, they burned it down. There-
> fore, the prefect wrote Theodosius, accusing the citizens. And
> he determined a punishment to impose on those who had done
> this and to rebuild the synagogue. The citizens fled to
> Ambrose the Great. . . .
>
> p. 572.19–22: And when Ambrose had said these things,
> the sovereign cancelled the punishment, having promulgated
> a law that Jews not have a synagogue in Byzantium or dare
> to pray in public.

153   The incident occurred on February 25 or 26, 387. Flavianus I
(*EEC* I, p. 325), bishop of Antioch from 381–404, left Antioch for
Constantinople on February 22. Though Flavianus certainly played

some role in assuaging Theodosius' anger, more credit is perhaps due to Theodosius *magister officorum* Flavius Caesarius 6 (*PLRE* I, p. 171), who had been dispatched to Antioch and, upon his return to Constantinople, had reported the results of his investigation to the emperor. For sources and critical discussion, see F. van de Paverd, *St. John Chrysostom: The Homilies on the Statues.*

154 Chrysostom's twenty-one *Homilies on the Statues* (*PG* 49, cols. 15–222), delivered while Flavianus was in Constantinople, culminate with the Easter Sunday, April 25, 387, announcement of Theodosius' pardon of Antioch, by which time Flavianus had returned to Antioch. *Cf.* Ced. pp. 560.9–22, 570.21–571.2 (both translated in n. 151), and Sym. 95.10–11, p. 122:

> In Antioch the image of his wife Placilla was pulled down because of very great imposts. Enraged by this, the sovereign threatened the city with utter destruction and was hindered through the law about anger which Ambrose had made him write. 11. Then, too, John Chrysostom, being a presbyter in Antioch, wrote *The Statues.*

155 Gregory the Theologian is Gregory of Nazianzus (*EEC* I, pp. 361–362). Gregory of Nyssa (*EEC* I, pp. 363–365) and Amphilochius of Iconium (*EEC* I, p. 32) were fellow champions of the Nicene theology. In 379 the Nicene minority of Constantinople had convinced Gregory to come to their aid. Since Valens had closed their churches, Gregory operated from the so-called Church of Holy Anastasia, actually the home of one of his relatives, until December 24, 380, when Theodosius restored the churches of the Nicene community. From 379 to 380, Gregory composed his *Five Theological Orations* (*Or.* 27–31, *PG* 36, cols. 9–172), which earned him his nickname. In 381, Theodosius prompted the First Council of Constantinople (the Second Ecumenical Council), which, among its actions, appointed Gregory bishop of the city. When the process and timing of the appointment drew objections, Gregory resigned. The *Farewell Address* is *Or.* 42, *PG* 36, cols. 453–492. Gregory's successor was Nectarius (2 *PLRE* I, p. 621; *EEC* I, p. 584). For Zonaras' commentary on the proceedings of this Council, see R-P II, pp. 165–191. Canon I excommunicates Macedonius and those who shared his views. See R-P II, pp. 165–167, for Zonaras' comments. *Cf.*:

Theod. Lect. *Epit*. 228, p. 77.8–13: Gregory the Theologian instructed the orthodox in the current church of the martyr Anastasia, it being a small chapel. The historian says that the house was named Anastasia either through the resurrection of the right faith or through the death of a pregnant woman who had fallen from above, and, when there had been a communal prayer by the orthodox, the dead woman had returned to life. And they say that great and incredible wonders happened in this church from the manifestation of the all-holy Mother of God.

Epit. 229, p. 77. 14–22: After he had entered Constantinople, Theodosius the Great ordered Demophilus [*EEC*I, p. 228] either to turn from the Arian error and to accept the *homoousios* or to withdraw speedily from the churches. And when he had gathered the multitude of the base-believers outside of the city, he held services, having with him, too, Lucius of Alexandria [*EEC* I, p. 509], who already had been driven out. And thus the godly Gregory, with those whom he himself baptized in the orthodox faith, thereafter took possession of all the churches, the Arians having controlled all the churches for forty years. And hence Gregory says that after forty years the curtain had been lifted and Anastasia had become a new Salem.

Epit. 231–232, pp. 77.26–78.9: [The approval of the Nicene theology and the expulsion of Macedonius and his supporters.]

Epit. 234, p. 78.10–15: And the synod of the one-hundred and fifty and the sovereign Theodosius assigned to Gregory the Theologian the episcopate of Constantinople, compelling him, reluctant to assume

Sym. 95.7–8, pp. 121–122: Under Theodosius the Great, Gregory the Theologian instructed the orthodox in the current church of the martyr Anastasia, it being a small chapel. The historian says that the big dwelling was named Anastasia either through the resurrection of the right faith or through the death of a pregnant woman who had fallen from above, and, when there had been a communal prayer by the orthodox, the dead woman had returned to life. 8. Theodosius ordered Demophilus either to turn from the Arian error or to withdraw from the churches. He then departed, the Arians having controlled the churches for forty years. Then the synod [122] and the sovereign forcibly settled Gregory on the throne, though he was unwilling, on the grounds that he had labored much and had freed the city from the disgrace of the heresies. And when he had noted men from Egypt who had rejected the rationale behind this, after he had delivered the *Farewell Oration*, he retired from the episcopate, Nectarius having been chosen instead of him by the sovereign.

the throne on the grounds that he had labored much and had freed the city from the blight of the heresies. And when he had learned of a few men from Egypt who had refused to recognize the rationale behind this, the godly Gregory, after he had delivered the *Farewell Oration*, willingly relinquished the episcopate.

Epit. 235, p. 78.16–19: When Gregory had retired from the episcopate, the sovereign and the synod chose Nectarius. He was at Tarsian by birth, then holding the office of praetor, up to that time being unbaptized, and devout and reverent and wondrous with respect to the way he lived.

Ced. pp. 551.14–552.6: . . . he [Gratian; *cf.* Theod. *HE* V.1.1–2,3, pp. 278.3–279.7] recalled the bishops in exile and restored their own churches to them, having driven out the Arians with the help of Damasus, the pope of Rome. Then, too, Gregory the Theologian forthrightly preached the doctrine of the truth in Constantinople in the chapel of the holy Anastasia, which was still small, having done so there on a bit more than ten occasions. Unusual marvels, too, occurred there as a result of the appearance of our immaculate lady, the Mother of God. For the explanation of the name of the Church of the Holy Anastasia is twofold: on the one hand, resurrection through [552] the resurrection therein of the orthodox doctrine; on the other hand, resurrection through the miracle working which occurred in it. For it is said that a woman who had fallen from above died and that after there had been a communal prayer by the orthodox she came back to life. The chapel, then being small, later, under

Scut. p. 60.10–14: Under him [Valens] the great theologian Gregory taught in Constantinople, having concealed himself in the Church of Holy Anastasia. For this church alone was left to the orthodox. And he converted the whole populace to the orthodox faith.

pp. 62.25–63.5: Theodosius the Great, 16 years. This most godly sovereign, being most orthodox, when first he entered Constantinople immediately ordered Demophilus, patriarch of the Arians, either to turn from the Arian error or forthwith depart the church. And after he had gathered the multitude of Arians, he lived with them outside the city, having Lucius Alexander [*sic*] with him. And so the divine Gregory the Theologian, [63] when he had received the churches, forthrightly taught the rest orthodoxy, and by the sovereign Theodosius, though unwilling, was made to ascend the patriarchal throne, and he controlled it six years. And after they had controlled the churches fifty years, the blessed Marcianus, is said to have been rebuilt as is seen.

pp. 552.15–553.2: When he had been taken ill while in Thessalonica, he [Theodosius] was baptized by Ascholius the bishop. And he wrote a law on behalf of the *homoousios* of the orthodox, which they sent to Constantinople. And he himself, too, after he had entered Constantinople, ordered Demophilus either to turn from the Arian error or withdraw speedily from the church. And having gathered the multitude of Arians outside the city, he held services, having with him, too, Lucius the bishop of Alexandria, an Arian. And thus the godly Gregory, with those whom he himself taught the orthodox faith, [553], thereafter took possession of all the churches, the Arians having controlled them for a bit more than forty years.

p. 553.6–9: In year 6, the great and ecumenical second holy synod of one hundred and fifty orthodox bishops was convened in Constantinople for confirmation of the doctrines laid down in Nicaea and against Macedonius the Spirit-fighter.

pp. 553.16–554.1: The synod assigned Gregory the Theologian bishop of Constantinople, on the grounds that he had labored much and had freed the church from the blight of the heresies. And the most blessed one, having learned that some of those from Egypt had refused to recognize the act, after he had delivered the *Farewell Oration*, willingly relinquished the throne of the Queen of Cities, having alone served two times as her bishop. The sovereign and the synod chose Nectarius, until then un-baptized. And it also added to the formula the theology [554] of the Spirit.

the Arians were then persecuted by command of the sovereign.

p. 64.10–16: And to Gregory the Theologian the synod assigned the episcopate of Constantinople, on the grounds that he had labored much and had freed the church from the blight of the heresies. But when he ascertained that some of the bishops were not in agreement, after he had read the *Farewell Oration*, he retired from the throne, and chosen by the head of the synod was Nectarius, a senatorial official, having been enlightened by baptism at this time. For he was still unbaptized. And he held the position six years.

pp. 554.16–555.14: In year 6 of the
reign of the great Theodosius there
took place in Constantinople the
second holy and ecumenical synod of
150 fathers, under Damasus, pope of
Rome [*EEC* I, pp. 218–219], which
Timotheus of Alexandria [*EEC* II,
p. 84, *s.v.* Timotheus I], Meletius of
Antioch [*EEC* I, p. 150], Cyril of
Jerusalem [*EEC* I, p. 215], and
Gregory the Theologian led against
Macedonius, who had become
bishop of Constantinople, who,
still being alive, continued to
blaspheme similarly to Arius. And
likewise, too, he supposed the Holy
Spirit not to be True God but a
creation and distinct. And when a
brief moment had elapsed, [555] the
godly Gregory, after he had learned
that some of those from Egypt had
refused his word, after he had
presented the *Farewell Oration*,
abdicated the episcopal
administration. And when he had
departed to his estate in Cappadocia,
after he had remained quiet there a
bit and refrained from the many
disturbances and become greater in
contemplation, he exchanged life,
an old man and full of days, replete
with all knowledge and
contemplation of matters of the
Spirit. And the holy synod
anathematized Macedonius, with him
also Sabellius the Libyan [*EEC* II,
pp. 748–749], who had maintained
the doctrine of one visage upon the
holy trinity, and yet indeed
Apolinarius of Laodicea [*EEC* I,
pp. 58–59] too, who said that the
Logos, having become incarnate,
was human, instead of the notion
that the *Logos* suffices for the soul.
And he proclaimed the Holy Spirit
to be vivifying and *homousios* to the
Father and the Son, having added
to the holy formula with regard to
the Holy Spirit "the Lord, the
Vivifier, etc."

156   For Zonaras' support and exegesis of Canon III on the relative ranks of the Old and New Romes, see R-P II, pp. 173–174, trans. *NPNF*, 2nd series, XIV, p. 178). *Cf.* Soc. *HE* V.8, p. 221, Soz. *HE* VII.9.2, p. 312.1–2, and:

Theod. Lect. *Epit.* 235, p. 78.20–24: And the synod of the one hundred and fifty bishops confirmed the *Homousios*. And it added to the creed all the theology of the Holy Spirit. And it also set forth the canons affording like prerogative of the bishop of Rome to the throne of Constantinople.	Ced. p. 554.1–2: And it also set out the canons which assigned to the throne of Constantinople the prerogatives of Rome.	Scut. p. 65.11–14: And then the throne of Constantinople received prerogative, and the patriarch of Constantinople was judged to rank after the pope of Rome, he being held in higher esteem than the other patriarchs.

157   For Theodosius' directive, see *Cod. Theod.* 16.5.6—issued at Constantinople, January 10, 381—and 16.1.3—issued July 30, 381 at Heraclea and mentioning Amphilochius. *Cf. Cod. Theod.* 16.5.20 of May 19, 391. The popular anecdote about Amphilochius and Theodosius is suspect. The earliest version of the alleged incident (Soz. *HE* VII.6.4–7, pp. 307.23–308.13) features a nameless "old priest of an insignificant city" rather than Amiphilochius. Theod. *HE* V.16.1, p. 305.12, names Amphilochius and directly or indirectly influenced the anonymous *Life of Amphilochius* (*PG* 39, cols. 9–35) 5, cols 24A-25B) and Symeon Metaphrastes' *Life of Amphilochius* (*PG* 116, cols. 955–970) 7–8, cols. 965D-968C). *Cf.*:

Ced. pp. 555.15–556.16: Amphilochius the Great began importuning the sovereign to drive the Arians out of all the cities. And after he had considered the request too cruel, he rejected it. And then, on the one hand, Amphilochius the most wise was silent, when he was in the palace shortly thereafter, while he saluted the sovereign as expected, disrespectfully ignored his son, who,	Scut. p. 64.18–65.4: And then the holy Amphilochius of Iconium, a member of the synod, kept exhorting the sovereign that the Arians be removed from all the cities. And when he had received the very harsh request, he rejected it. And Amphilochius then was silent, but after this he tended to the matter most wisely. For when he had come to the palace and observed the son

royally attired, was with him. And the sovereign, having reckoned that Amphilochius had forgotten, commanded that his son, too, be royally saluted. And he said that the respect he gave him privately sufficed. The sovereign, angry with him, began to say that the disrespect toward his son was [556] disrespect toward him. And Amphilochius cried out, "Do you see, Sovereign, how you do not endure the disrespect of your son? Trust then that God, too, both loathes and turns away from those who blaspheme his son." When he had heard this and been exceedingly astonished, the sovereign immediately wrote a law banning the congregations of the heretics.

Arcadius enthroned with his father, he granted the father the honor appropriate to a sovereign, but thus neglected the son. And the sovereign, having thought that Amphilochius had forgotten, ordered him to honor this son as a sovereign. And he said that the honor offered him sufficed and not to seek another for his son. And, having become angry with him, the sovereign kept saying that the neglect of the son befit insobriety. And Amphilochius cried out, "Do you see, Sovereign, how you do not endure the neglect of your son? Know then, [65] too, that God loathes and hates those blasphemous to his son." And when he had heard Amphilochius and been astonished, the sovereign wrote a law checking the gathering of the heretics.

158 Arcadius became Augustus, January 19, 383, Honorius on January 23, 393.

159 Arsenius the Great (*EEC* I, p. 83) is said to have left Constantinople to become a follower of the abbot John Colobus at Scete, perhaps in 394, though any motive other than a "fear of God" is unspecified (Theodore the Studite, *Encomium of Arsenius* [*PG* 99, cols. 849–882] 5–6, col. 851–853). The Desert of Scete, modern Wadi al-Natrun, lies between Alexandria and Cairo (*EEC* II, p. 759). *Encomium of Arsenius* 3, col. 851, makes him a native of Rome and from one of its elite families. *Cf.*:

| Sym. 95.4, pp. 120–121: And he brought Arsenius the Great from Rome, having heard of his love of wisdom and divine knowledge, and to him he gave his sons Arcadius and Honorius to be taught the Holy Scriptures from him. And he also made him | Ced. p. 573.11–17: At the beginning of his reign, Theodosius the Great brought Arsenius the Great from Rome, having heard about his wisdom and divine knowledge, and to him gave his sons Arcadius and Honorius to be taught the Holy Scriptures by him. He | Scut. pp. 66.30–67.4: From her, then, Theodosius had sons, Honorius and Arcadius, whom, too, he consigned to the sainted Arsenius the Great [65] to be educated, having appointed him Father of the Sovereign, who, not much later, as a result of a divine voice, after |

Father of the Sovereign. Beseeching God in the night, he heard a voice saying, "Arsenius, flee mankind and be safe."	had also made him Father of the Sovereign. Praying in the night, he heard the voice of God saying to him, "Arsenius, flee mankind and be safe."	he had abandoned everything, fled and, after he had been a slave to God for fifty years alone on Mount Sinai, was deemed worthy of abiding with angels.
	576.10–13: After he had disdained all things of the cosmos and withdrawn from the cosmos, Arsenius the Great, in the habit of a monk, sought godly philosophy in Egypt.	

160   Theodosius died on January 17, 395. *Cf.* Ced. pp. 573.18–574.4:

> Theodosius razed to their foundations all the idolatrous temples which the great Constantine only commanded be closed. And when he had taken ill in Mediolanum, he died in power, being 60 years old, after he had reigned 16 years, having left behind his two sons, Arcadius, the elder, of the East, and Honorius, with Placidia, of the West. And Honorius had his court in Ravenna, and Placidia, the daughter of Gratian, in Rome. And Arcadius transferred his body to Constantinople, having placed it in the Church of the Holy Apostles. And Nectarius was holding the seat of archpriest, in the 5888th year of the cosmos, the 394th of the divine incarnation.

BIBLIOGRAPHY

Texts and Translations

The Acts of the Synod of Constantinople of 1166, ΤΑ ΠΡΑΚΤΙΚΑ ΤΗΣ ΕΝ ΚΩΝΣΤΑΝΤΙΝΟΥΠΟΛΕΙ ΣΥΝΟΔΟΥ ΤΟΥ 1166, ed. S. N. Sakkos, "Ο ΠΑΤΗΡ ΜΟΥ ΜΕΙΖΩΝ ΜΟΥ ΕΣΤΙΝ," ΣΠΟΥΔΑΣΤΗΕΡΙΟΝ ΕΚΚΛΕΣΙΑΣΤΙΚΗΣ ΓΡΑΜΜΑΤΟΛΟΓΙΑΣ 8, Thessalonica, 1968.

Agathias, *Agathiae Myrinaei Historiarum Libri Quinque*, ed. R. Keydell, *CFHB* II, Berlin: Walter de Gruyter, 1967.

—— *The Histories*, trans. J. D. Fredo. *CFHB* IIA, Berlin: Walter de Gruyter, 1975.

Alexander the Monk, *De Venerandae ac Vivificae Crucis Inventione*, *PG* 87, cols 4015–4088.

Ammianus Marcellinus, *Ammiani Marcellini Rerum Gestarum*, ed. W. Seyfarth, 2 vols, Leipzig: B. G. Teubner, 1978.

—— *Res Gestae*, trans. J. C. Rolfe, 3 vols, *LCL*, reprint of 1935–1939 edn, Cambridge MA: Harvard University Press, 1964–1971.

Amphilochius, *Life of St Basil. Sanctorum patrum Amphilochii Iconiensis, Methodii Patarensis et Andreae Cretensis Opera Omnia*, ed. R. P. F. Combefis, Paris: S. Piget, 1644.

Anonymous, *Life of Amphilochius*, *PG* 39, cols 9–35.

Anonymous Continuator of Dio Cassius, *FHG* IV, pp. 191–199.

Athanasius, *Apologia ad Constantium Imperatorem*, *PG* 25, cols 595–642.

Aurelius Victor, *De Caesaribus*, eds F. Pichlmayr and R. Gruendel, 2nd edn, Leipzig: B. G. Teubner, 1970.

—— *De Caesaribus*, trans. H. W. Bird, *Translated Texts for Historians*, Liverpool: Liverpool University Press, 1994.

Basil of Caesarea, *Correspondence*, ed. Y. Courtonne, 3 vols, Collection Budé, Paris: Les Belles Lettres, 1957–1961.

—— *Letters*, trans. R. J. Deferrari and M. R. P. McGuire, 4 vols, *LCL*, Cambridge MA: Harvard University Press, 1926–1939.

Basilicorum Libri LX, eds H. J. Scheltema, N. van der Wal, and D. Holwerda, 17 vols, Groningen: J. B. Wolters, 1953–1988.

Basilika, ed. I. D. Zepos, 5 vols, Athens: G. D. Phexes, 1910–1912.

Bryennius, Nicephorus, *Hylê Historias*, ed. A. Meineke, *CSHB*, Bonn: Weber, 1836.

Cassius Dio, *Cassii Dionis Cocceiani Historiarum Romanarum Quae Supersunt*, ed. U. P. Boissevain, 3 vols, reprint of 1895 edn, Berlin: Weidmann, 1941.

—— *Roman History*, trans. E. Cary, 9 vols, *LCL*, Cambridge MA: Harvard University Press, 1914–1927.

Cedrenus, *Georgii Cedreni Historiarum Compendium*, ed. I. Bekker, 2 vols, *CSHB*, Bonn: Weber, 1838.

Chronographer of 354, *Chronographus Anni CCCLIIII*, ed. T. Mommsen, *Chronica Minora Saec. IV. V. VI. VII*, Vol. I. *MGH. Auctores Antiquissimi* 9, Berlin: Weidmann, 1892, pp. 13–148.

Chronicon Paschale, ed. L. Dindorf, 2 vols, *CSHB*, Bonn: Weber, 1832.

Chronicon Paschale 284–628 AD, trans. M. and M. Whitby, *TTH*, Liverpool: Liverpool University Press, 1989.

Comnena, Anna, *Annae Comnenae Alexias*, eds D. R. Reinsch and A. Kambylis, 2 vols, *CFHB* 40.1–2, Berlin: Walter de Gruyter, 2001.

—— *The Alexiad*, trans. E. R. A. Sweter, London and New York: Penguin Books, 1969.

Crates, *Epistulae*, ed. R. Hercher, *Epistolographi Graeci*, Paris: Didot, 1873, pp. 208–217.

Cyprianus, *S. Thasci Caecili Cypriani Opera Omnia*, ed. W. A. Hartel, *Corpus Scriptorum Ecclesiasticorum Latinorum*, Vol. III.2, Vienna: C. Geroldi Filium Bibliopolam Academiae, 1871.

—— *The Letters of Cyprian*, Vol. IV, trans. G. W. Clarke, *Ancient Christian Writers*, Vol. XLVII, New York and Mahwah NJ: Newman Press, 1989.

XII Panegyrici Latini, ed. R. A. B. Mynors, Oxford: Oxford University Press, 1964.

——, trans. C. E. V. Nixon, and B. S. Rodgers, *In Praise of Later Roman Emperors*, Berkeley CA: University of California Press, 1994.

Epitome de Caesaribus, eds F. Pichlmayr and R. Gruendel, 2nd edn, Leipzig: B. G. Teubner, 1970.

—— *A Booklet About the Style of Life and the Manners of the* Imperatores, trans. T. M. Banchich, Buffalo NY: *Canisius College Translated Texts*, 2000, available at www.roman-emperors.org/epitome.htm.

Etymologicum Graecae linguae Gudianum, ed. F. W. Sturz, reprint of 1818 edn, Hildesheim: Georg Olms, 1973.

Eunapius. *History. FHG* IV, pp. 7–56.

—— *History*, ed. and trans. R. C. Blockley, *The Fragmentary Classicising Historians of the Later Roman Empire*, Vol. II, Liverpool: Francis Cairns, 1983, pp. 2–150.

—— *Lives of the Philosophers*, trans. W. Wright, *Philostratus and Eunapius, LCL*, reprint of 1921 edn, Cambridge MA: Harvard University Press, 1968.

—— *Vitae Sophistarum*, ed. J. Giangrande, Rome: Instituto poligrafico dello stato, 1956.

Eusebius. *Ecclesiastica Theologia*, eds E. Klostermann and G. C. Hanson, 2nd edn, *Eusebius Werke,* Vol. IV, *GCS* 14, Berlin: Akademie-Verlag, 1972.

—— *The History of the Church*, trans. G. A. Williamson, New York: Penguin Books, 1965.

—— *Die Kirchengeschichte*, eds E. Schwartz, T. Mommsen, and F. Winkelmann, 2nd edn, *Eusebius Werke*, Vol.II.1–3, *GCS* N.F. 6.1–3, Berlin: Akademie Verlag, 1999.

Eustathius of Thessalonica, *Commentarium in Dionysii periegetae orbis descriptionem*, ed. C. Müller, *Geographi Graeci Minores*, Vol. II, Paris: Didot, 1861, pp. 201–407.

Eutropius, *Eutropi Breviarium ab Urbe Condita*, ed. H. Droysen, *MGH. Auctores Antiquissimi 2*, Berlin: Weidmann, 1879.

—— *Breviarium*, trans. H. W. Bird, *TTH*, Liverpool: Liverpool University Press, 1993.

Evagrius Scholasticus, *The Ecclesiastical History of Evagrius with the Scholia*, eds J. Bidez and L. Parmentier, London: Methuen & Co., 1898.

—— *The Ecclesiastical History of Evagrius Scholasticus*, trans. M. Whitby, *TTH*, Liverpool: Liverpool University Press, 2000.

Excerpta Historica Iussu Imperatoris Constantini Porphyrogeniti Confecta, eds U. Boissevain, C. de Boor, and T. Büttner-Wobst, 4 vols, Berlin: Weidmann 1903–1910.

Excerpta de Insidiis, ed. C. de Boor, *EH*, Vol. III, Berlin: Weidmann, 1905.

Excerpta de Legationibus Gentium ad Romanos, ed. C. de Boor, *EH*, Vol. I.2, Berlin: Weidmann, 1903.

Excerpta de Legationibus Romanorum ad Gentes, ed. C. de Boor, *EH*, Vol. I.1, Berlin: Weidmann, 1903.

Excerpta de Sententiis, ed. U. Boissevain, *EH*, Vol. IV, Berlin: Weidmann, 1906.

Excerpta Valesiana, eds J. Moreau and V. Velkov, Leipzig: B. G. Teubner, 1968.

Excerpta de Virtutibus et Vitiis, ed. T. Büttner-Wobst and A. G. Roos, *EH*, Vol. II.1–2, Berlin: Weidmann, 1910.

Gelasius of Caesarea, *Epitome of the Ecclesiastical History of Gelasius of Caesarea, Anhang to Theodore Anagnostes*, ed. G. C. Hansen, 2nd edn, *GCS N.F. 3. Kirchengeschichte*. Berlin: Akademie Verlag, 1995, pp. 158–159.

Gelasius Cyzicenus, *Anonyme Kirchengeschichte*, ed. G. C. Hansen, *GCS N.F. 9*, Berlin and New York: Walter de Gruyter, 2002.

—— *Gelasii Cyziceni Actorum Concilii Nicaeni Commentarius*, *PG* 85, cols 1185–1360.

George the Monk, *Georgii Monachi Chronicon*, eds C. de Boor and P. Wirth, 2 vols, reprint of 1904 edn, Stuttgart: B. G. Teubner, 1978.

Glycas, Michael, *Michaelis Glycae Annales*, ed. I. Bekker, *CSHB*, Bonn: Weber, 1836.

Greek Anthology, ed. and trans. W. R. Patton, 5 vols, *LCL*, Cambridge MA: Harvard University Press, 1916–1918.

Gregory of Nazianzus, *Or.* 8, *PG* 35, cols 789–817.

—— *Or.* 24, *PG* 35, cols 1169–1194.

—— *Or.* 43, *PG* 36, cols, 493–606.

Gregory the Wonderworker, *Canonical Letter*, *PG* 10, cols 1020–1048.

—— trans. P. Heather and J. Matthews, *The Goths in the Fourth Century*, *TTH* 11, Liverpool: Liverpool University Press, 1991, pp. 5–11.

Guida Life of Constantine, ed. M.Guida, "Un BIOS di Constantino." *Rendiconti della Reale Accademia dei Lincei. Classe di Scienze Morali, Storiche e Filologiche*, Series 5, Vol. XVI, Rome: Tipografia della Accademia, 1907, pp. 304–340 and 637–662.

Herodian, ed. C. R. Whittaker, 2 vols, *LCL*, Cambridge MA: Harvard University Press, 1969–1970.

Homer, *Iliad*, eds D. Munro and T. Allen, 2 vols, 3rd edn, Oxford: Oxford University Press, 1920.

—— *Odyssey*, ed. T. Allen, 2 vols, 2nd edn, Oxford: Oxford University Press, 1917.

Jerome, *Die Chronik des Hieronymus*, ed. R. Helm, *Eusebius Werke*, Vol. VII.,*GCS*, 2nd edn, Berlin: Akademie Verlag, 1956.

—— *A Translation of Jerome's* Chronicon *with Historical Commentary*, trans. M. D. Donalson, Lewiston NY: Mellen University Press, 1996.

John of Antioch, *FHG* IV, pp. 535–622.

—— *Ioannis Antiocheni Fragmenta ex Historia Chronica*, ed. and trans. Umberto Roberto, *Texte und Untersuchungen zur Geschichte der altchristichen Literatur* 154, Berlin and New York: Walter de Gruyter, 2005.

John Chrysostom, *Homilies on the Statues*, *PG* 49, cols 15–222.

John of Rhodes, *S. Artemii Passio*, *PG* 96, cols 1251–1320.

Jordanes, *Getica. Iordanis Romana et Getica*, ed. T. Mommsen, *MGH, Auctores Antiquissimi* 5.1, Berlin: Weidmann, 1882, pp. 53–138.

—— *The Gothic History of Jordanes*, trans. C. C. Meirow, reprint of 1915 edn, New York: Barnes & Noble, 1960.

—— *Romana. Iordanis Romana et Getica*, ed. T. Mommsen, *MGH. Auctores Antiquissimi* 5.1, Berlin: Weidmann, 1882, pp. 1–52.

Josephus, *Antiquitatum Iudicarum Libri XX*, ed. B. Niese, *Flavii Iosephi Opera*, Vols. I–IV, reprint of 1887–1889 edn, Berlin: Weidmann, 1955.

—— *De Bello Iudaico Libri VII*, ed. B. Niese, *Flavii Iosephi Opera*, Vol. VI, reprint of 1887–1889 edn, Berlin: Weidmann, 1955.

Julian, *Discours de Julien César* (I–V), ed. J. Bidez. *Oeuvres complètes*, Vol. I, Paris: Les Belles Lettres, 1932.

—— *Discours de Julien Empereur (X–XII)*, ed. C. Lacombrade, *Oeuvres completes*, Vol. II.2, Paris: Les Belles Lettres, 1965.

—— *The Works of the Emperor Julian*, trans. W. Wright, Vol. I, *LCL*, reprint of 1913 edn, Cambridge MA: Harvard University Press, 1962.

—— *The Works of the Emperor Julian*, trans. W. Wright, Vol. II, *LCL*, reprint of 1913 edn, Cambridge MA: Harvard University Press, 1969.

Jus Graecoromanum, eds J. Zepos and P. Zepos, Vol. I, Athens: George Fexis, 1931.

Justinian, *Digesta*, eds T. Mommsen and P. Krueger, reprint of 1905 edn, *Corpus Iuris Civilis*, Vol. I, Berlin: Weidmann, 1973.

—— *The Digest of Justinian*, trans. A. Watson, 2 vols, Philadelphia PA: University of Pennsylvania Press, 1998.

Lactantius, *De Mortibus Persecutorum*, ed. and trans. J. L. Creed, Oxford: Oxford University Press, 1984.

Laterculus Imperatorum Malalianus, ed. T. Mommsen, *Chronica Minora Saec. IV. V. VI. VII*, Vol. III, *MGH. Auctores Antiquissimi* 13, Berlin: Weidmann, 1898, pp. 426–437.

Leges Novellae ad Theodosianum Pertinentes, ed. P. Meyer, reprint of 1905 edn, Dublin and Zürich: Weidmann, 1971.

Leo the Grammarian, *Leonis Grammatici Chronographia*, ed. I. Bekker, *CSHB*, Bonn: Weber, 1842.

Libanius, *The Julianic Orations*, ed. and trans. A. F. Norman, *Selected Works*, Vol. I, *LCL*, Cambridge MA: Harvard University Press, 1969.

Life of Silvester, *ΒΙΟΣ ΚΑΙ ΠΟΛΙΤΕΙΑ ΤΟΥ ΕΝ ΑΓΙΟΙΣ ΠΑΤΡΟΣ ΗΜΩΝ ΣΙΛΒΕΣΤΡΟΥ ΠΑΠΑ ΡΩΜΗΣ*, *Roma e l'Oriente* 6 (1913), pp. 340–367.

Macarius of Magnesias, *Apocriticus*, eds C. Blondel and P. Foucart, *Macarii Magnetis quae supersunt ex inedito codica*, Paris: Typographia Publica, 1876.

Malalas, John, *Chronographia*, ed. I. Thurn, *CFHB, Series Berolinenesis* 35, Berlin: Walter de Gruyter, 2000.

——— *The Chronicle of John Malalas*, trans. E. Jeffreys, M. Jeffreys, R. Scott, *et al.*, Melbourne: Australian Association for Byzantine Studies, 1986.

Martyrdom of Eugenia, *PG* 116, cols 609–652.

Nicephorus Callistus Xanpthopoulus, *Ecclesiastical History*, *PG* 145, col. 559– *PG* 147, col. 448.

Opitz Life of Constantine, ed. H. G. Opitz, "Die *Vita Constantini* des *Codex Angelicus* 22," *Byzantion* 9 (1934), pp. 535–593.

Origen, *Adamantius Dialogue*, *PG* 11, cols 1713–1884.

——— *Contra Celsum*, ed. P. Koetschau, 2 vols, *Origenes Werke, GCS* 2–3, Berlin: Akademie Verlag, 1899.

——— *Exhoration to Martyrdom*, ed. P. Koetschau, *Origenes Werke, GCS* 2, reprint of 1899 edn, Berlin: Akademie Verlag, 1941.

——— *Exhoration to Martyrdom*, trans. J. O'Meara, *Ancient Christian Writers* 19, Westminster MD: Newman Press, 1954, pp. 141–196.

Origo Constantini, trans. J. Stevenson, *From Constantine to Julian*, eds S. N. C. Lieu and D. Montserrat, London: Routledge, 1996, pp. 39–62.

Orosius, *Pauli Orosii Historiarum Adversum Paganos Libri VII*, ed. K. Zangemeister, *Corpus Scriptorum Ecclesiasticorum Latinorum*, Vol. V, Vienna: C. Geroldi Filium Bibliopolam Academiae, 1872.

——— *Seven Books of History Against the Pagans*, trans. I. Raymond. Columbia NY: Columbia University Press, 1936.

Paeanius, *ΠΑΙΑΝΙΟΥ ΜΕΤΑΦΡΑΣΙΣ*, ed. H. Droysen. *MGH, Auctores Antiquissimi* 2, Berlin: Weidmann, 1879.

Peter the Patrician, *FHG* IV, pp. 181–191.

Philostorgius, *Kirchengeschichte*, eds J. Bidez and F. Winkelmann, 2nd edn, *GCS*, Berlin: Akademie Verlag, 1972.

——— *Church History*, trans. P. Amidon, Atlanta GA: Society of Biblical Literature, 2007.

Photius, *Bibiotheca*, ed. and trans. R. Henry, 8 vols, Paris: Les Belles Lettres, 1959–1977.

Plutarch, *Parallel Lives*, ed. and trans. B. Perrin, 11 vols, *LCL*, Cambridge MA: Harvard University Press, 1914–1926.

—— *Roman Questions*, ed. and trans. F. C. Babbit, Vol. IV of *Plutarch's Moralia*, *LCL*, Cambridge MA: Harvard University Press, 1936, pp. 2–169.

Polemius Silvius, *Polemii Silvii Laterculus*, ed. T. Mommsen, *Chronica Minora Saec. IV. V. VI. VII*, Vol. I, *MGH, Auctores Antiquissimi* 9, Berlin: Weidmann, 1892, pp. 511–551.

Porphyry, *Life of Plotinus*, ed. and trans. A. H. Armstrong, *Plotinus*, Vol. 1, *LCL*, London and Cambridge MA: Harvard University Press, 1966, pp. 1–85.

Rufinus. *Kirchengeschichte*, ed. E. Schwartz and T. Mommsen. *Eusebius Werke* II.2 *GCS*. Leipzig: J. C. Hinrichs'sche Buchhandlung, 1908.

Rufinus, *The Church History of Rufinus of Aquileia. Books 10 and 11*, trans. P. R. Amidon, New York: Oxford University Press, 1997.

Scholia in Thucydidem, ed. K. Hude, Leipzig: B. G. Teubner, 1927.

Scriptores Historiae Augustae, ed. and trans. D. Magie, 3 vols, *LCL*, Cambridge MA: Harvard University Press, 1921–1932.

Scriptores Originum Constantinopolitanarum, ed. T. Preger, reprint of 1901–1907 edn, New York: Arno Press, 1975.

Scutariotes, *ΑΝΟΝΥΜΟΥ ΣΥΝΟΨΙΣ ΧΡΟΝΙΚΗ*, ed. K. N. Sathas, *Bibliotheca Graeca Medii Aevi*, Vol. 7, reprint of 1894 edn, Hildesheim: Georg Olms, 1972.

—— *Theodori Scutariotae Chronica*, ed. R. Tocci, *CFHB, Series Berolinensis* 46, Berlin: Walter de Gruyter, forthcoming, 2008.

Scylitzes Continuatus, *Ἡ συνέχεια τῆς χρονογραφίας τοῦ Ἰωάννου Σκυλίτση*. Ἑταιρεία Μακεδονικῶν Σπουδῶν. Ἵδρυμα Μελετῶν Χερσονήσου τοῦ Αἵμου 105, ed. E. T. Tsolakes, Thessalonica, 1968.

Socrates, *Ecclesiastical History*, ed. R. Hussey, Oxford: Oxford University Press, 1878.

—— *Ecclesiastical History*, trans. A. Zenos, *NPNF*, 2nd series, Vol II, reprint of 1890 edn, Grand Rapids MI: W. B. Eerdmans, 1976.

Sozomenus, *Kirchengeschichte*, eds J. Bidez and G. C. Hansen, 2 vols, *GCS*, Berlin: Akademie-Verlag, 1960.

—— *Ecclesiastical History*, trans. C. Hartranft, *NPNF*, 2nd series, Vol. II, reprint of 1890 edn, Grand Rapids MI: W. B. Eerdmans, 1976.

Suda, *Suidae Lexicon*, ed. A. Adler, 5 vols, Leipzig: B. G. Teubner, 1937.

Symeon Magister, *Symeonis Magistri et Logothetae Chronicon*, ed. S. Wahlgren, *CFHB, Series Berolinensis* 44.1, Berlin: Walter de Gruyter, 2006.

Symeon Metaphrastes, *Life of Amphilochius*, *PG* 116, cols 955–970.

Syncellus, *Georgii Syncelli Ecloga Chronographica*, ed. A. A. Mosshammer. Leipzig: B. G. Teubner, 1984.

—— *The Chronography of George Synkellos*, trans. W. Adler and P. Tuffin, Oxford: Oxford University Press, 2002.

Theodore Anagnostes, *Kirchengeschichte*, ed. G. C. Hansen, 2nd edn, *GCS N.F.* 3, Berlin: Akademie Verlag, 1995.

Theodore the Studite, *Encomium of Arsenius*, *PG* 99, cols 849–882.

Theodoret. *Kirchengeschichte*, eds L. Parmentier and F. Scheidweiler, 2nd edn, GCS, Berlin: Akademie Verlag, 1954.

—— *The Ecclesiastical History, Dialogues, and Letters of Theodoret*, trans. B. Jackson, *NPNF*, 2nd series, Vol. III, New York: The Christian Literature Company, 1892.

—— *Eranistes*, *PG* 83, cols 27–336.

Theodosian Code. *Theodosiani libri XVI cum Constitutionibus Sirmondianis et Leges novellae ad Theodosium pertinentes*, ed. T. Mommsen, reprint of 1905 edn, Berlin: Weidmann, 1954.

Theophanes, *Chronographia*, ed. C. de Boor, 2 vols, Leipzig: B. G. Teubner, 1883.

—— *The Chronicle of Theophanes Confessor*, ed. and trans. C. Mango and R. Scott, Oxford: Oxford University Press, 1997.

Theophylact Simocatta, *Historiae*, eds C. de Boor and P. Wirth, reprint of 1887 edn, Stuttgart: B. G. Teubner, 1972.

—— *The History of Theophylact Simocatta*, trans. M. and M. Whitby. Oxford: Oxford University Press, 1986.

Valerius Maximus, *Memorable Doings and Sayings*, ed. and trans. D. R. Shackleton Bailey, 2 vols, *LCL*, Cambridge MA: Harvard University Press, 2000.

Xiphilinus, *Xiphilini Epitome librorum 36–80*, ed. U. Boissevain, *Cassii Dionis Cocceiani Historiarum Romanarum Quae Supersunt*, Vol. III, Appendix 1, Berlin: Weidmann, 1901, pp. 657–730.

Zonaras, John, *Commentary on Gregory the Wonderworker's Canonical Letter*, *PG* 10, cols 1023–1026.

—— *Commentary on Gregory the Wonderworker's Canonical Letter*, R-P IV, pp. 46–47.

—— *De Canone, Hirmo, Tropario et Oda*, *PG* 135, cols 422–428.

—— *De Matrimonio Sobrinorum*, *PG* 135, cols 429–438.

—— Ἐπιτομὴ Ἱστοριῶν, trans. I. Gregoriades, 3 vols, *Keimena vyzantines logotechnias* 5, Athens: Kanake, 1995–2001.

—— *Ioannis Zonarae Epitomae Historiarum*, eds M. Pinder and T. Büttner-Wobst, 3 vols, *CSHB*, Bonn: Weber, 1841–1897.

—— *Ioannis Zonarae Epitome Historiarum*, ed. L. Dindorf, 6 vols, Leipzig: B. G. Teubner, 1868–1874.

—— *Lexicon*. *Ioannis Zonarae Lexicon*, ed. J. A. H. Tittmann, reprint of 1808 edn, Amsterdam: A. M. Hakkert, 1967.

—— *Oratio ad Eos Qui Naturalem Seminis Fluxum Immunditiem Existimant*, *PG* 119, cols 1011–1031.

—— ΥΠΟΜΝΗΜΑ ΕΙΣ ΤΟΝ ΟΣΙΟΝ ΠΑΤΕΡΑ ΗΜΩΝ ΣΩΦΡΟΝΙΟΝ, ed. A. Papadopoulos-Kerameus, Vol. V of ΑΝΑΛΕΚΤΑ ΙΕΡΟΣΟΛΥΜΙΤΙΚΗΣ ΣΤΑΧΥΟΛΟΓΙΑΣ, reprint of 1888 edn, Brussels: Culture et Civilisation, 1963, pp. 137–150.

Zosimus, *Zosime Histoire Nouvelle*, ed. and trans. F. Paschoud, Vol. I, 2nd edn, Collection Budé, Paris: Les Belles Lettres, 2003.

—— *Zosime Histoire Nouvelle*, ed. F. Paschoud. Vols. II–III, Collection Budé, Paris: Les Belles Lettres, 1971–1989.

—— ed. I. Bekker, *CSHB*, Bonn: Weber, 1837.

—— *New History*, trans. R. T. Ridley, Canberra: Australian Association for Byzantine Studies, 1982.

Modern scholarship

Afinogenov, D., "Le manuscrit grec Coislin. 305: la version primitive de la *Chronique* de Georges le Moine," *Revue des Études Byzantines* 62 (2004), pp. 239–246.

Anecdota Graeca e Codd. Manuscriptis Bibliothecae Regiae Pariensis, ed. A. J. Cramer, 3 vols, reprint of 1839–1841 edn, Hildesheim: Georg Olms, 1967.

Angold, M., *Church and Society in Byzantium Under the Comneni, 1081–1261*, Cambridge: Cambridge University Press, 1995.

Banchich, T. M., "Eutychianos," *BNJ* 226, Leiden: Brill, 2008.

—— *The Historical Fragments of Eunapius of Sardis*, 1985 State University of New York at Buffalo PhD Dissertation, Ann Arbor MI: University Microfilms International, 1986.

—— "Review of S. Wahlgren, *Symeonis Magistri et Logothetae Chronicon*," *BMCR* 2007.09.34, available at: http://ccat.sas.upenn.edu/bmcr/2007/2007-09-34. html.

Barnes, T. D., *Athanasius and Constantius*, Cambridge MA: Harvard University Press, 1993.

—— *The New Empire of Diocletian and Constantine*, Cambridge MA and London: Harvard University Press, 1982.

The Barrington Atlas of the Greek and Roman World, ed. R. A. J. Talbert, Princeton NJ: Princeton University Press, 2000.

Berve, H., *Das Alexanderreich*, Vol. II, Munich: C. H. Beck, 1926.

Bibliotheca hagiographica Graeca, ed. F. Halkin, 3rd edn, 3 vols, Brussels: Société des Bollandistes, 1957.

Bleckmann, B., *Die Reichskrise des III. Jahrhundert in der spätantiken und byzantinischen Geschichtsschreibung. Untersuchungen zu den nachdionischen Quellen der Chronik des Johannes Zonaras*, Munich: tuduv, 1992.

Brecht, S., *Die römische Reichskrise von ihrem Ausbruch bis zu ihrem Höhepunkt in der Darstellung byzantinischer Autoren. Althistorische Studien der Universität Würzburg*, Band 1, Rahden, Westf.: Verlag Marie Leidorf GmbH, 1999.

Brill's New Jacoby, ed. I. Worthington. Leiden: Brill, 2006–.

Brill's New Pauly, eds H. Cancik and H. Schneider, Leiden: Brill, 2003–.

Burgess, R., *Studies in Eusebian and Post-Eusebian Chronography, Historia Einzelschriften* 135, Stuttgart: Franz Steiner Verlag, 1999.

The Byzantine Empire: Byzantium and Its Neighbours, Vol. IV.1 *CMH*, ed. J. M. Hussey, 2nd edn, Cambridge: Cambridge University Press, 1966.

Cameron, A. "Review of U. Roberto, *Ioannis Antiocheni Fragmenta ex Historia Chronica*," *BMCR* 2006.07.37, available at http://ccat.sas.upenn.edu/bmcr/2006/2006-07-37.html.

Carlyle, E. "Agnes Wenman," *The Dictionary of National Biography*, eds L. Stephen and S. Lee, 22 vols, Oxford: Oxford University Press, 1921–1922, Vol. XX, p. 1166.

Chronologies of the Ancient World, BNP, Supplement I, eds W. Eder and W. J. Renger, trans. W. Henkelman, Brill: Leiden, 2007.

The Crisis of Empire, Vol. XII of *CAH*, eds A. K. Bowman, P. Garnsey, and A. Cameron, 2nd edn, Cambridge: Cambridge University Press, 2005.

Demandt, A. *Die Spätantike: Römische Geschichte von Diocletian bis Justinian, 284–565 n. Chr.*, Munich: C. H. Beck, 1978.

DiMaio, Michael, "The Antiochene Connection: Zonaras, Ammianus Marcellinus, and John of Antioch on the Reigns of the Emperors Constantius II and Julian," *Byzantion* 50 (1980), pp. 158–185.

—— "Infaustis Ductoribus Praeviis: The Antiochene Connection, Part II," *Byzantion* 51 (1981), pp. 502–510.

—— " Smoke in the Wind: Zonaras' Use of Philostorgius, Zosimus, John of Antioch, and John of Rhodes in his Narrative on the Neo-Flavian Emperors," *Byzantion* 58 (1988), pp. 230–255.

—— *Zonaras' Account of the Neo-Flavian Emperors: A Commentary*, 1977 University of Missouri PhD Dissertation, Ann Arbor MI: University Microfilms International, 1992.

Dodgeon, M. H. and Lieu, S. N. C., *The Roman Eastern Frontier and the Persian Wars. A.D. 226–363*, London and New York: Routledge, 1991.

Enmann, Alexander, *Eine Verlorene Geschichte der römischen Kaiser, Philologus* Supplementband IV (1884), pp. 337–501.

Encyclopedia of the Early Church, ed. A. Di Berardino, trans. A. Walford, 2 vols, New York: Oxford University Press, 1992.

Fragmenta Historicorum Graecorum, ed. C. Müller, 5 vols, Paris: Didot, 1841–1883.

Die Fragmente der griechischen Historiker, ed. F. Jacoby, 15 vols, Leiden: Brill, 1923–1999.

Gautier, John P., *"Le synod des Blachernes (fin 1094). Étude prosopographique,"* *Revue des Études Byzantines* 29 (1971), pp. 213–284.

Geographi Graeci Minores, ed. C. Müller, 2 vols, Paris: Didot, 1855–1861.

Greatrex, G., and Lieu, S. N. C., *The Roman Eastern Frontier and the Persian Wars. Part II, A.D. 363–630*, Routledge: London and New York, 2002.

Grigoriadis, I., "A Study of the *Prooimion* of Zonaras' *Chronicle*," *Byzantinische Zeitschrift* 91 (1999), pp. 327–344.

—— *Linguistic and Literary Studies in the* Epitomê Historiôn *of John Zonaras*, *BYZANTINA KEIMENA KAI MEΛETAI* 26, Thessalonica: Byzantine Research Centre, 1998.

Halkin, F. "Le Synaxaire grec de Christ Church a Oxford," *Analecta Bollandiana* 66 (1948), pp. 59–90.

Hunger, H., *Die Hochsprachliche Profane Literatur der Byzantiner*, 2 vols, Munich: C. H. Beck, 1978.

Hussey, J. M., *The Orthodox Church in the Byzantine Empire*, Oxford: Oxford University Press, 1990.

Janin, R., *Les Églises et les Monastères des Grands Centres Byzantins. La Géographie Ecclésiastique de l'Empire Byzantin*, Paris: Institut Français d'Études Byzantines, 1975.

Jeffreys, E. M., "The Attitudes of Byzantine Chroniclers towards Ancient History," *Byzantion* 49 (1979), pp. 199–238.

Kienast, D., *Römische Kaisertabelle*, 3rd edn, Darmstadt: Wissenschaftliche Buchgesellschaft, 2004.

Krumbacher, K., *Geschichte der byzantinischen Litteratur*, 2 vols, reprint of 1897 edn, New York: Burt Franklin, 1970.

Laiou, A. E., "Imperial Marriages and Their Critics in the Eleventh Century: The Case of Skylitzes," *Dumbarton Oaks Papers* 46, Dumbarton Oaks, Washington DC: Trustees for Harvard University, 1992, pp. 165–176.

The Late Empire, A.D. 337–425, eds A. Cameron and P. Garnsey, Vol. XIII of *CAH*, 2nd edn, Cambridge: Cambridge University Press, 1998.

Lenski, N., *Failure of Empire*, Berkeley CA: University of California Press, 2002.

Leone, P. M. L., "La tradizione manoscritta dell' *Epitome historiarum* di Giovanni Zonaras," *Syndesmos. Studi in onore di Rosario Anastasi*, 2 vols, Catane: Facoltà di lettere e filosofia, Istituto di studi bizantini e neoellenici, 1991, pp. 221–262.

Lieu, S. N. C., and Montserrat, D., *From Constantine to Julian*, London and New York: Routledge, 1996.

McInerney, J., "Dexippos," *BNJ* 100, Leiden: Brill, 2008.

McLynn, N. B., *Ambrose of Milan*, Berkeley CA: University of California Press, 1994.

Macrides, R., "Nomos and Kanon on Paper and in Court," *Kinship and Justice in Byzantium, 11th-15th Centuries. Variorum Collected Studies*, Aldershot: Ashgate, 1999, pp. 61–86.

—— "Perceptions of the Past in the Twelfth-Century Canonists," *Byzantium in the 12th Century: Canon Law, State and Society*, ed. N. Oikonomides, Society of Byzantine and Post-Byzantine Studies 3, Athens, 1991, pp. 589–599.

Macrides, R. J. and Magdalino, P., "The Fourth Kingdom and the Rhetoric of Hellenism," *The Perception of the Past in Twelfth-Century Europe*, ed. P. Magdalino, London and Rio Grande: Hambledon Press, 1992, pp. 117–156.

Magdalino, P., "Aspects of Twelfth-Century Byzantine *Kaiserkritik*," *Speculum* 58 (1983), pp. 326–346.

—— *The Empire of Manuel I Komnenos*, Cambridge: Cambridge University Press, 1993.

Mango, C., "Twelfth-Century Notices from Cod. Christ Church Gr. 53," *Jahrbuch der Österreichischen Byzantinistik* 42 (1992), pp. 221–228.

Mitchell, S., *A History of the Later Roman Empire*, Oxford: Blackwell Publishing, 2007.

Nicholson, J., *The Vita Sancti Basilii of Pseudo-Amphilochius: A Critical Edition with Commentary and English Translation*, MA thesis, Athens GA: University of Georgia, 1986.

Oxford Classical Dictionary, eds S. Hornblower and A. Spawforth, 3rd edn, Oxford: Oxford University Press, 1996.

Oxford Dictionary of Byzantium, ed. A. Kazhdan, 3 vols, Oxford: Oxford University Press, 1991.

The Oxyrhynchus Papyri, Part XXXI, eds J. W. B. Barns, P. Parsons, J. Rea, and E. G. Turner, London: Egypt Exploration Society, 1966.

Patrologia Cursus Completus. Series Graeca, ed. J.-P. Migne, 161 vols, Paris: Garnier Fratres, 1857–1866.

Patzig, E., "Über einige Quellen des Zonaras," *Byzantinische Zeitschrift* 5 (1896), pp. 24–53.

—— "Über einige Quellen des Zonaras II," *Byzantinische Zeitschrift* 6 (1897), pp. 322–356.

Paverd, F. van de, *St. John Chrysostom: The Homilies on the Statues. Orientalia Christiana Analecta* 239, Rome: Pont. Institutum Studiorum Orientalum, 1991.

The Perception of the Past in Twelfth-Century Europe, ed. P. Magdalino, London and Rio Grande: Hambledon Press, 1992.

Pingree, D., "The Horoscope of Constantinople," *PRISMATA: Naturwissenschaftsgeschichtliche Studien*, eds Y. Maeyama and W. G. Saltzer, Wiesbaden: Franz Steiner, 1977, pp. 305–315.

Potter, D., *The Roman Empire at Bay*, London and New York: Routledge, 2004.

Prosopographia Imperii Romani, Pars III, eds P. de Rohden and H. Dessau, Berlin: G. Reimer, 1897.

Prosopographia Imperii Romani[2], eds E. Groag, L. Peterson, A. Stein, and K. Wachtel, 6 parts, Berlin and New York: W. de Gruyter, 1933–.

Prosopography of the Byzantine World 2006.2, available at www.pbw.kcl.ac.uk.

The Prosopography of the Later Roman Empire, eds A. H. M. Jones, J. R. Martindale, and J. Morris, Vol. I, Cambridge: Cambridge University Press, 1971.

Schmidt, W. A., "Ueber die Quellen des Zonaras," *Zeitschrift für die Altertumswissenschaft* 30–36 (1839), pp. 238–285, reprinted in *Ioannis Zonarae Epitome Historiarum*, ed. L. Dindorf, Leipzig: B. G. Teubner, 1874, Vol. VI, pp. iii–lx.

Schreiner, P., "Die Historikerhandschrift Vaticanus Graecus 977: ein Handexemplar zur Vorbereitung des Konstantinischen Exzerptenwerkes?" *Jahrbuch der Österreichischen Byzantinistik* 37, Wein: Österreichischen Akademie der Wissenschaften, 1987, pp. 1–29.

Sotiroudis, P., *Untersuchungen zum Geschichtswerk des Johannes von Antiocheia.* ΕΠΙΣΤΗΜΟΝΙΚΗ ΕΠΕΤΗΡΙΔΑ ΤΗΣ ΦΙΛΟΣΟΦΙΚΗΣ ΣΧΟΛΗΣ 67. Thessalonica: ΑΡΙΣΤΟΤΕΛΕΙΟ ΠΑΝΕΠΙΣΤΗΜΙΟ ΘΕΣΣΑΛΟΝΙΚΗΣ, 1989.

Southern, P., *The Roman Empire from Severus to Constantine*, London and New York: Routledge, 2001.

ΣΥΝΤΑΓΑΜΑΤΑ ΤΩΝ ΘΕΙΩΝ ΚΑΙ ΙΕΡΩΝ ΚΑΝΩΝ, 6 vols, eds G. A. Rhalles and M. Potles, Athens: G. Chartophylax, 1852–1859.

Tada, R., *John Zonaras' Account of the Reign of Alexius I Comnenus (1081–1118): Translation and Commentary*, University of Washington MA Thesis, 1999.

Thevet, A., *Les Vrais Pourtraits et Vies des Hommes Illustres*, 2 vols, reprint of 1584 edn, Delmar NY: Scholars' Facsimiles & Reprints, 1973.

Tocci, R., "Zu Genese und Kompositionsvorgang der ΣΥΝΟΨΙΣ ΧΡΟΝΙΚΗ des Theodoros Skutariotes," *Byzantinische Zeitschrift* 98 (2005), pp. 551–568.

Winkelmann, F., *Untersuchungen zur Kirchengeschichte des Gelasios von Kaisareia. Sitzungsberichte der Deutschen Akademie der Wissenschaften zu Berlin, Klasse für Sprachen, Literatur und Kunst*, Jahrgang, 1965, Nr. 3, Berlin: Akademie Verlag, 1966.

Woods, D., "The Church of 'St.' Acacius at Constantinople," *Vigiliae Christianae* 55 (2001), pp. 201–207.

Ziegler, K., "Zonaras," Vol XA.1 of *Paulys Realencyclopädie der classischen Altertumswissenschaft*, Munich: Alfred Druckenmüller, 1972, cols 718–732.

Ziegler, K., "Zonarae Lexicon," Vol XA.1 of *Paulys Realencyclopädie der classischen Altertumswissenschaft*, Munich: Alfred Druckenmüller, 1972, cols 732–763.

ZONARAS' MILITARY AND ADMINISTRATIVE TERMINOLOGY

Archer, *toxotês*: XII.573.23
Attendant, *phrontistês*: XII.597.4
Cavalry commander, *hipparchôn*:
XII.597.10, 599.4, 604.8
Censor, timêtês: *Prologue* 13.2
Centurion, *hekatonarchos*:
XII.574.13
Colleague, *koiônos*: XII.583.2, 614.4,
624.1, 4; XIII.4.16, 49.14, 73.16,
82.16
Comes, komês: XII.613.17;
XIII.31.10, 70.6
Commander, *archôn*: *Prologue* 13.3, 7;
XII.590.16, 591.14, 607.14,
610.7, 13, 15, 614.6, 619.22,
622.17; XIII.37.2, 59.15
Consul, *hypatos*: *Prologue* 12.21,
13.5
Consulship, *hypateia*: *Prologue* 13.1
Corps commander, *chiliarchos*:
XIII.70.5, 72.11
Detachment, *tagma*: XIII.31.10
Domesticus, domestikos: XII.613.17,
18
Dux, doux: XII.613.16; XIII.58.13
Emperor, *autokratôr*: *Prologue* 6.3,
15.8; XII.575.15, 577.8, 578.18,
580.2, 582.5, 8, 11, 15, 584.1,
590.23, 591.5, 9, 594.4, 597.7,
597.15, 606.14, 608.1, 18,
609.17, 610.8, 612.1, 618.5,
619.11; XIII.13.5, 14.6, 18.10,
19.14, 23.7, 25.3, 12, 37.15,
39.6, 40.12, 43.5, 45.4, 46.8,
48.11, 49.5, 54.4, 56.7, 60.1,
61.5, 74.4, 75.2, 84.5, 18

General, *stratêgos*: *Prologue* 6.3;
XII.575.15, 577.2, 591.12, 595.3,
10, 22, 599.6, 600.9, 617.7;
XIII.28.1, 83.10, 84.15, 85.11
Guardsman, *doryphoros*: XII.571.10,
579.13, 610.16; XIII.32.4
Javelinier, *akontistês*: XII.573.23
Leadership, *hêgemonia*: *Prologue* 14.4;
XII.580.8, 582.19, 585.3, 592.20,
596.16, 606.7, 607.13, 613.14,
614.5, XIII.26.6, 56.9
Magister, magistros: XIII.51.12
Master, *despotês*: XIII.38.10, 85.8
(*bis*)
Praepositus, praipositos: XIII.47.9,
74.18, 75.1, 3, 7
Praetorian, *praitôrianos*: XII.6.15
Praetorian, *praitôrion*: XIII.46.3,
53.4, 72.2
Prefect, *eparchos*: XII.582.1, 3, 6,
583.17, 602.20, 611.23, 615.11;
XIII.46. 3, 11, 53.4, 80.15, 86.1,
87.9, 12, 15
Prefect, *hyparchos*: XII.608.13;
XIII.72.2
Prefecture, *eparchia*: XIII.20.11
Protector, protiktôr: XIII.31.9
Quaestor, koaistôr: XIII.46.12, 15,
52.12, 53.2, 5, 10, 16, 17
Realm, *basileia*: *Prologue* 6.16, 10.5
(Assyria), 7 (Assyria), 8, 11.6, 17
(Judaea), 21 (Herod), 12.2, 17,
15.1; XII.572.8 (Parthia), 574.15,
579.3, 584.7, 17, 587.2, 591.7,
12, 21, 597.16, 605.15, 18,
608.3, 19, 610.20, 614.3, 616.7

(Persia), 617.7, 18, 618.5, 10, 621.24, 622.2, 12, 623.2, 624.1, 4; XIII.1.1, 2.1, 4.9, 19.6, 22.2, 23.3, 27.14, 29.10, 17, 30.1, 32.4, b (*bis*), 35.7, 38.14, 41.10, 51.4, 15, 59.13, 60.3, 5, 61.9, 70.5, 72.7, 74.2, 75.18, 76.12, 82.17, 87.6, 93.11, 16

Reign, *basileuein*: Prologue 6.16, 11.5, 13, 12.16 (Romulus), 15.2; XII.572.9, 576.22, 578.10, 579.5, 580.16, 583.4, 584.3, 21, 23, 591.6, 601.4, 602.14, 604.10, 606.8, 9, 615.4, 616.4 (Narses), 5 (Persians); XIII.14, 24.13, 29.4, 55.6, 68.5, 70.8, 75.17, 81.5, 82.4, 84.16, 90.11

Senate, *boulê*: Prologue 6.5; XII.577.6, 11, 17, 578.18, 604.16; XIII.6.5

Senate, *gerousia*: XII.571.9, 582.15, 591.13, 617.9; XIII.6.6, 56.10

Senate, *sygklêtos*: Prologue 6.5; XII.576.5, 577.18, 22, 578.15, 584.4, 589.7, 591.10, 604.12, 605.16, 608.9, 23, 619.6, 621.23; XIII.6.3, 42.11, 59.12

Sovereign, *basileus*: XII.573.8 (Artaxerxes), 578.19, 584.13, 590.2, 593.20, 594.10, 598.7, 17, 599.5, 8, 10, 16, 21, 600.8, 601.4, 7, 10, 12, 19, 20, 602.6, 604.4, 5, 605.14, 16, 606.5, 607.20, 608.22, 609.14, 611.16, 615.7, 8, 617.12, 619.16; XIII.2.8, 10, 4.10, 21.6.3, 7.14,

9.2, 8, 10.1, 2, 7, 11.10, 20, 12.8, 10, 19.8, 20.10, 16, 24.4, 25.9, 10, 26.5, 27.2, 28.15, 31.3, 8, 37.2, 38.3, 15, 39.11, 42.15, 43.10 (Cambyses), 44.13, 47.16, 51.16, 52.6, 8, 55.12, 15, 56.18, 59.10, 60.8, 64.5, 65.17, 68.11, 71.20, 72.7, 73.3, 7, 74.11, 75.1, 5, 6, 15, 76.14, 77.8, 15, 78.2, 4, 19, 79.8, 12, 82.11, 15, 17, 84.2, 10, 18, 85.6, 86.3, 14, 87.3, 8, 15, 88.1, 4 (*bis*), 11, 14, 89.6, 11, 90.1, 9, 91.11, 16, 18, 92.7, 9, 14, 93.2, 13, 15

To comprise a rearguard, *opisthophylakein*: XIII.67.1

Tribune of the plebs, *dêmarchos*: Prologue 13.1

Tribune, *tribounos*: XIII.73.11

Triumph, *thriambos*: XII.618.16, 19, 619.4, 5

Triumph, *triambos*: XII.619.8

Tyrant, *tyrannos*: XII.576.9, 577.15, 598.16, 604.17, 620.11, 621.4, 625.1; XIII.2.10, 37.10, 38.3, 40.3, 41.8, 54.8, 86.17

Unit, *arithmos*: XIII.73.11

Unit commander, *taxiarchos*: Prologue 16.10 (Heavenly); XII.584.2; XIII.40.11, 51.1, 10, 66.11

Usurpation, *tyrannis*: Prologue 11.9, 12.17; XII.577.13, 598.20, 609.10, 613.5, 623.5; XIII.2.14, 6.9, 15.9, 31.14, 34.5, 11, 37.9, 38.6, 45.11, 46.13, 85.4, 14, 16

INDEX OF
PASSAGES CITED

Julian (332–363; *ODB* II, p. 1079)
  Caesares 36/335b: XIII, n. 42
—— *Ep. ad Athen.* 8/280C: XIII, n.
  79; 10–11/282B-285D: XIII, n.
  80; 12/285D-286D: XIII, n. 81
—— *Misopogon* 33/361B-C: XIII, n.
  108
—— *Or.* I.6 D: XII, n. 95
Lactantius (*ca.* 240–*ca.* 325; *ODB* II,
  p. 1168) *De Mortibus Persecutorum*
  29.1–2: XIII, n. 7; 50.3: XIII,
  n. 6
Libanius (314–393; *ODB* II, p.
  1222) *Or.* 12.42–42: XIII, n. 78;
  18.36–3: XIII, n. 78; *Or.*
  18.90–105: XIII, nn. 80 and 88.
Life of Amphilochius 5: XIII,
  n. 157
Life of Sylvester (10th-early 12th c.)
  XIII, n. 15
LIM (*ca.* 740; see *The* Chronicle *of
  John Malalas*, trans. E. Jeffreys, M.
  Jeffreys, R. Scott, *et al.*, p. xxxvii)
  pp. 436.12: XII, nn. 32–33;
  436.14–17: XII, n. 41; 436.19:
  XII, n. 82
Lucillius Tarrhaeus (perhaps 1st c.
  BC; *FHG* IV, pp. 440–441) *fr.* 1:
  XII, n. 87
Malalas (*ca.* 490–570s; *ODB* II, p.
  1275) XII.24–25: XII, n. 14; XII,
  p. 227, xvi.b: XII, n. 38; XII, p.
  227, xv.b: XII, n. 38; XII, p. 227,
  xii.c: XII, n. 39; XII, p. 227,
  xvii.e: XII, n. 49; XII, p. 227,
  xv.b: XII, n. 52; XII.27: XII, n.
  82; XII.28: XII, n. 94; XII.33:
  XII, nn. 108 and 110; XII.34–36:
  XII, n. 111; XIII.7: XIII, n. 27;
  XIII.19: XIII, n. 116; XIII.23:
  XIII, n. 116; XIII.25: XIII, n.
  117; XIII.31–32: XIII, n. 130;
  XIII.31: XIII, n. 132; XIII.42:
  XIII, n. 149
Martyrdom of Eugenia (10th c.; *ODB*
  III, pp. 1983–1984, *s.v.* Symeon
  Metaphrastes) XII, n. 36
Nazarius (4th c. AD; *PLRE* I, pp.
  618–619) *Pan. Lat.* IV(X).14.1–4:
  XIII, n. 13

New Testament: *Mark* 9.43–47: XIII,
  n. 43
Nicephorus Callistus Xanthopoulus
  (*ca.* 1256–*ca.* 1335; *ODB* III, p.
  2207, *s.v.* Xanthopoulos) *HE*
  X.11: XIII, n. 109; X.34: XIII, n.
  113; X.43: XIII, n. 114
Nov. Theod. (368; *ODB* I, p. 475, *s.v.*
  Codex Theodosianus) 3: XIII, n. 152
Opitz Life of Constantine (9th–11th c.;
  L-M, pp. 103–104) XIII, n. 15
Origen (*ca.* 185–254; *ODB* III, p.
  1534) *Exhortation to Martyrdom*:
  XII, n. 15
Origo Constantini (*ca.* 390; *ODB* II, p.
  768, *s.v. Excerpta Valesiana*) 2.3:
  XII, n. 154; 5.28: XIII, n. 11;
  6.31–32, 34: XIII, n. 21
Orosius (d. *ca.* 418; *ODB* III, p.
  1537) VII.18.6: XII, n. 11;
  VII.21.1: XII, n. 38; VII.21.2:
  XII, n. 43; VII.21.4: XII, n. 50;
  VII.21.5: XII, n. 52; VII.22.1–9:
  XII, n. 72; VII.22.10: XII, n. 73;
  VII.22.13: XII, n. 82
Paeanius (mid 4th c.; *PLRE* I, p.
  657) IX.2.2: XII, n. 23; IX.5:
  XII, nn. 50 and 52; IX.8.1: XII,
  n. 73; IX.11.1: XII, n. 82;
  IX.11.2: XII, nn. 85 and 94;
  IX.15.2: XII, n. 101; IX.19.2:
  XII, n. 121; IX.20.1: XII, n. 123;
  IX.20.3–23: XII, n. 129; IX.22.1:
  XII, nn. 95, 127–128; IX.22.2:
  XII, n. 129; IX.23: XII, nn. 127
  and 130; IX.24–25.1: XII, n.
  131; IX.25.2: XII, n. 133; IX.26:
  XII, n. 134; IX.27.1: XII, n. 137;
  IX.27.2: XII, n. 138; IX.27–28:
  XII, n. 148; X.1.1: XII, n. 141;
  X.2.3: XII, n. 141; X.2.3–4: XII,
  n. 149; X.2.3–3.2: XII, n. 150;
  X.4.1: XII, n. 155; X.4.4: XII, n.
  157; X.5: XII, n. 155; X.9.3:
  XIII, n. 53; X.9.4: XIII, n. 55
Pan. Lat. (*OCD*³, p. 1104, *s.v.*
  Panegyric) V(VIII).2.5: XII, n. 95;
  VI (VII).2.1–2: XII, n. 95
Pap. Ox. 2565: XII, n. 3; 2710: XII,
  n. 76

INDEX OF PEOPLE
AND PLACES